Connect the Dots ~ 1

Fun~Workbook for Kids

I0468910

Best Collection of "Connect the Dots" Exercises

Dot to Dot

Vol – 1

SATYANVESHI

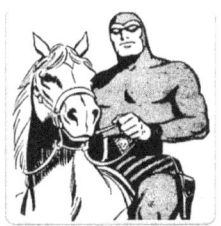

DIGITAL COMICS WORLD PUBLICATION

Published By Digital Comics World Publication
Fort, Mumbai – 400 001
digital.comics.world@gmail.com

Published in arrangement with
Amazon Digital Services, USA

Connect the Dots 1
2nd Edition-2016
ISBN-13: 978-1530765942
ISBN-10: 1530765943

I dedicate this book, with deep respect and great love, to Mother Nature.

You not only gave me the gift of life but an unrelenting passion

to live it fully. For that I am so very grateful

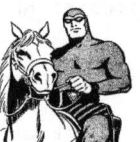

Features of "Connect the Dots-1" Funbook

"Connect the Dots-1" Fun-book is the fun and colorful way to introduce early learning concepts to young children and to give older children confidence for their first years at school.

This book has exclusive collection of 160+ "Connect the Dots" picture pages which is segregated into four levels to suit individual child's age and capability.

- **Level 1: 10 Working Dots – 31 Pictures**
- **Level 2: 20 Working Dots – 35 Pictures**
- **Level 3: 30 Working Dots – 57 Pictures**
- **Level 4: 50 Working Dots – 43 Pictures**

Salient Features:

- Suitable for the Age 3+
- Reverse side of each picture page has intentionally kept blank in order to withstand pressured pencil impressions. (Please insert one rough page between working page and next page in order to protect next page from pencil impressions)
- Guide your child to sharpen pencil, hold the pencil properly and to make use of eraser in case of mistake.
- Encourage your child to count aloud when joining the numbered dots to complete each picture.
- Your child can then color the picture selecting his or her own colors or by following the colors in the stickers.

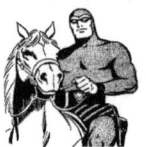

More Benefits of "Connect the Dots" Exercise

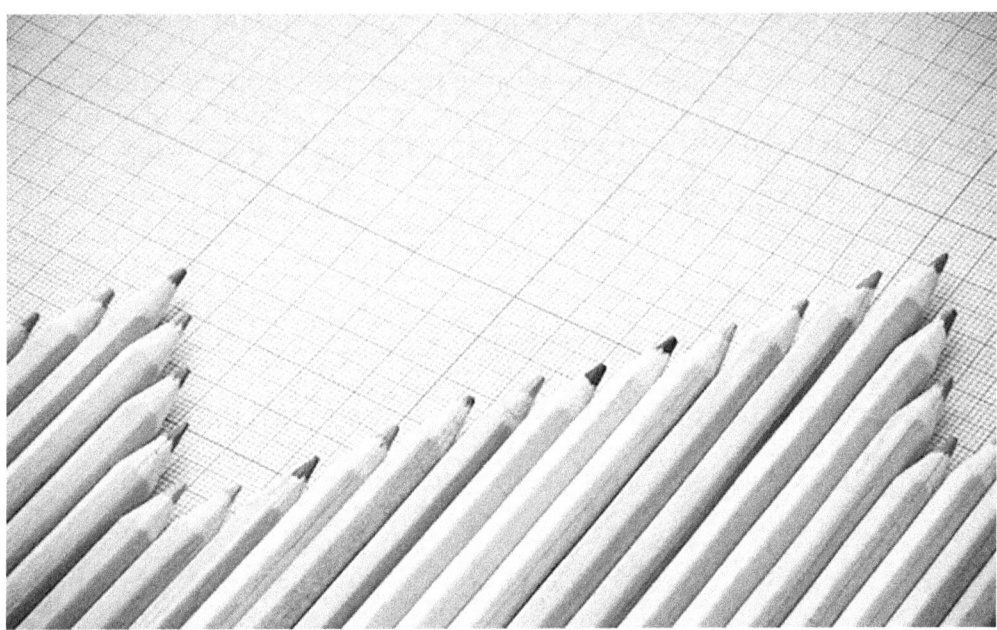

Dot-to-dot and counting:

Working on a dot-to-dot teaches children number order and help with counting. Little ones may need a little help, but as they get older, completing a dot-to-dot all by themselves is a great confidence booster.

Hand-eye co-ordination:

Dot-to-dot games are wonderful for improving hand-eye co-ordination. There's a lot of concentration that goes into completing a dot-to-dot! Visual motor control is developed through dot-to-dot work.

Handwriting skills

Doing dot-to-dot activities really helps improve handwriting skills and are a valuable pre-writing teaching tool. Children learn how to create shapes, focus their pencil and learn how much pressure to apply to the paper.

Fine motor skills:

Working on a dot-to-dot is a great way to strengthen hand and finger muscles in preparation for writing. During early childhood is the optimal time to help develop vital muscles we'll be using throughout our life. Children can concentrate on gripping their pencil and strengthen their hands while working on dot-to-dot.

Other skills:

Concentration and focus are built through working on dot-to-dot drawings. Completing a dot-to-dot drawing shows the benefits of hard work – and in a fun way.

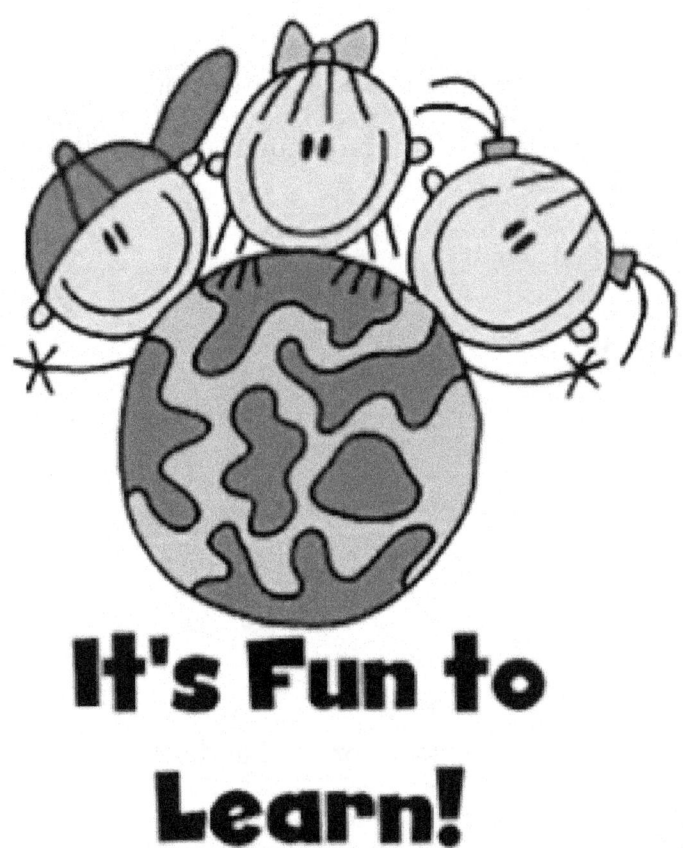

Level – 1

10 Dots per Picture

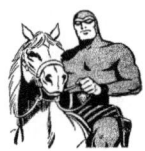

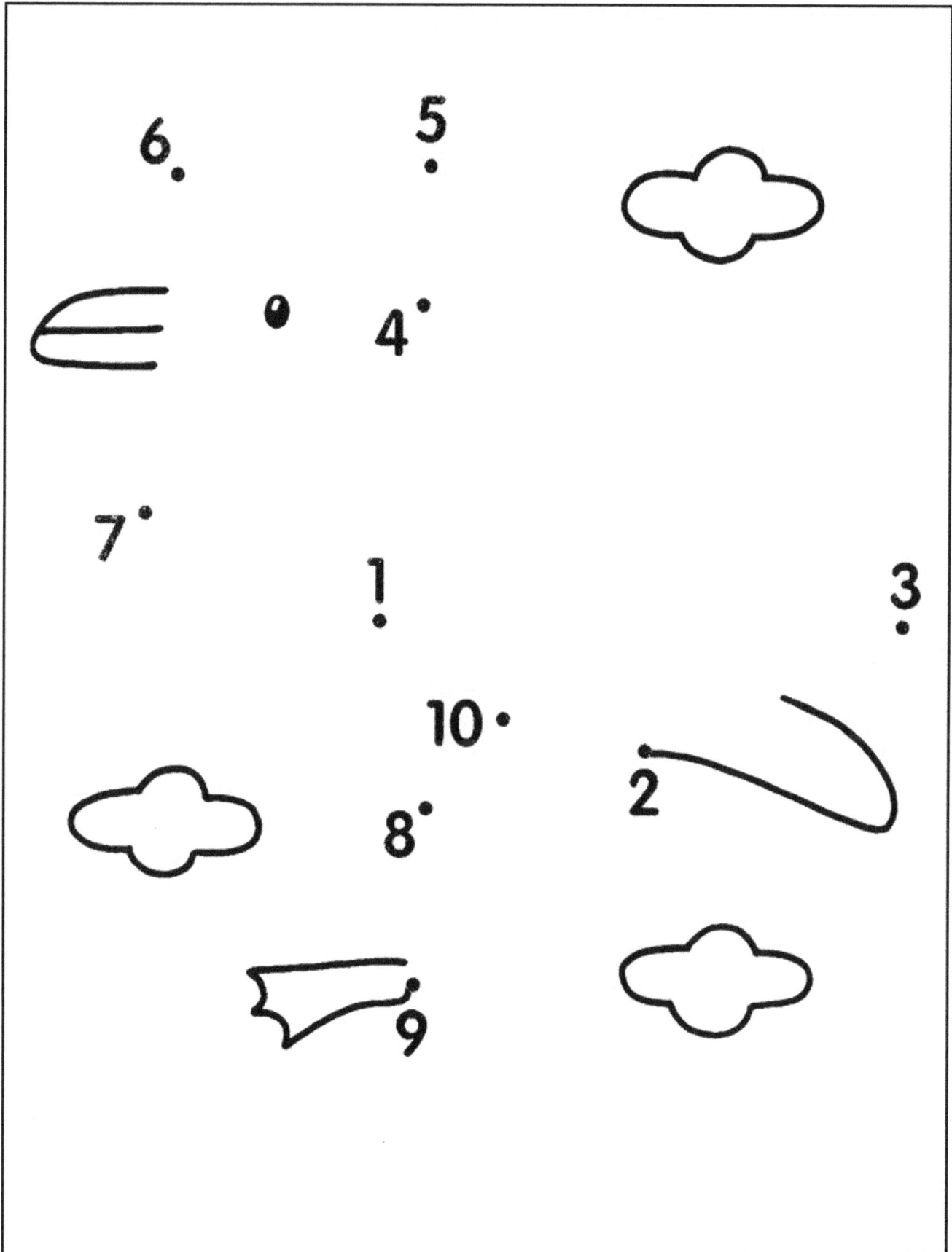

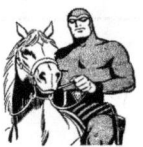

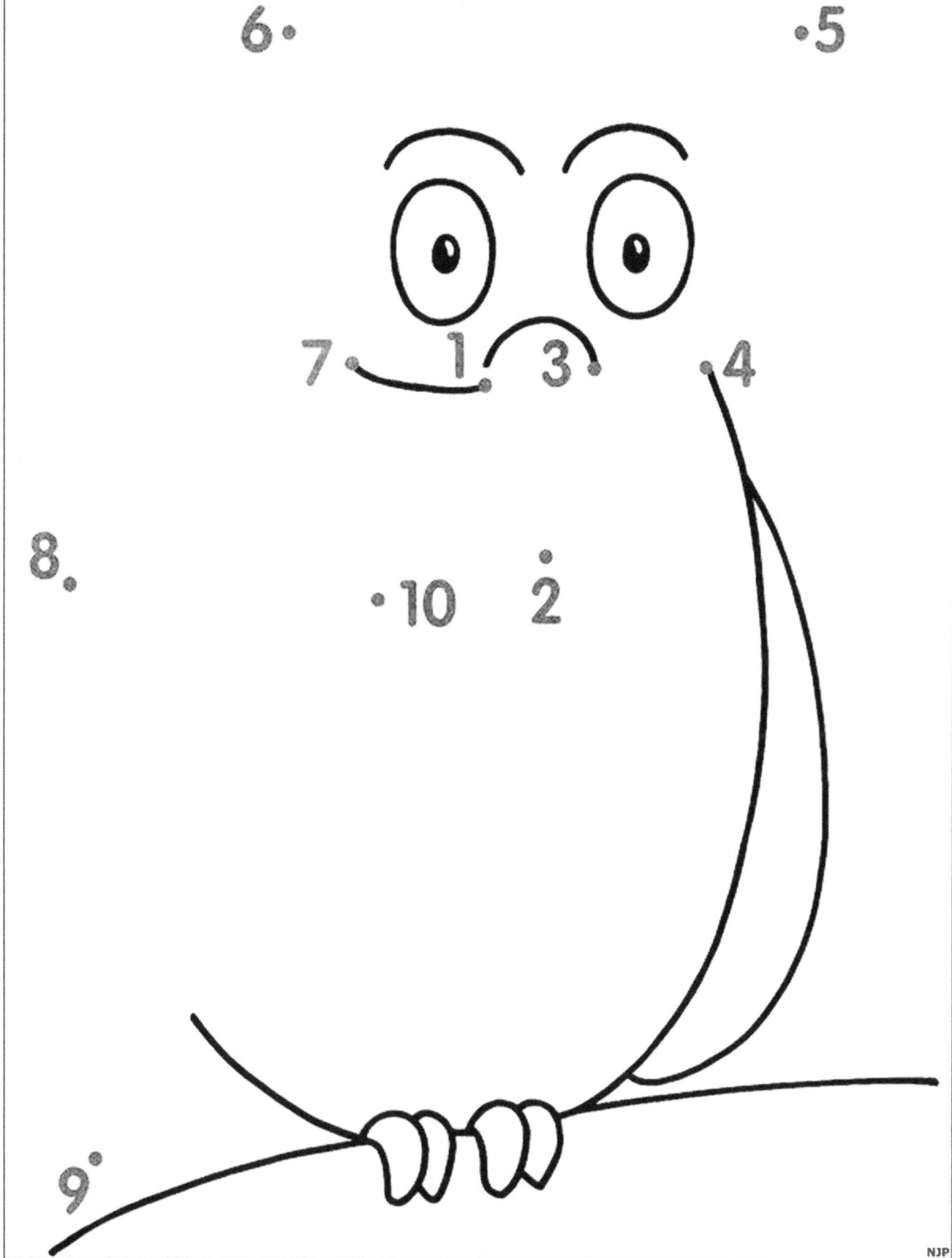

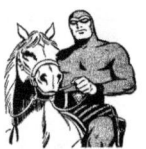

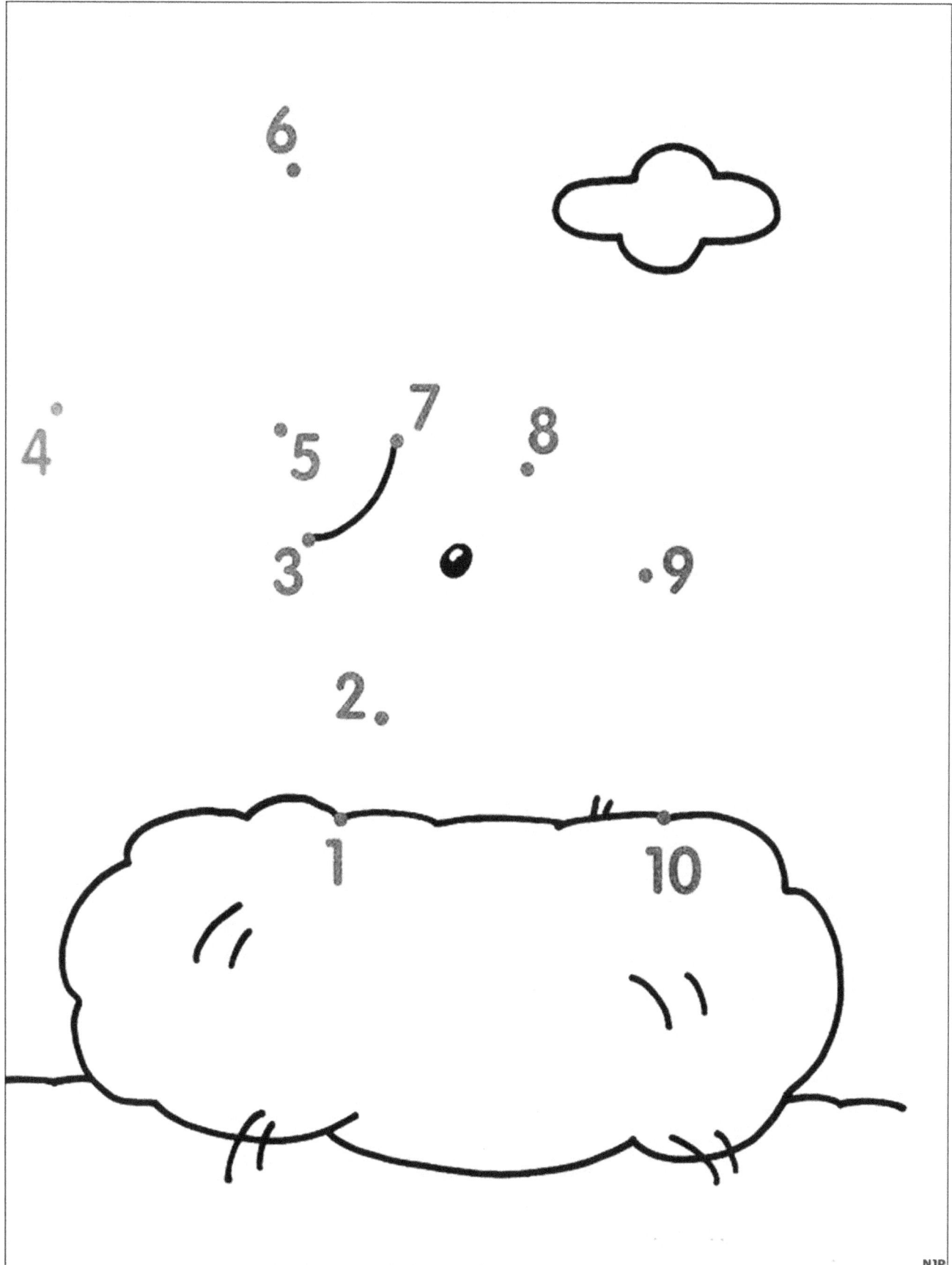

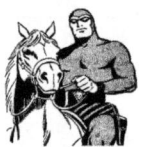

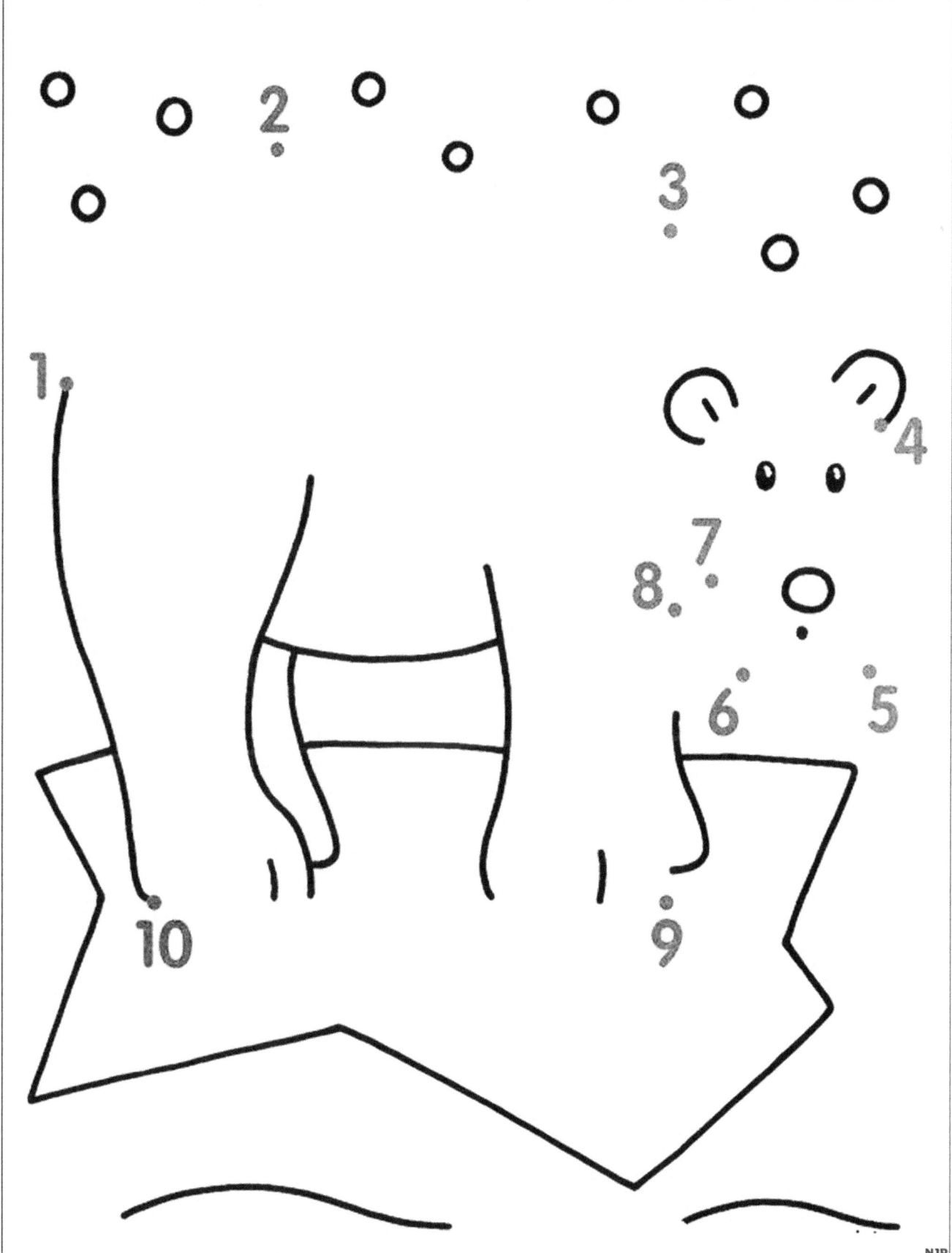

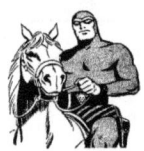

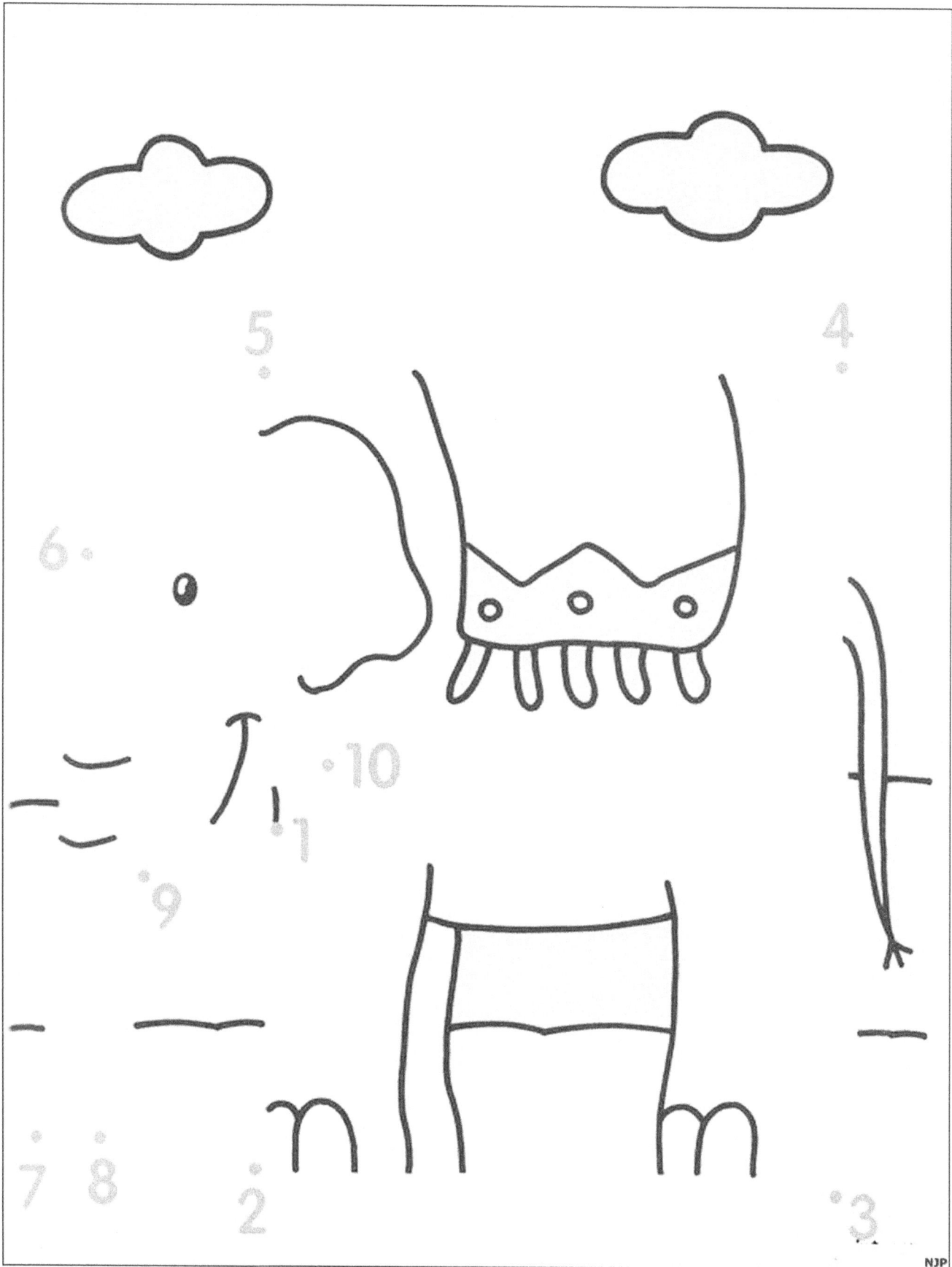

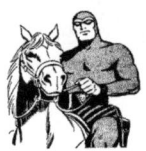

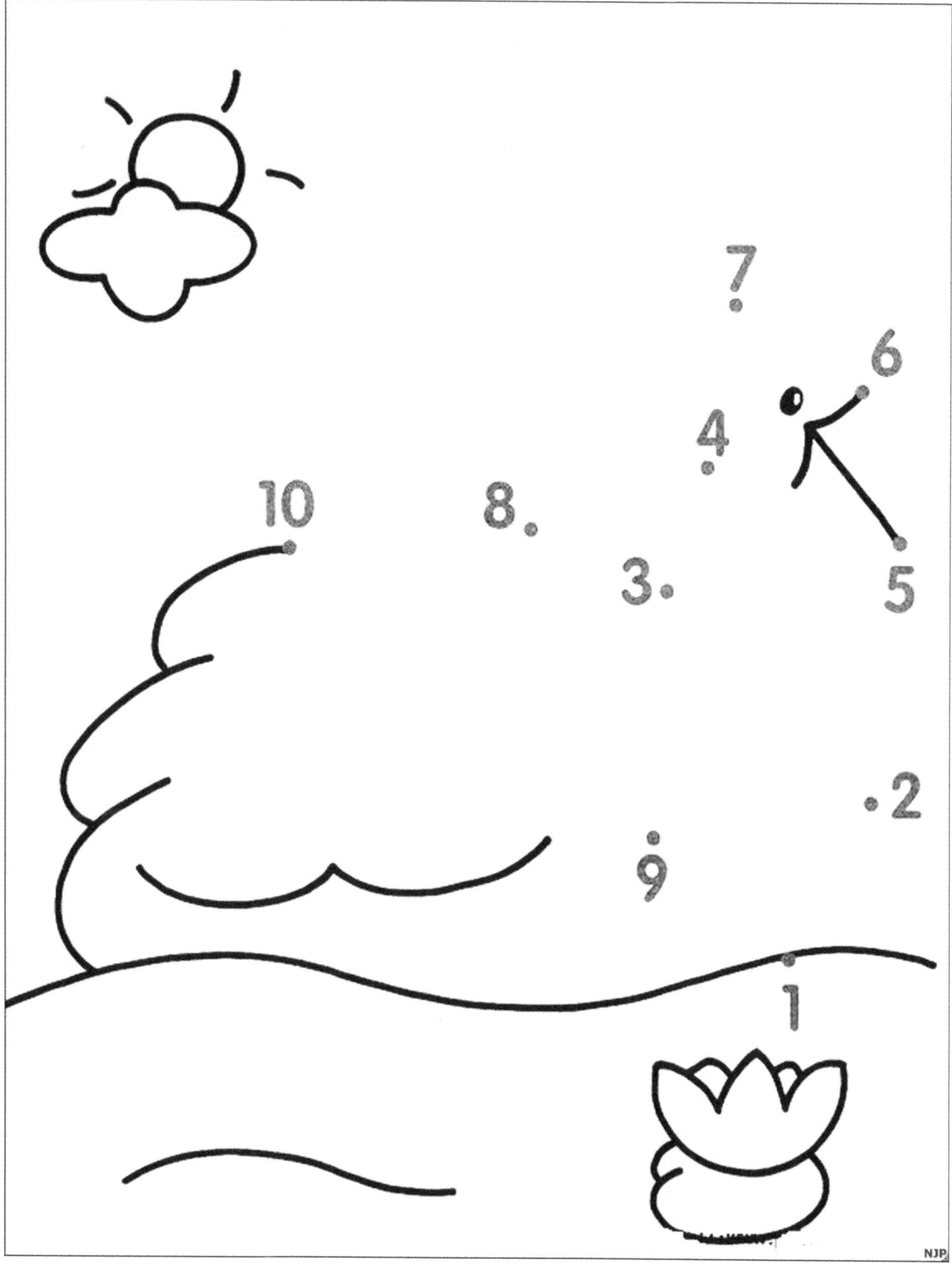

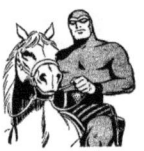

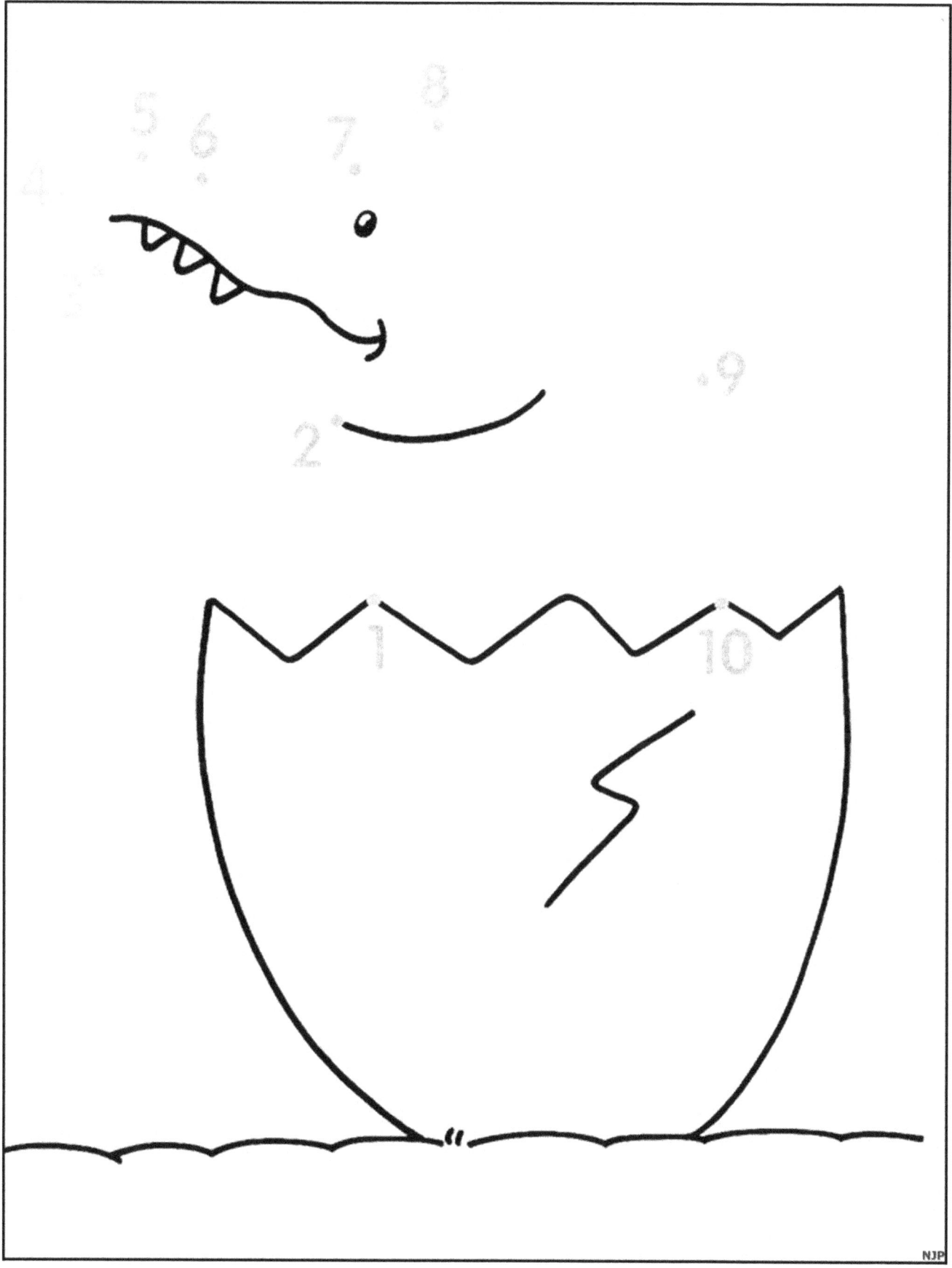

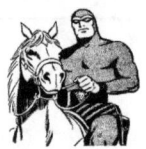

Connect the Dots -1

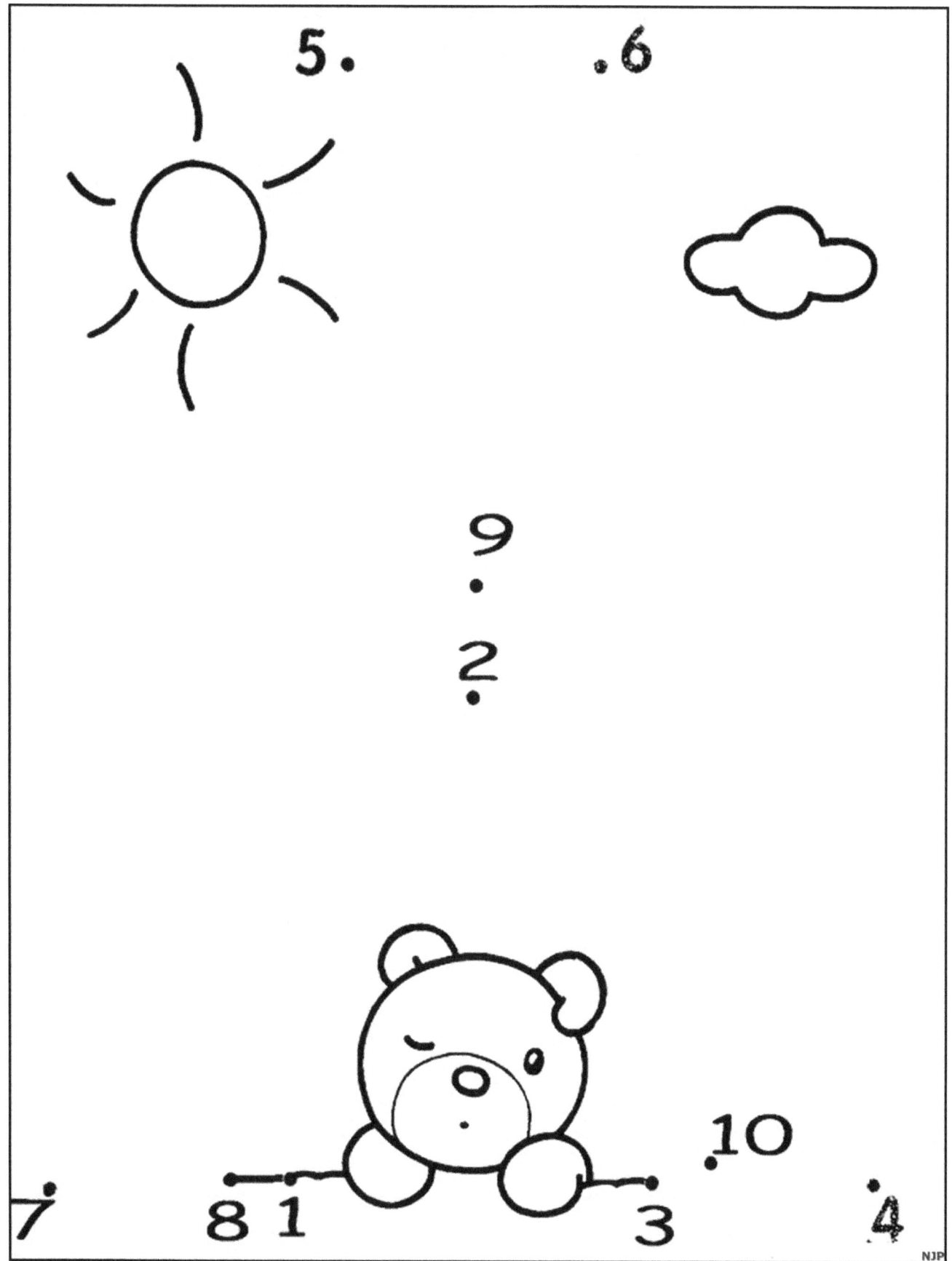

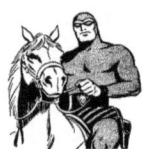

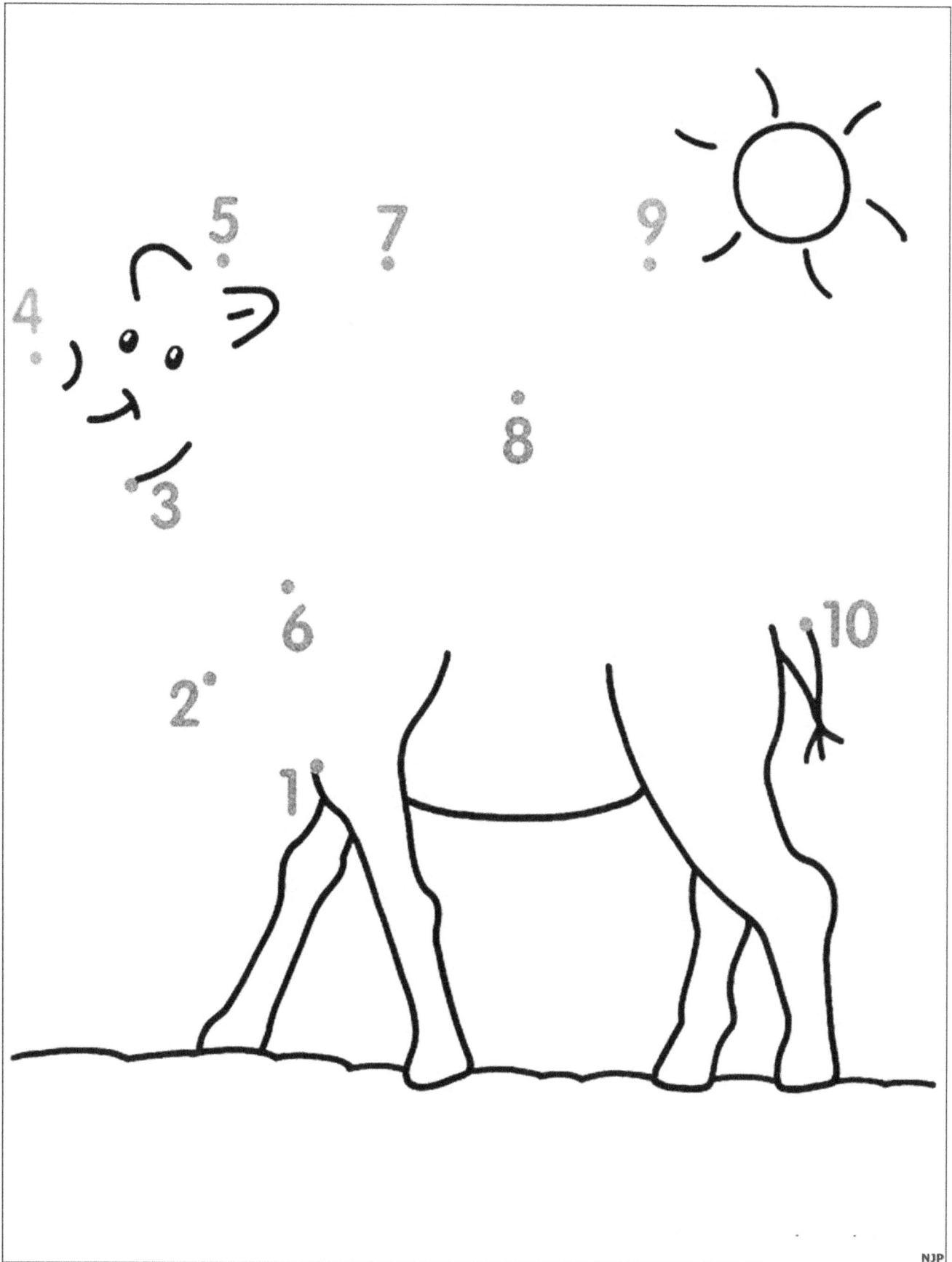

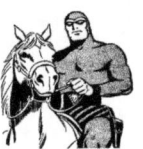

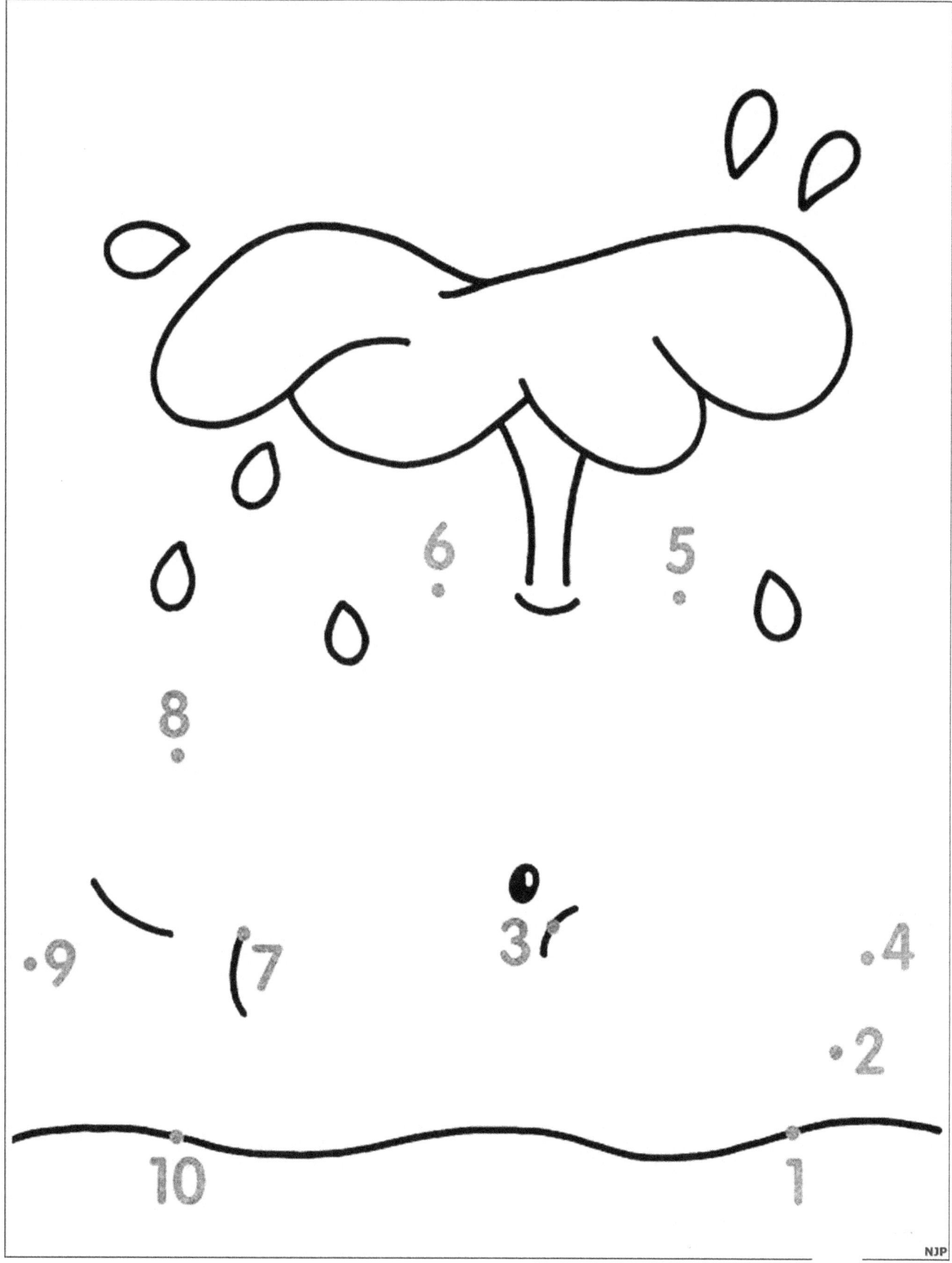

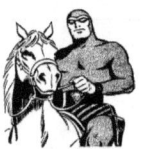

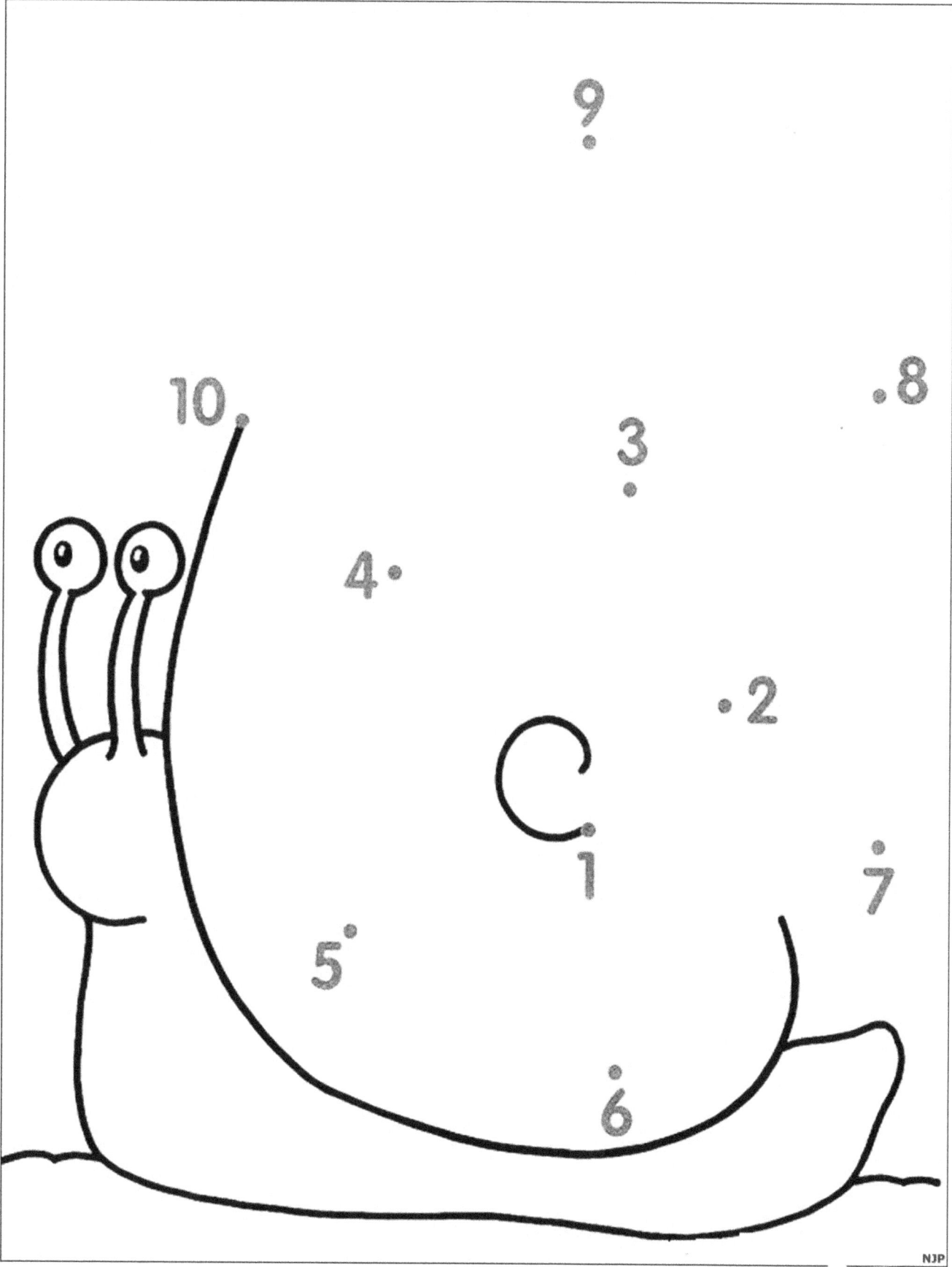

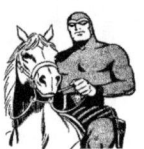

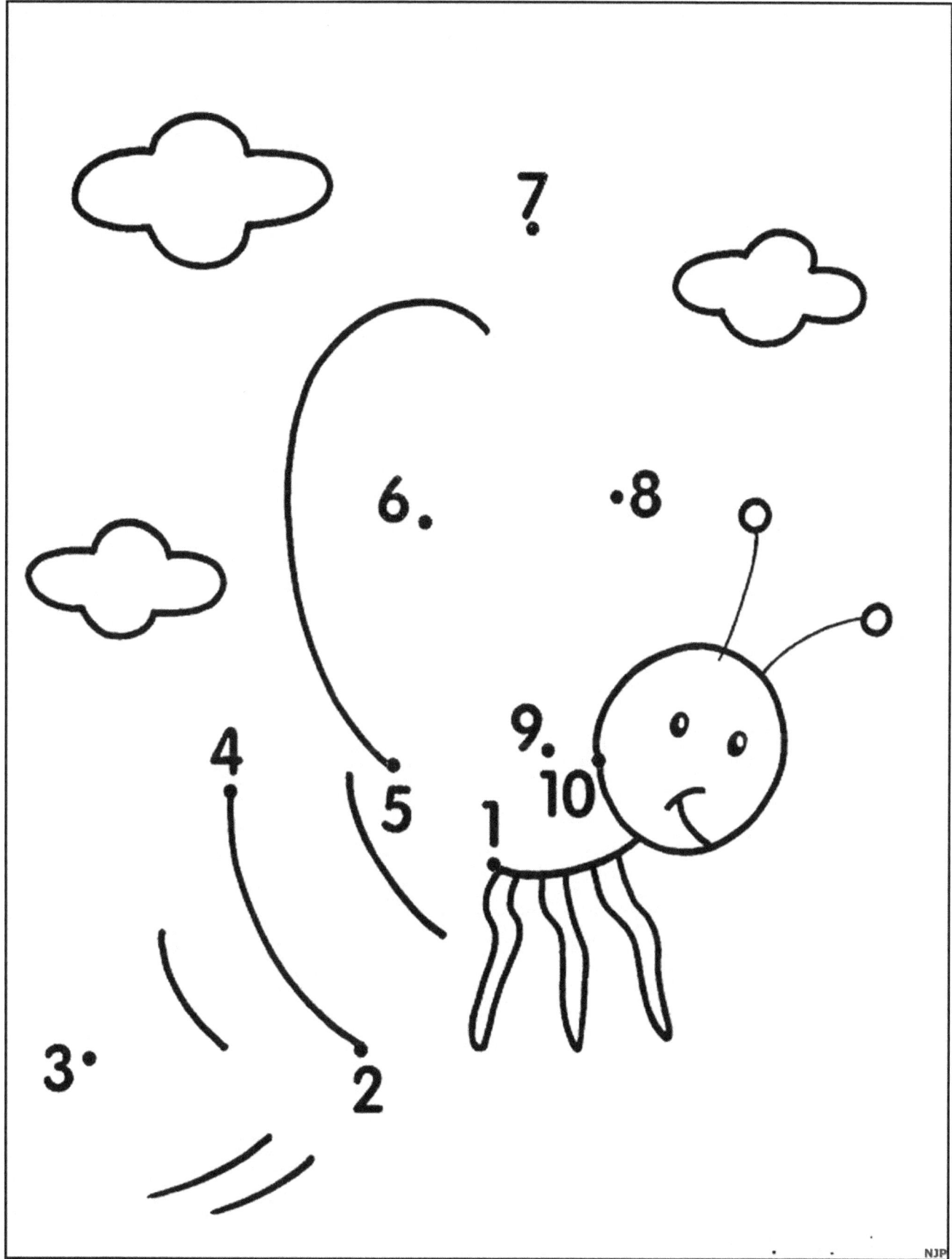

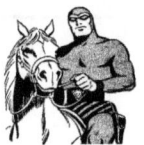

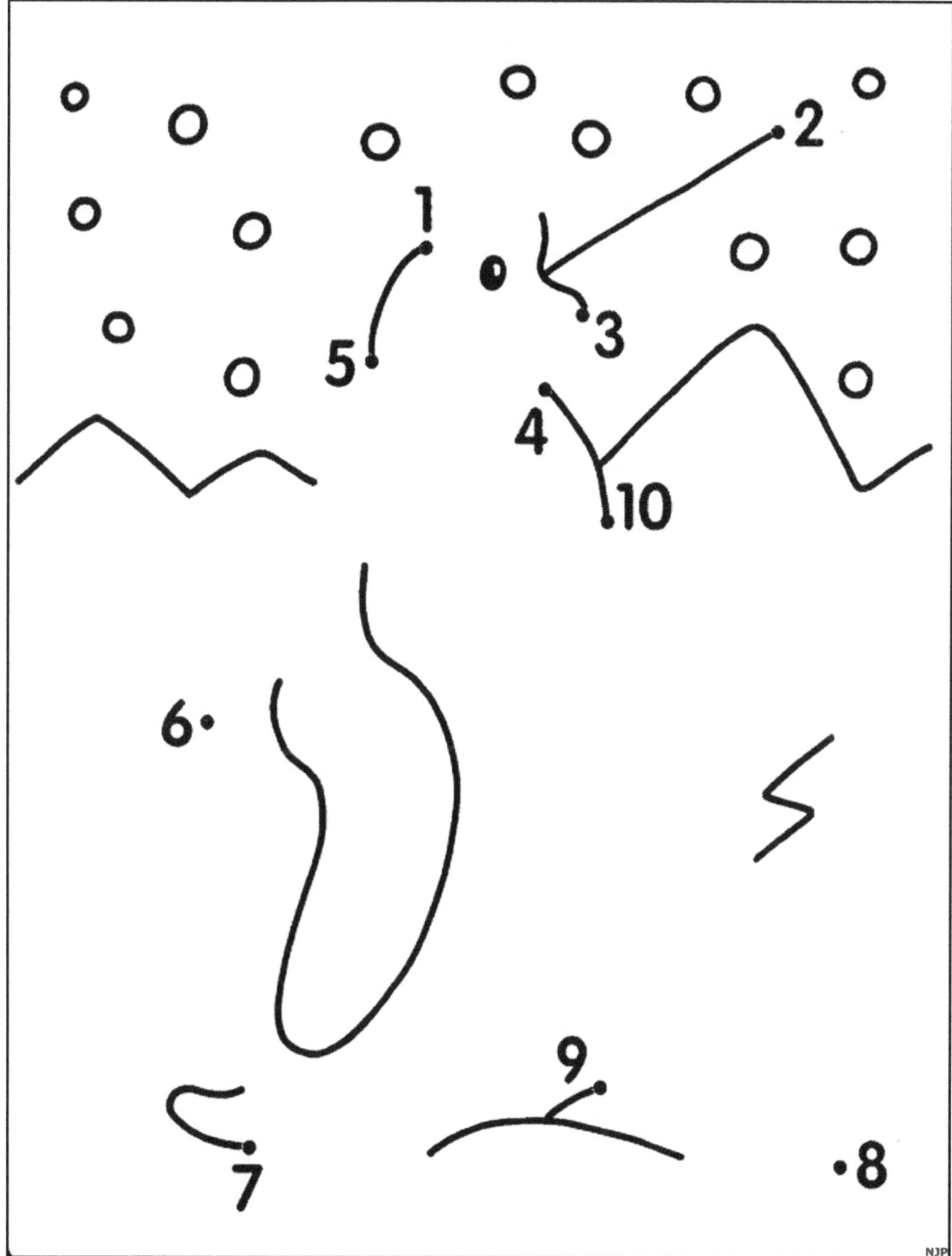

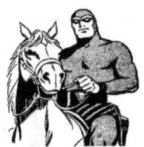

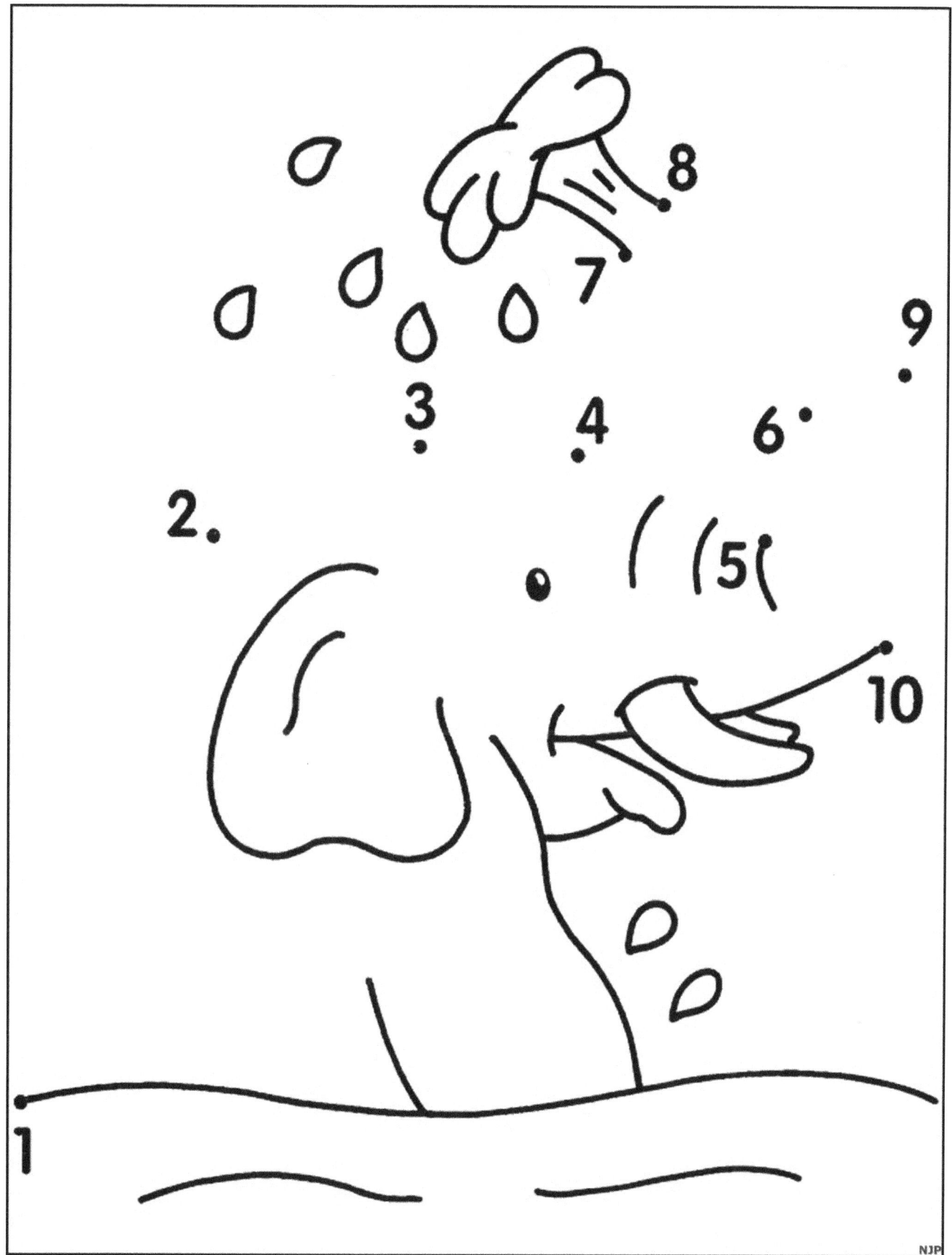

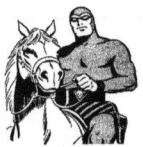

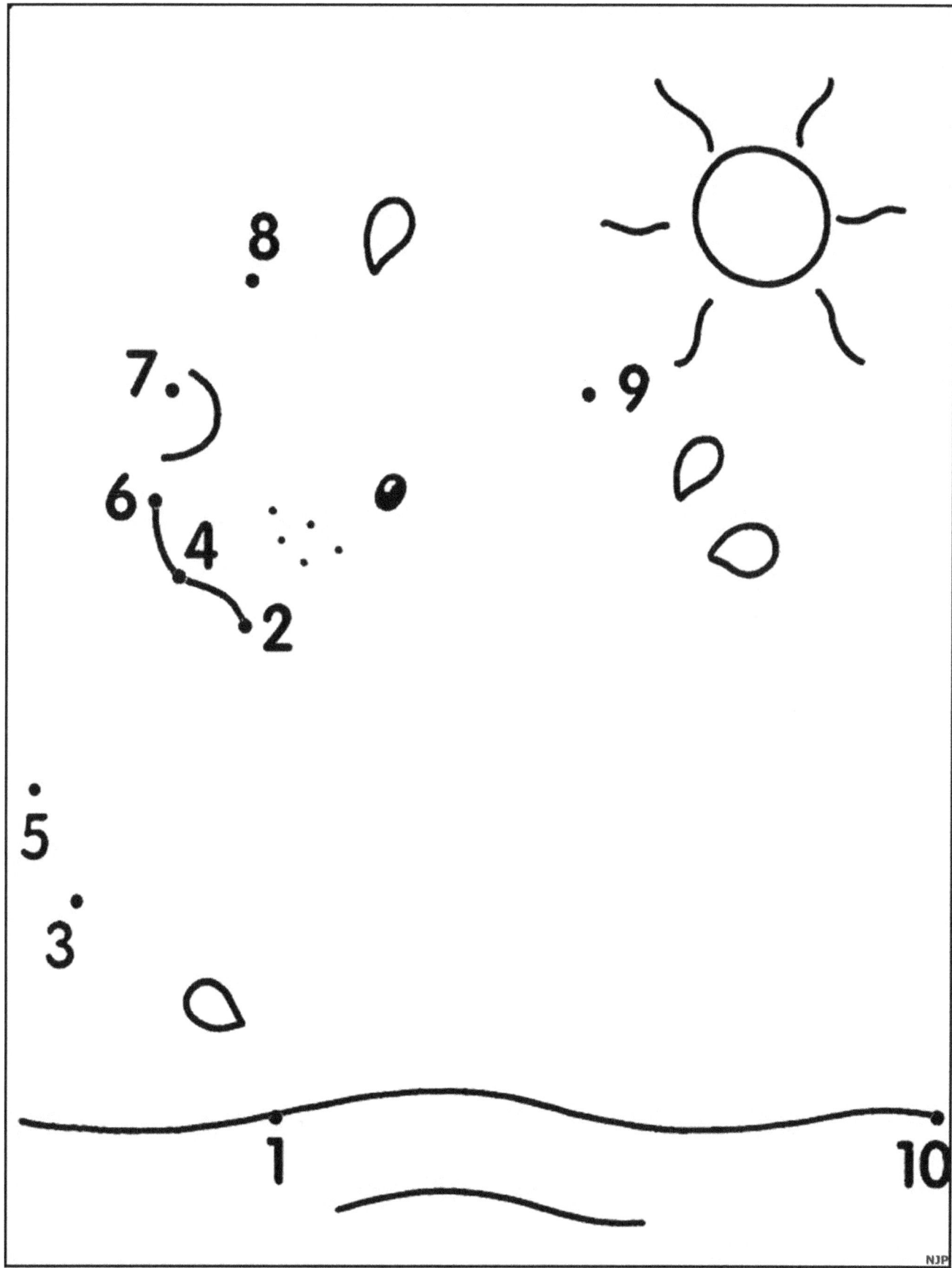

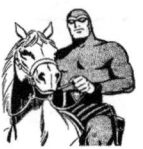

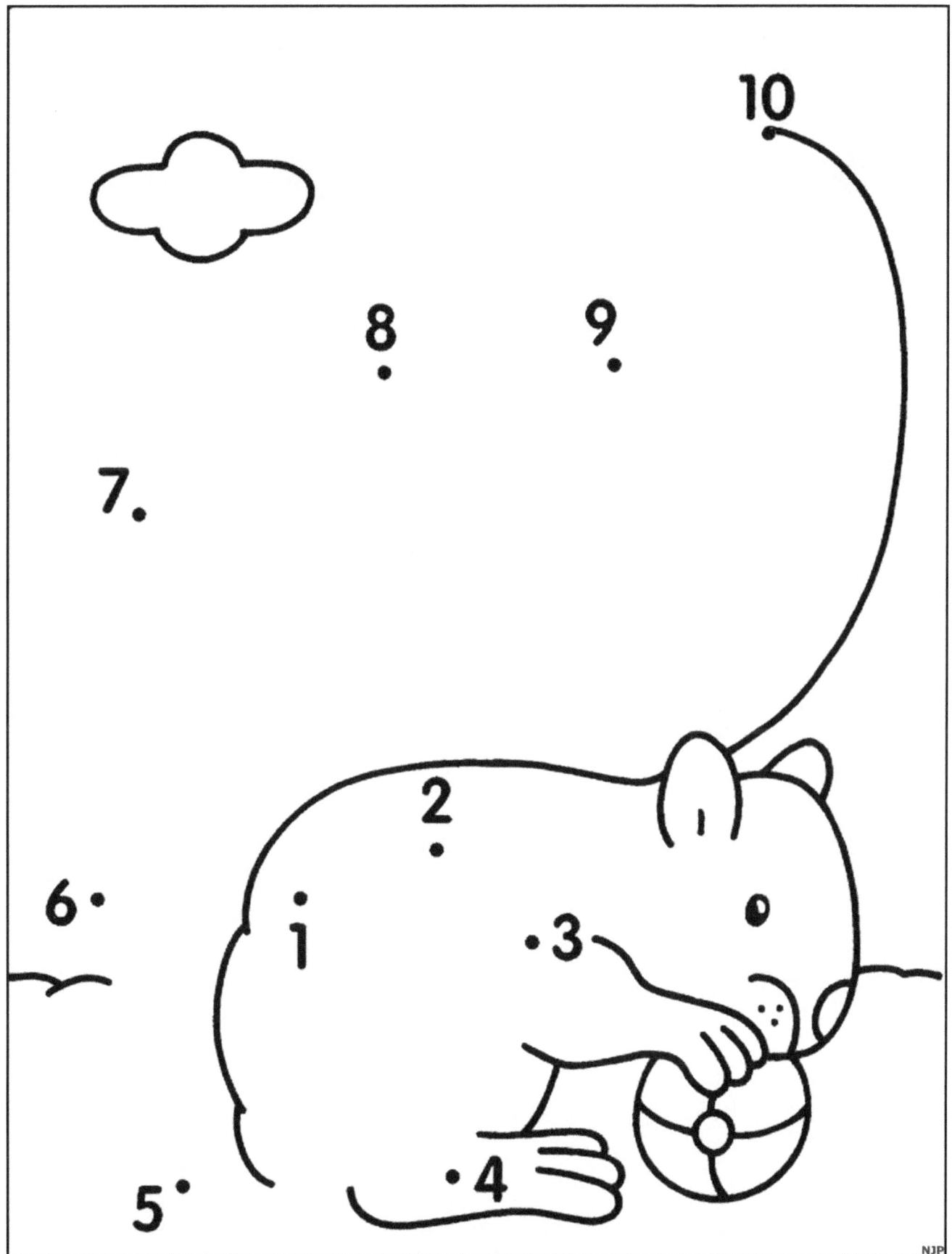

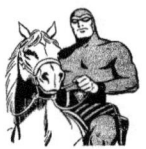

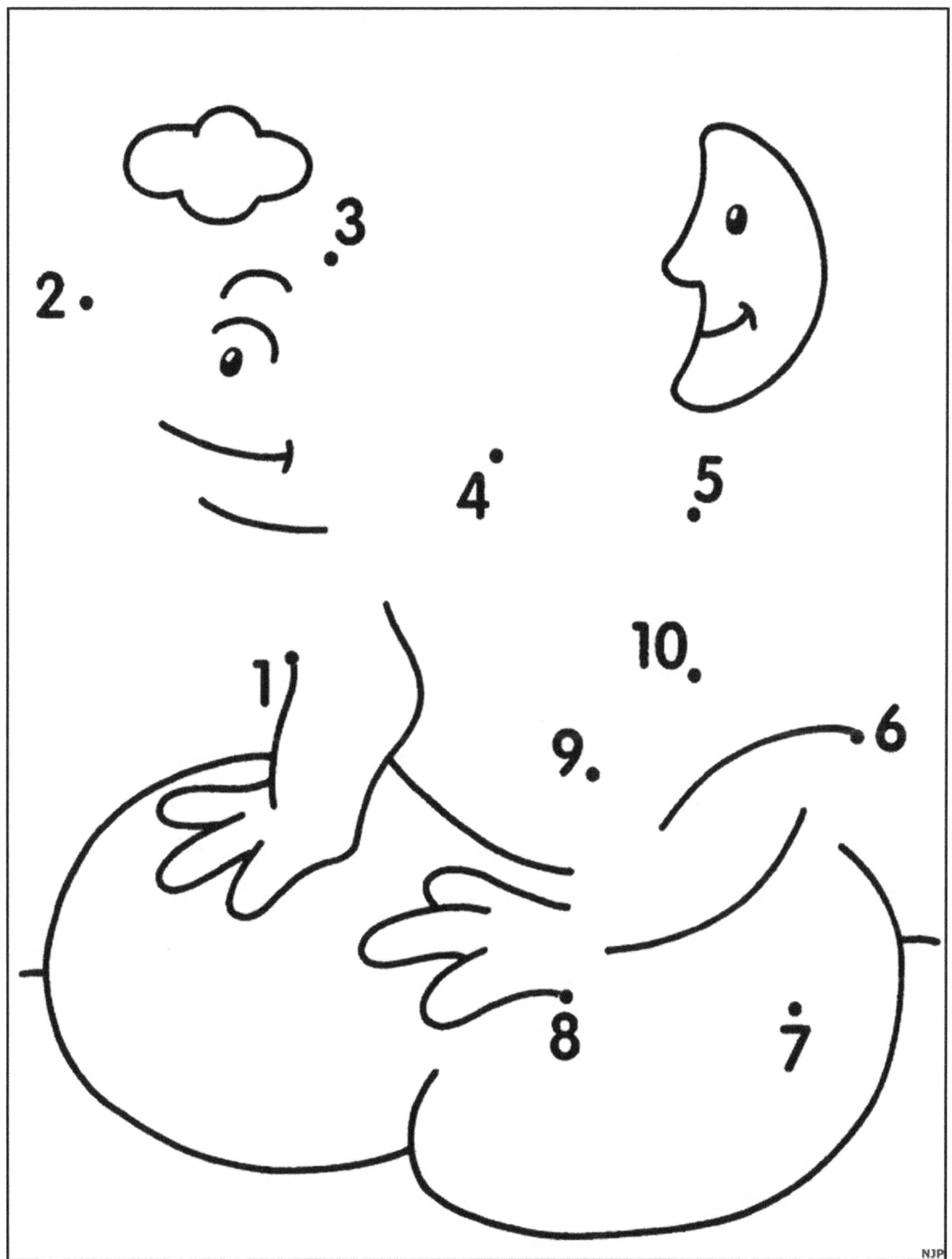

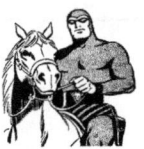

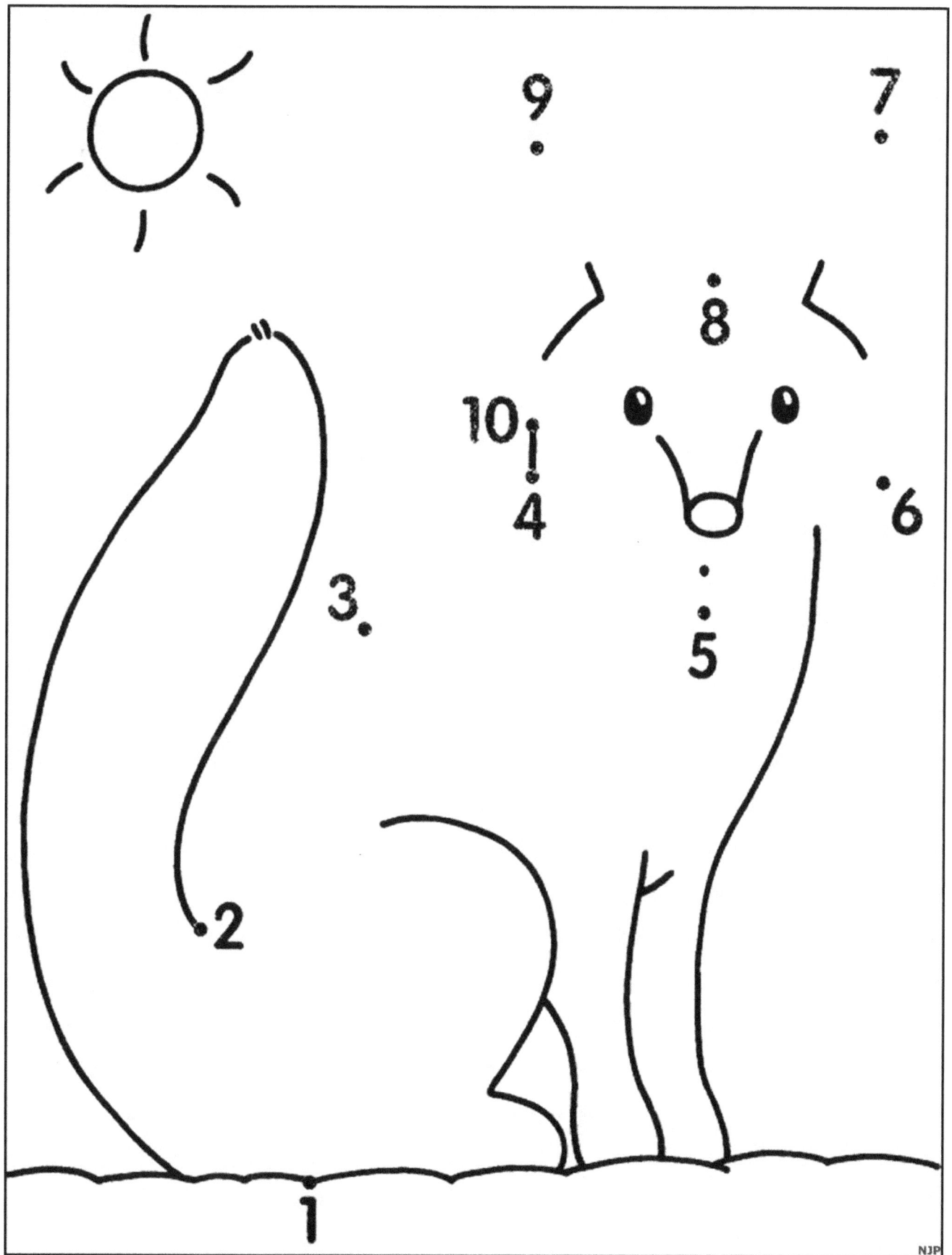

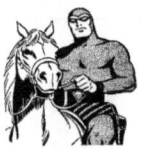

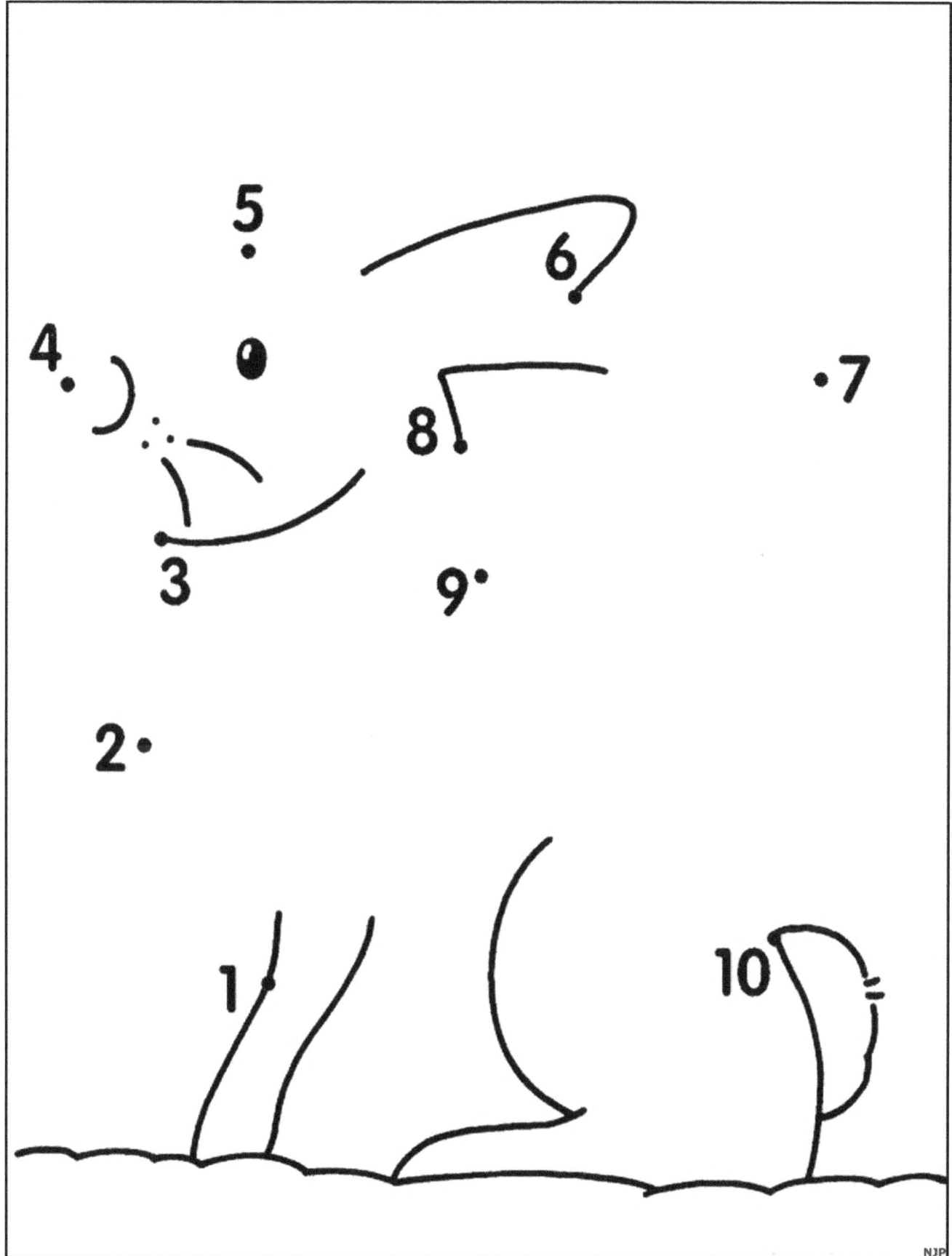

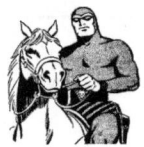

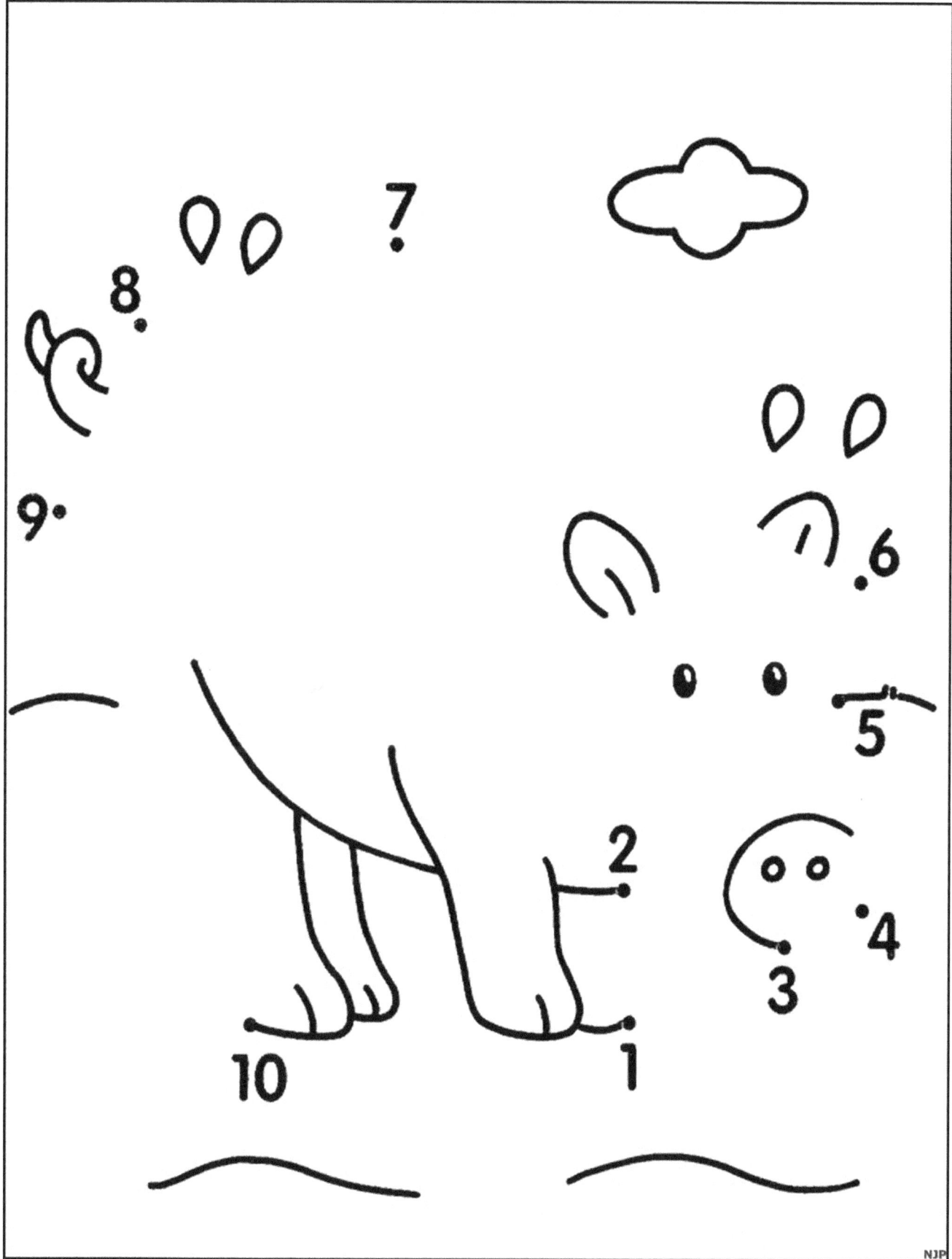

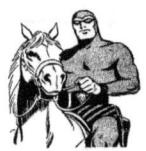

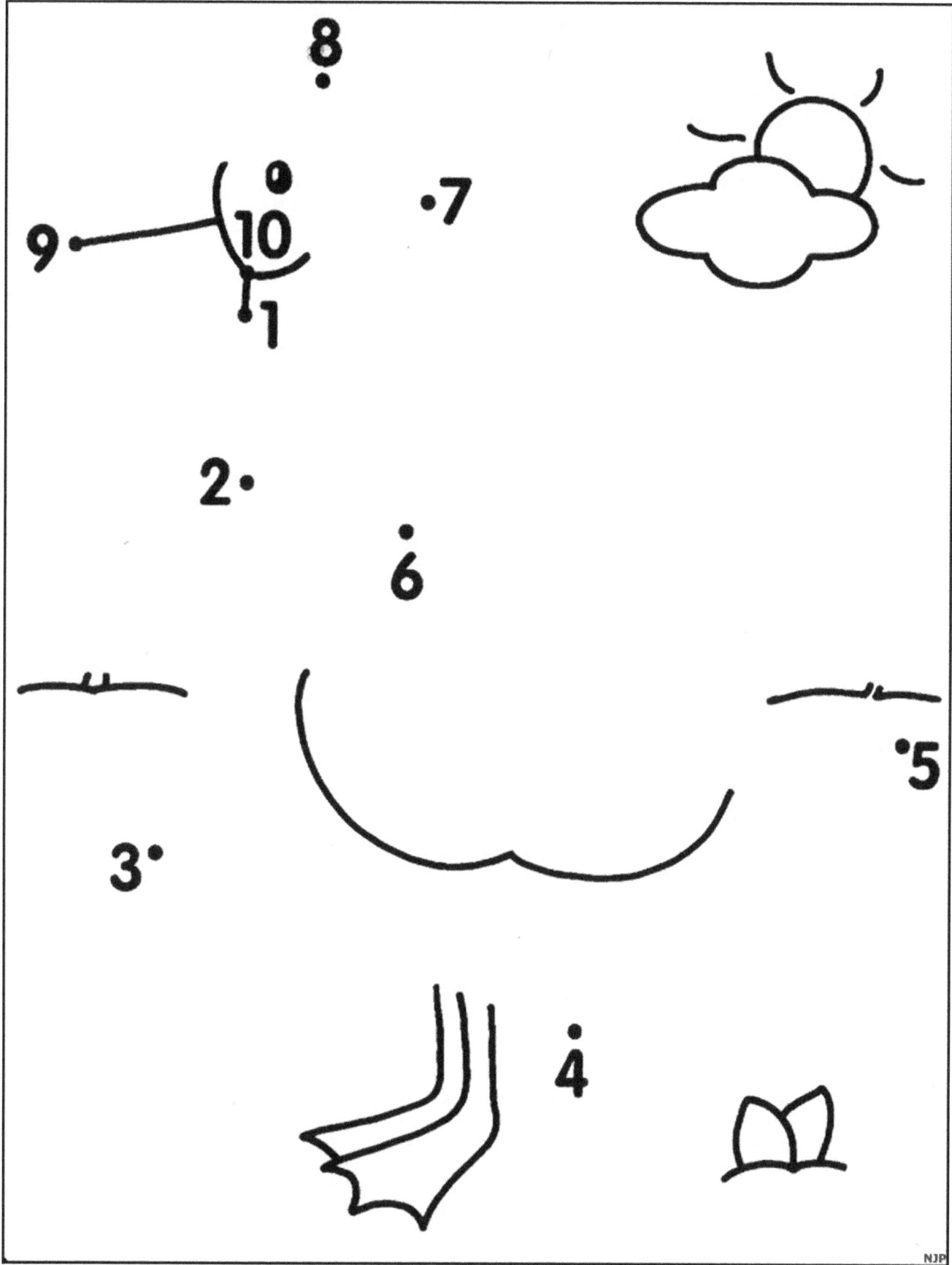

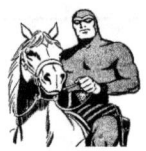

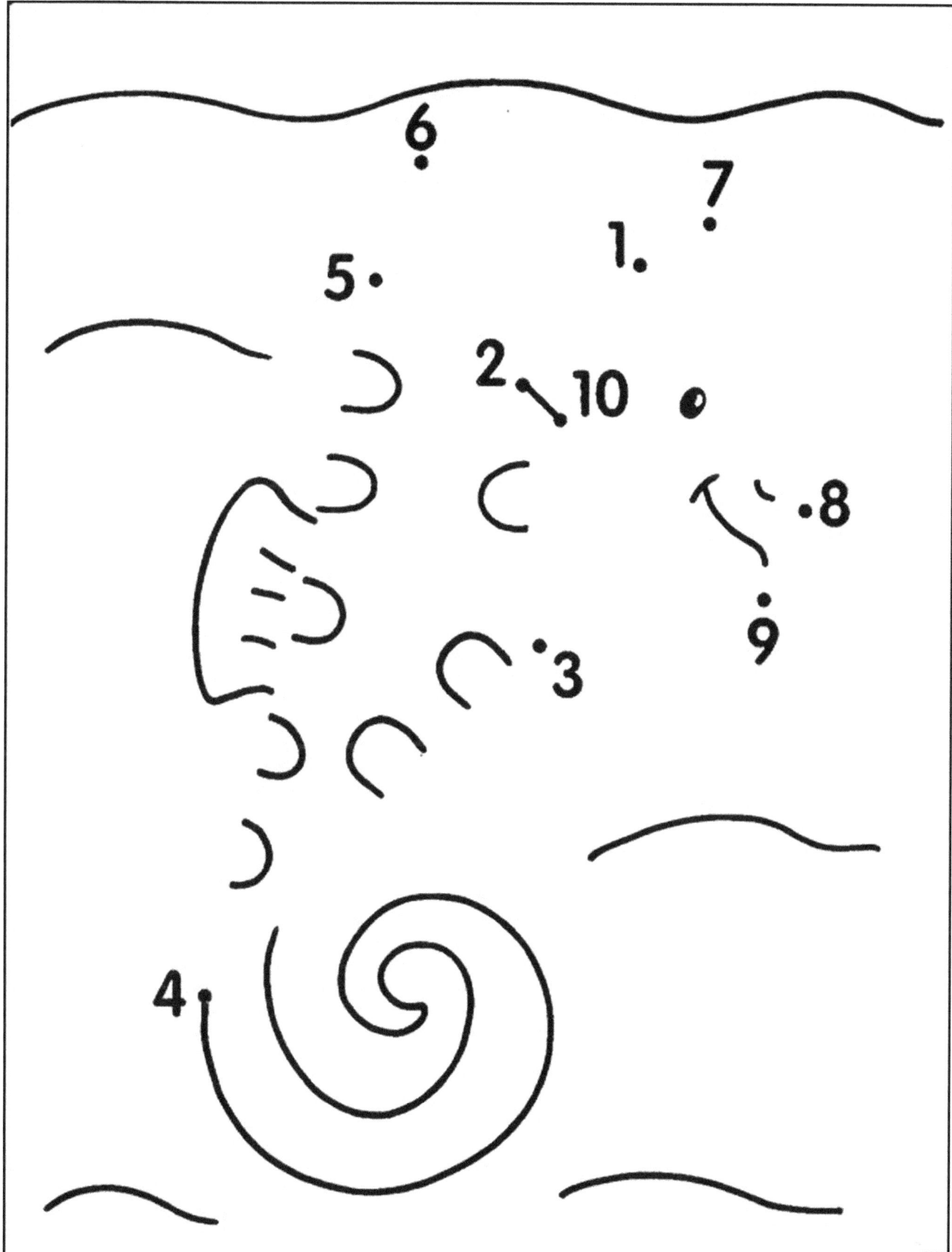

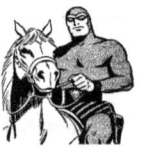

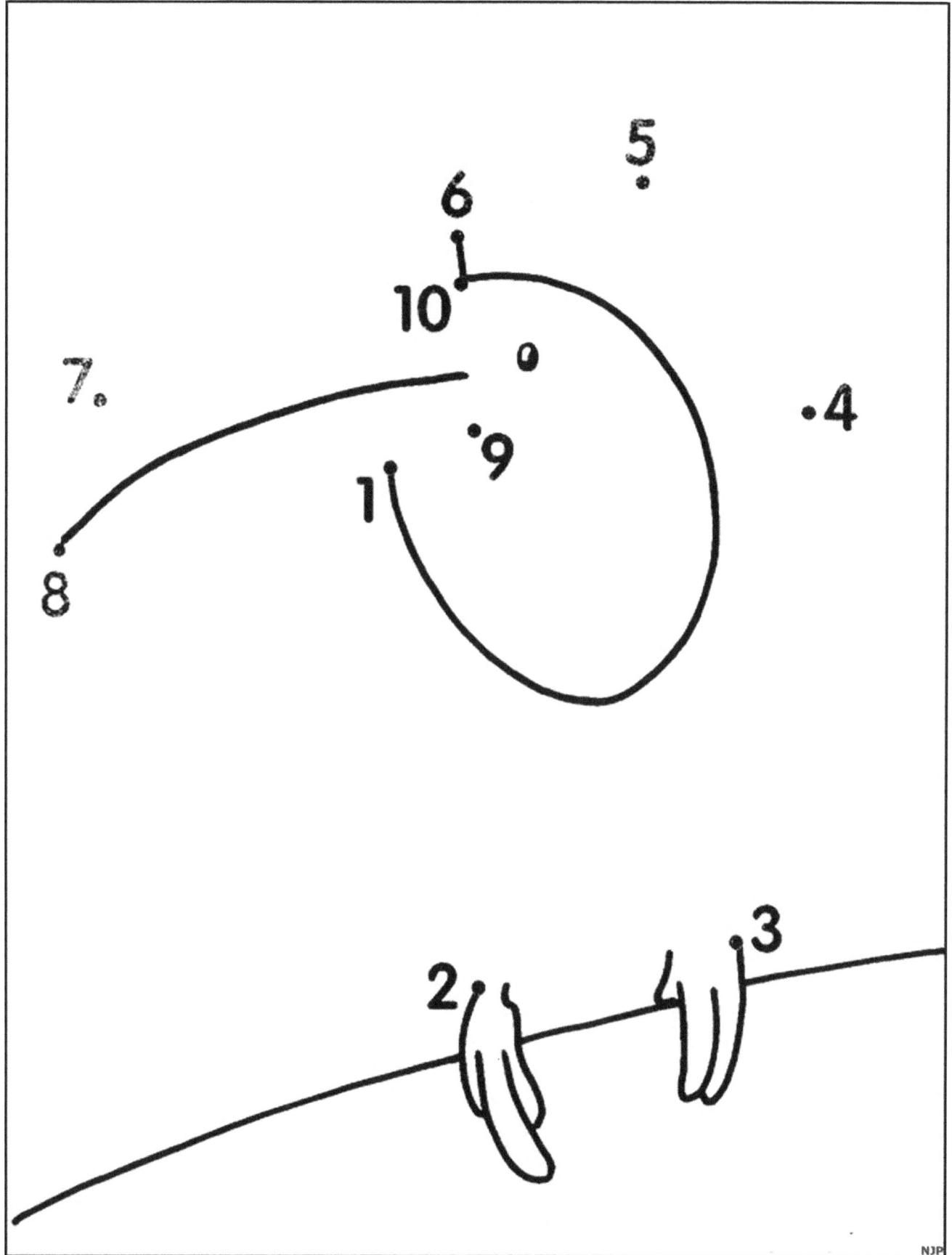

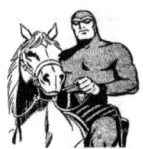

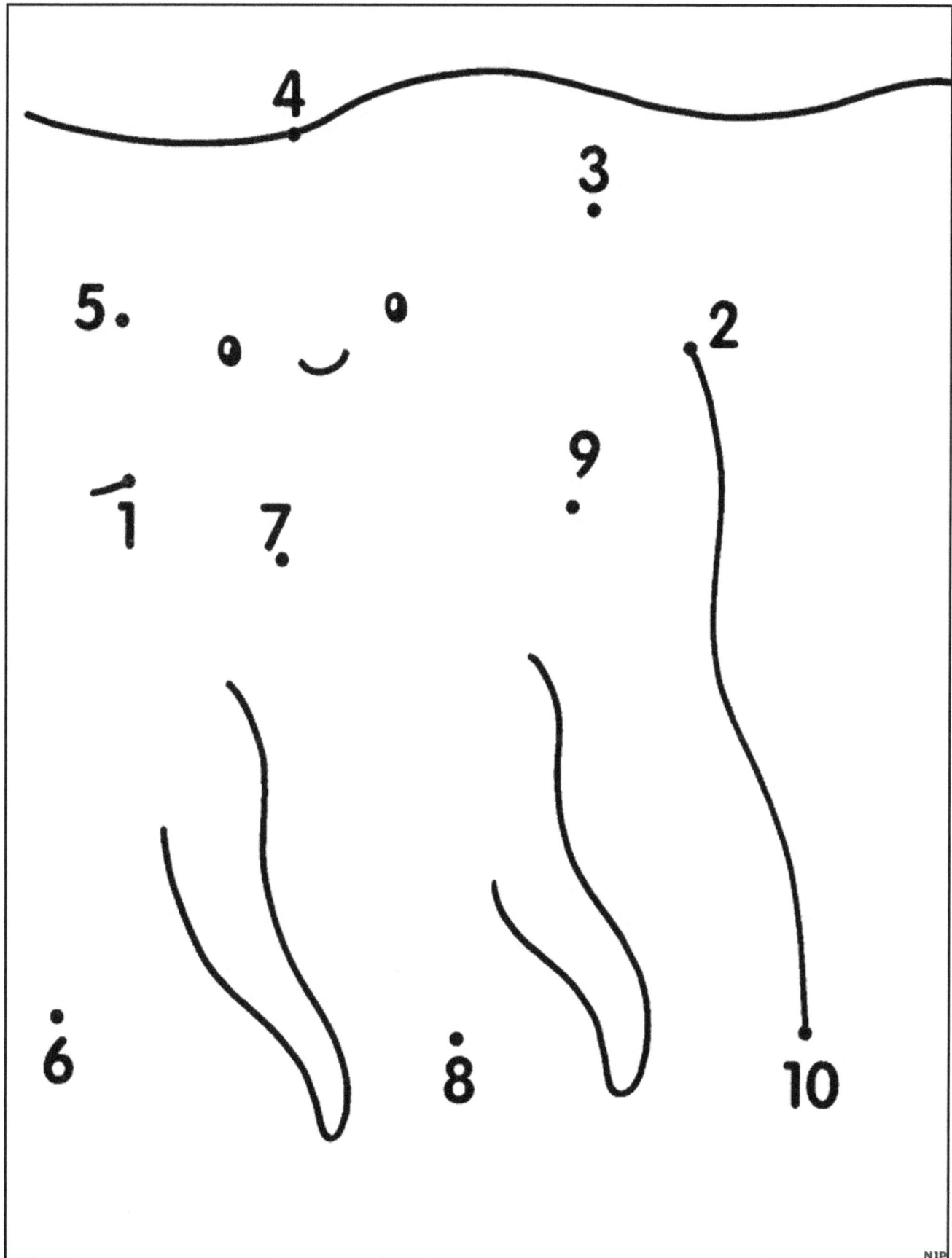

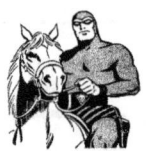

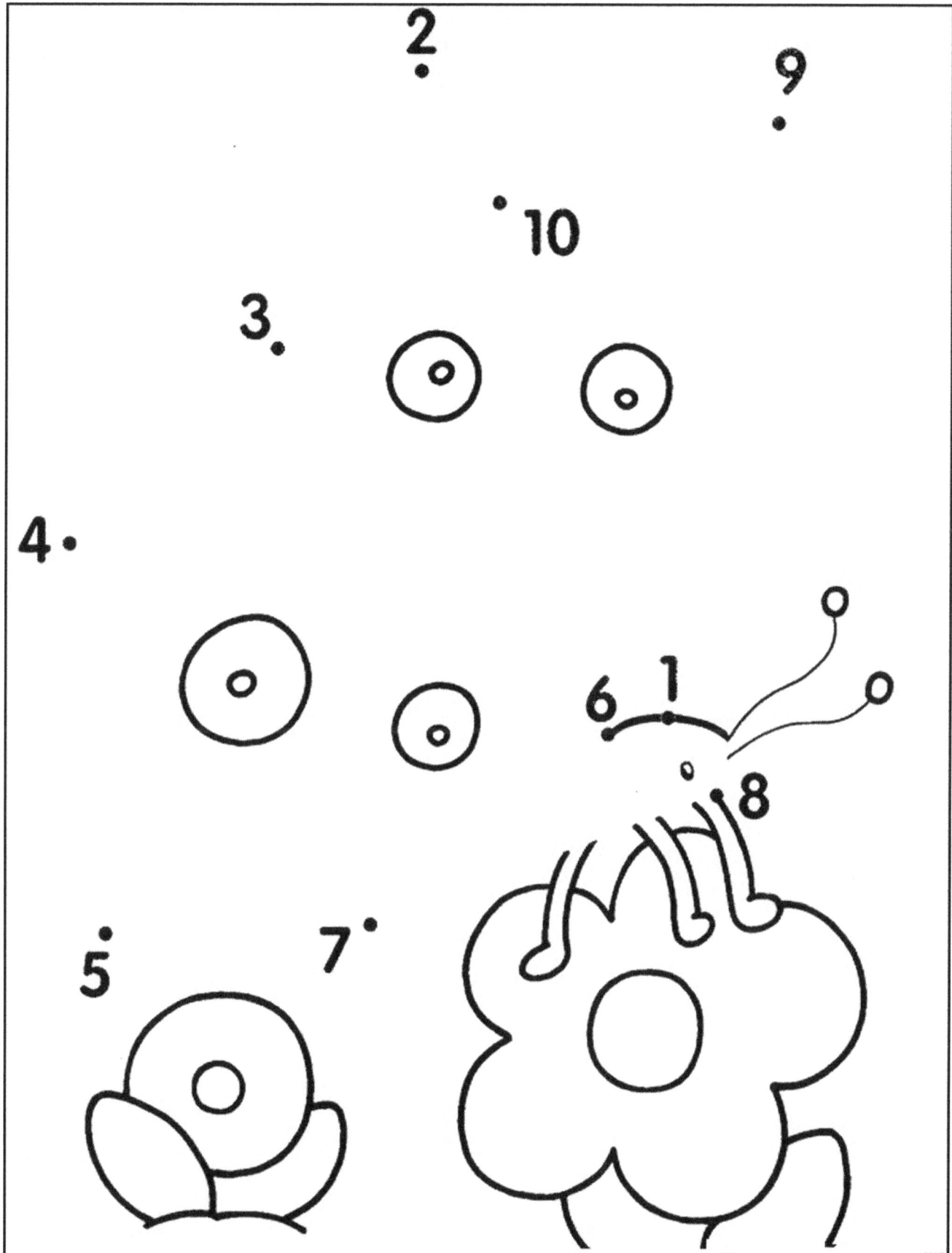

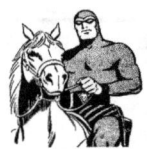

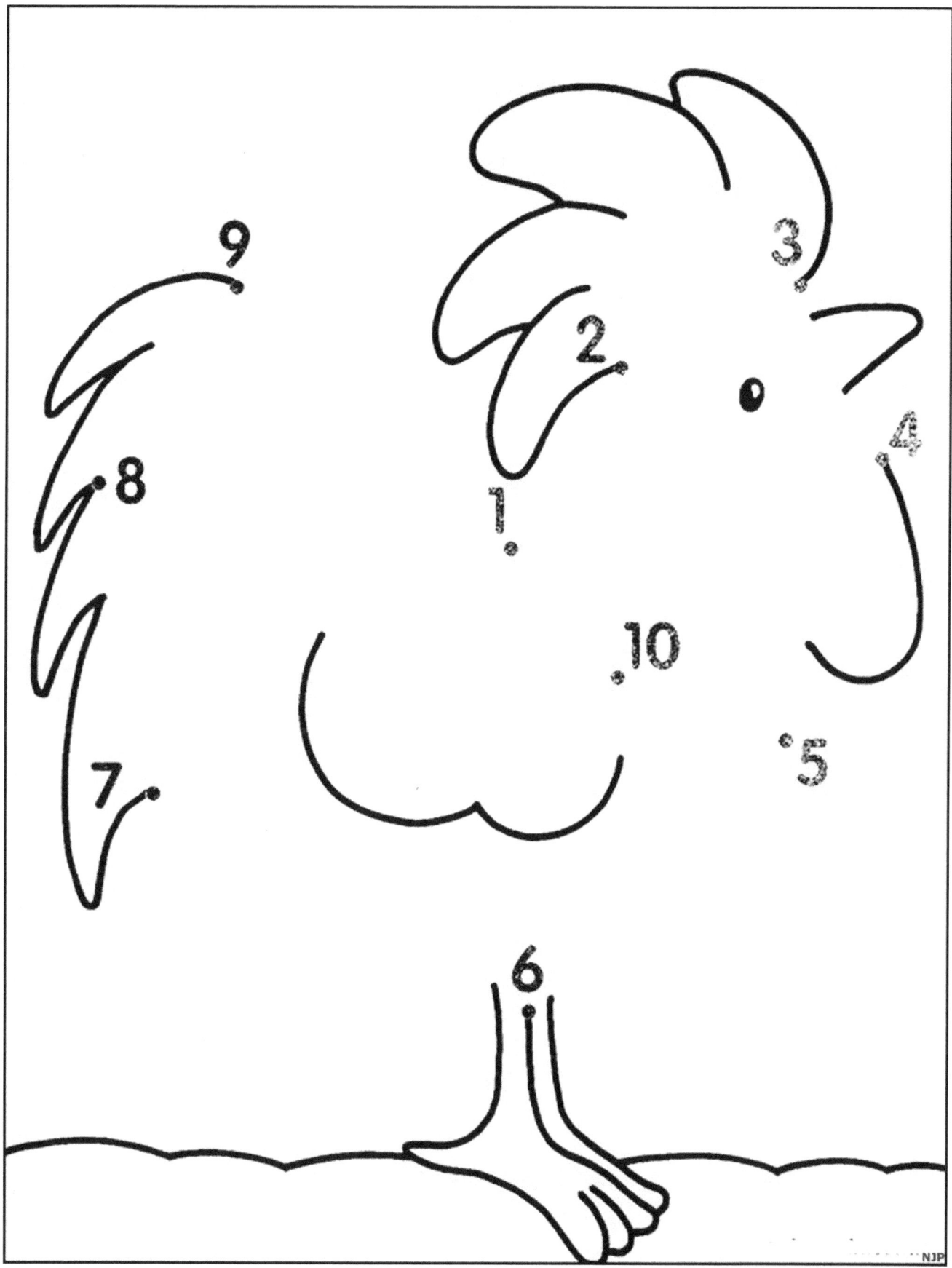

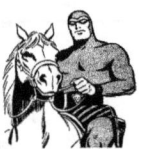

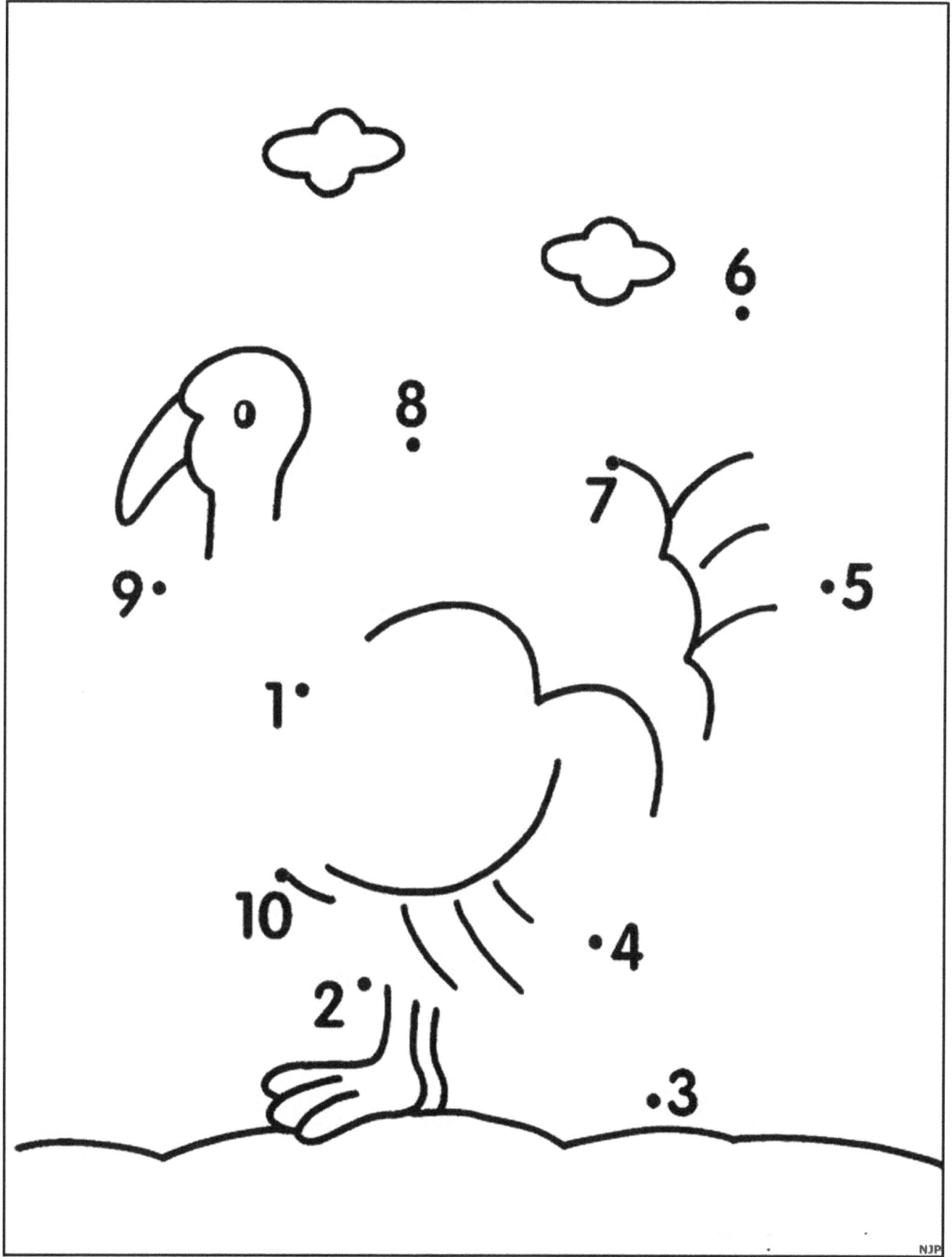

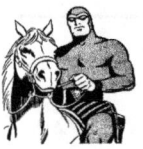

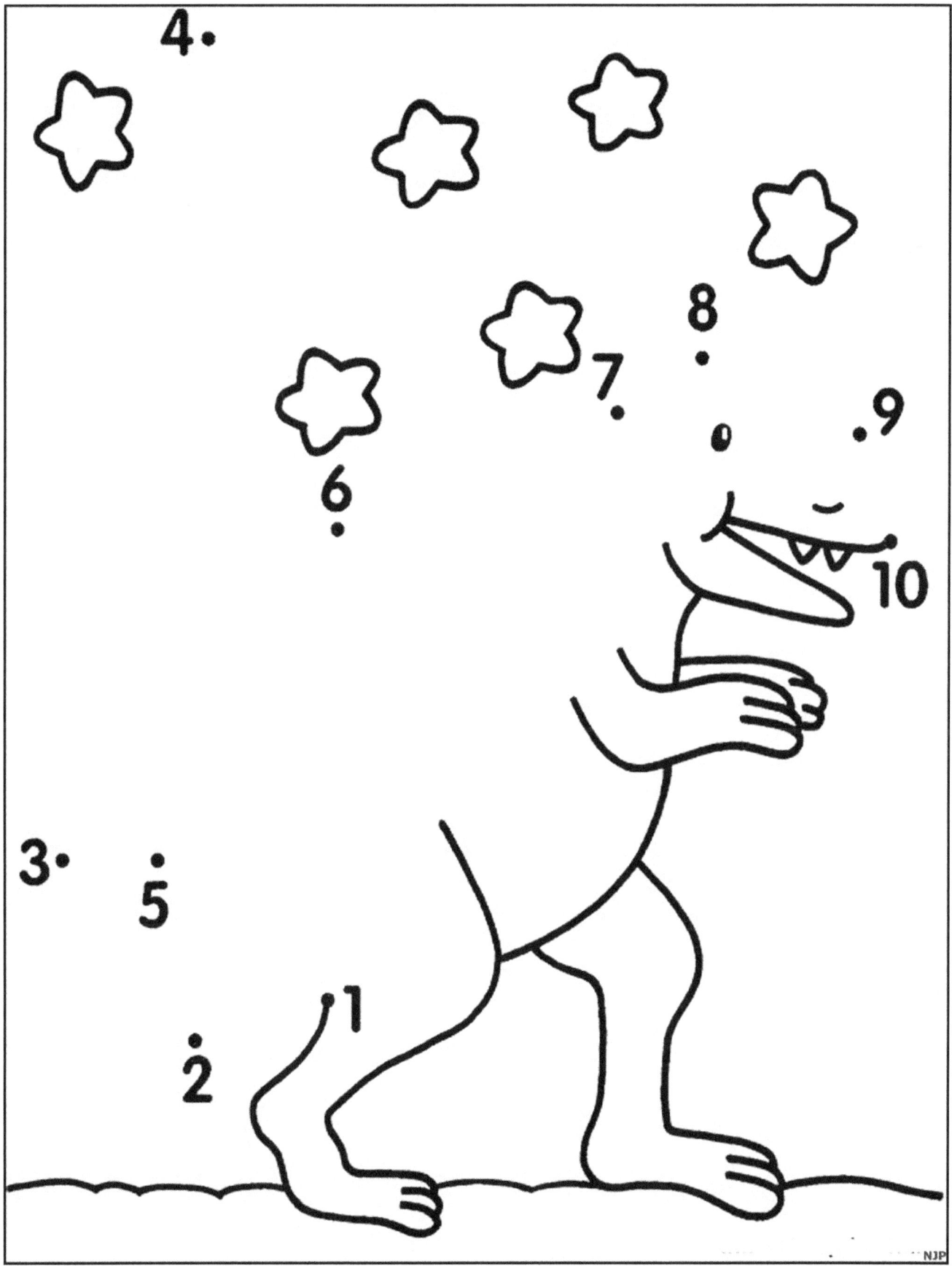

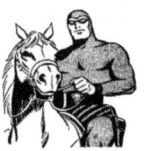

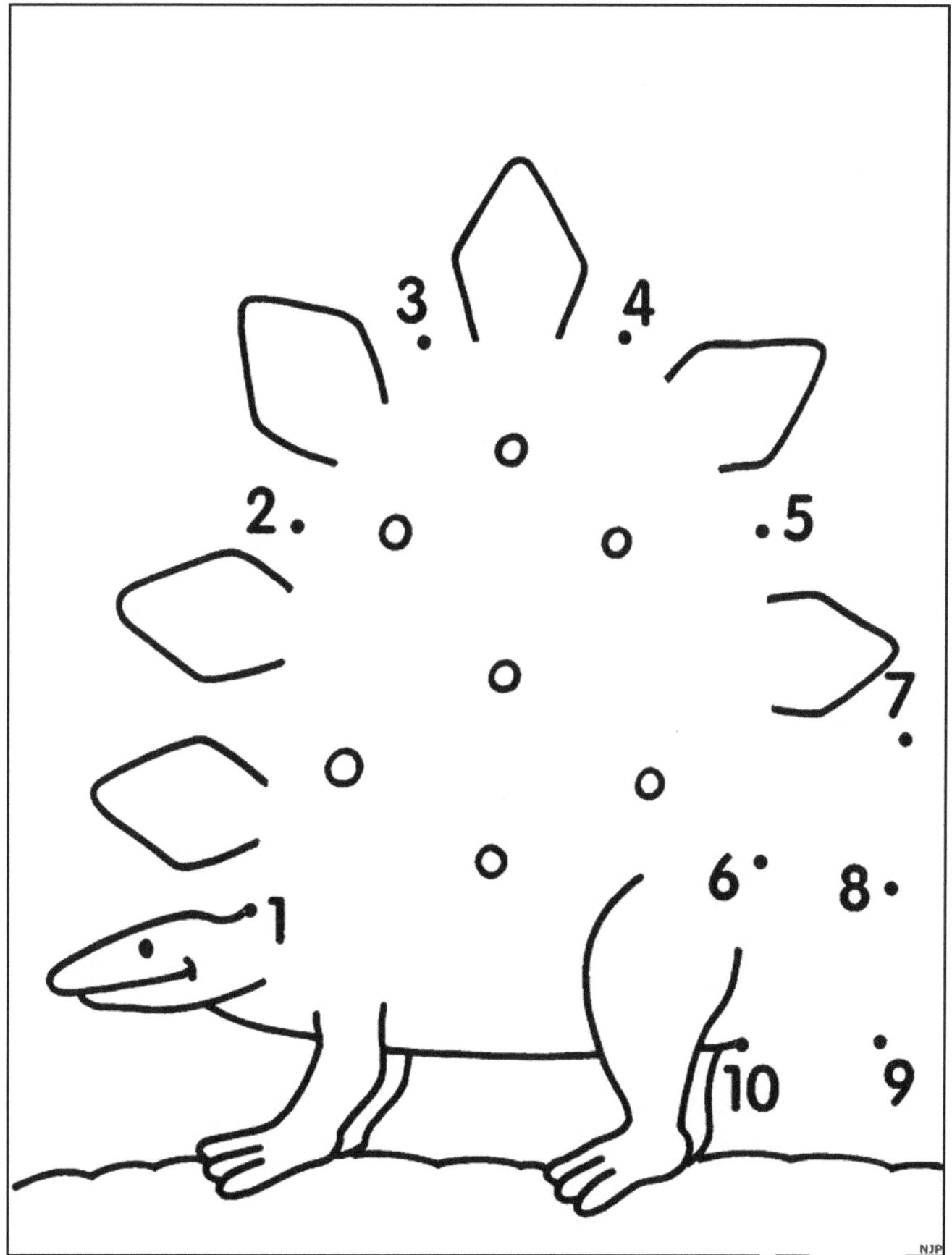

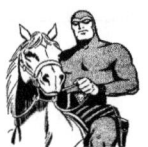

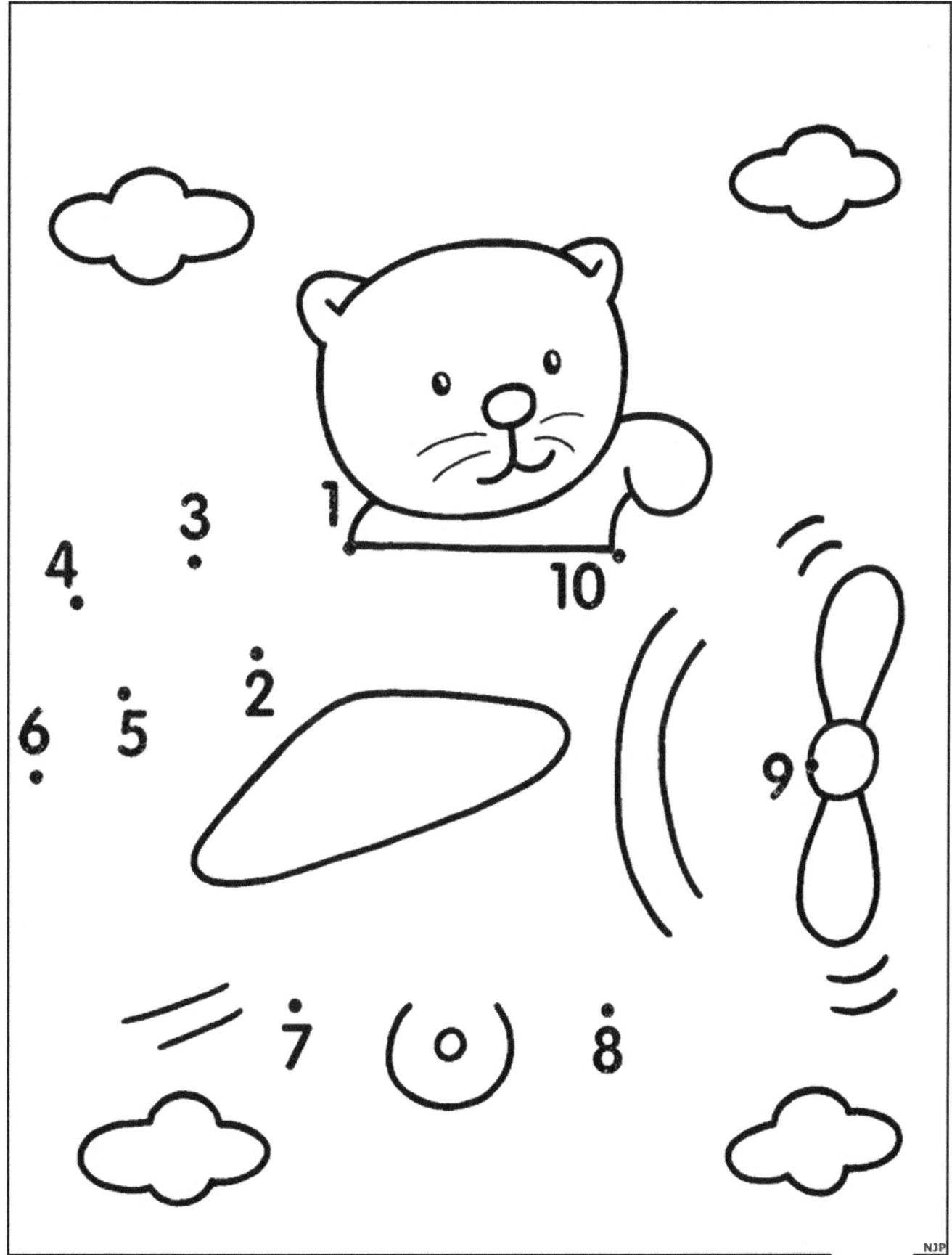

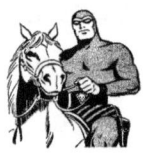

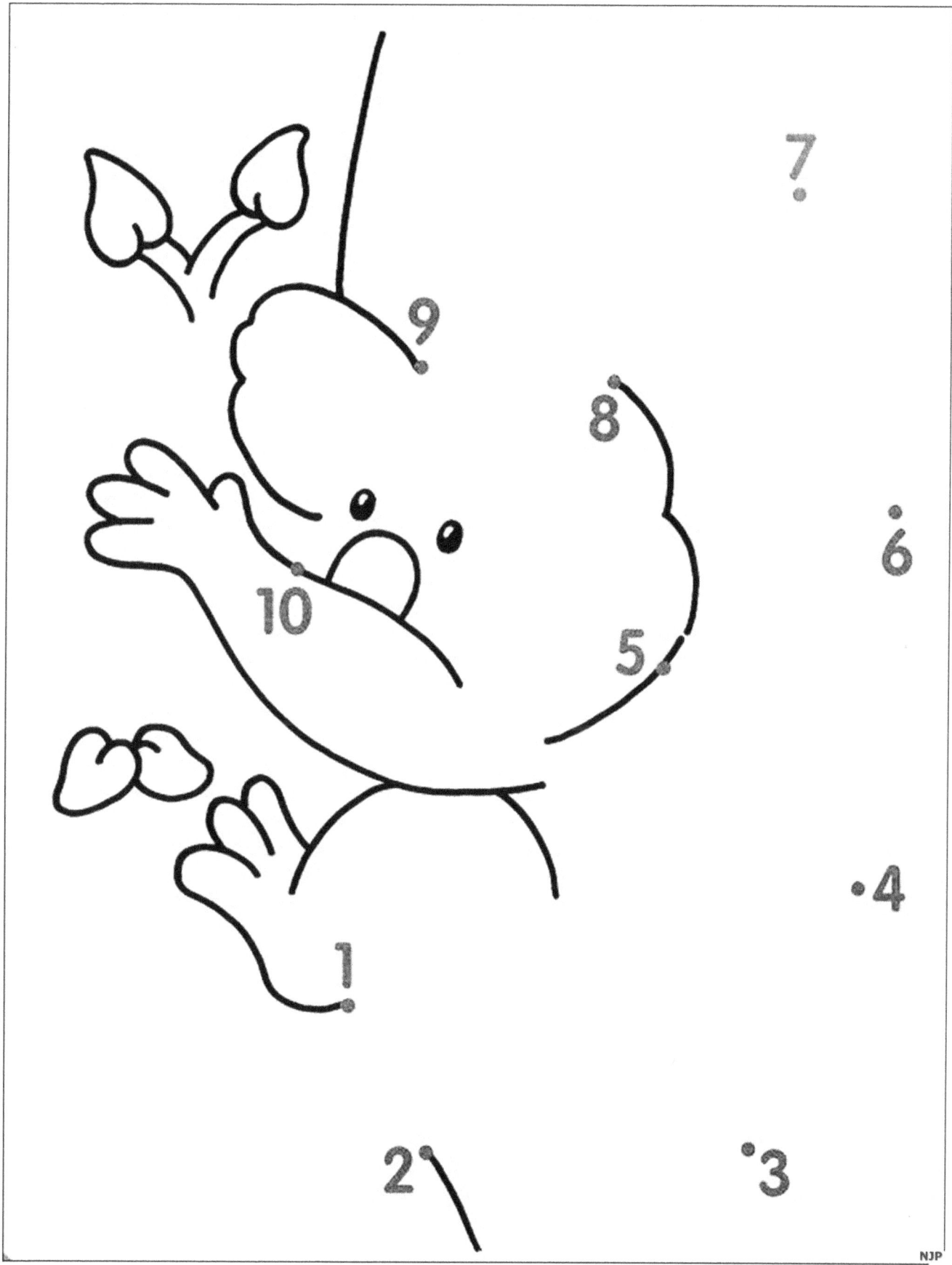

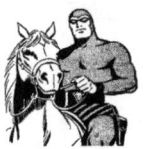

Level – 2

20 Dots per Picture

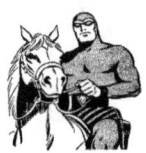

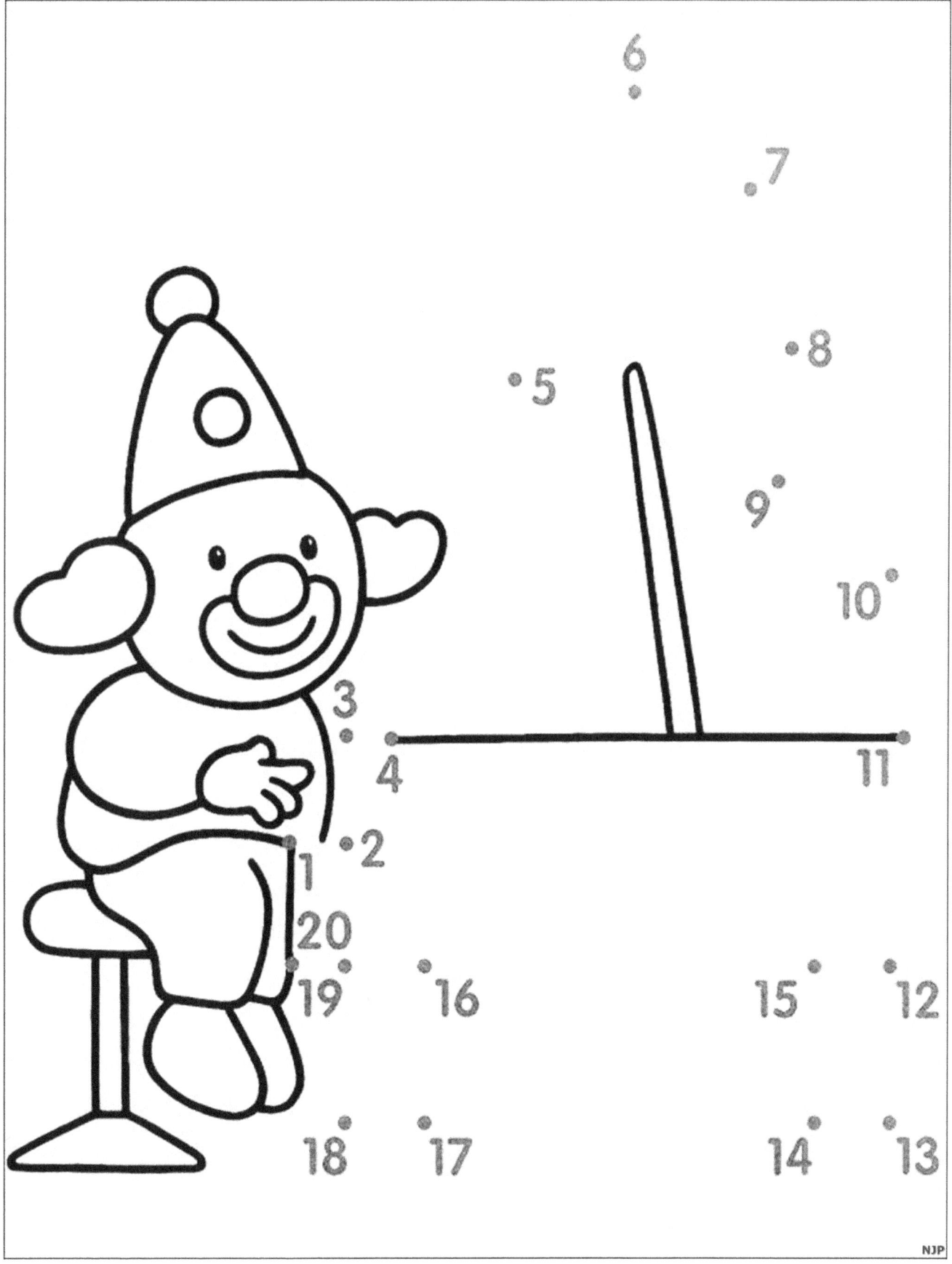

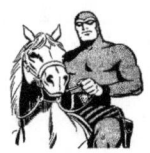

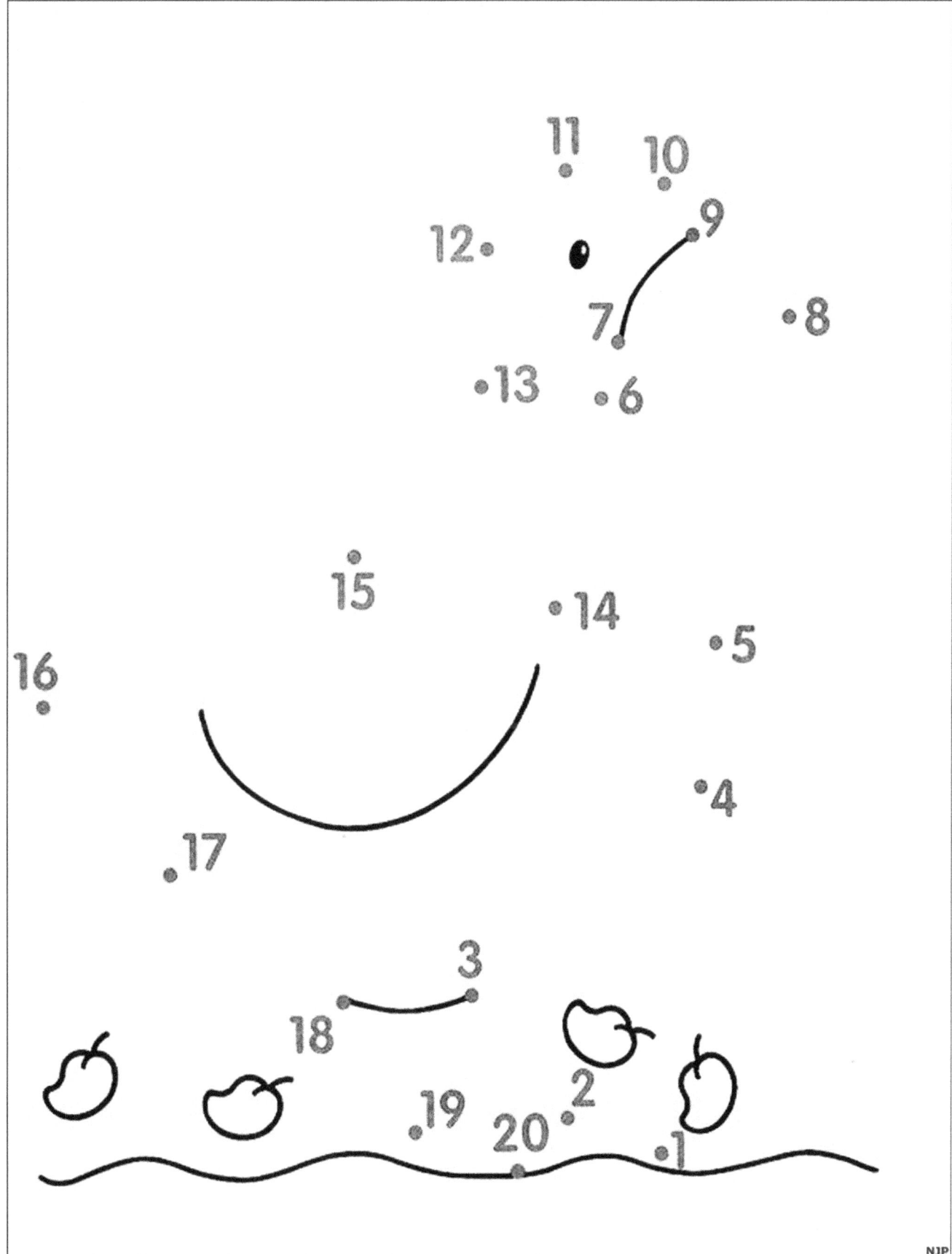

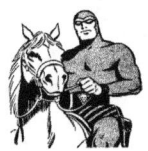

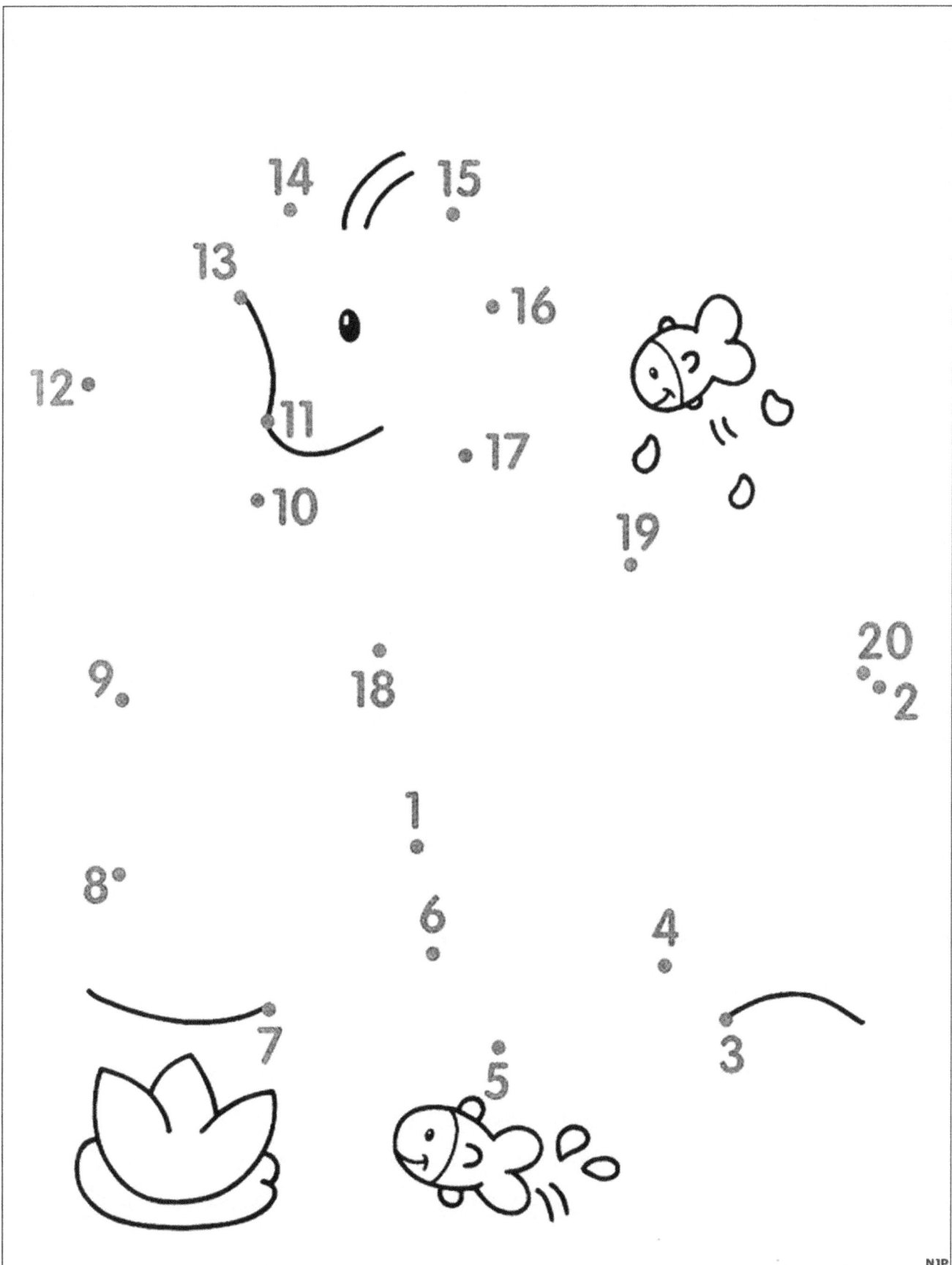

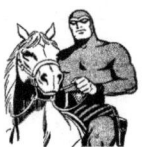

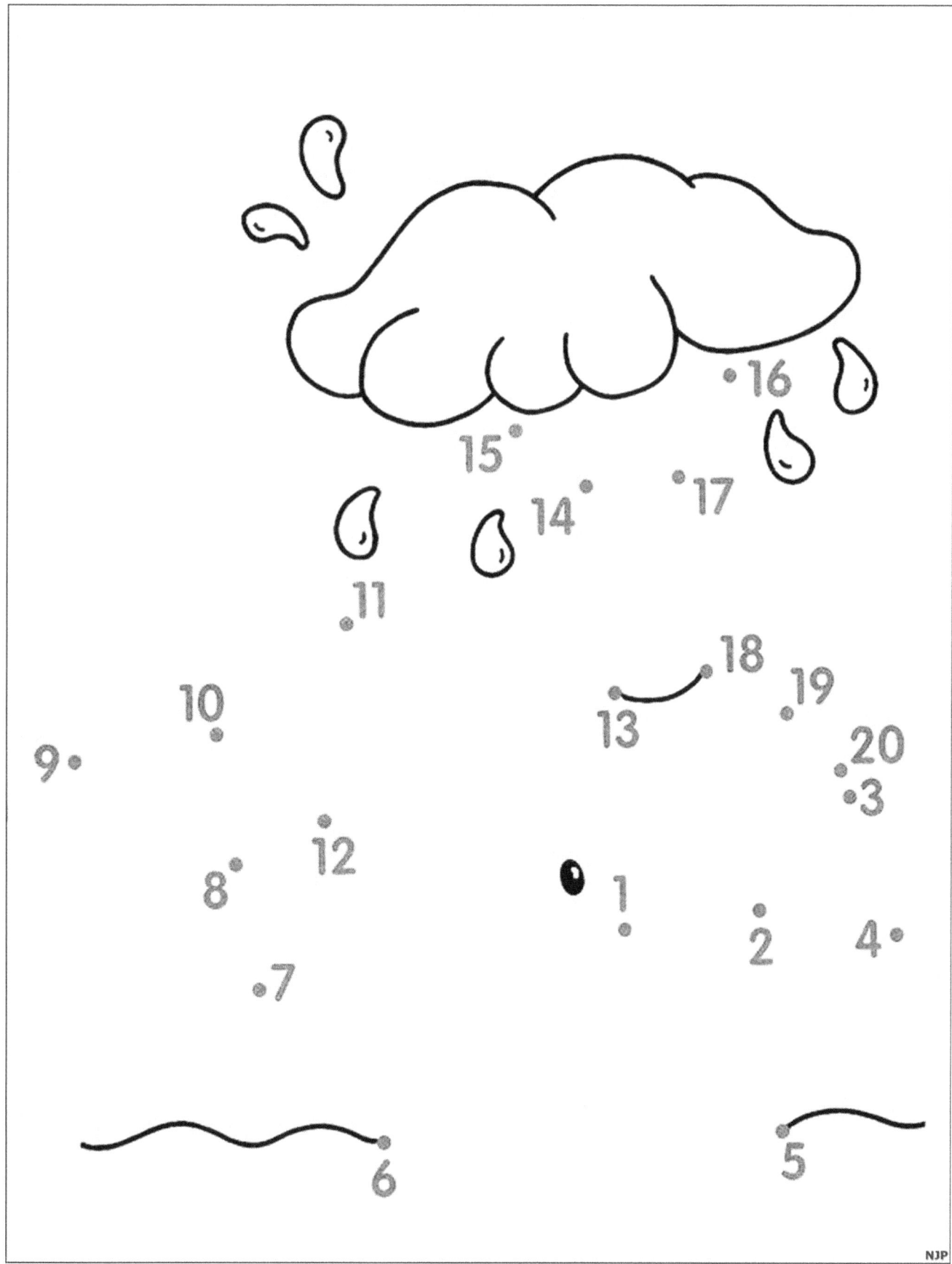

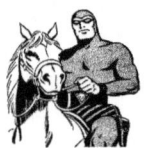

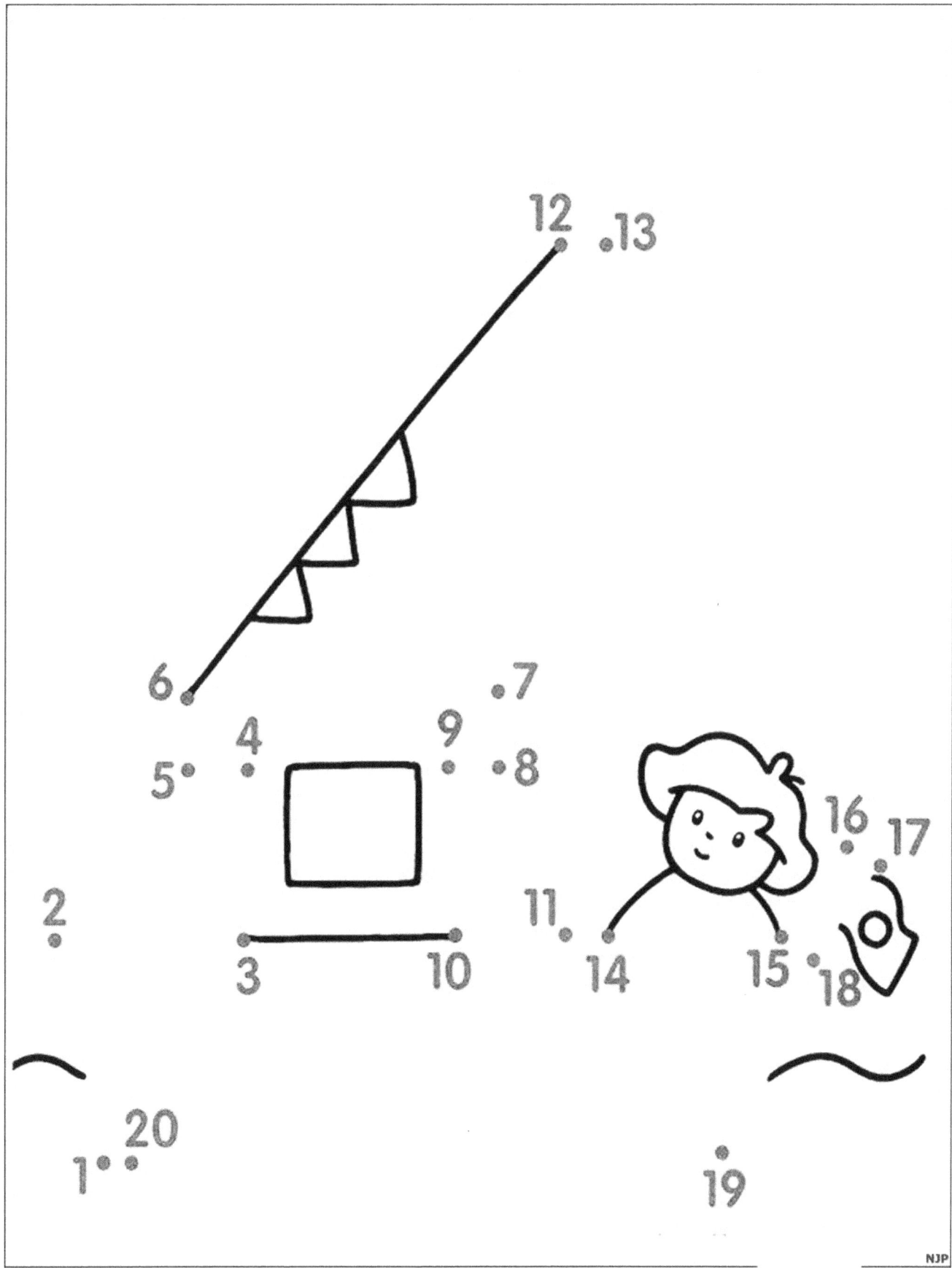

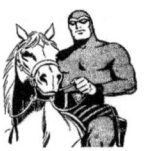

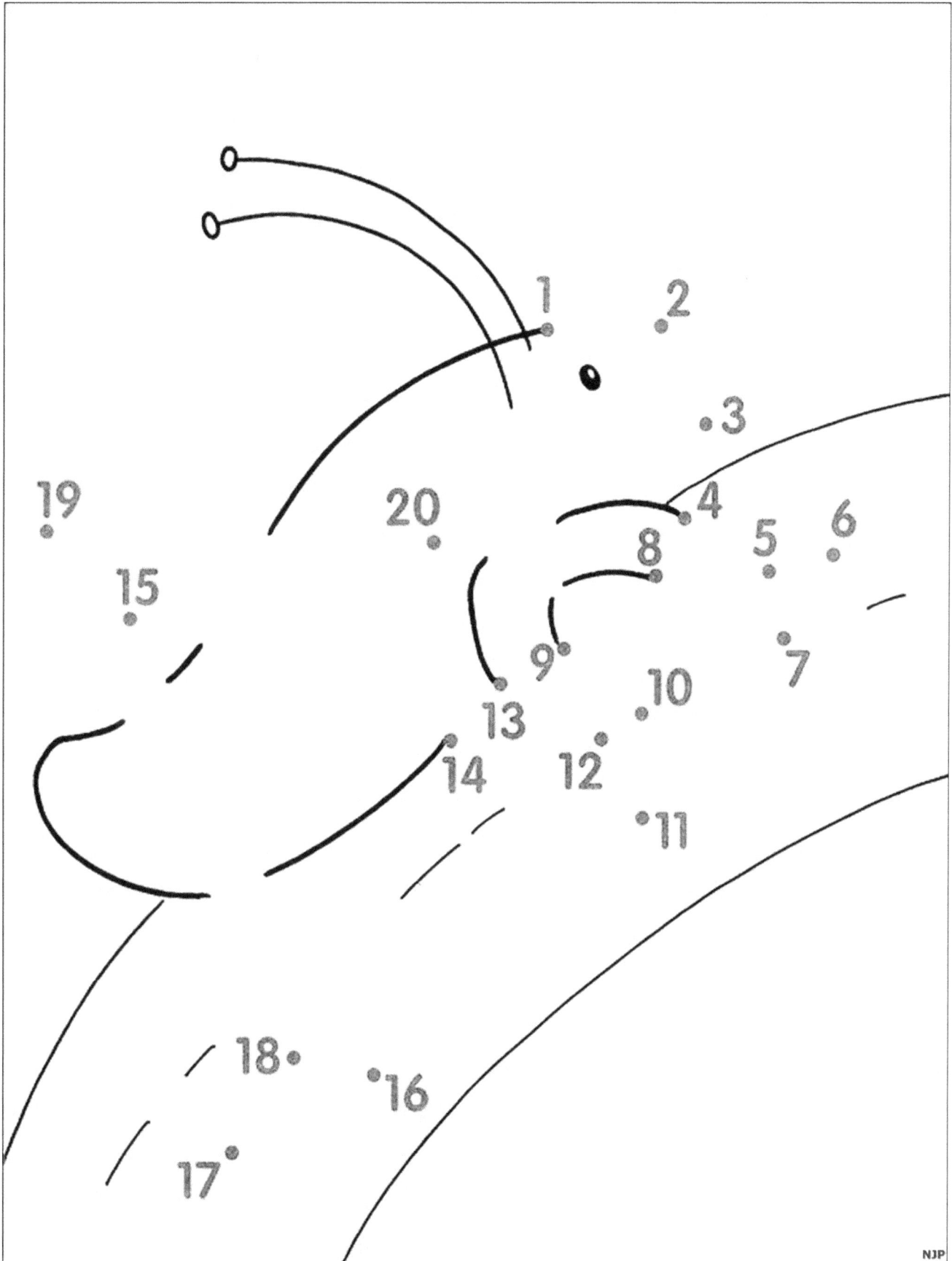

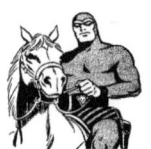

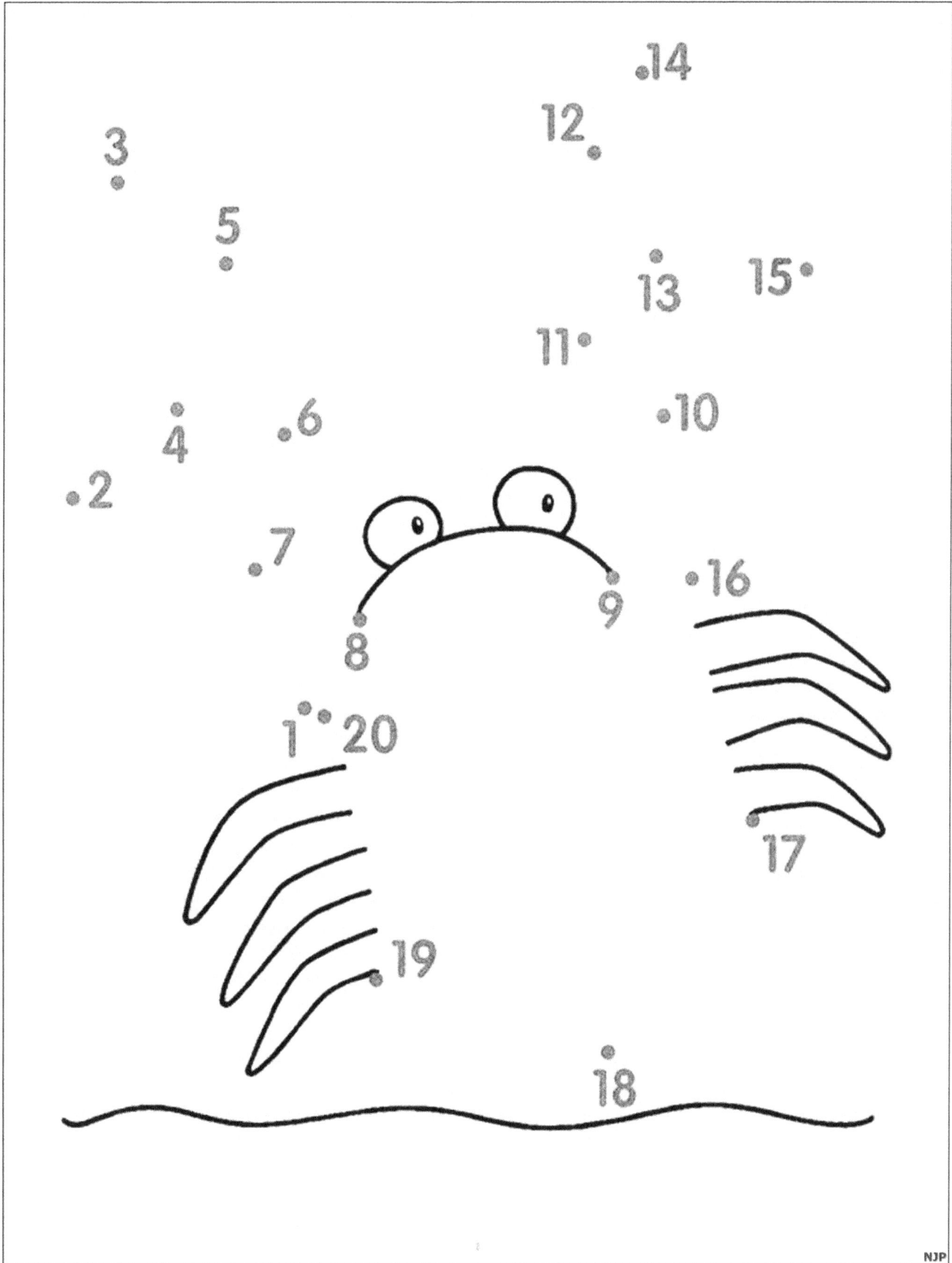

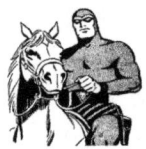

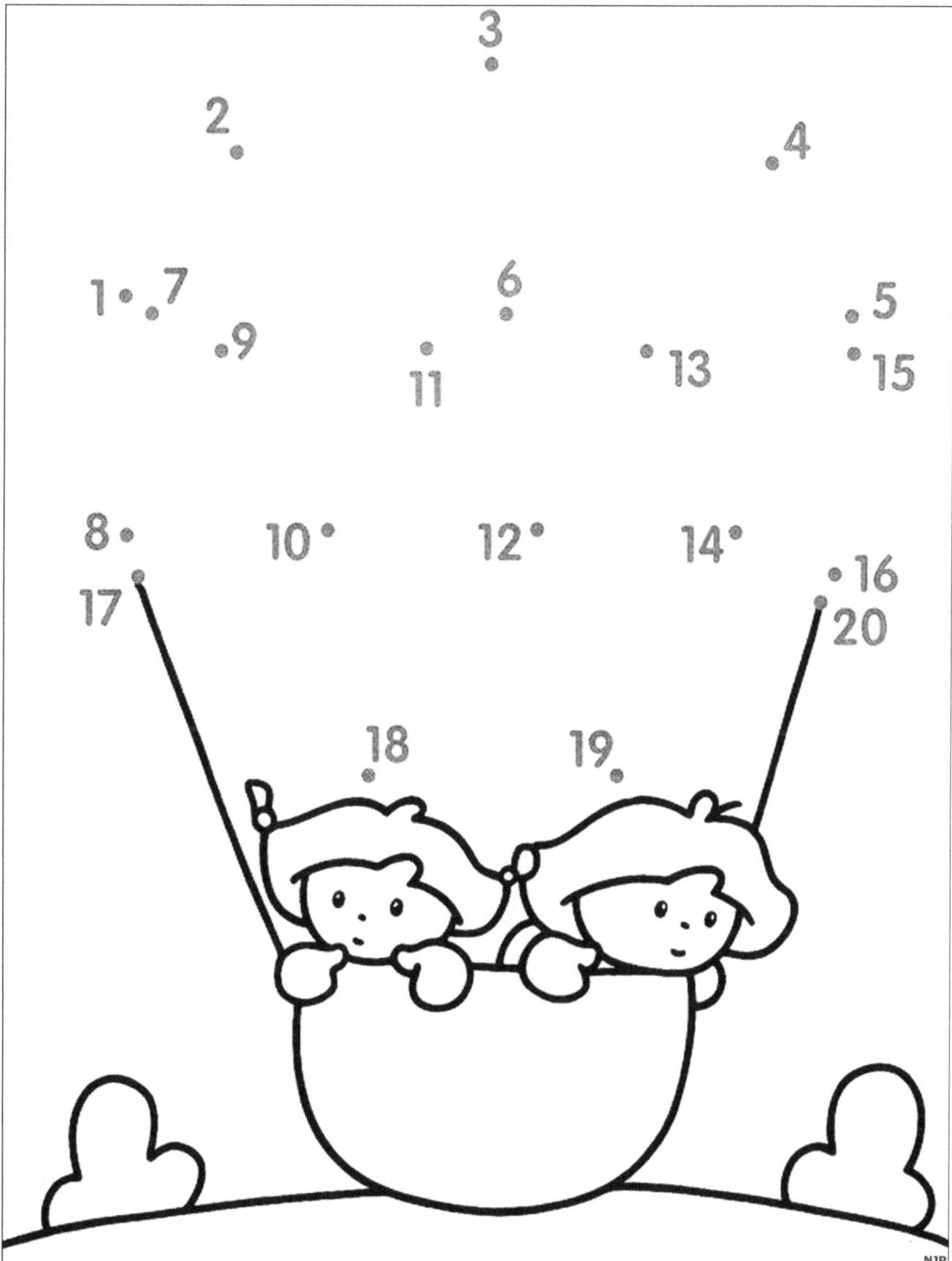

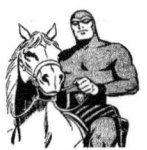

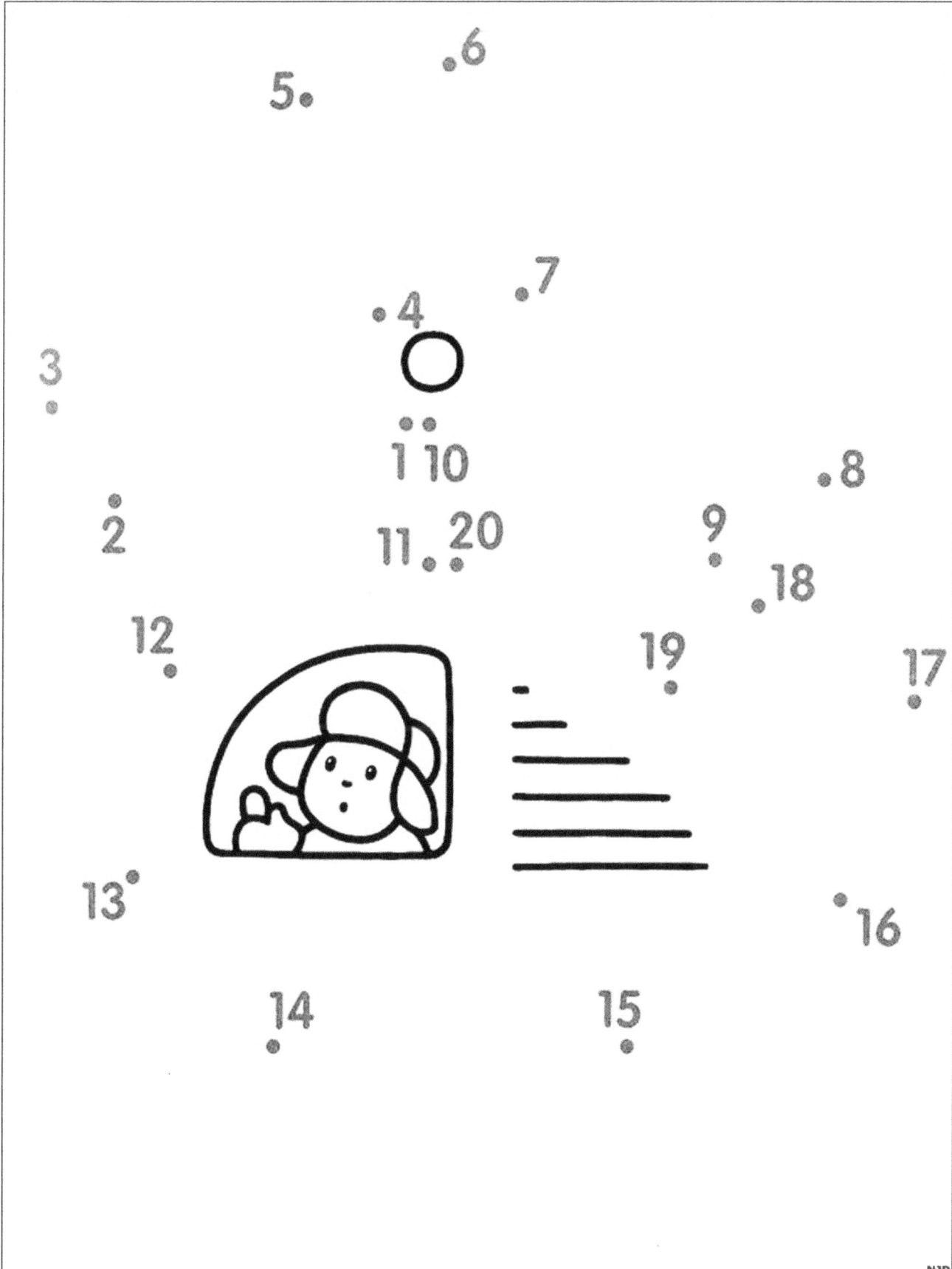

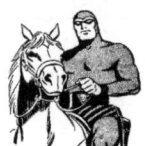

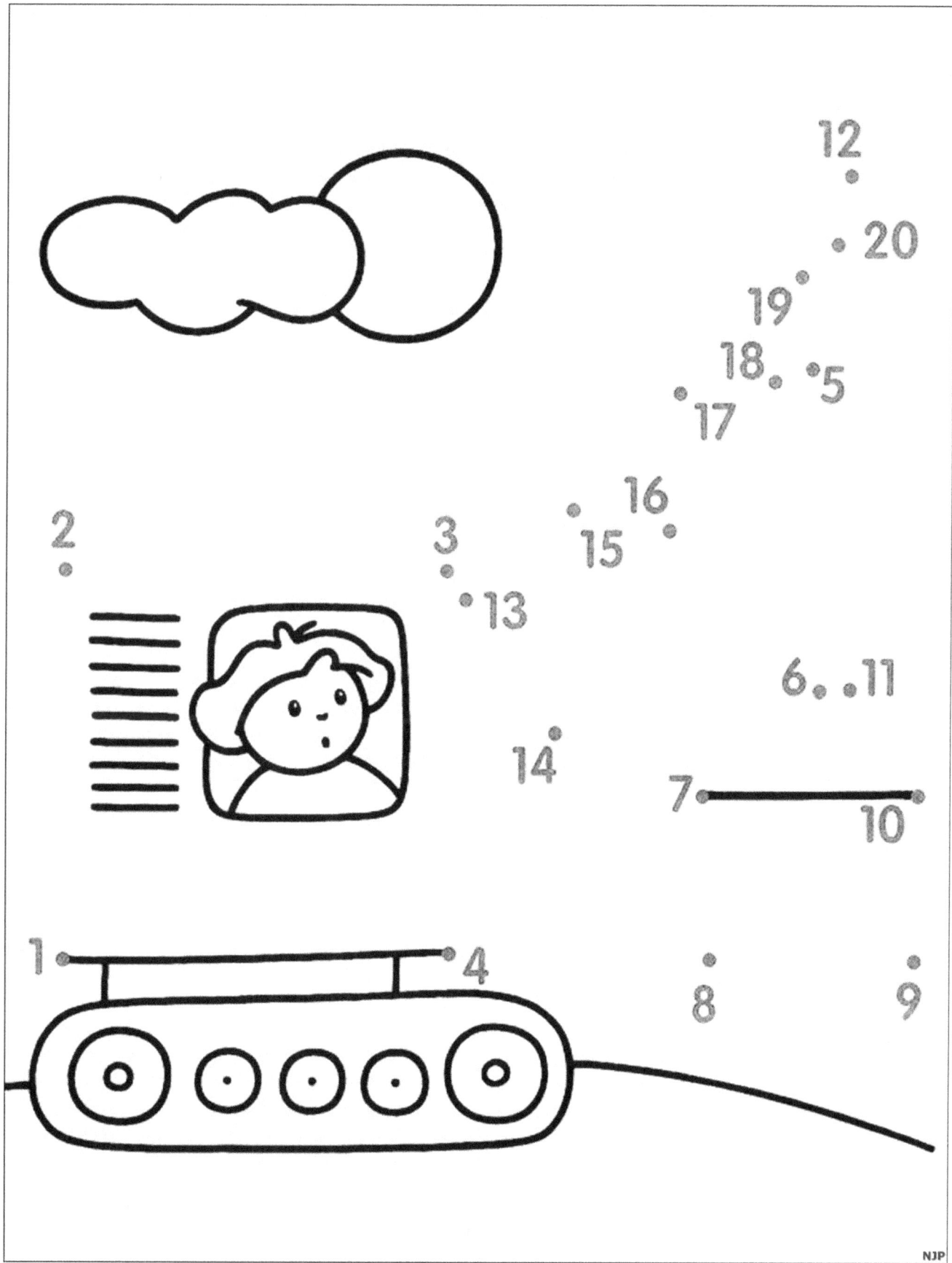

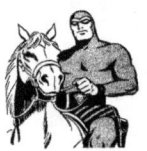

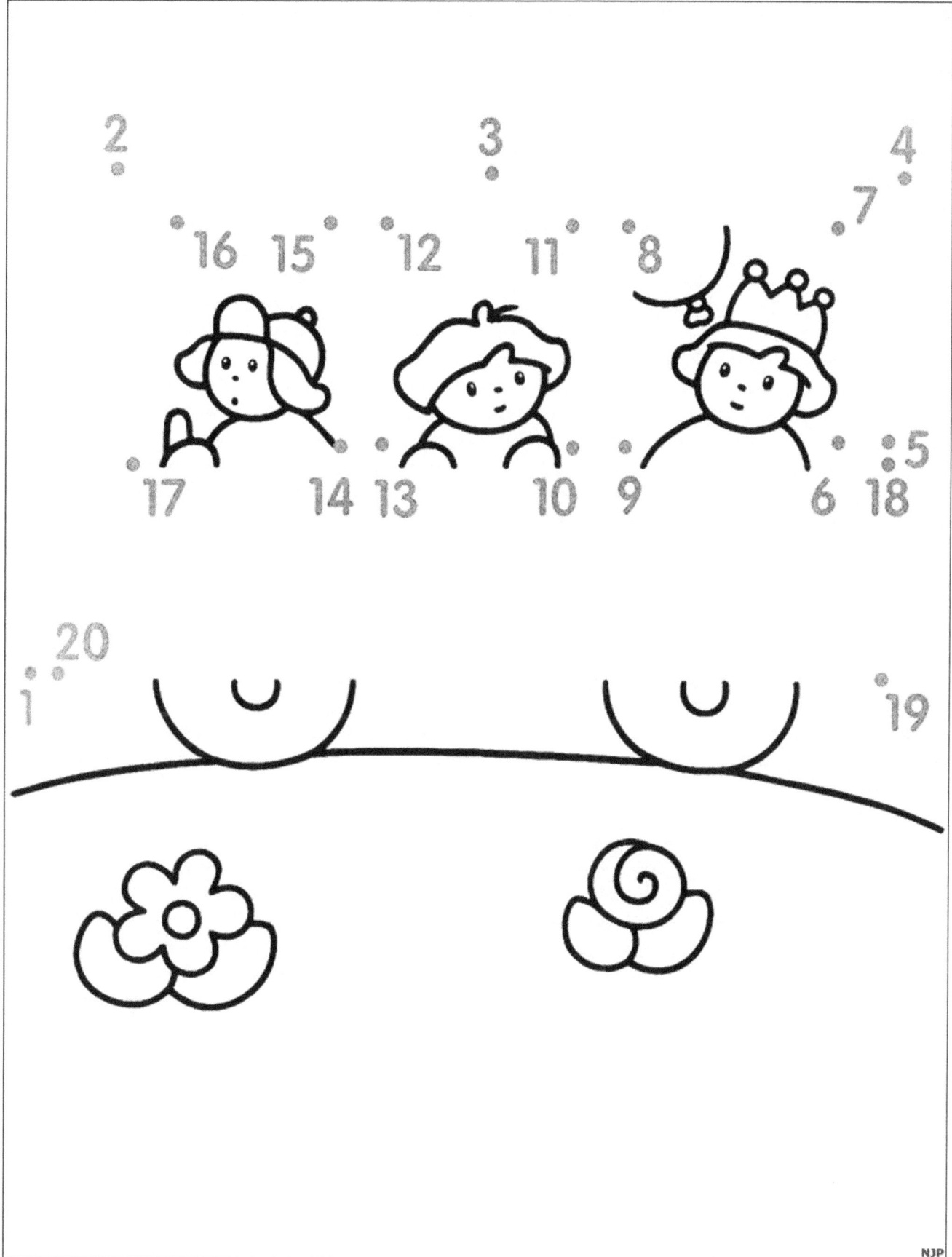

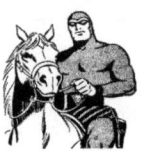

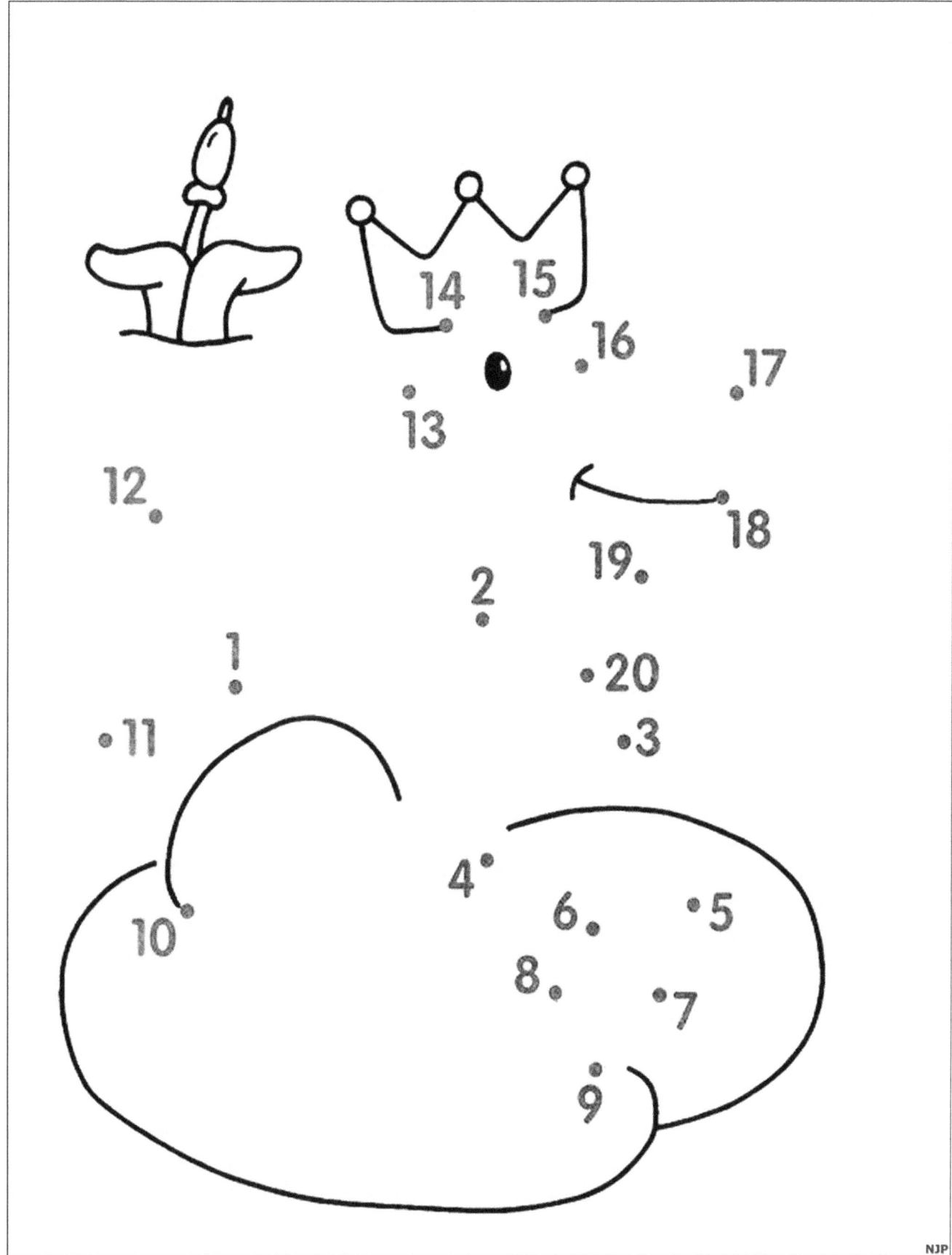

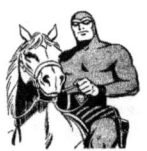

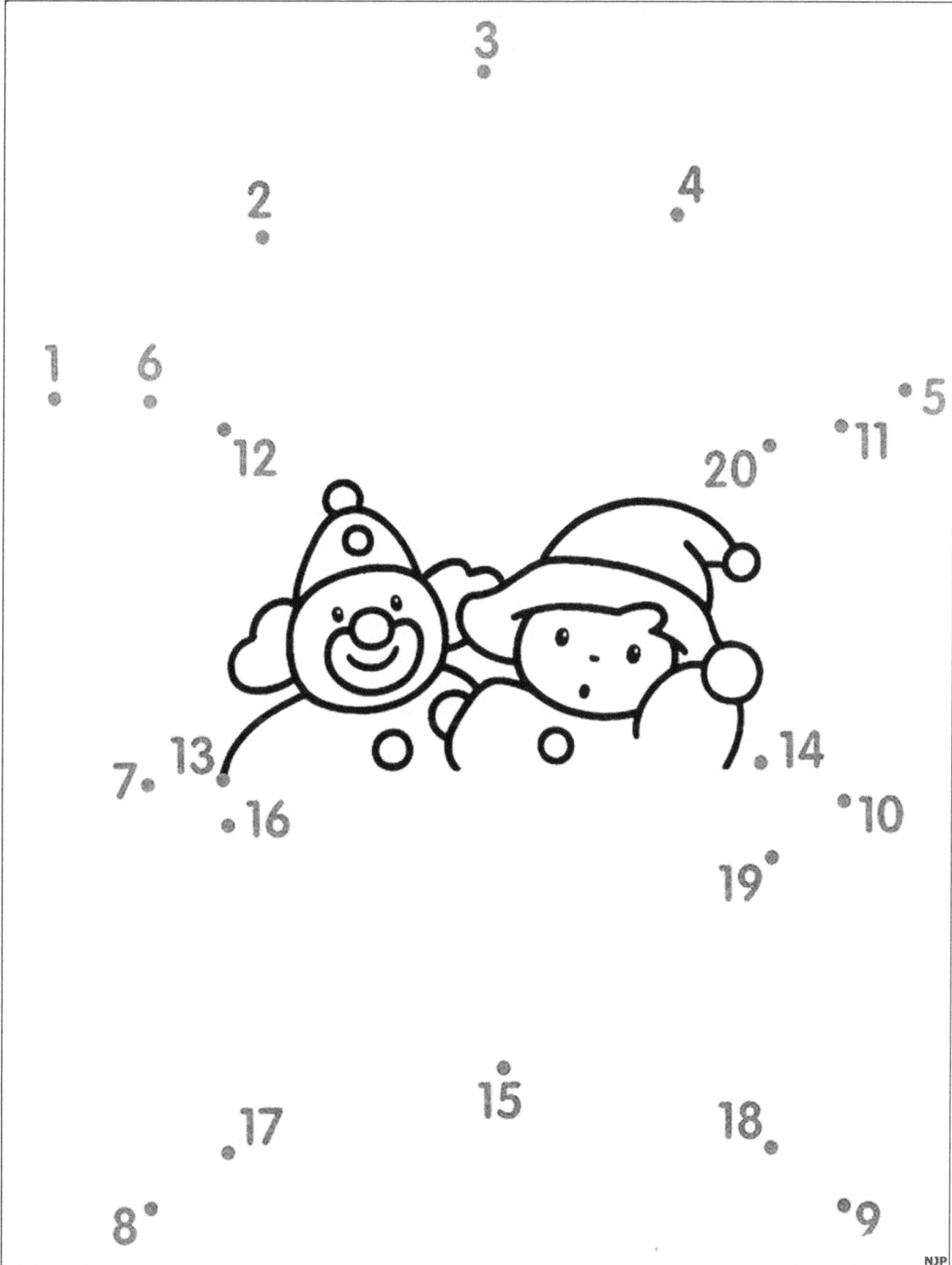

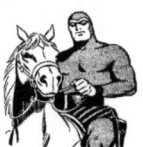

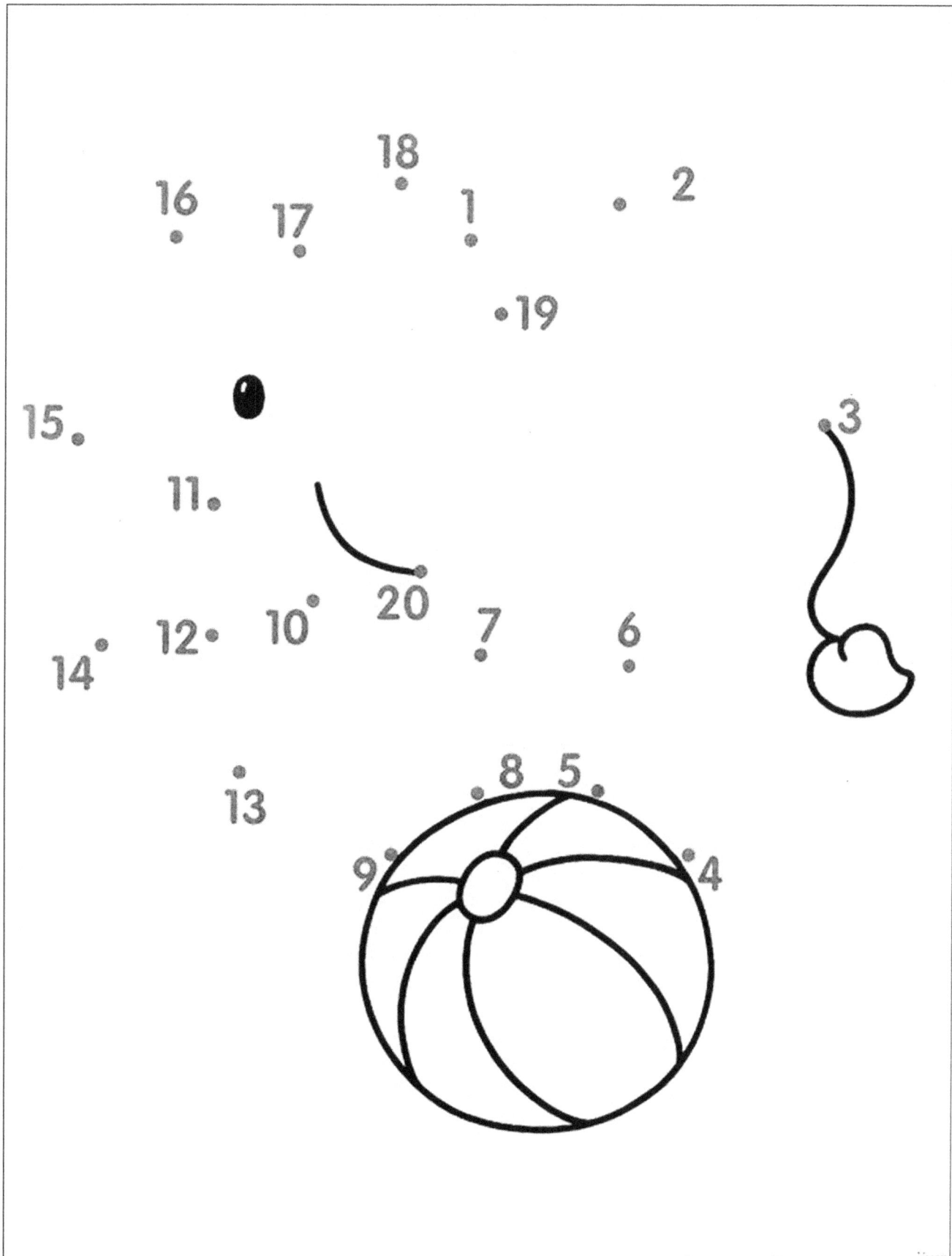

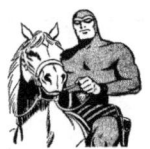

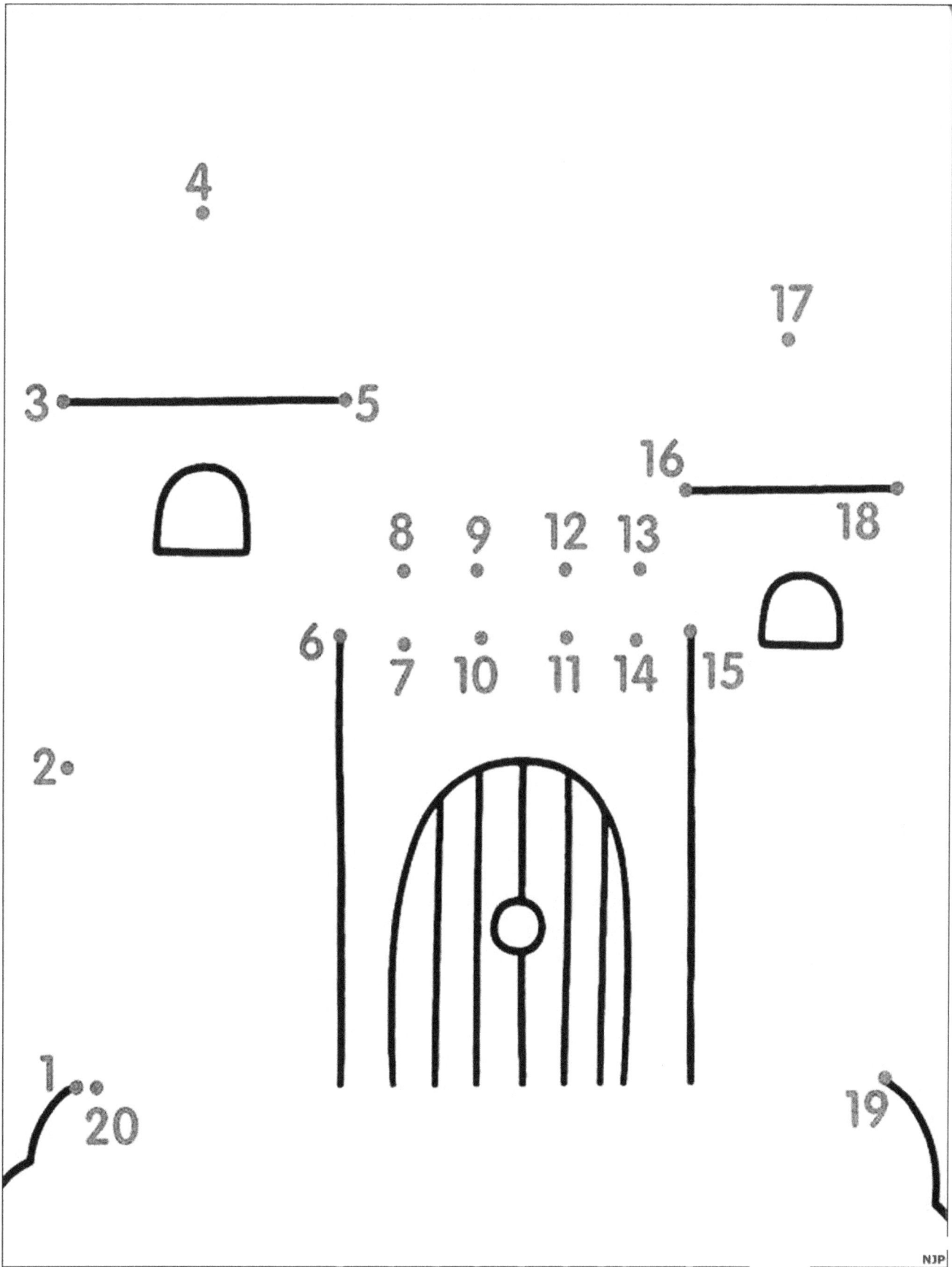

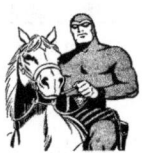

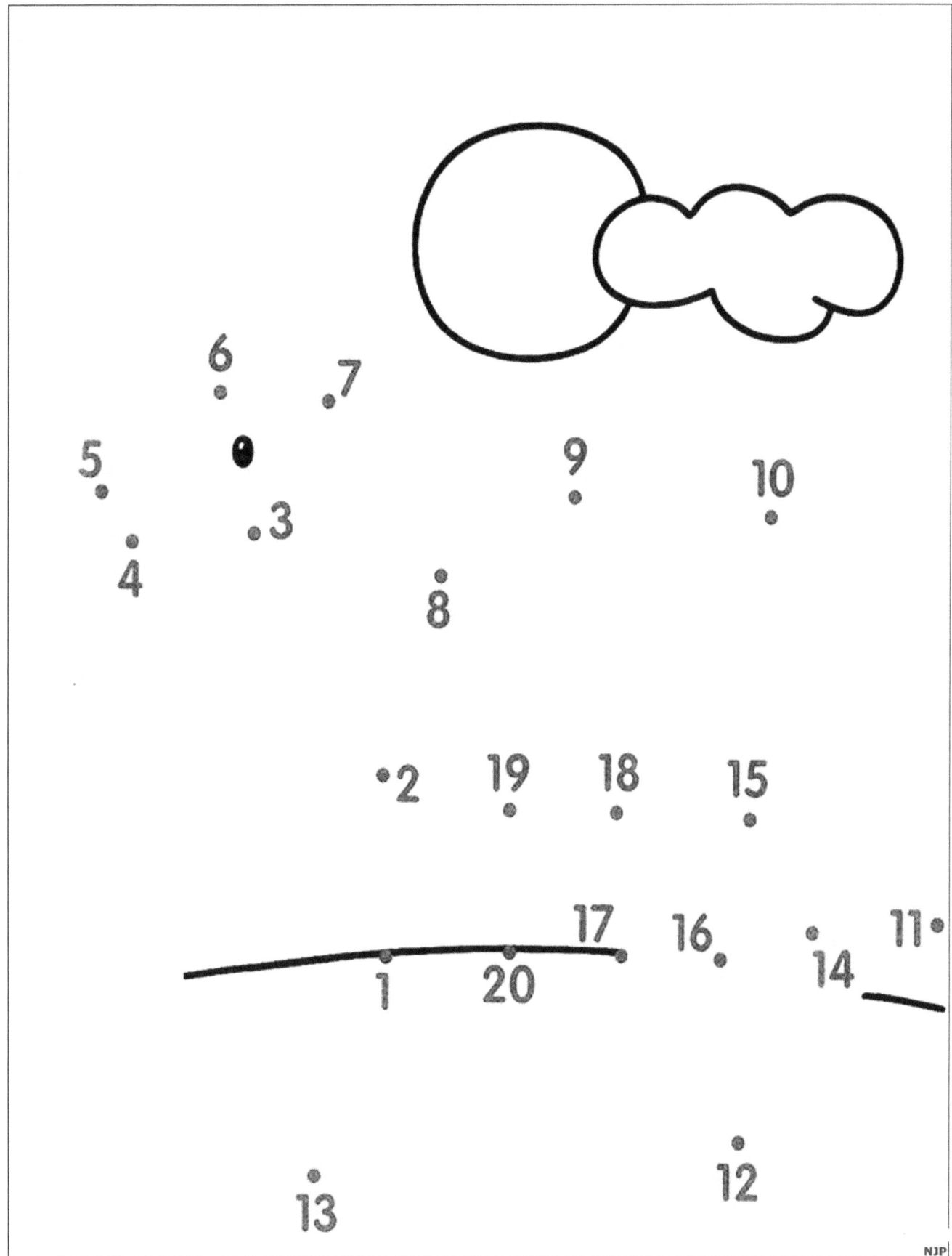

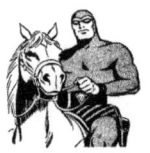

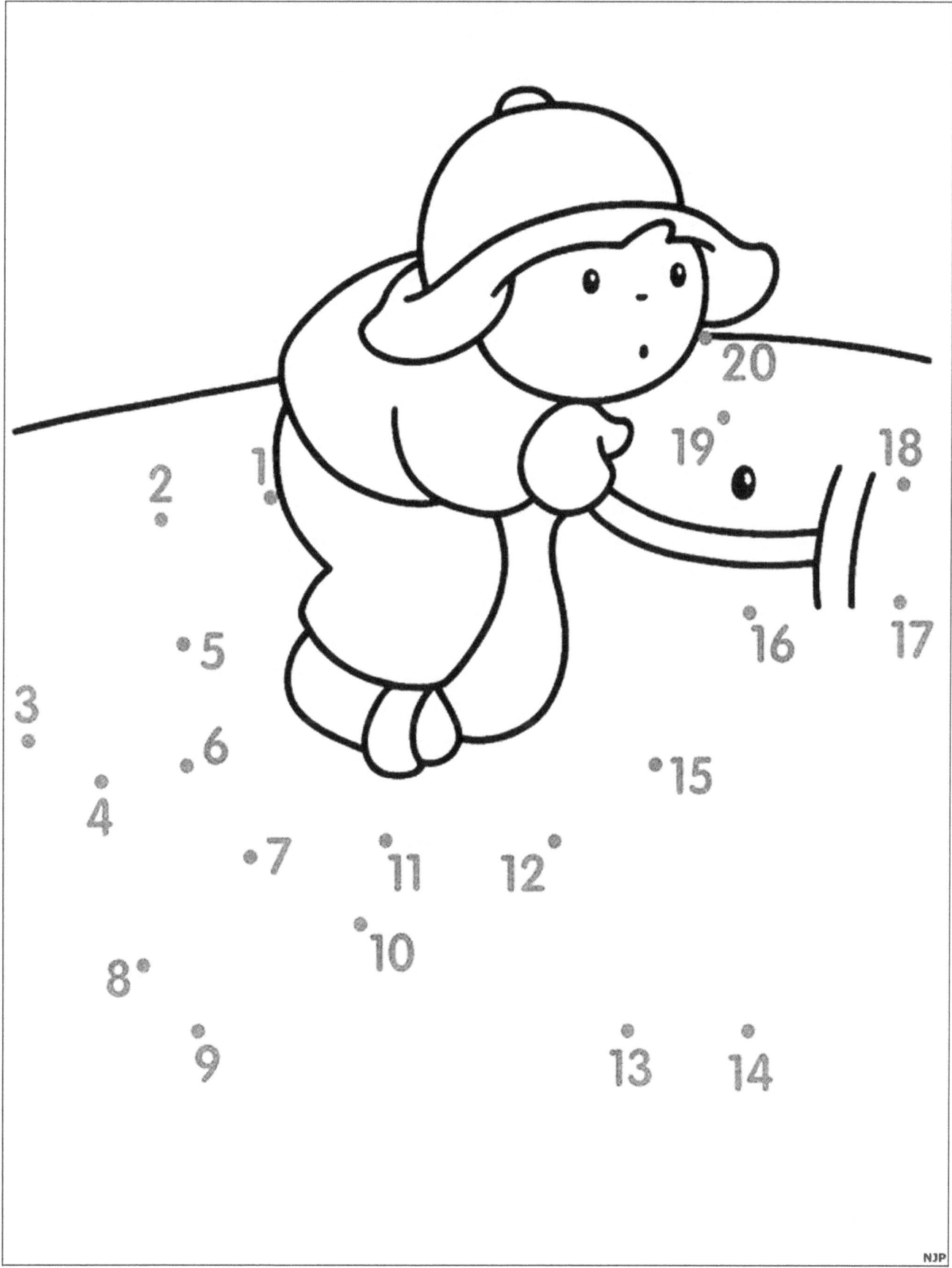

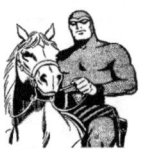

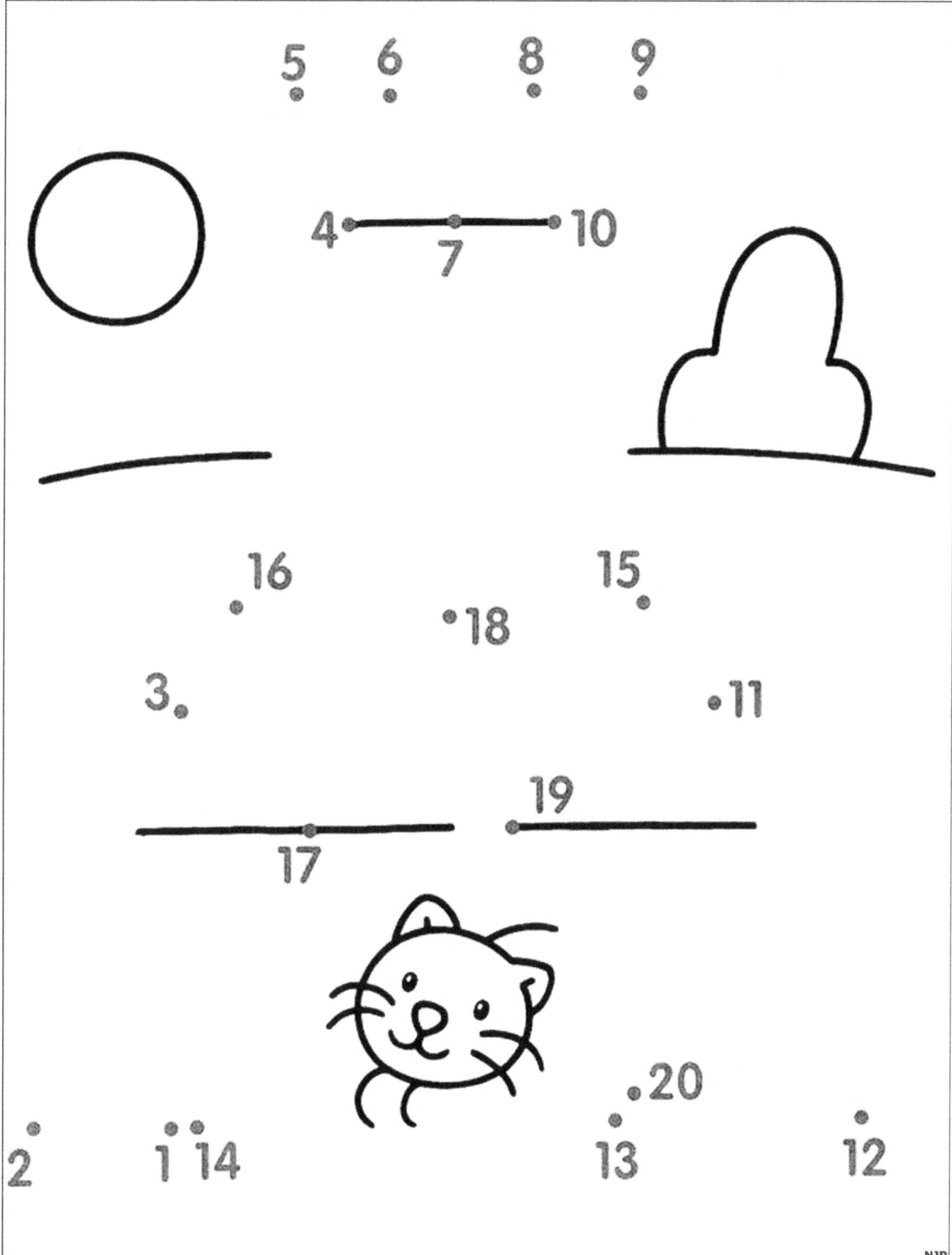

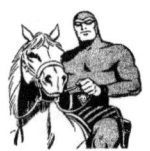

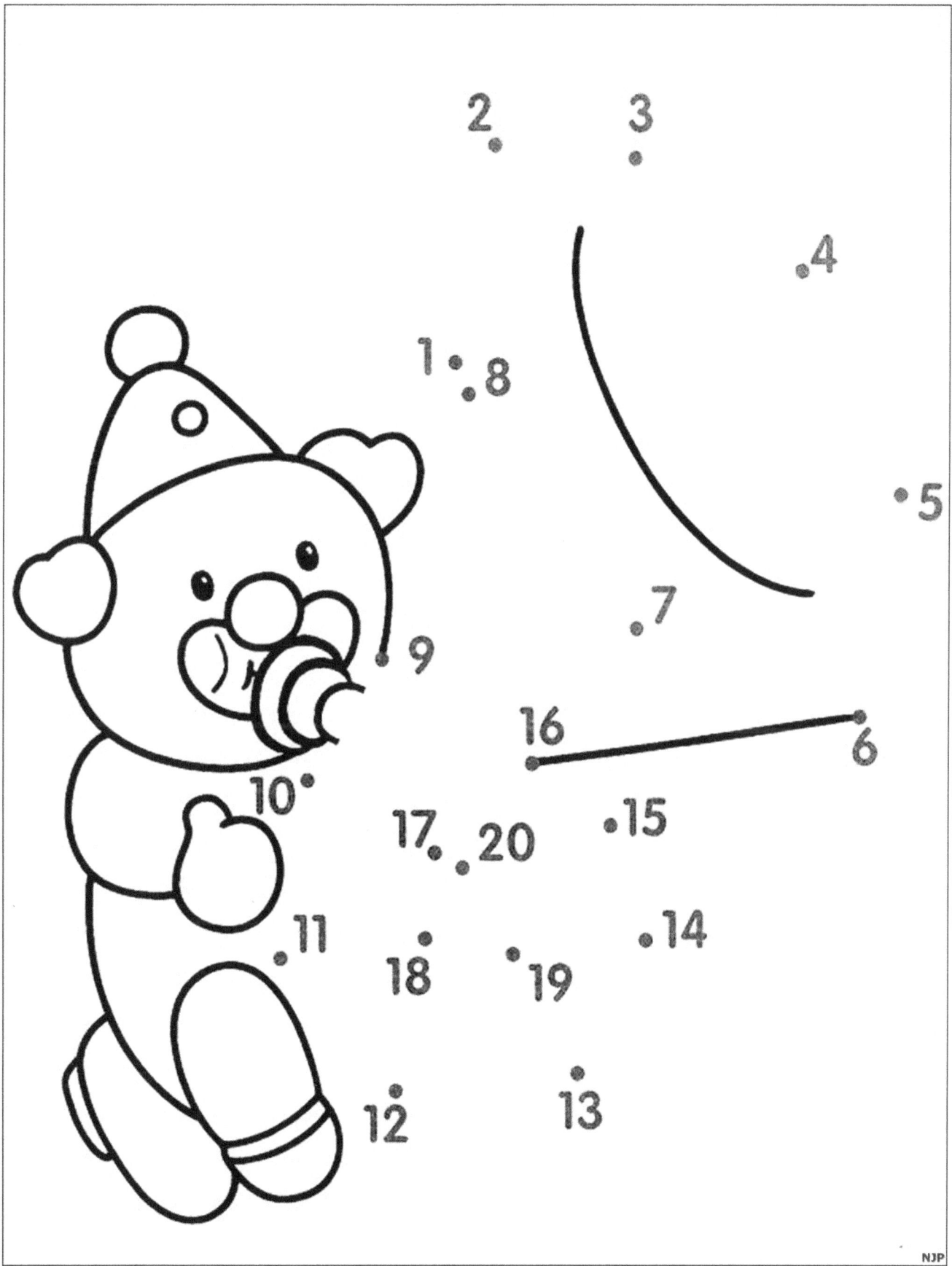

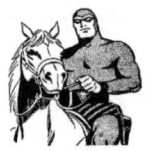

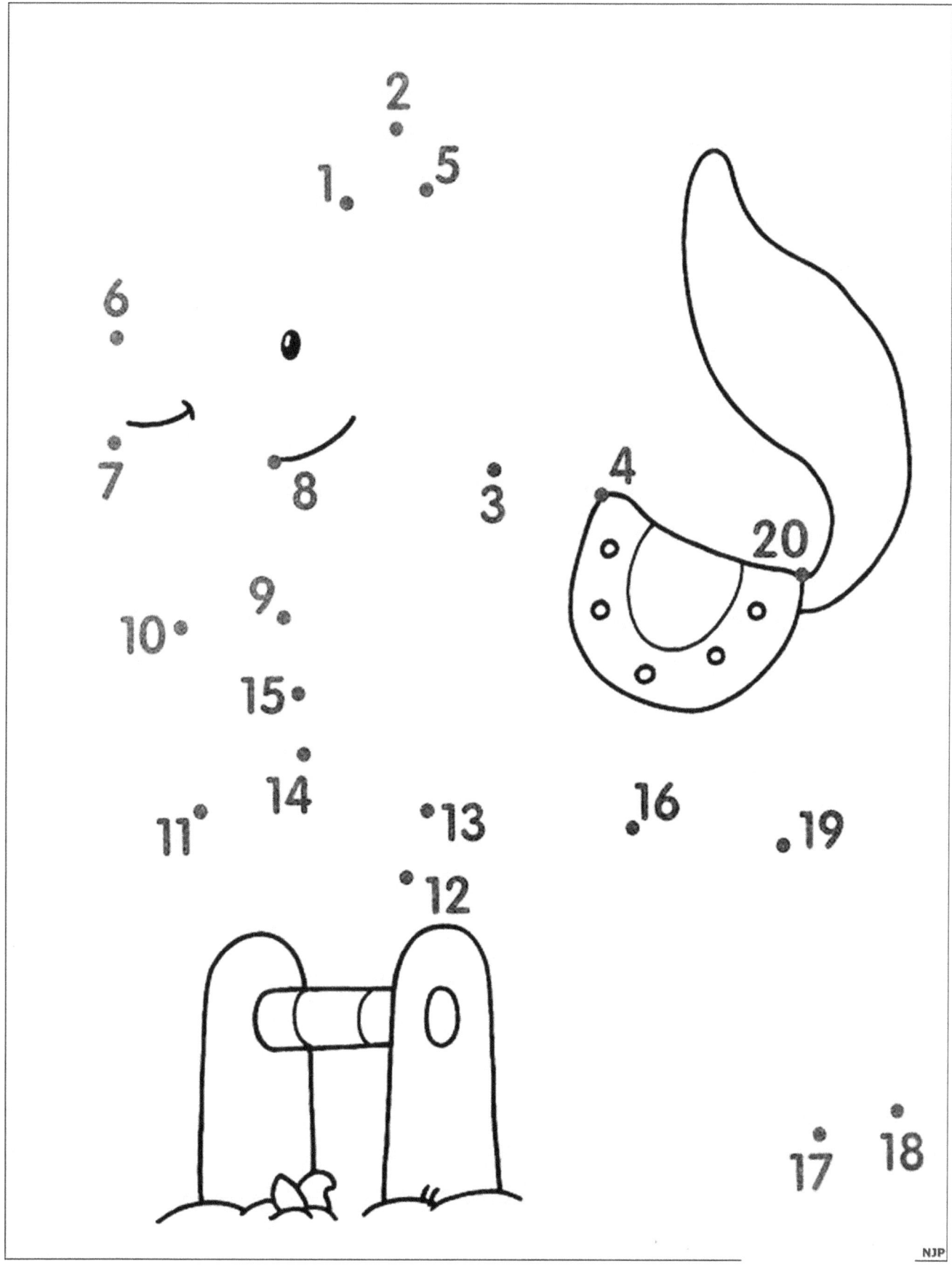

NJP

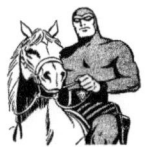

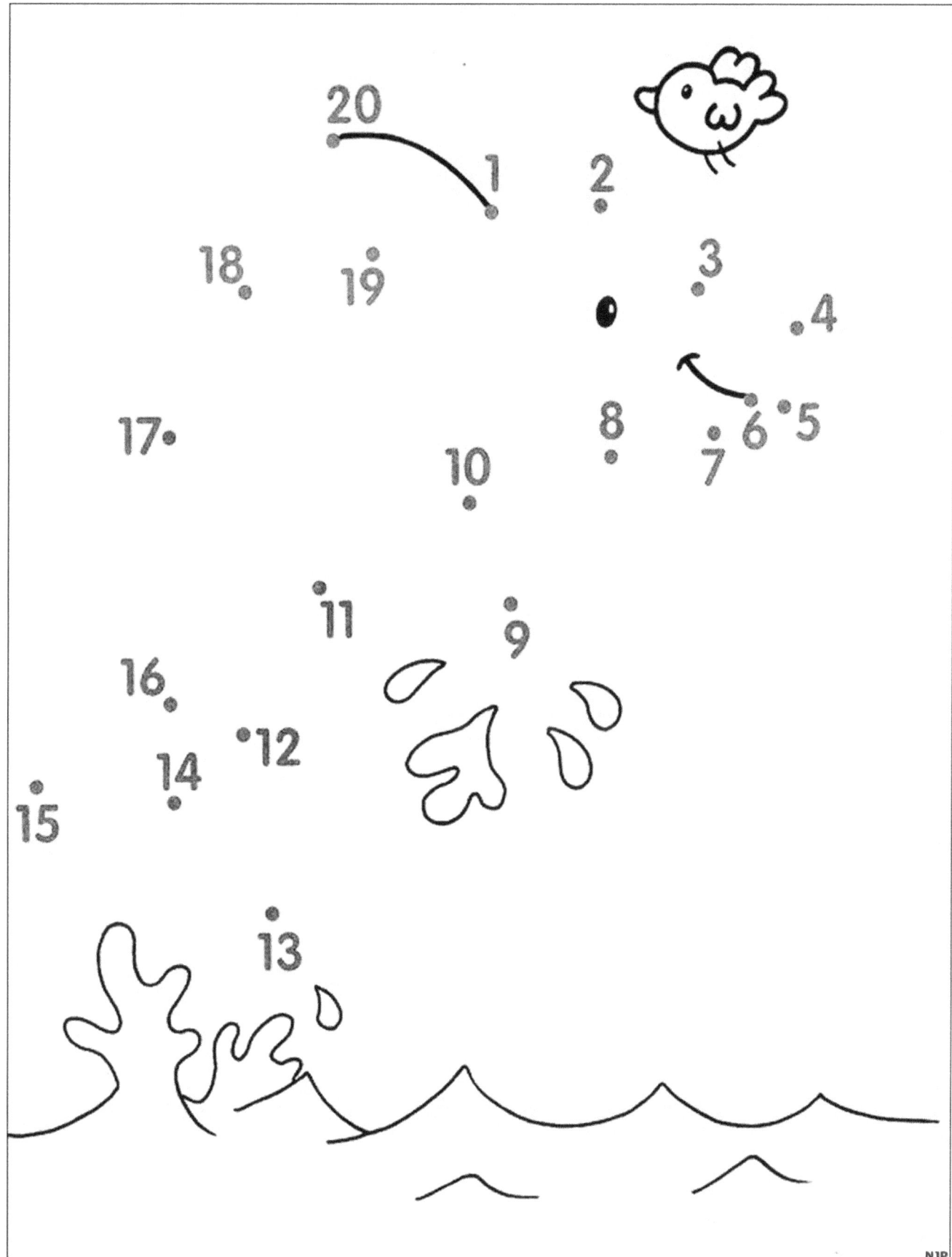

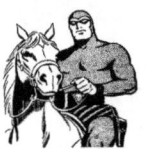

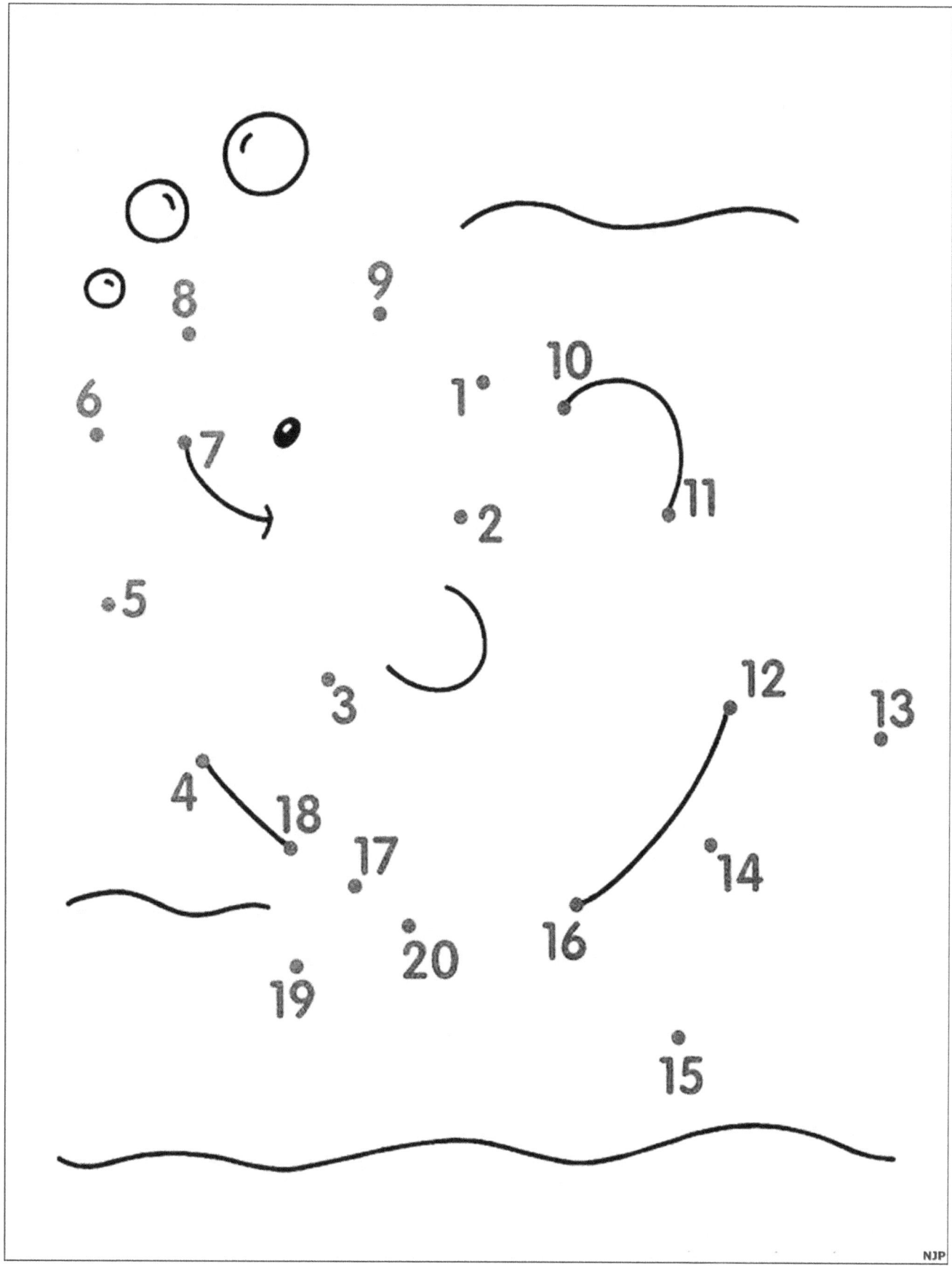

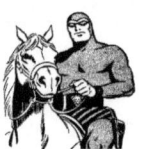

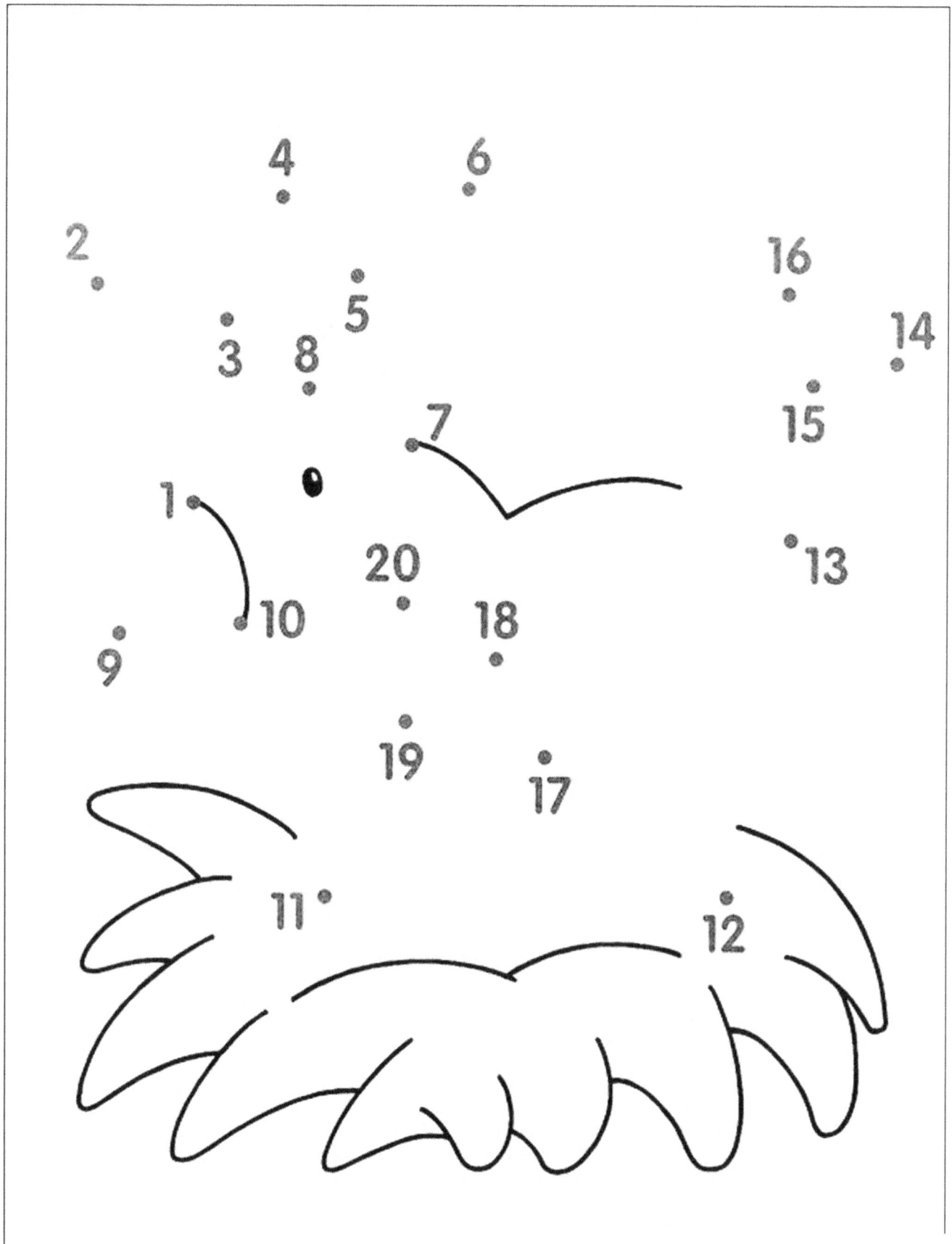

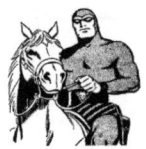

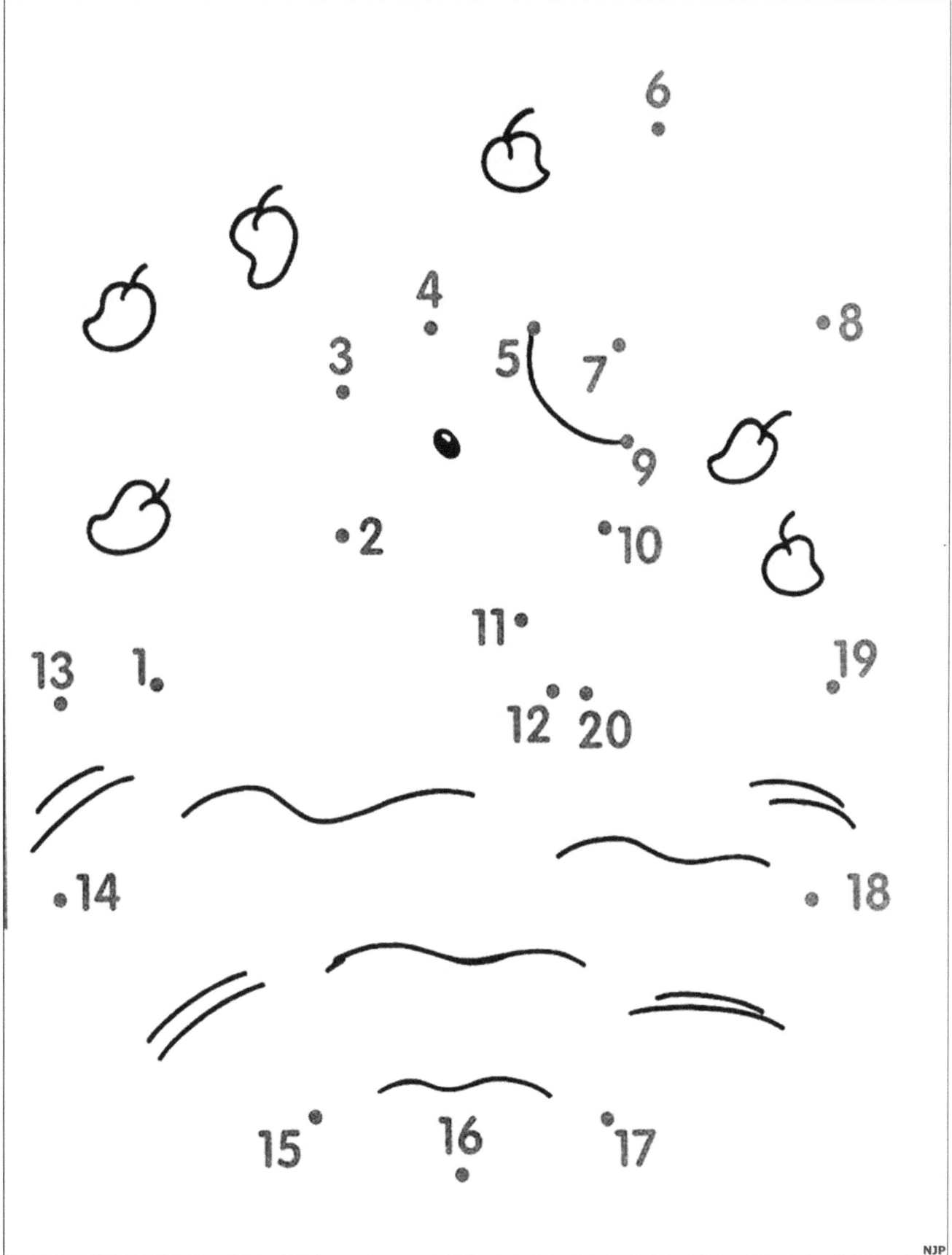

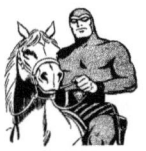

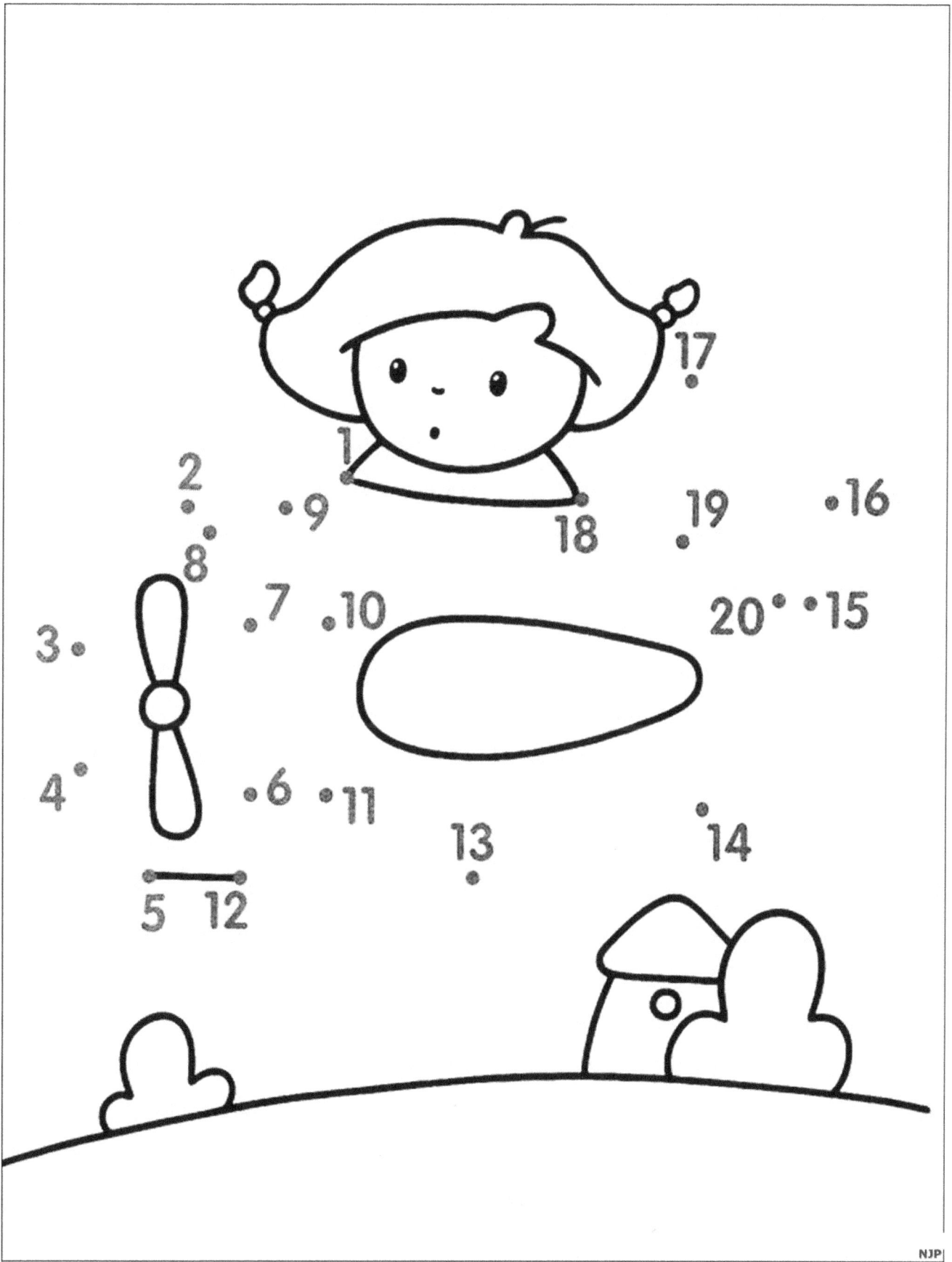

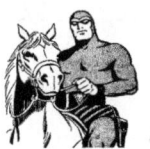

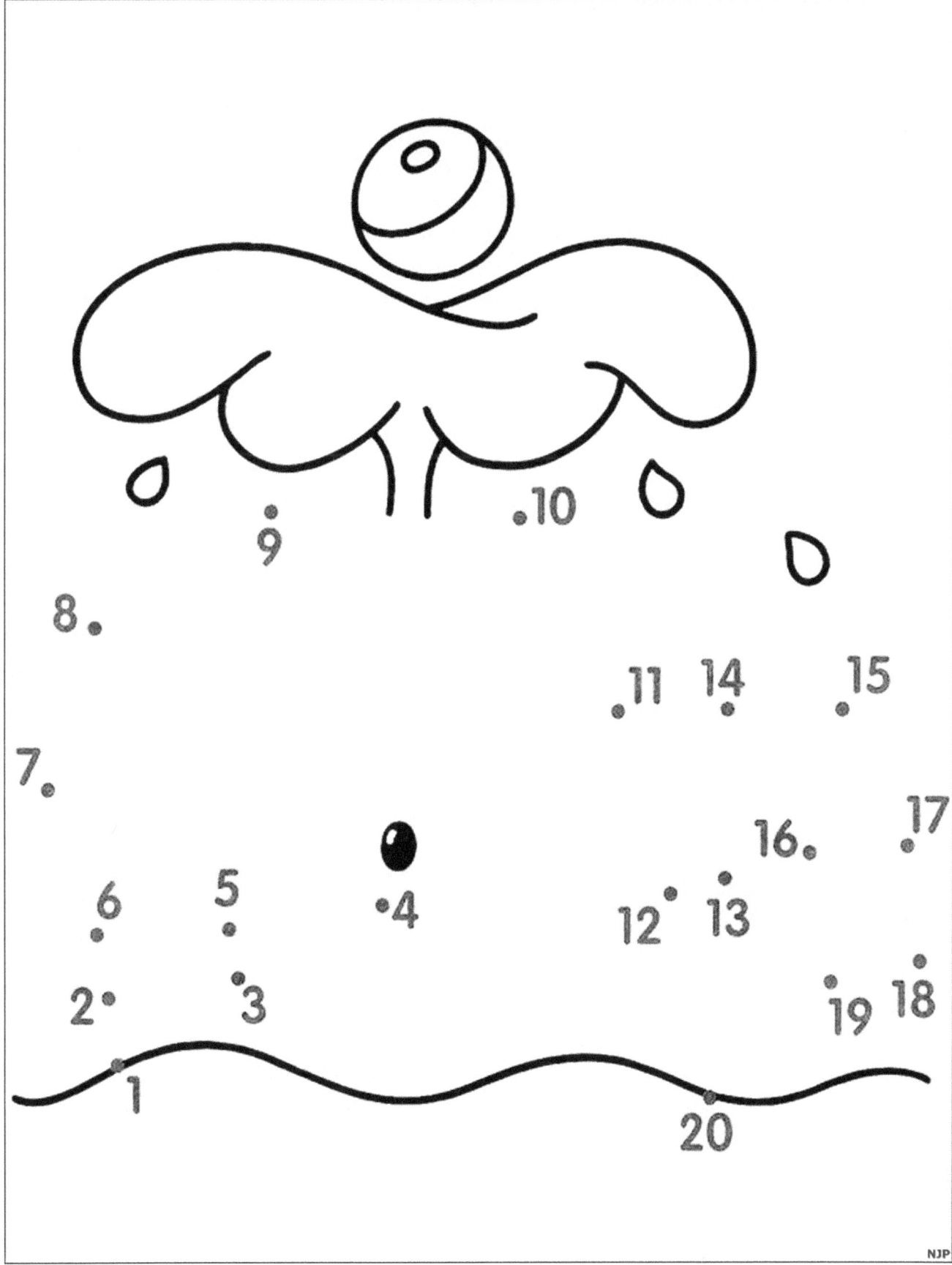

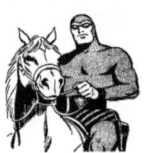

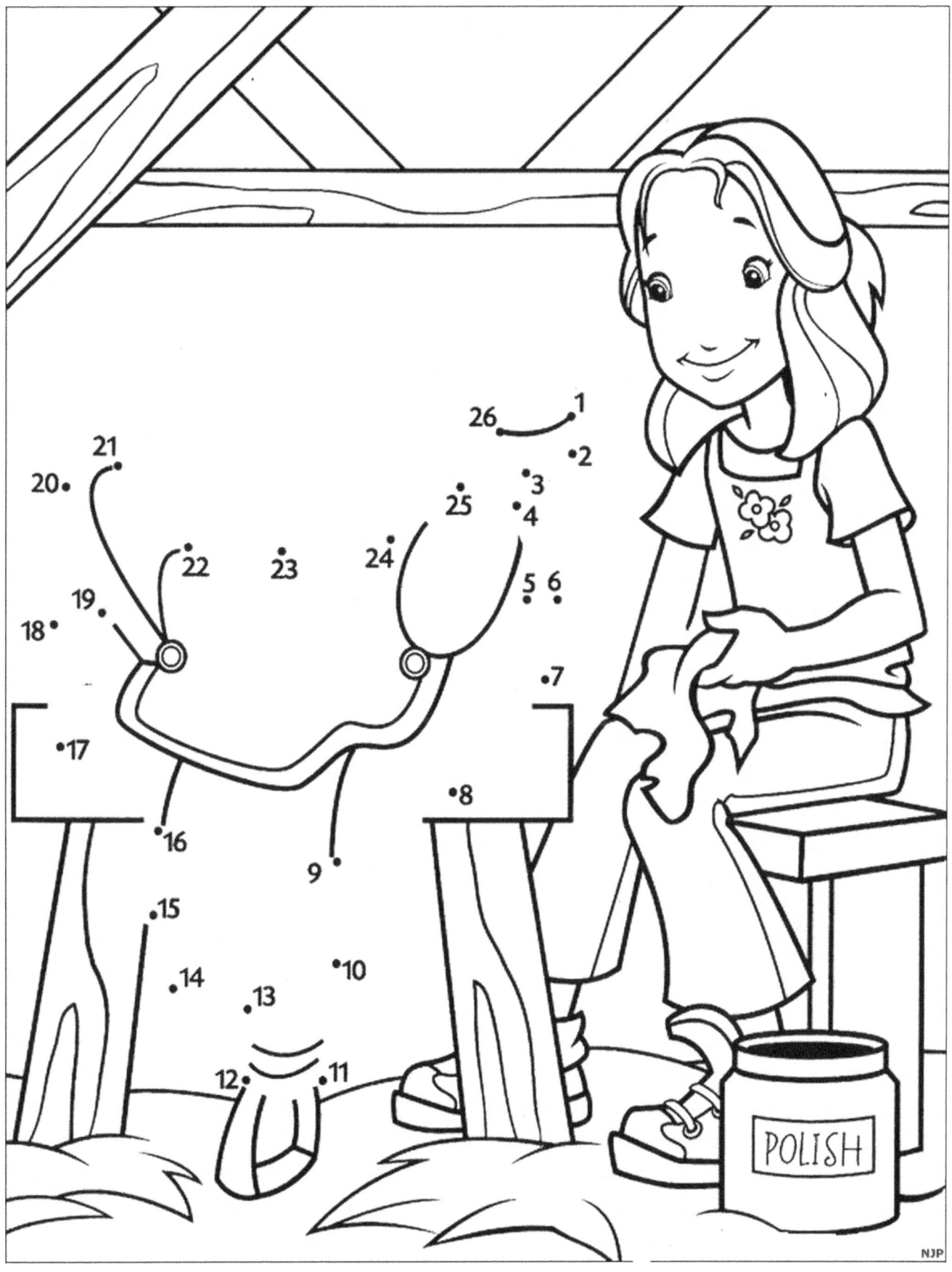

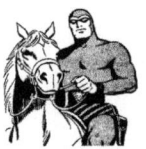

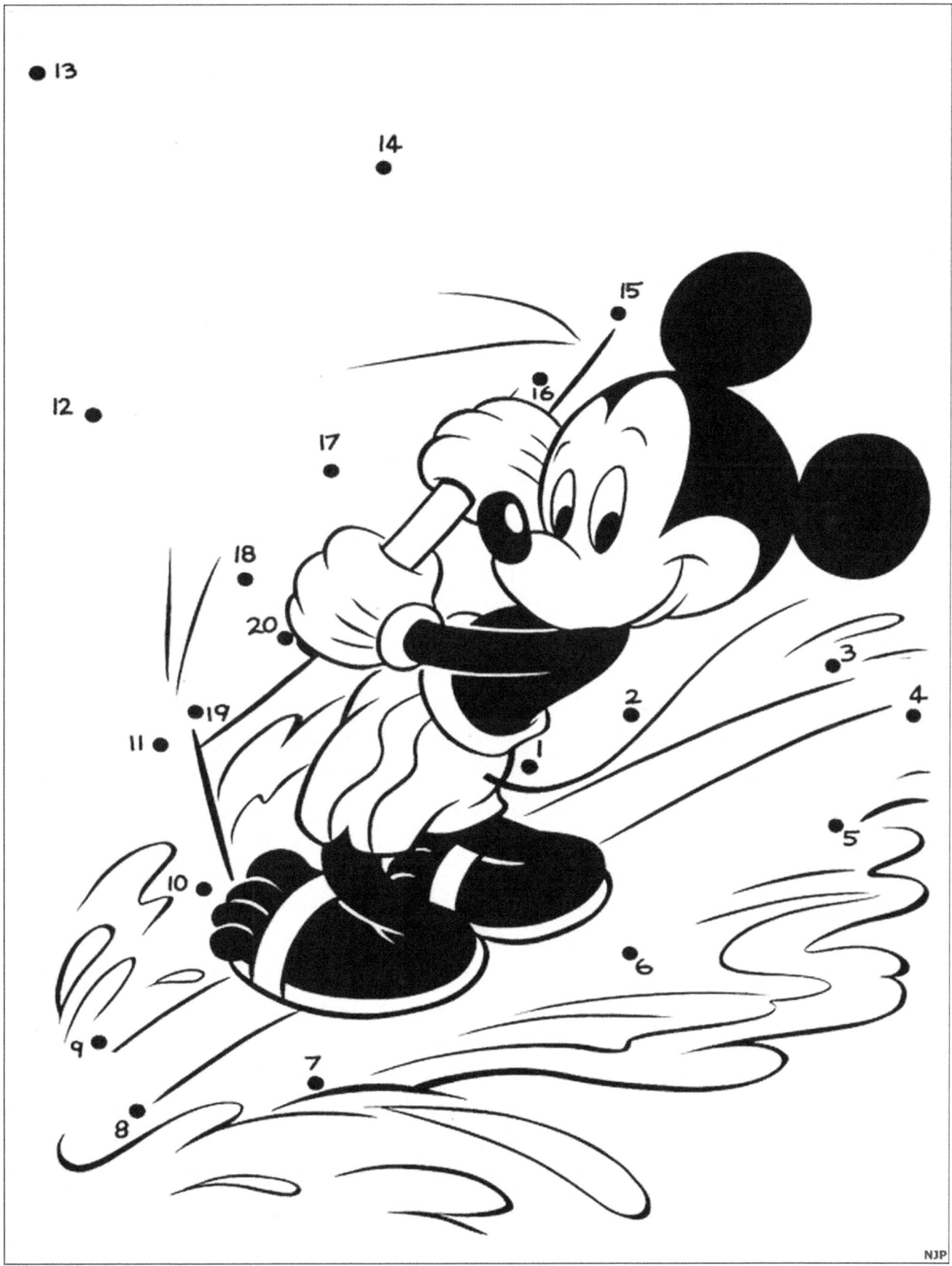

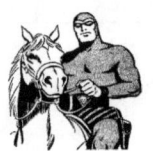

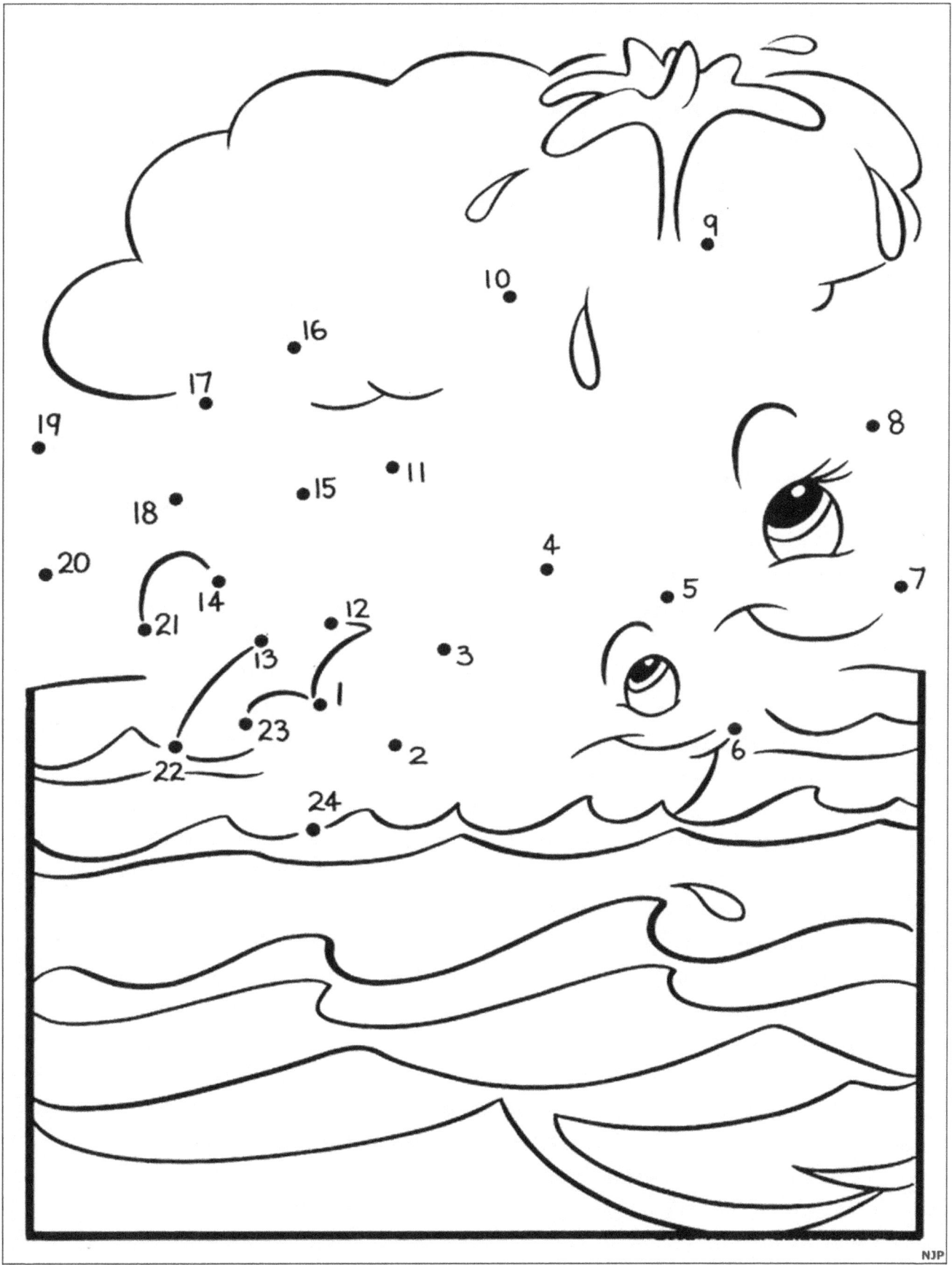

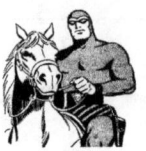

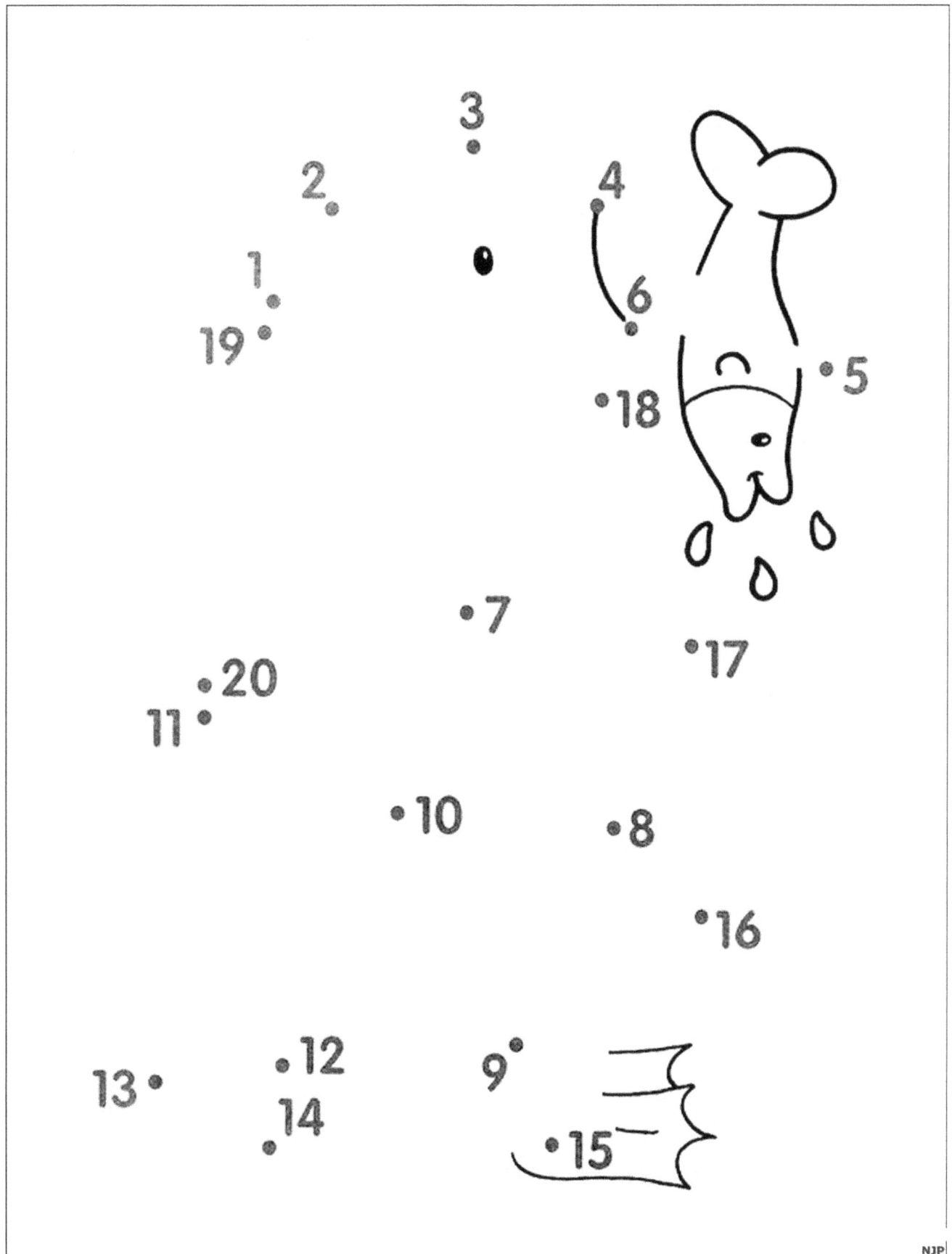

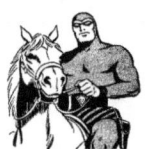

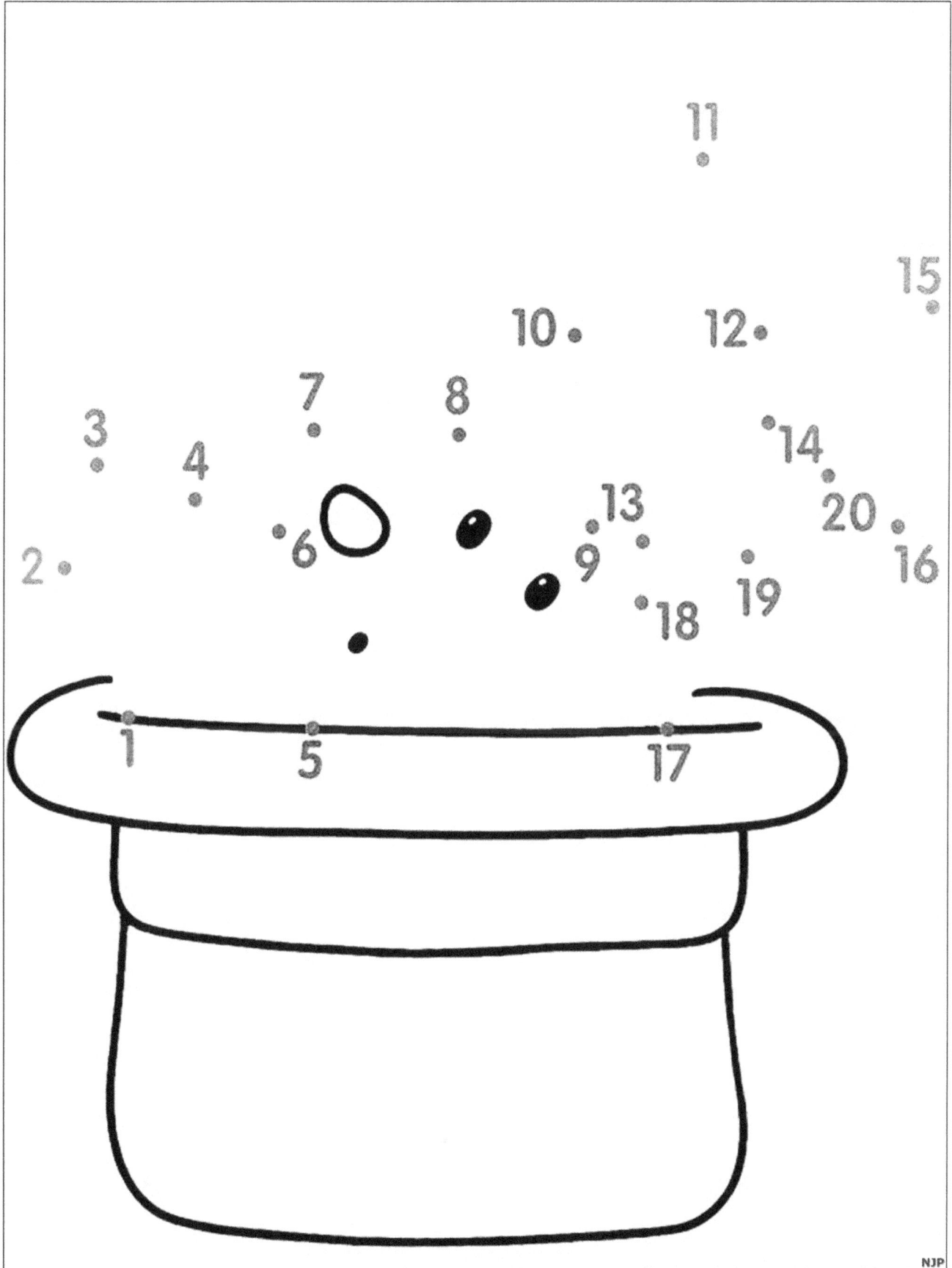

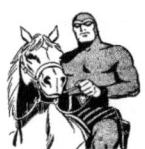

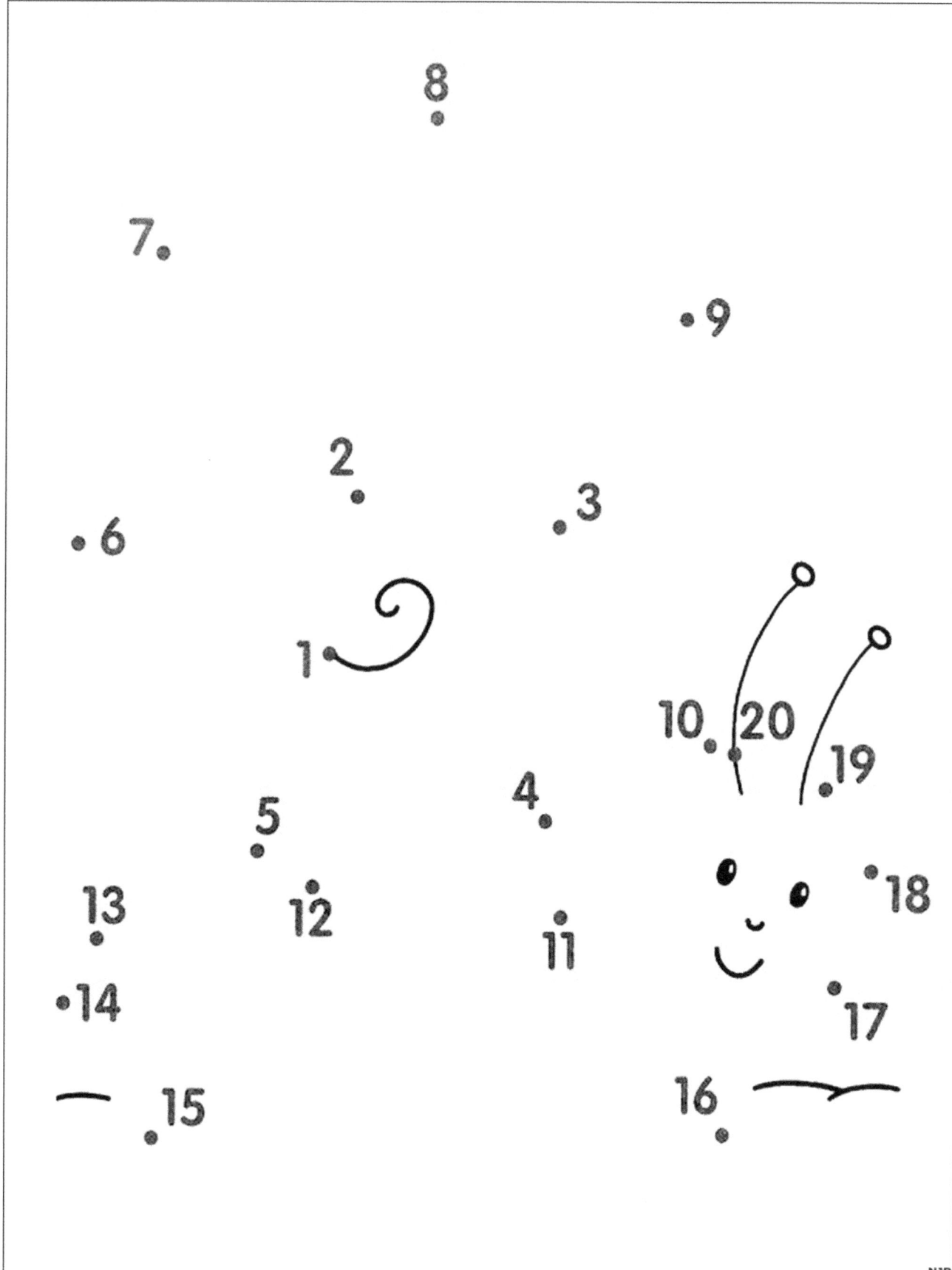

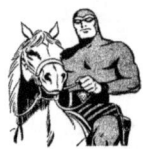

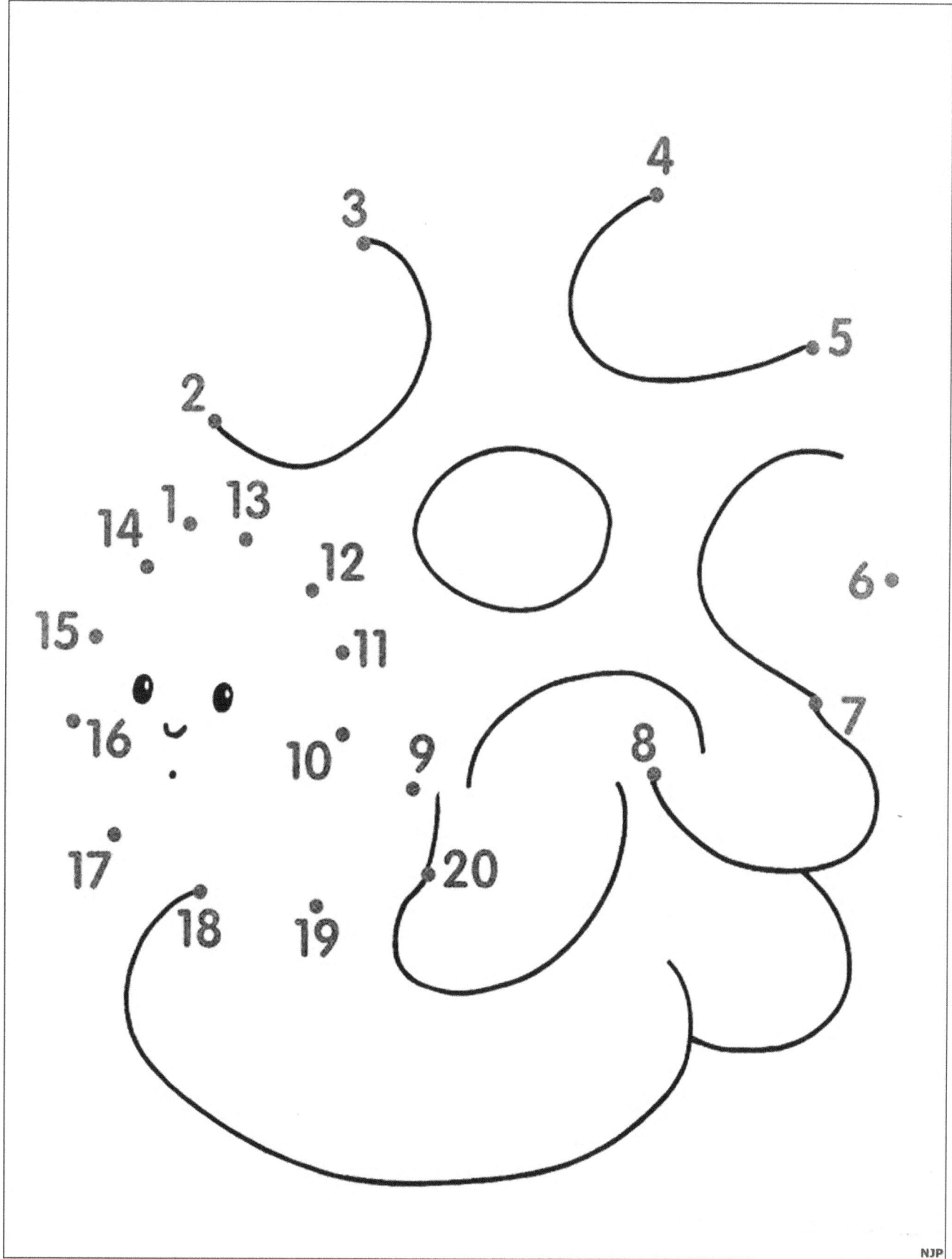

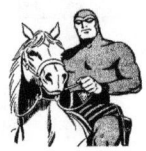

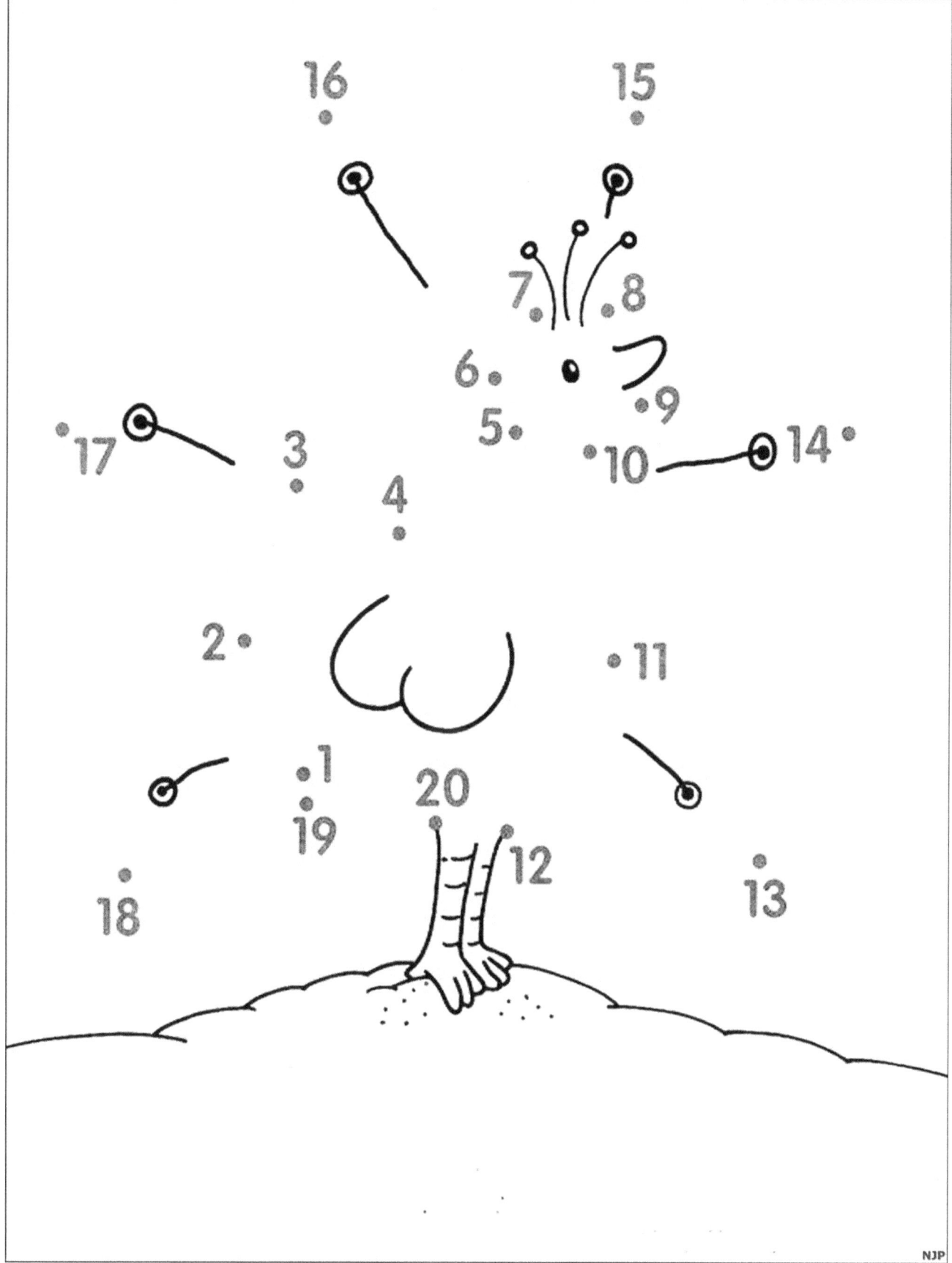

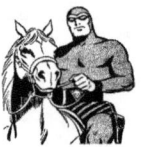

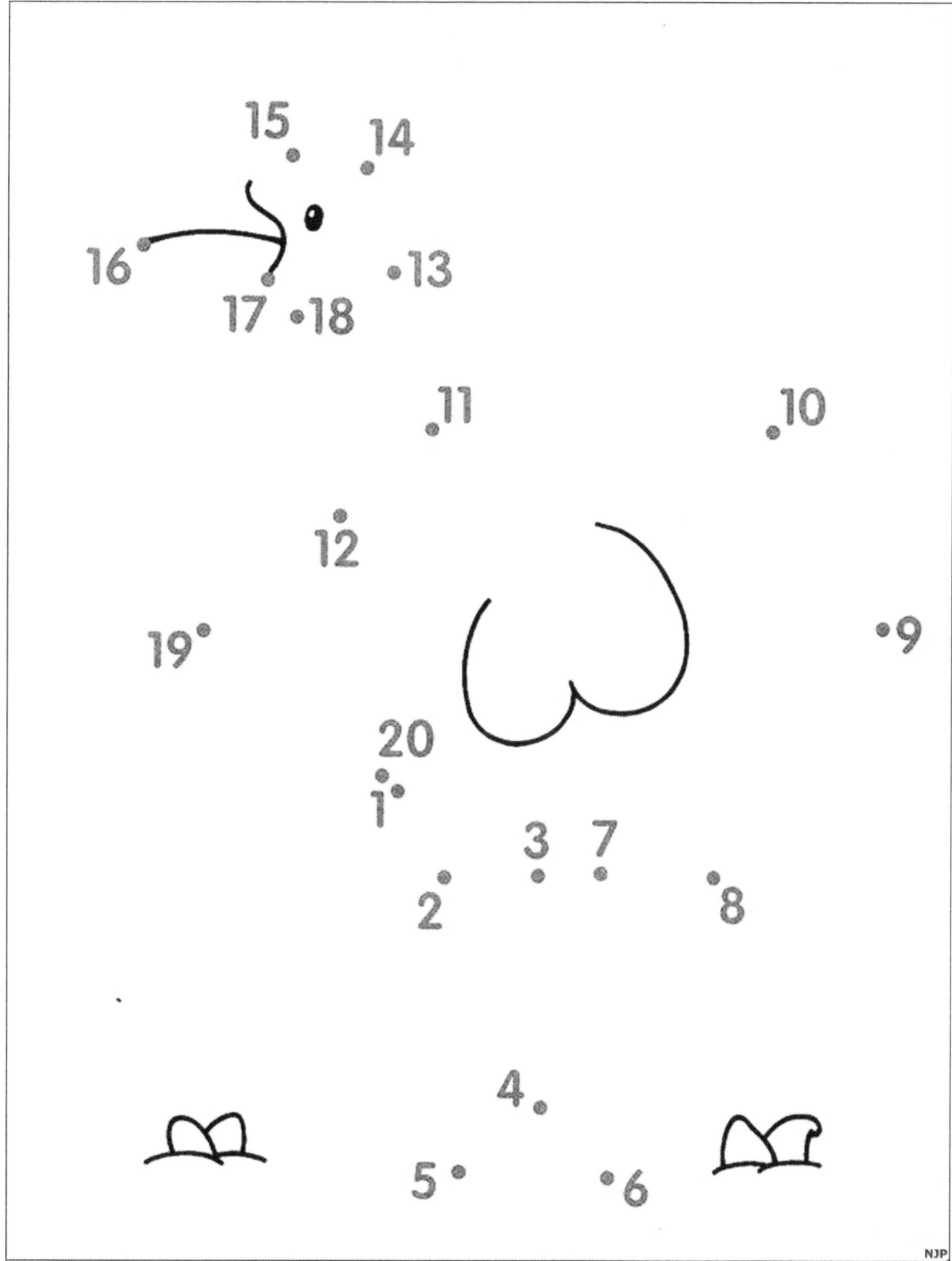

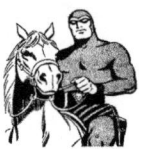

Level – 3

30 Dots per Picture

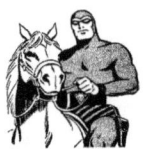

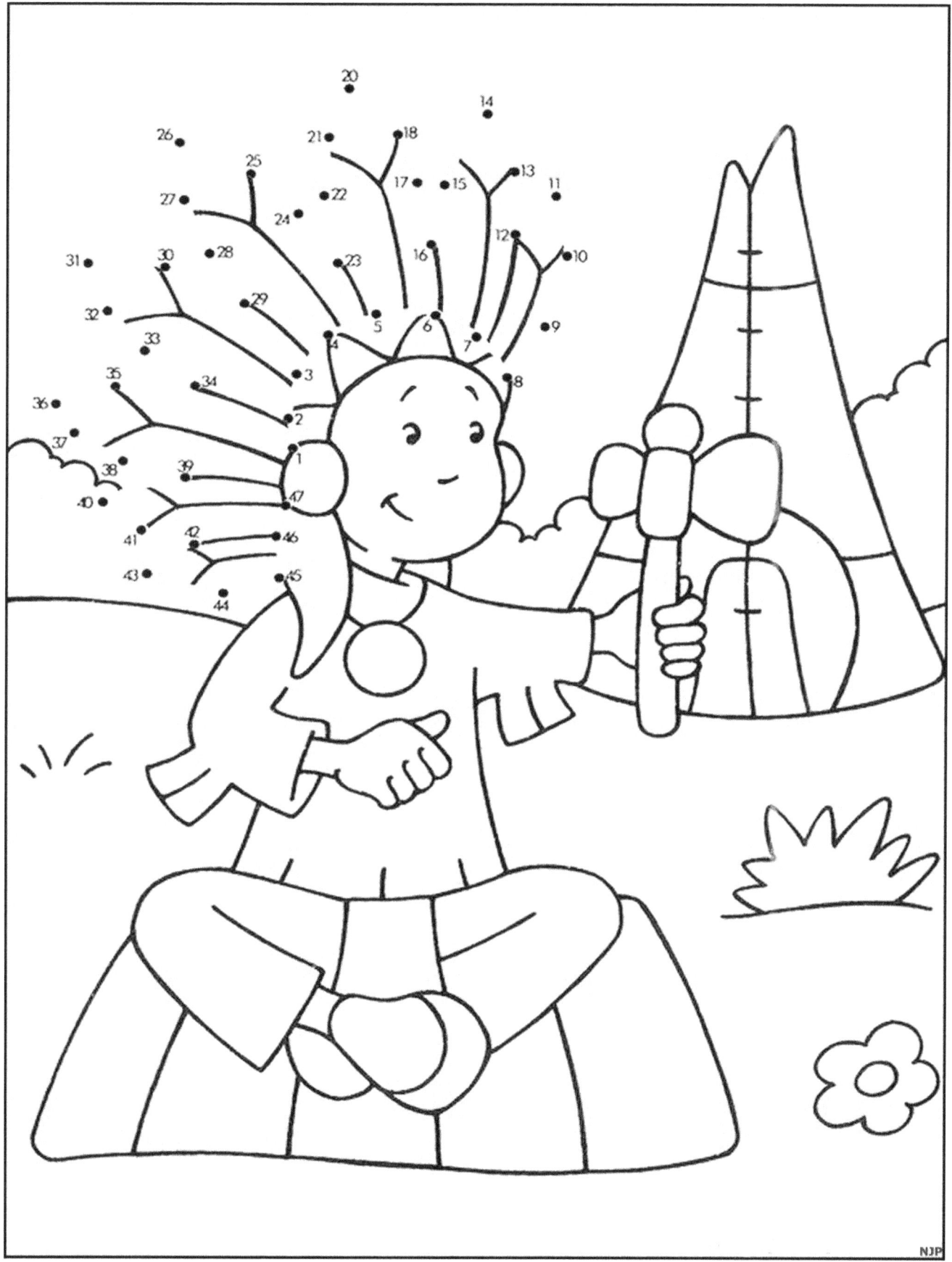

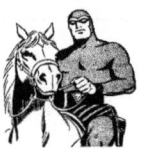

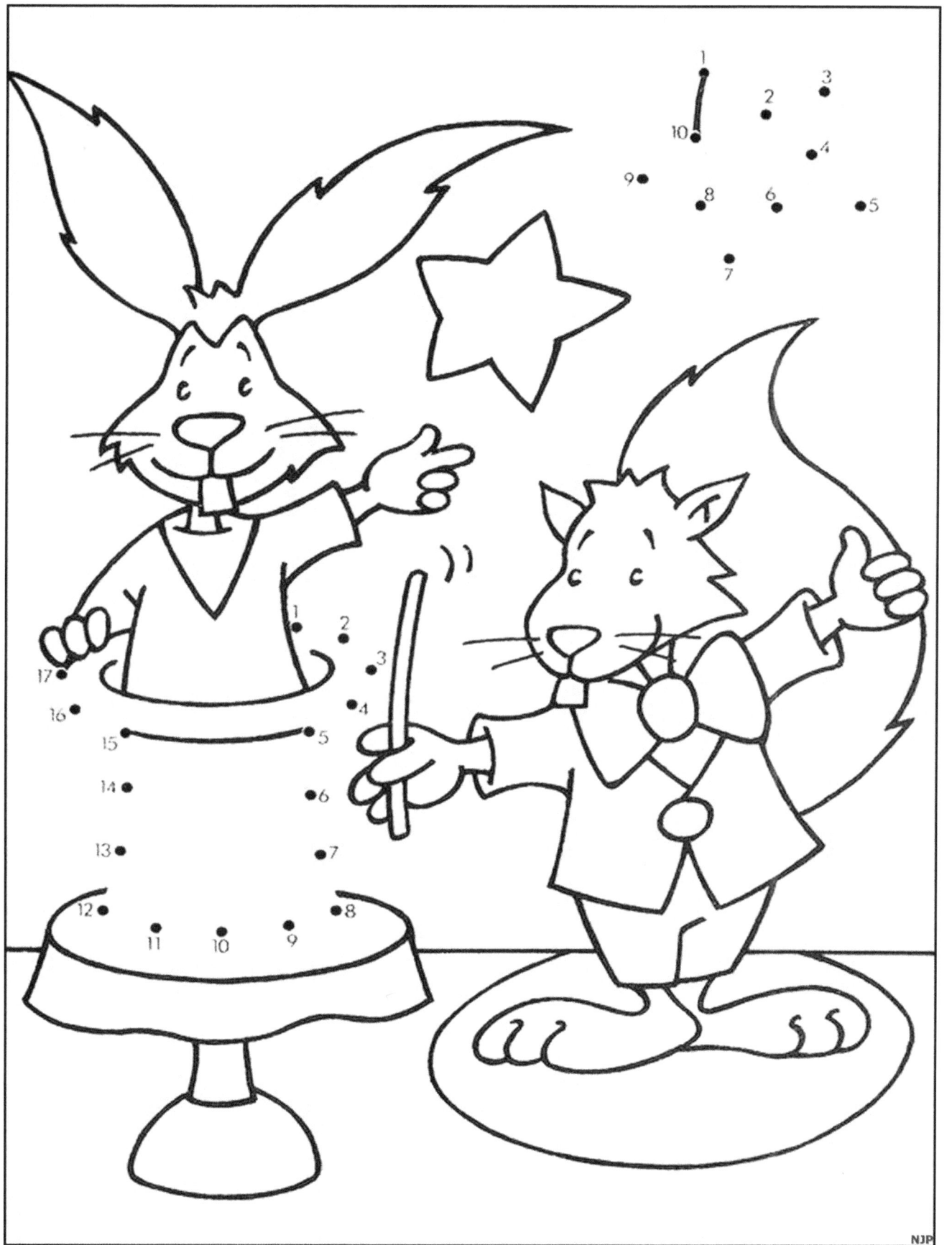

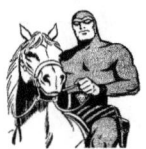

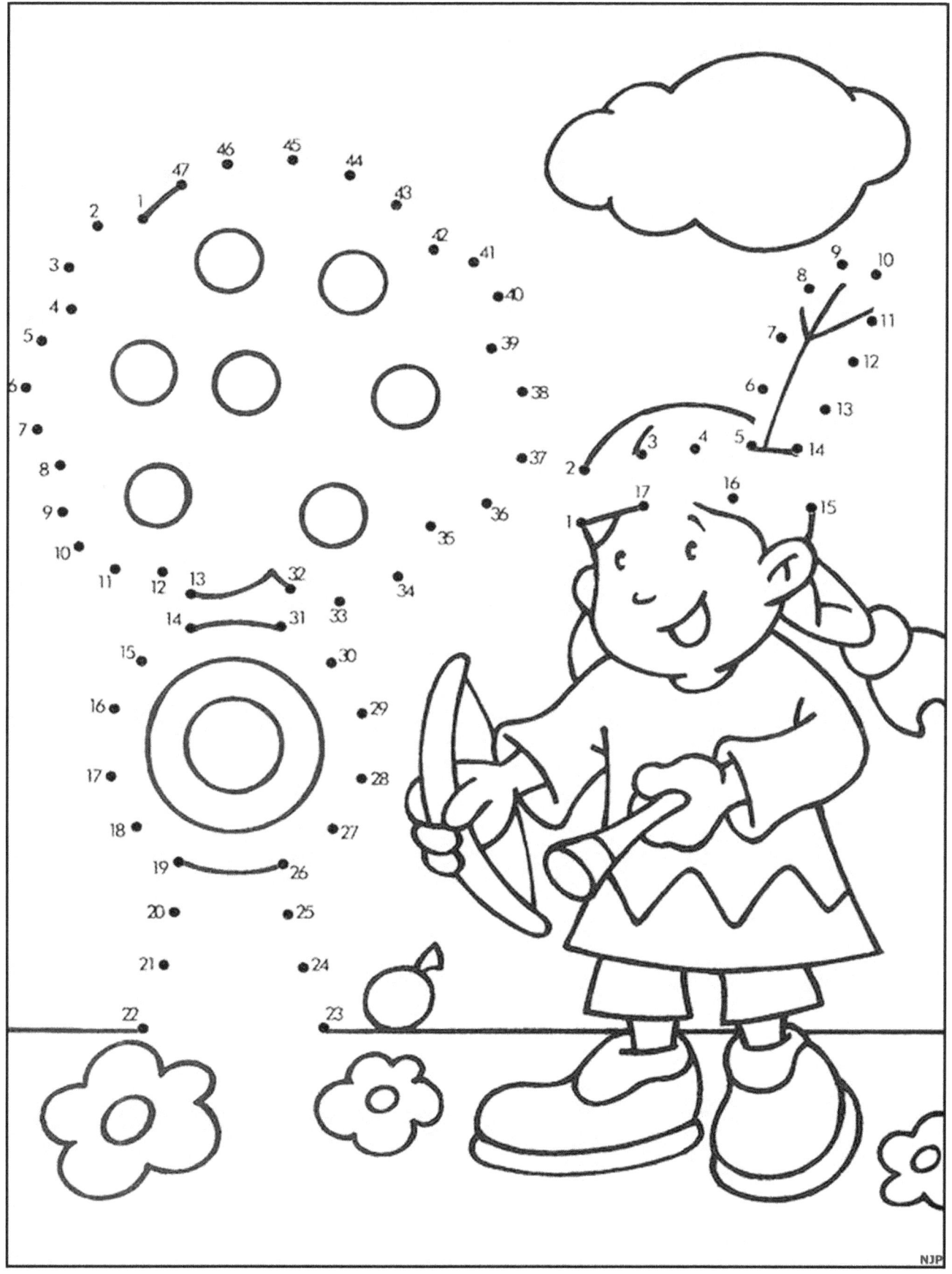

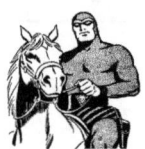

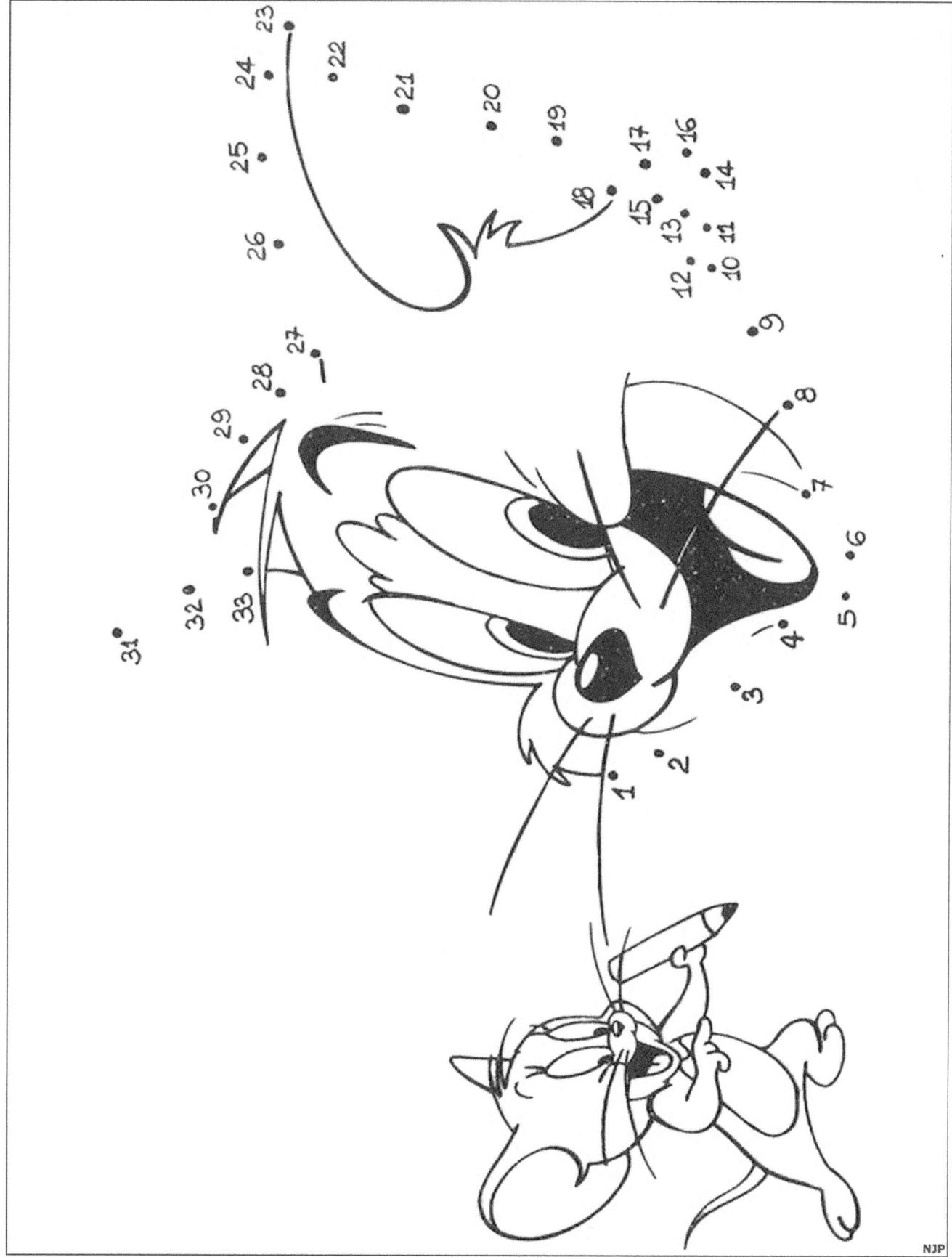

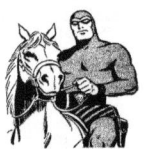

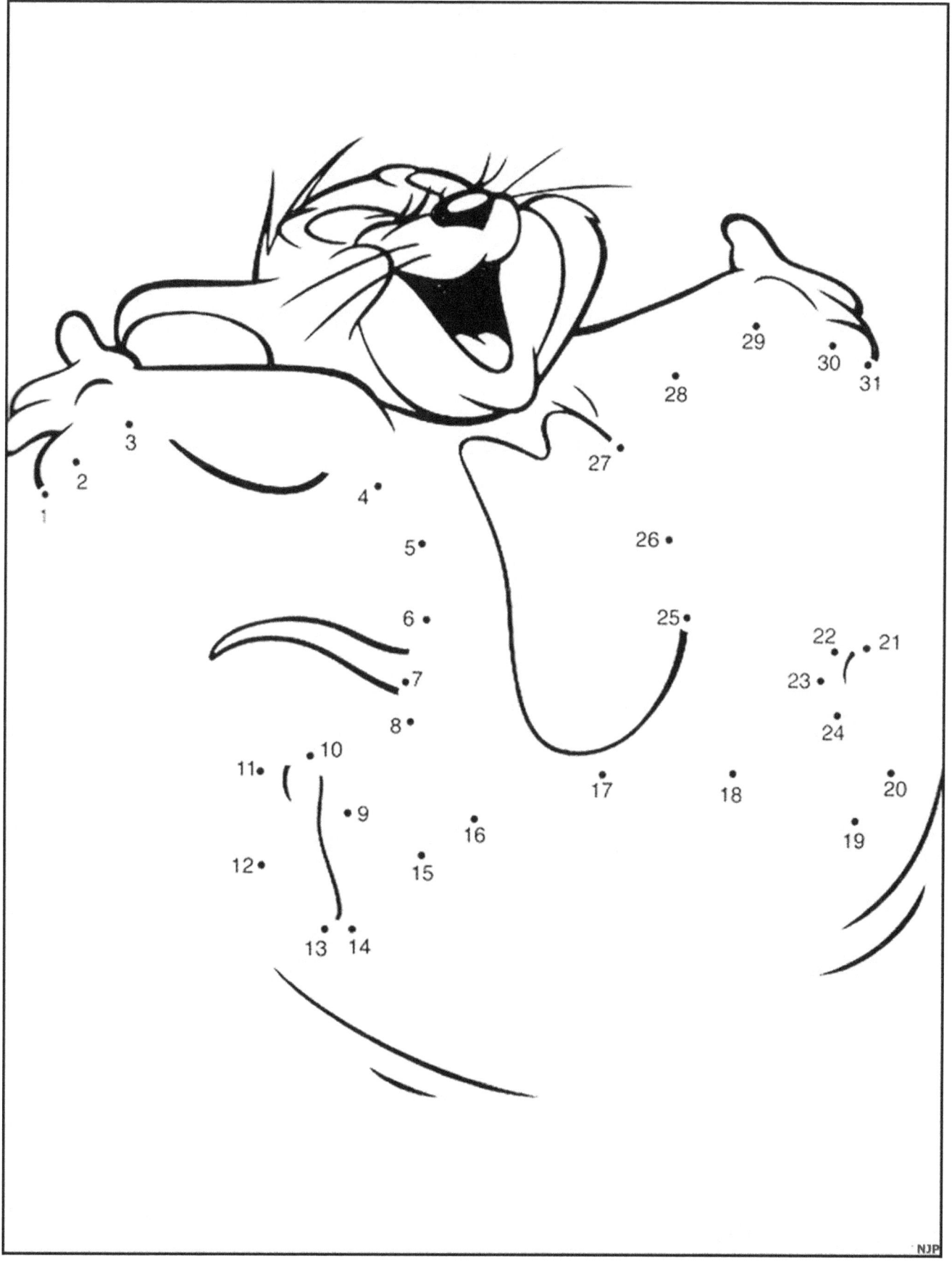

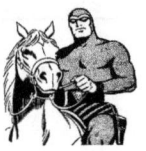

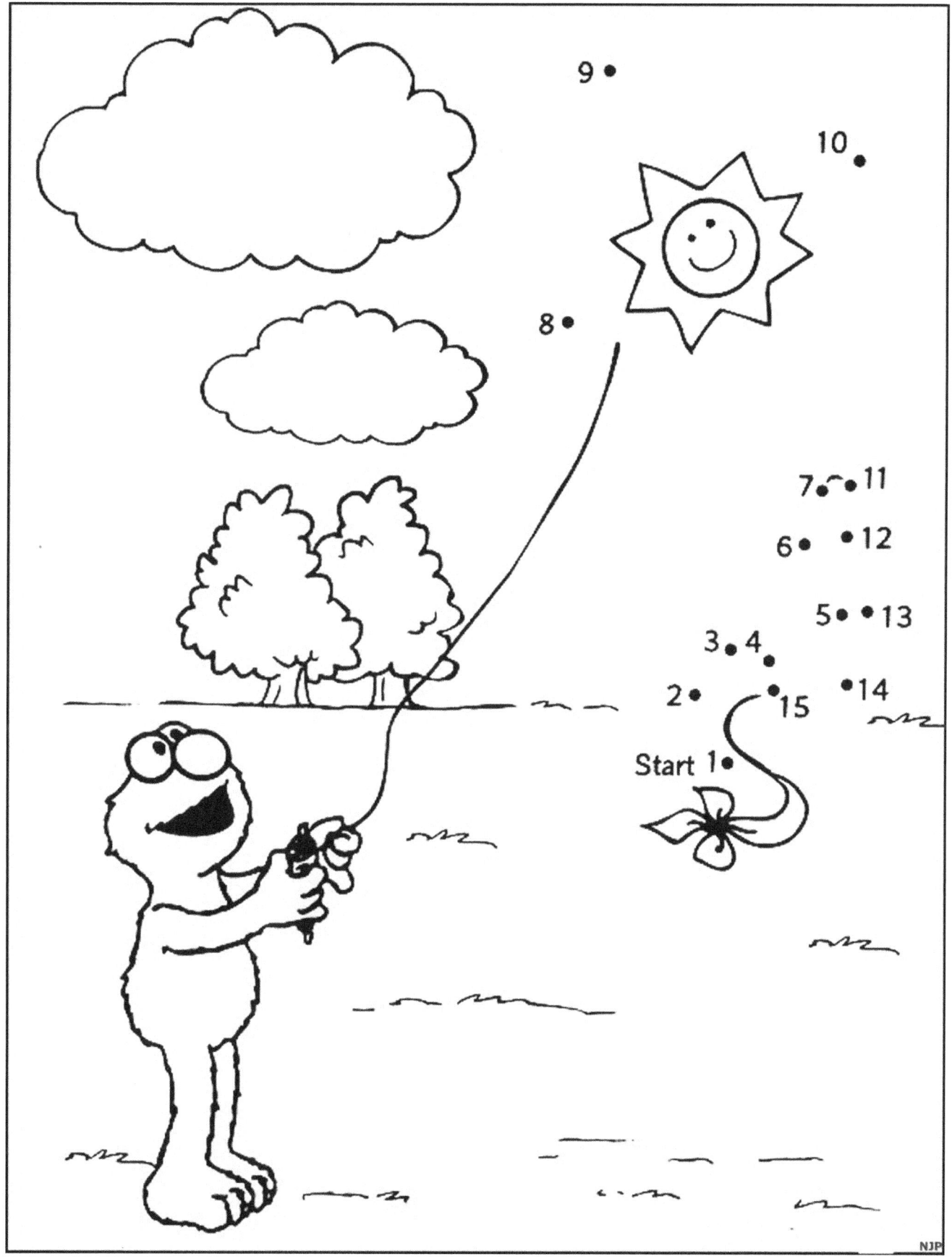

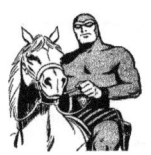

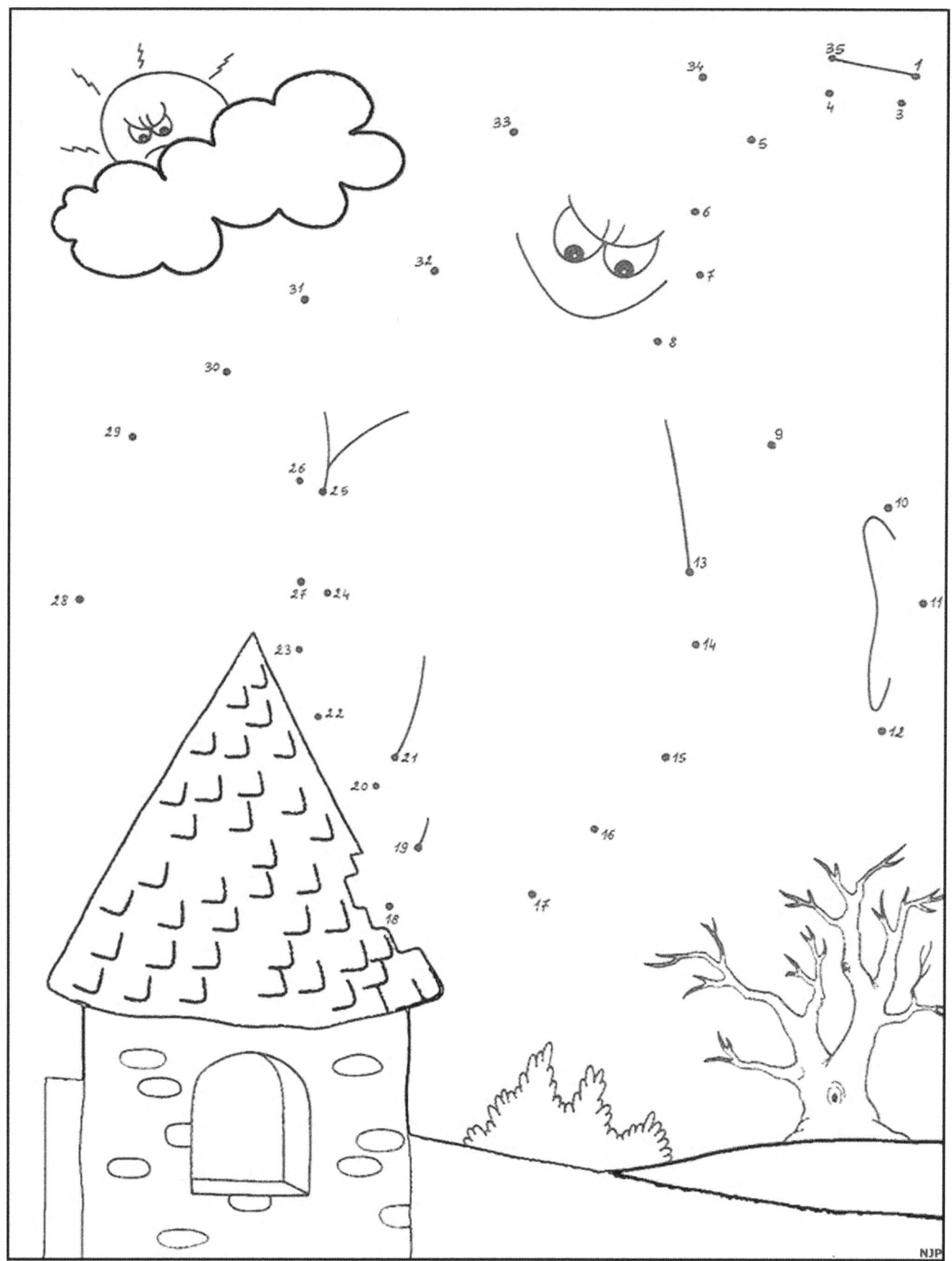

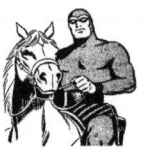

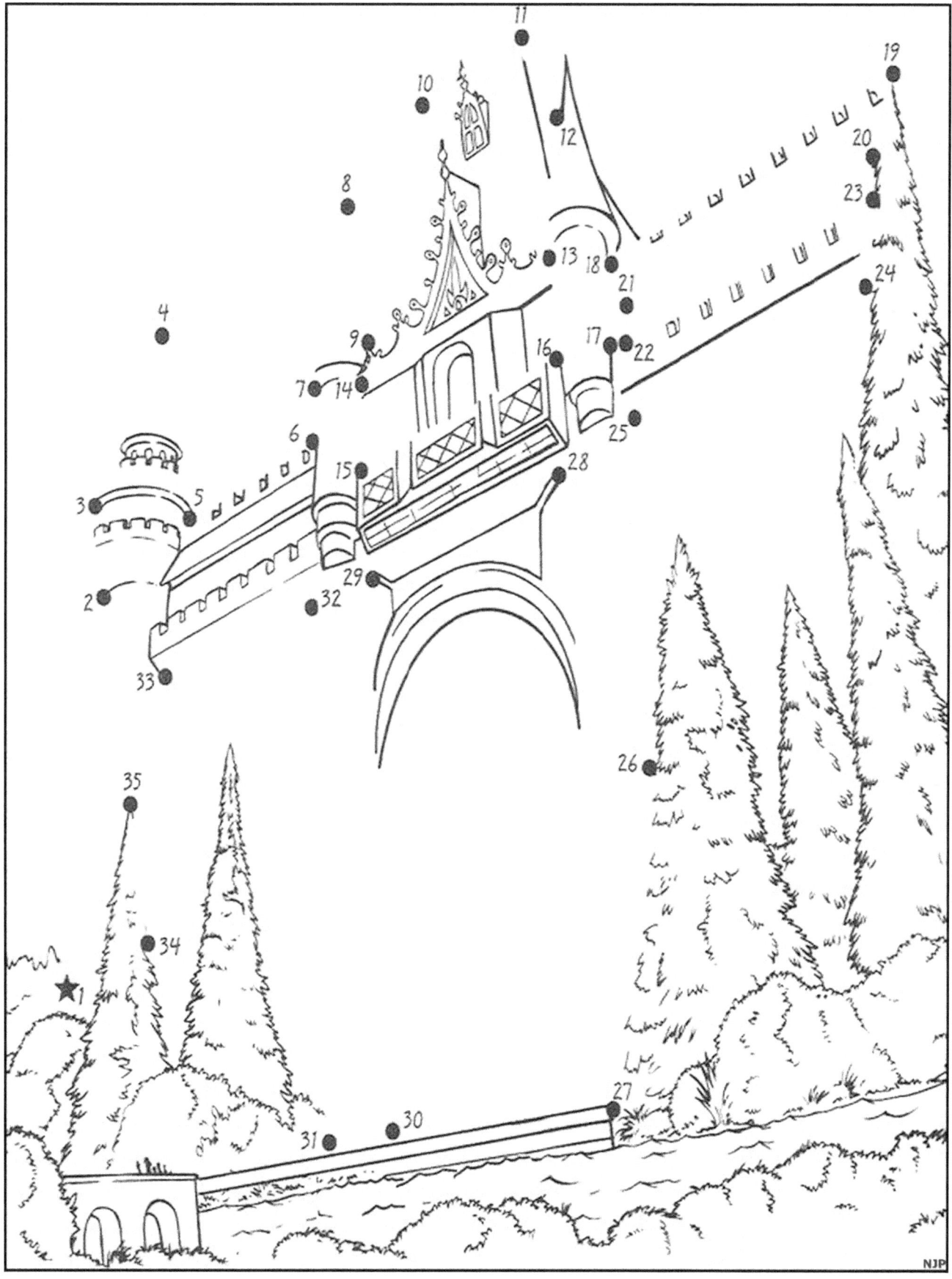

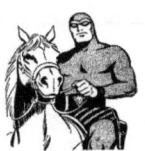

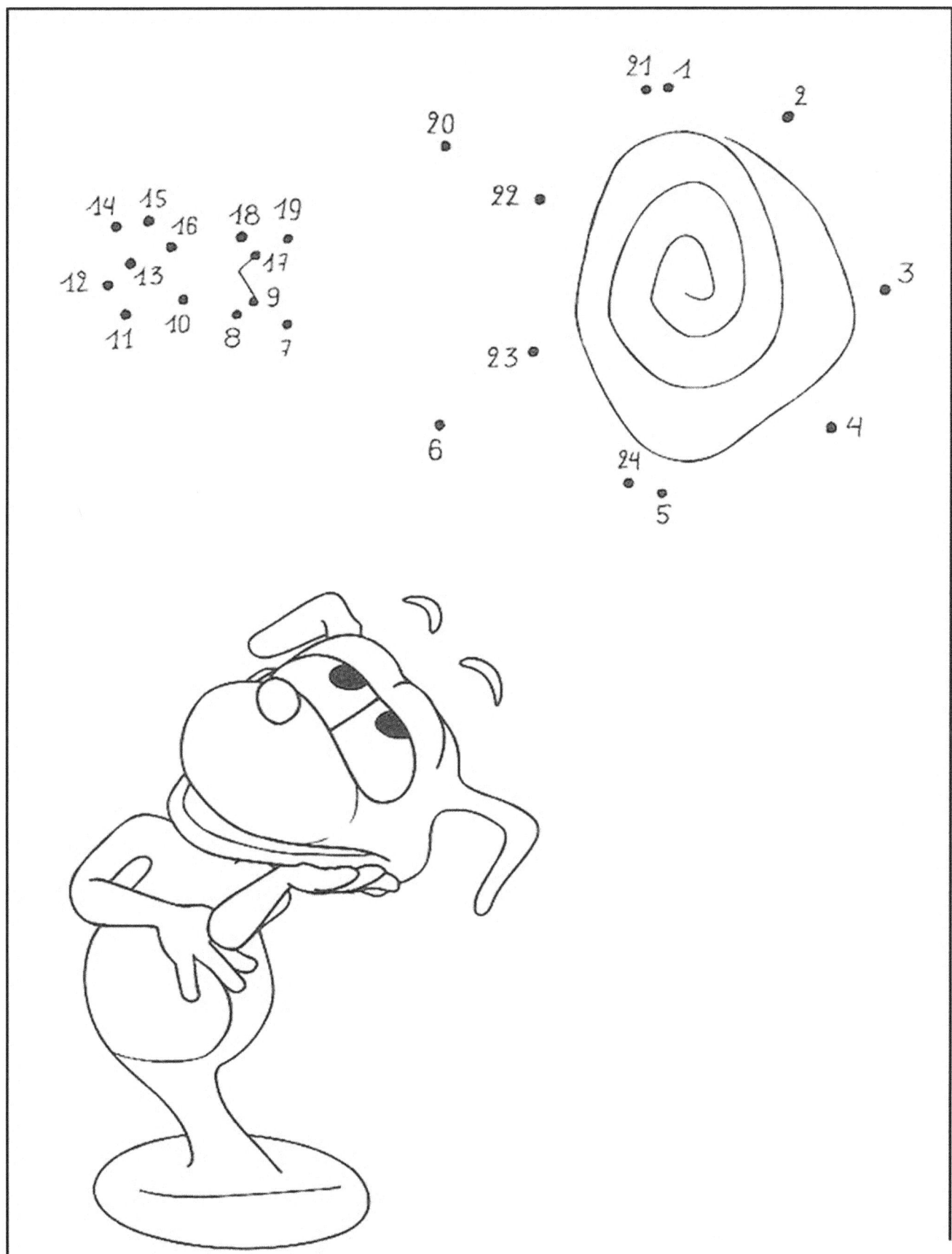

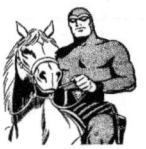

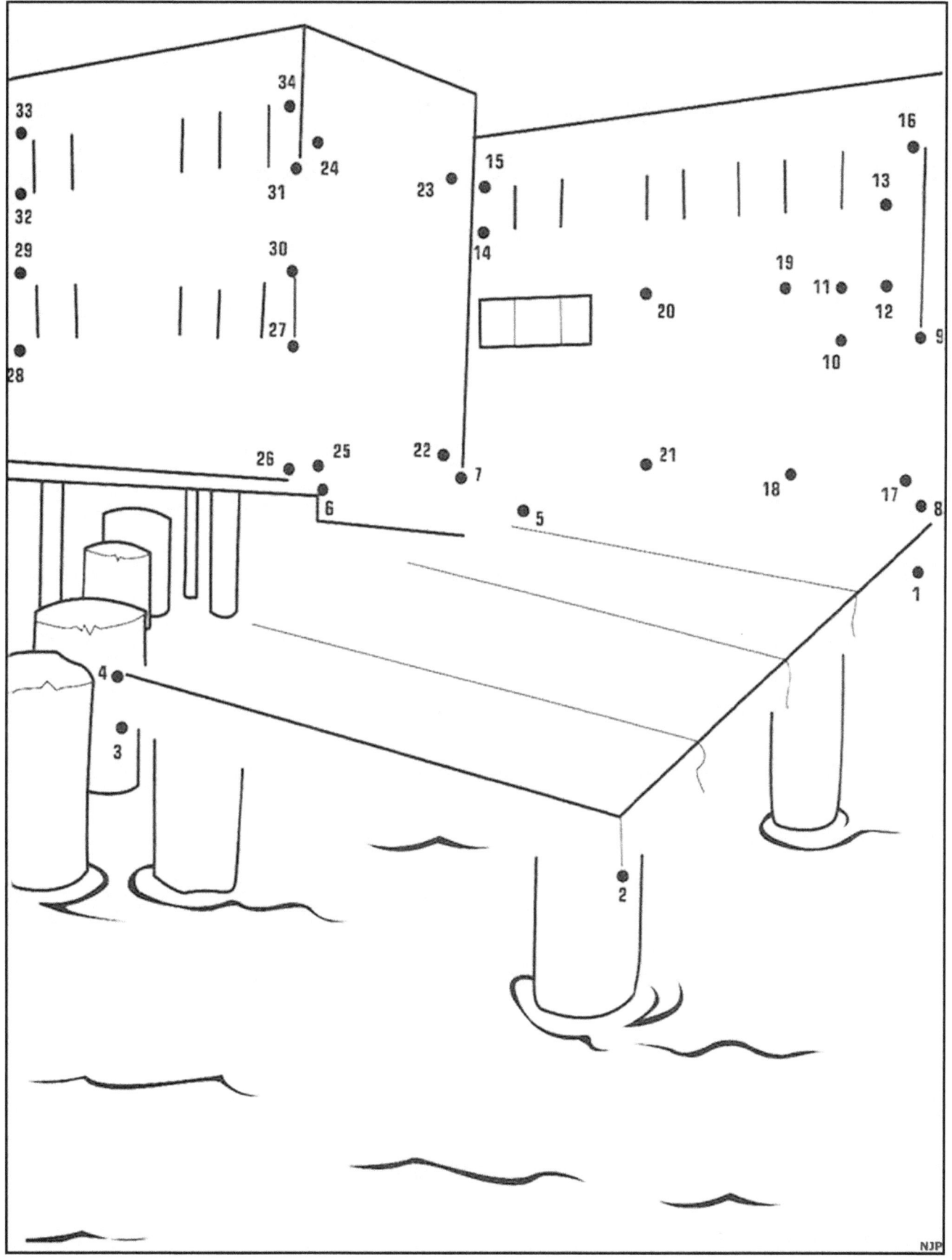

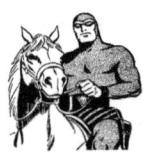

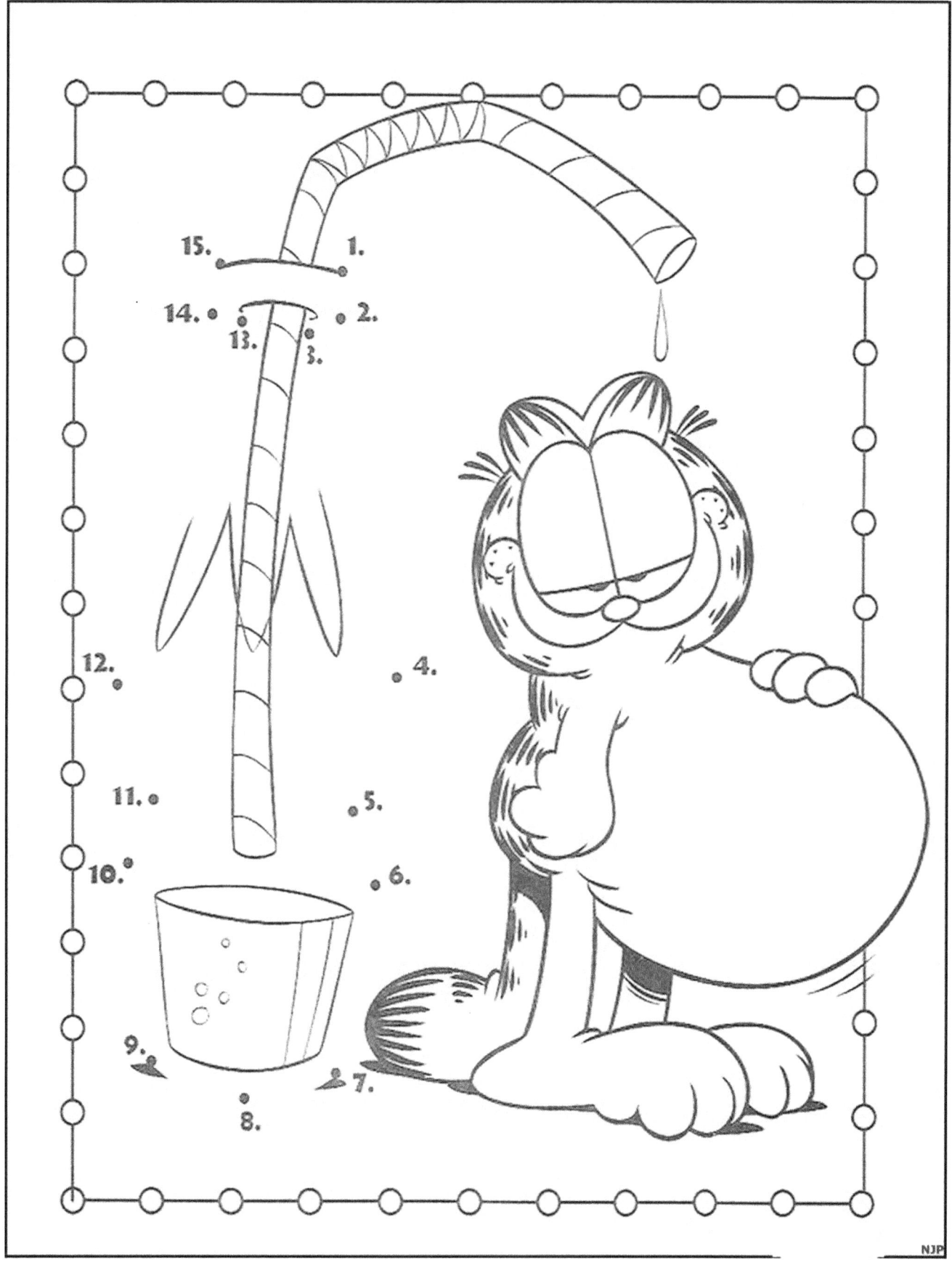

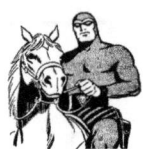

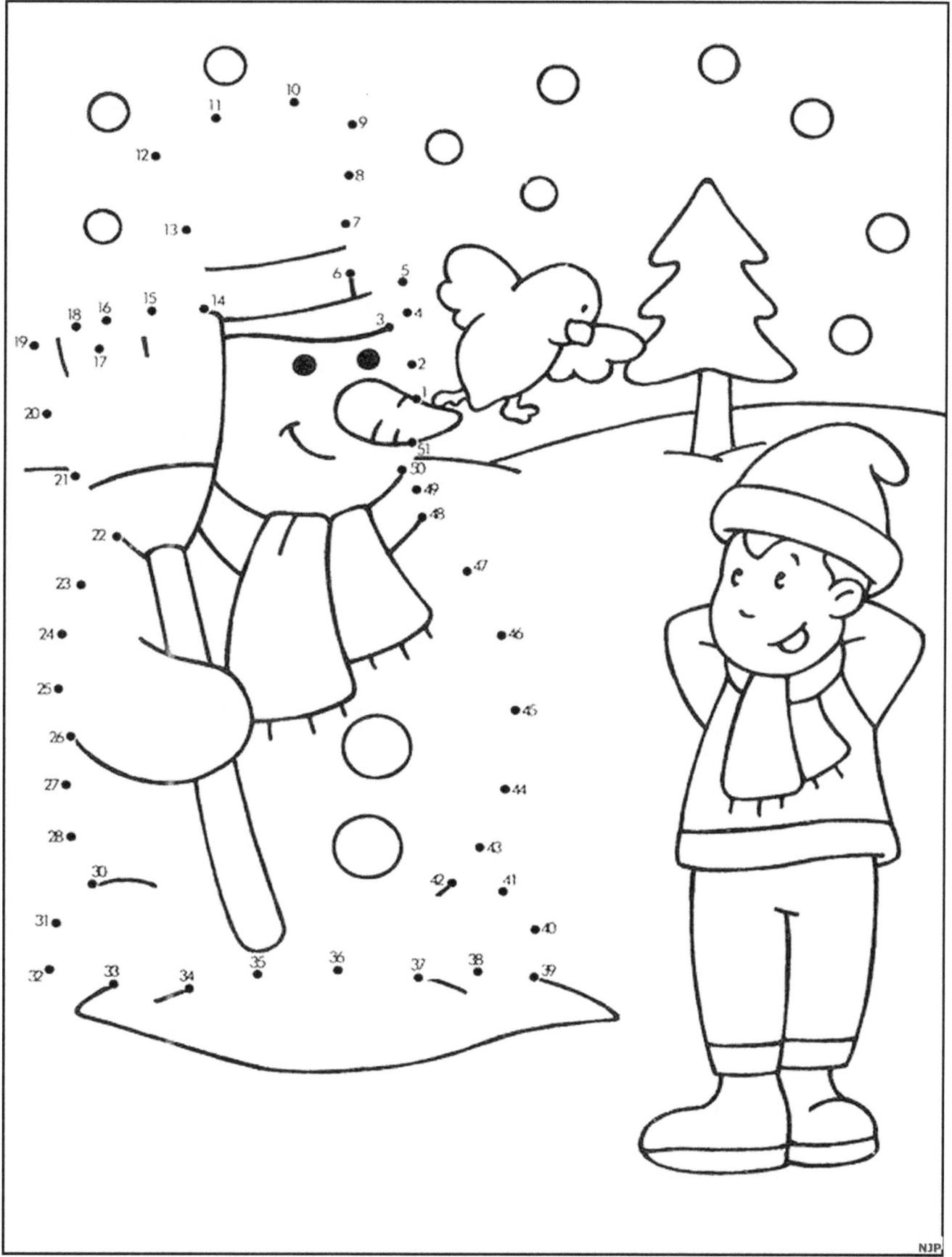

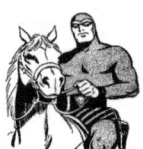

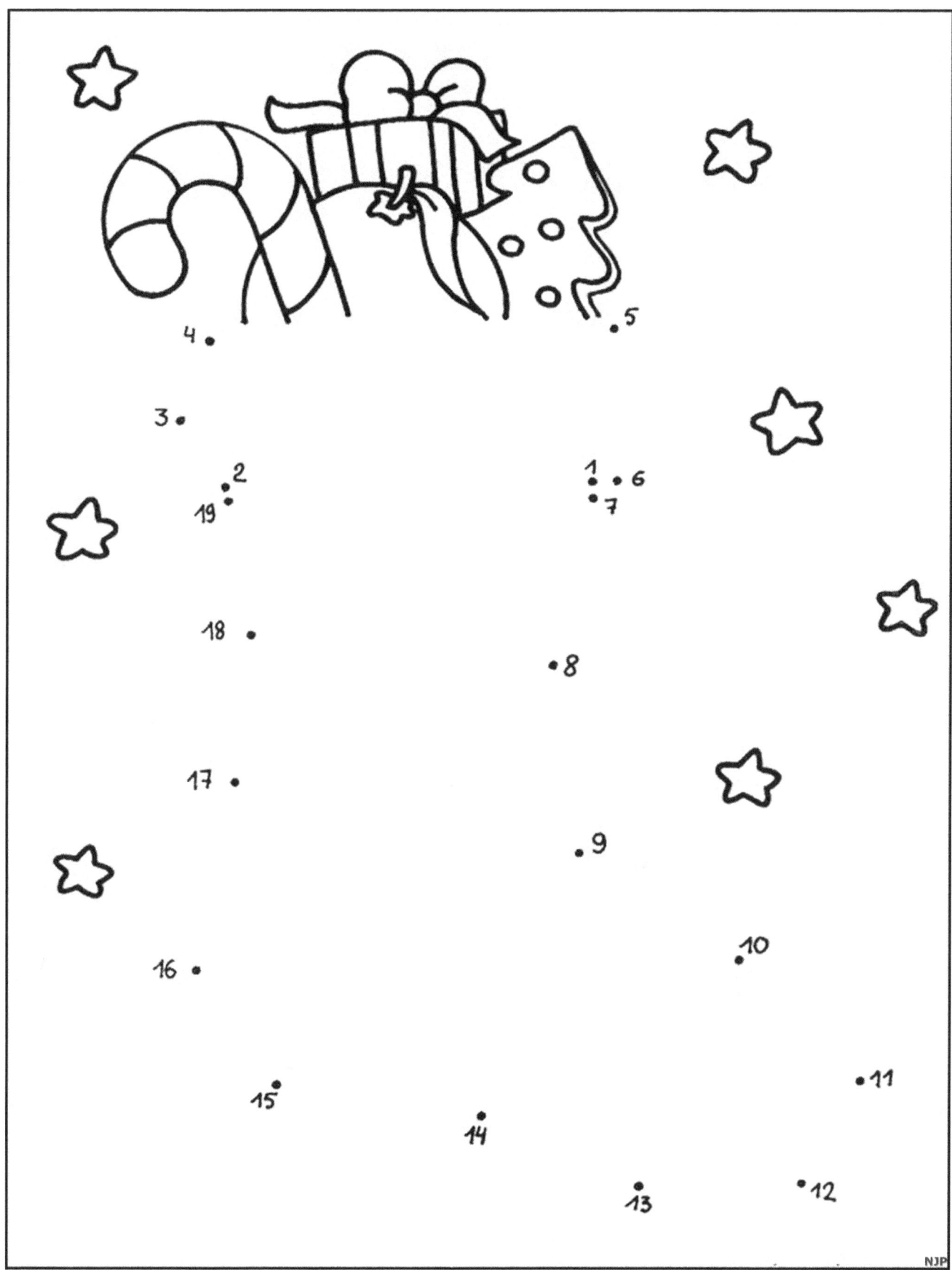

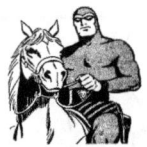

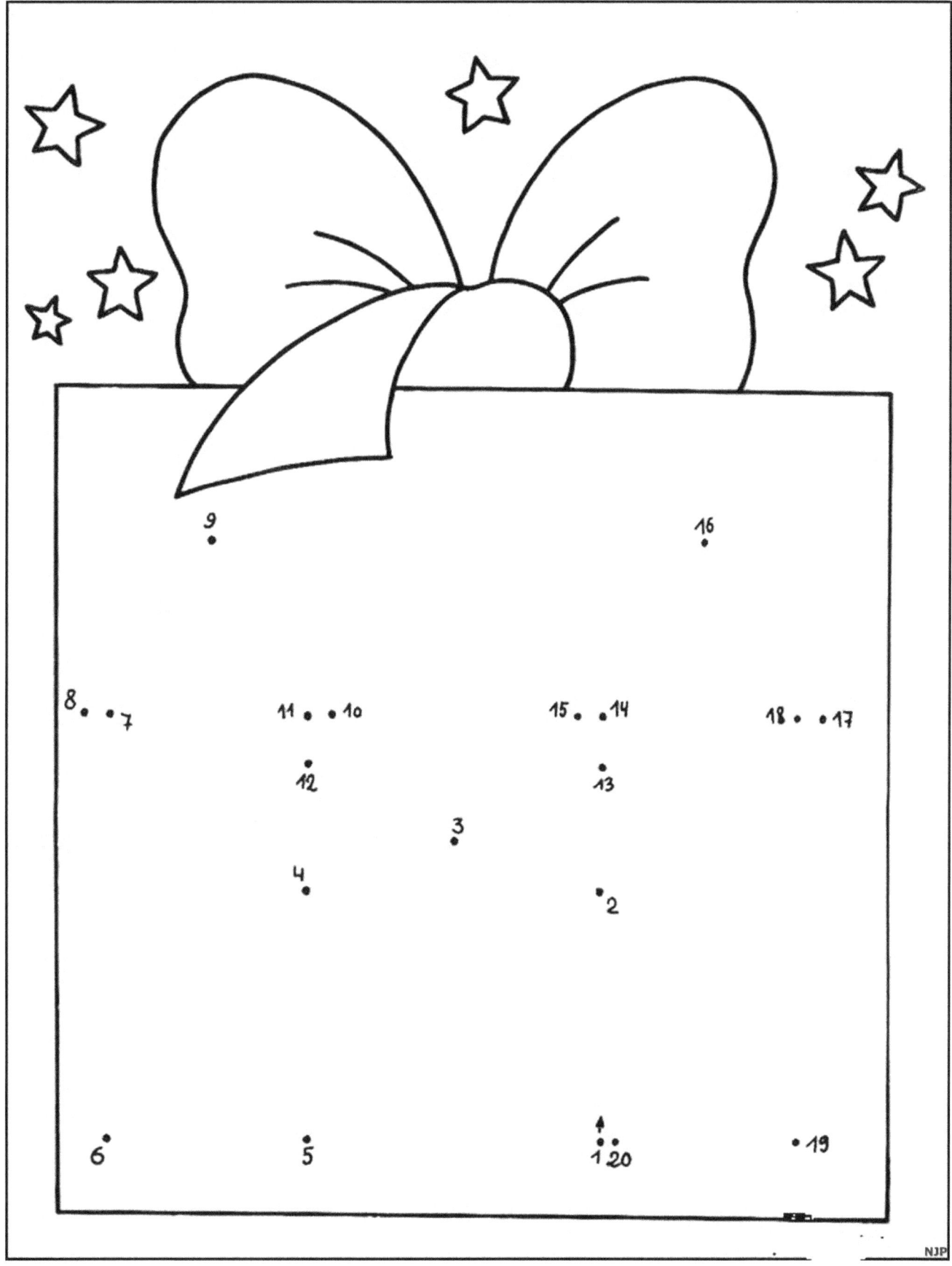

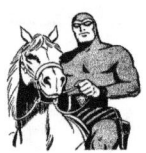

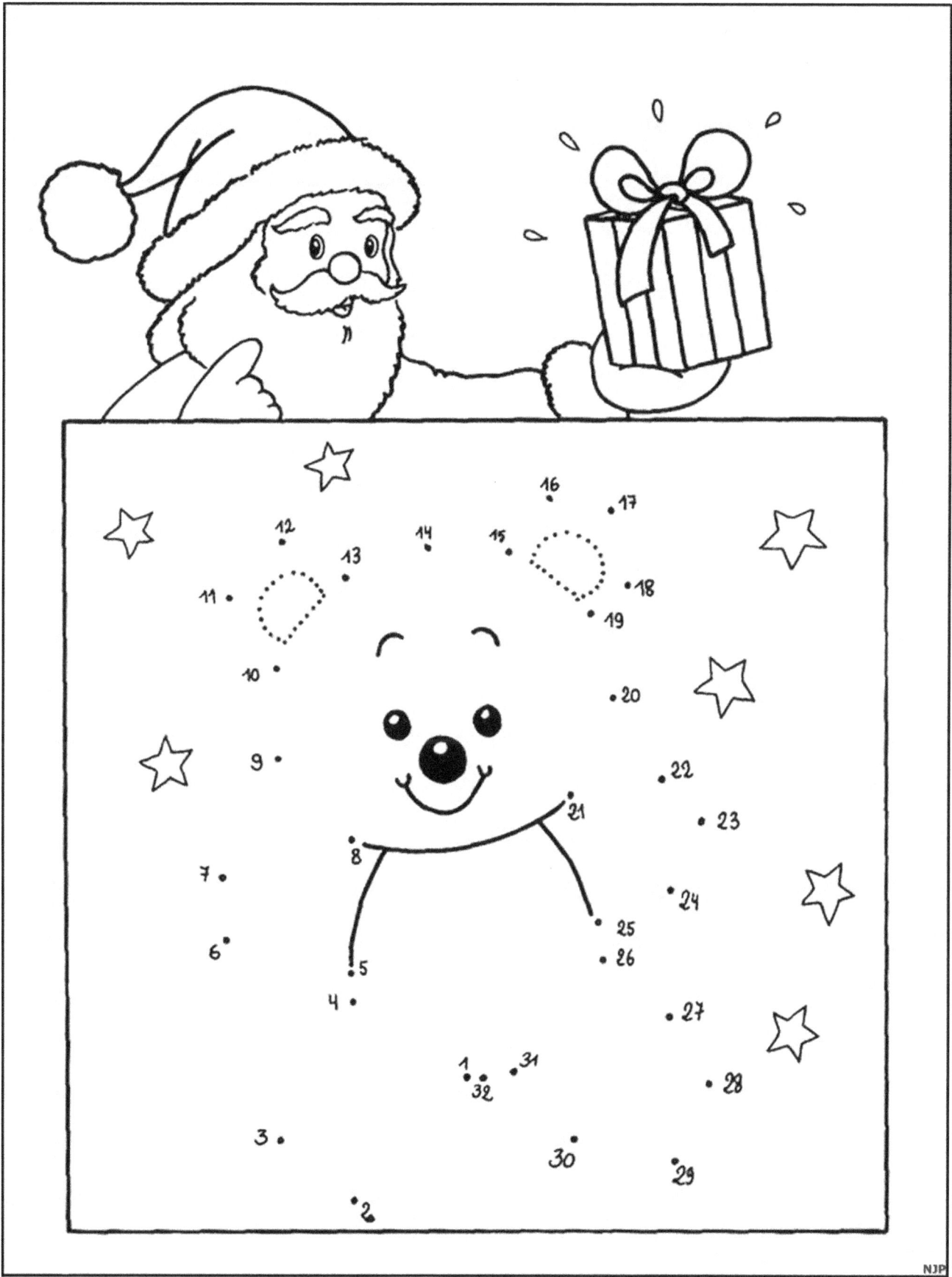

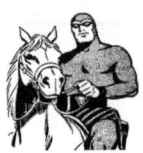

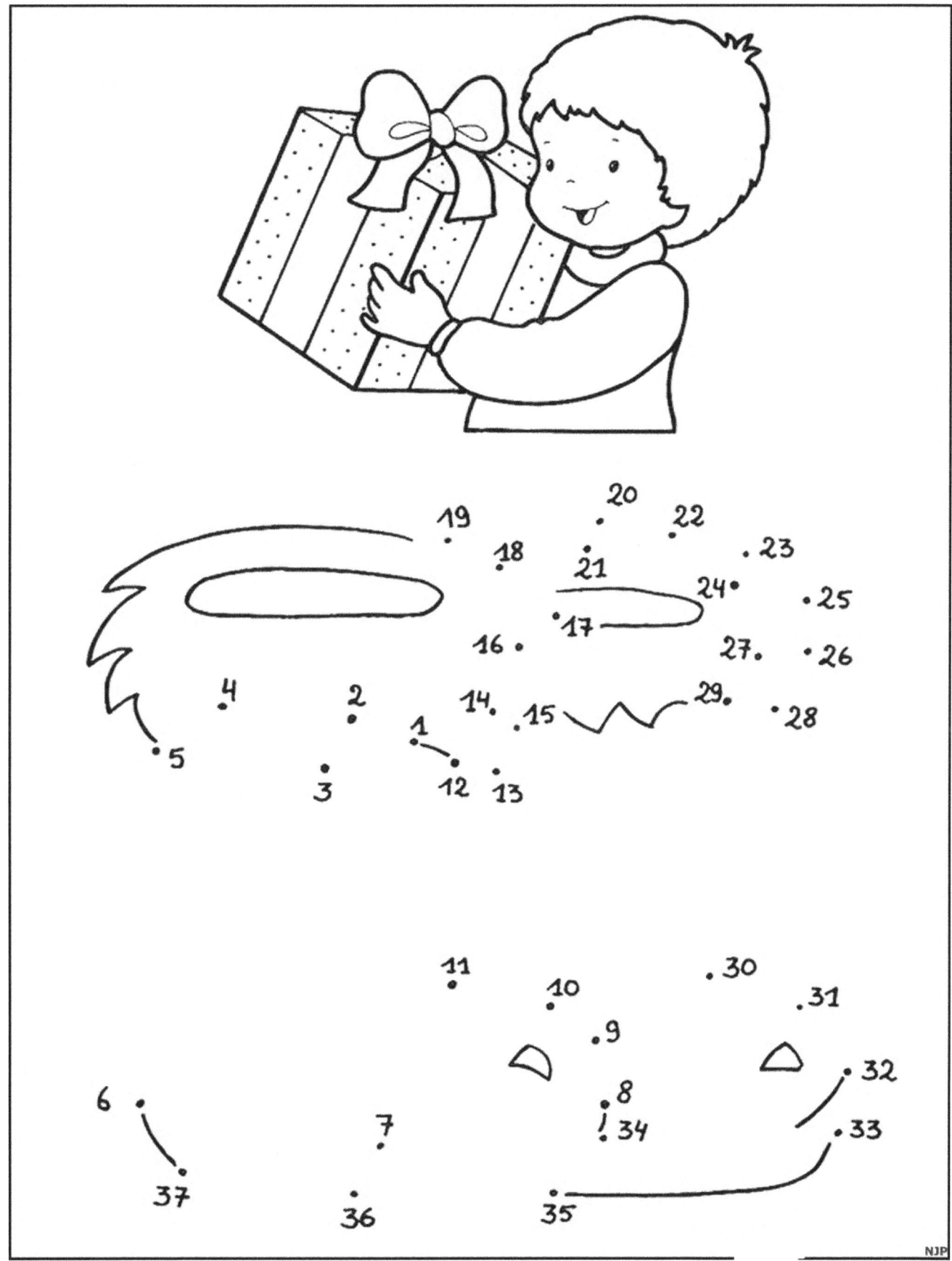

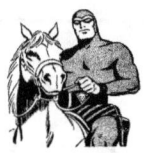

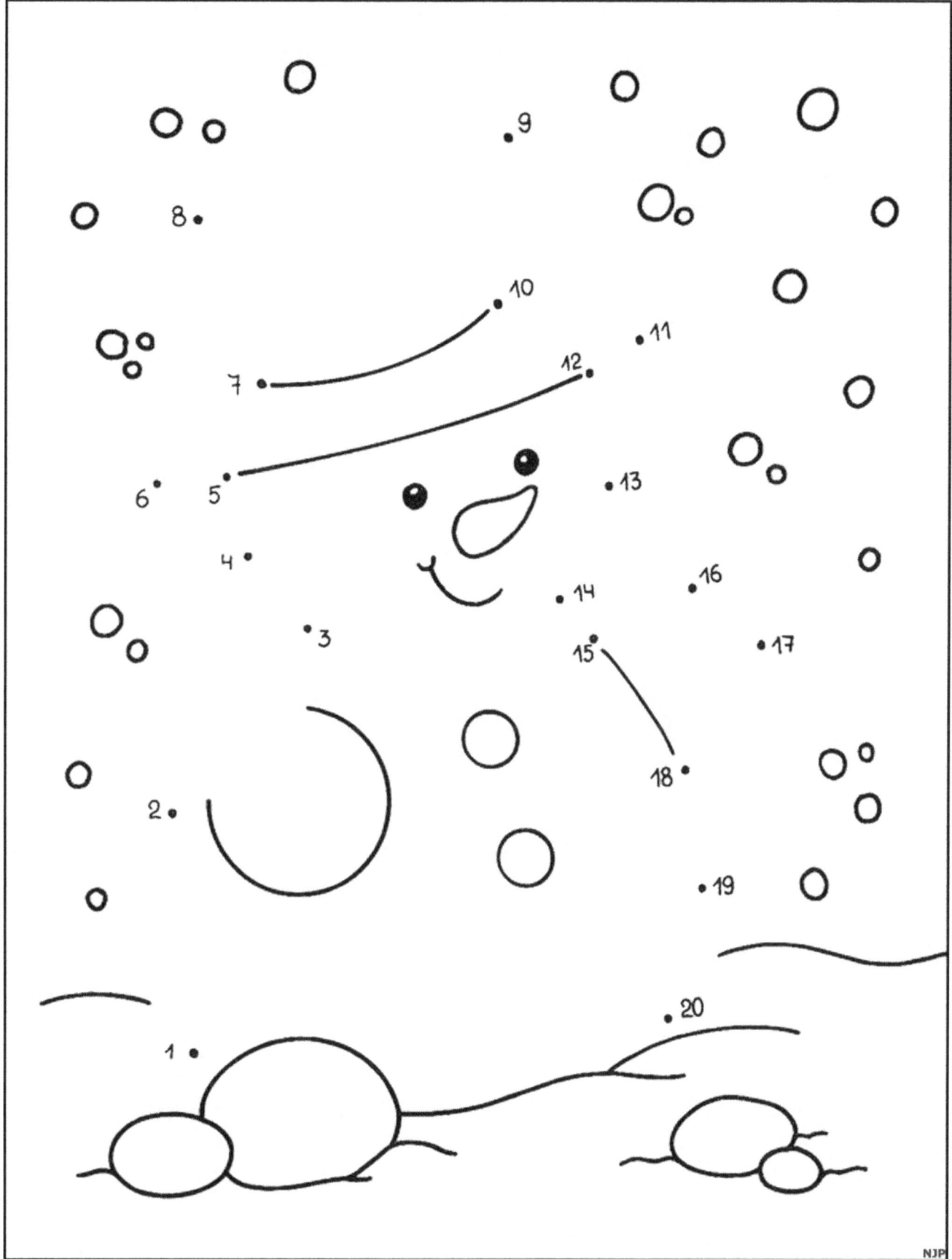

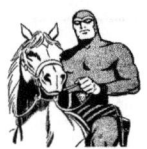

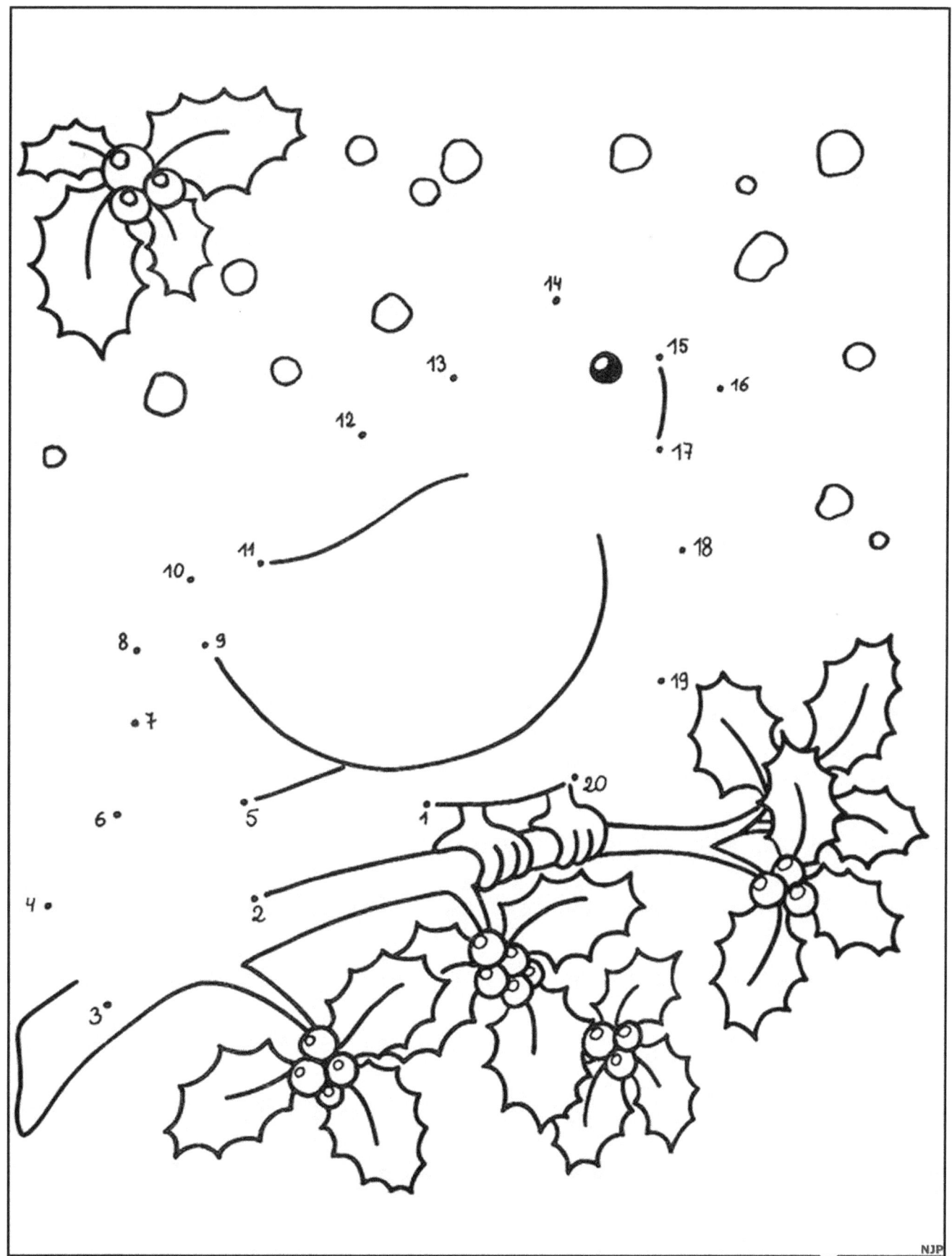

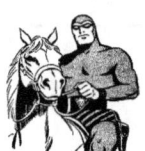

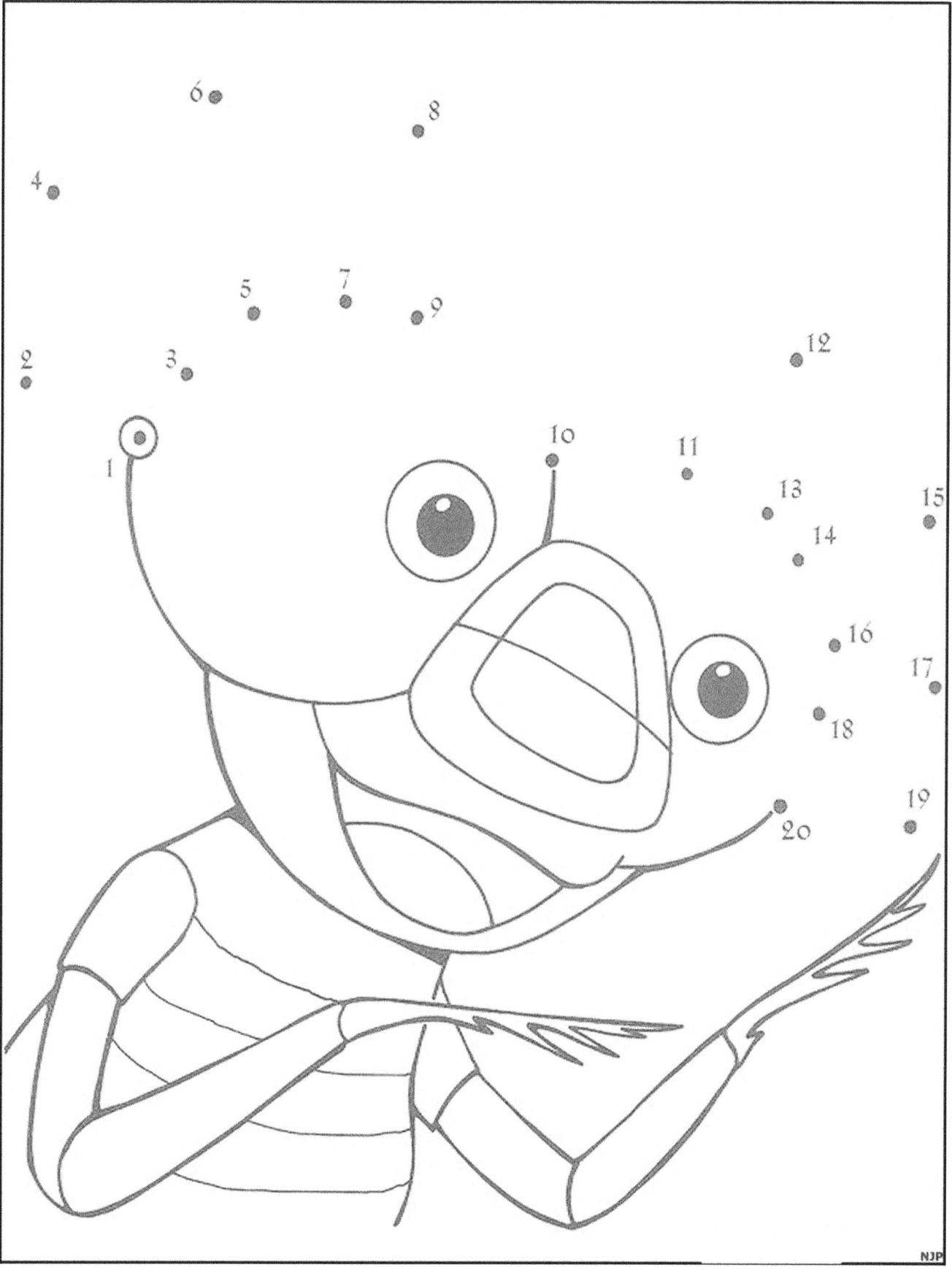

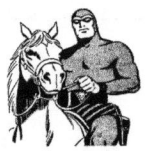

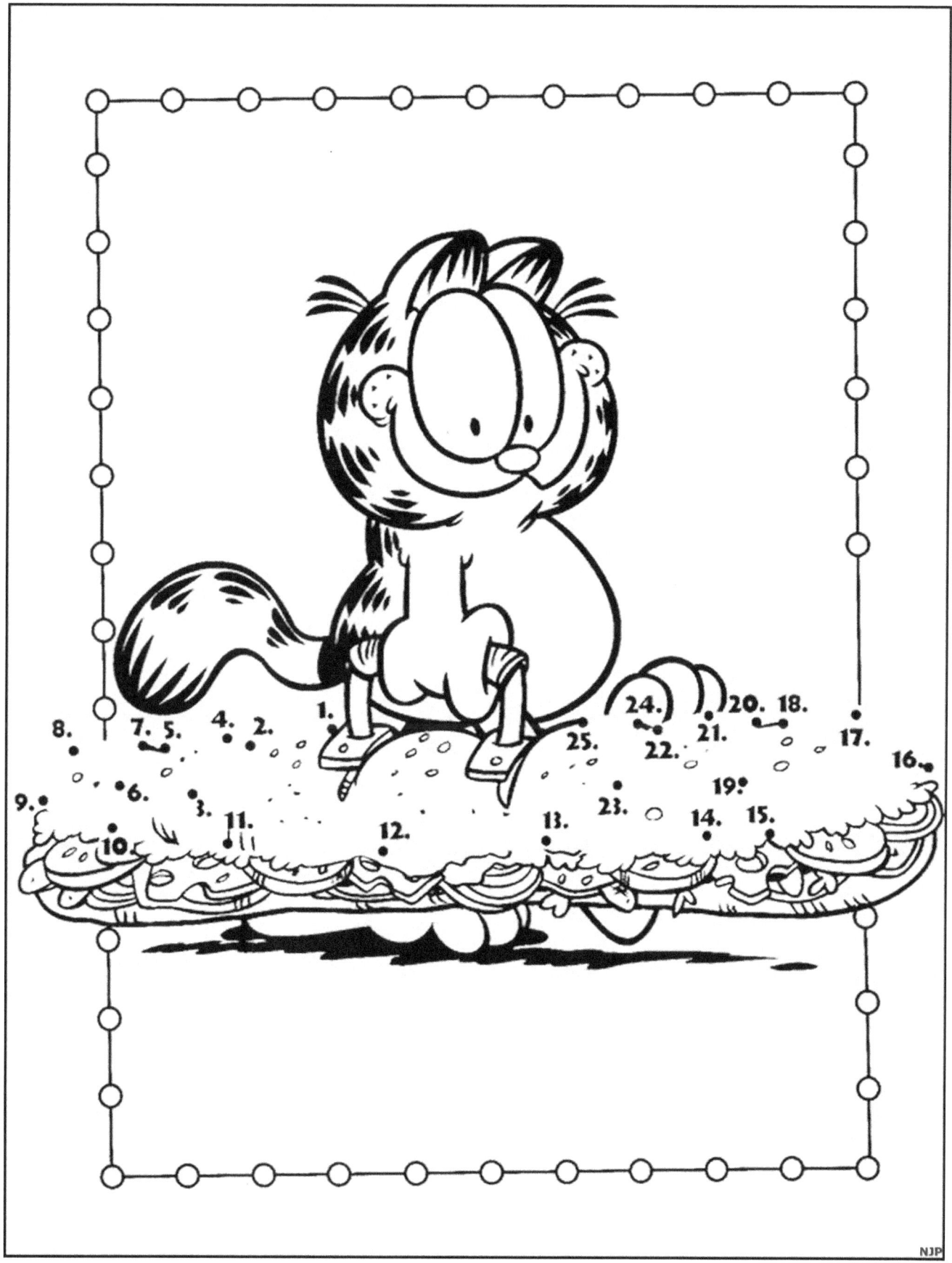

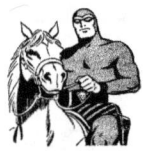

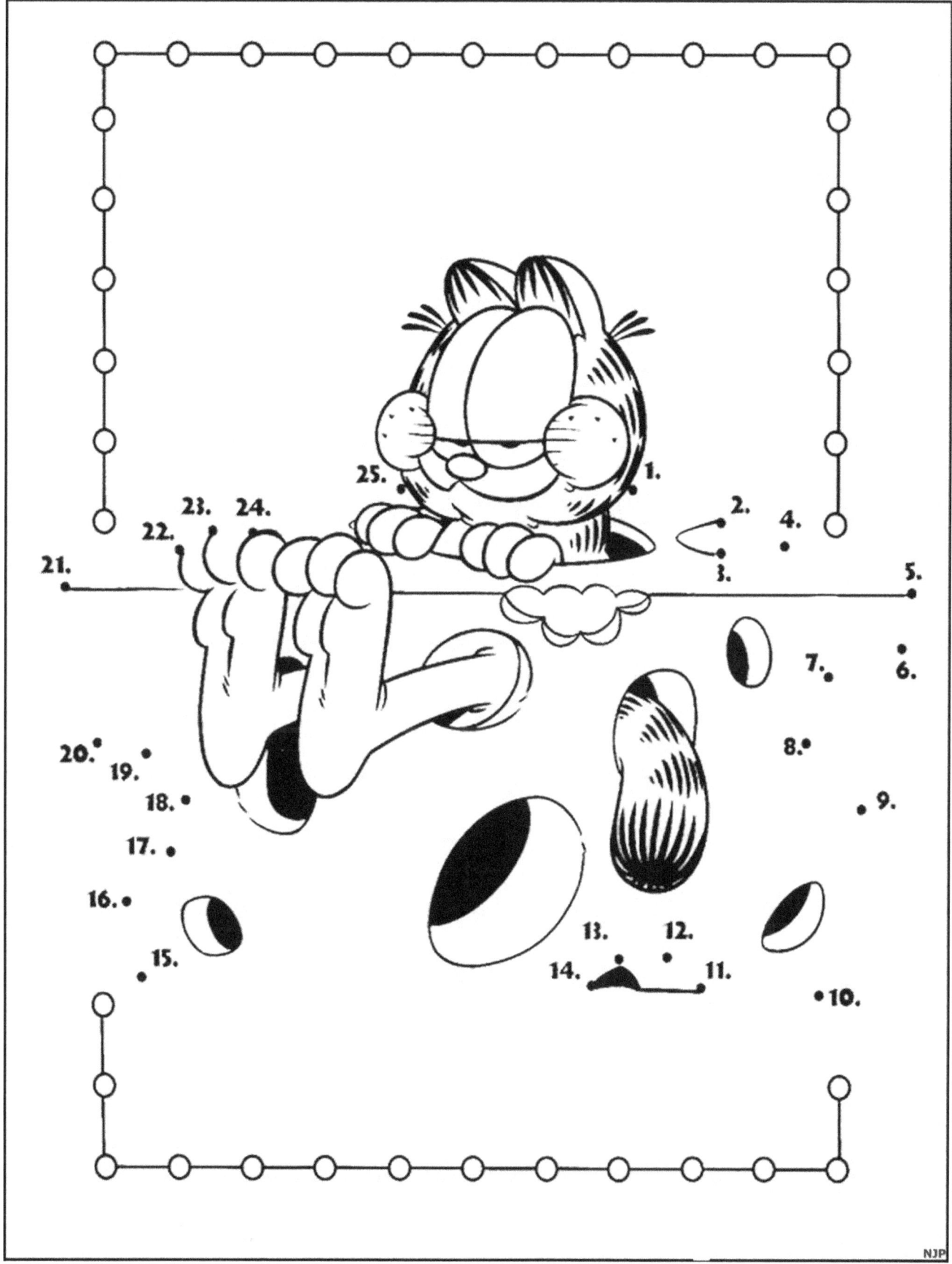

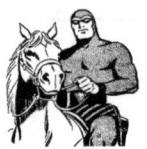

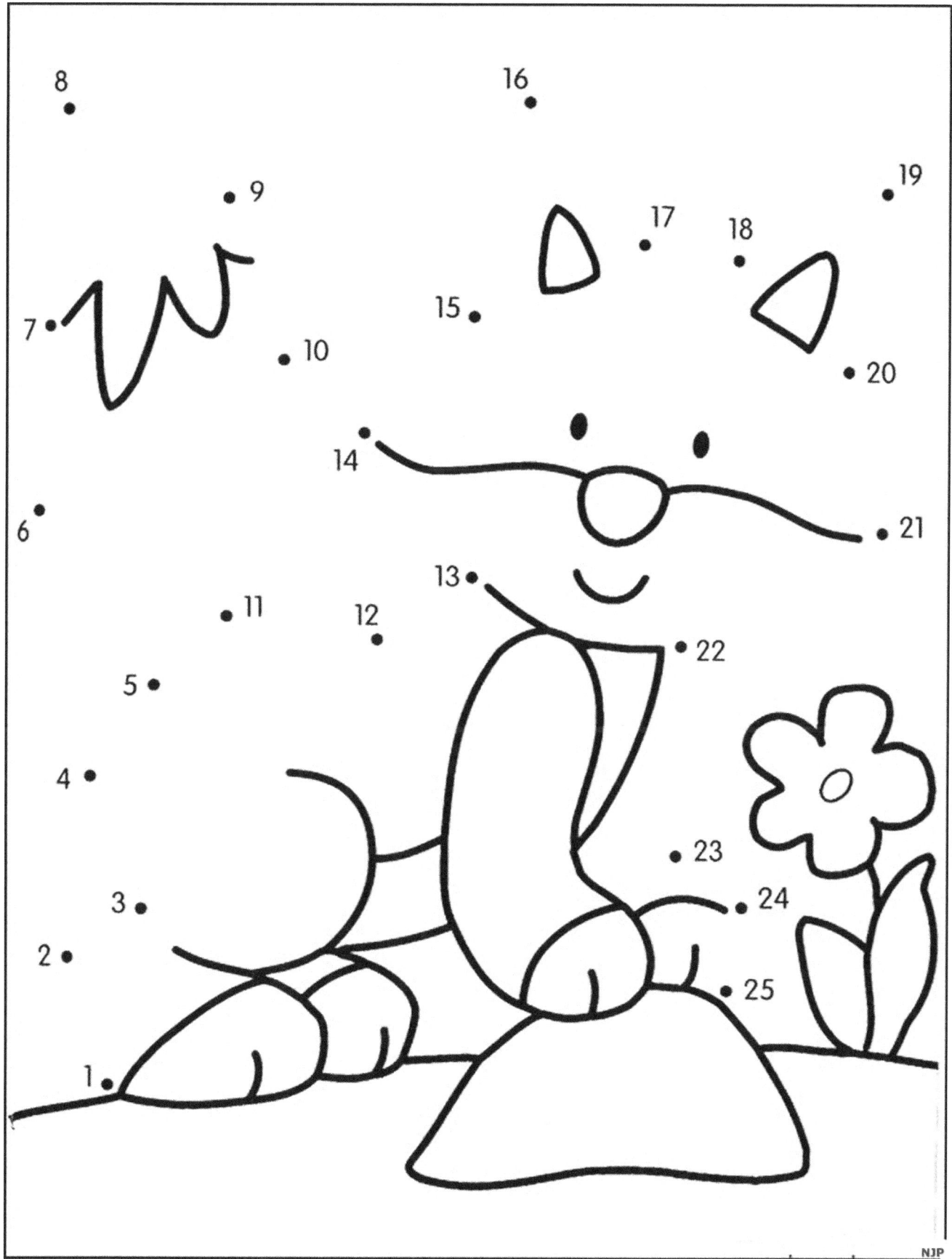

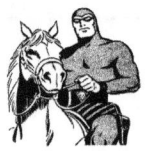

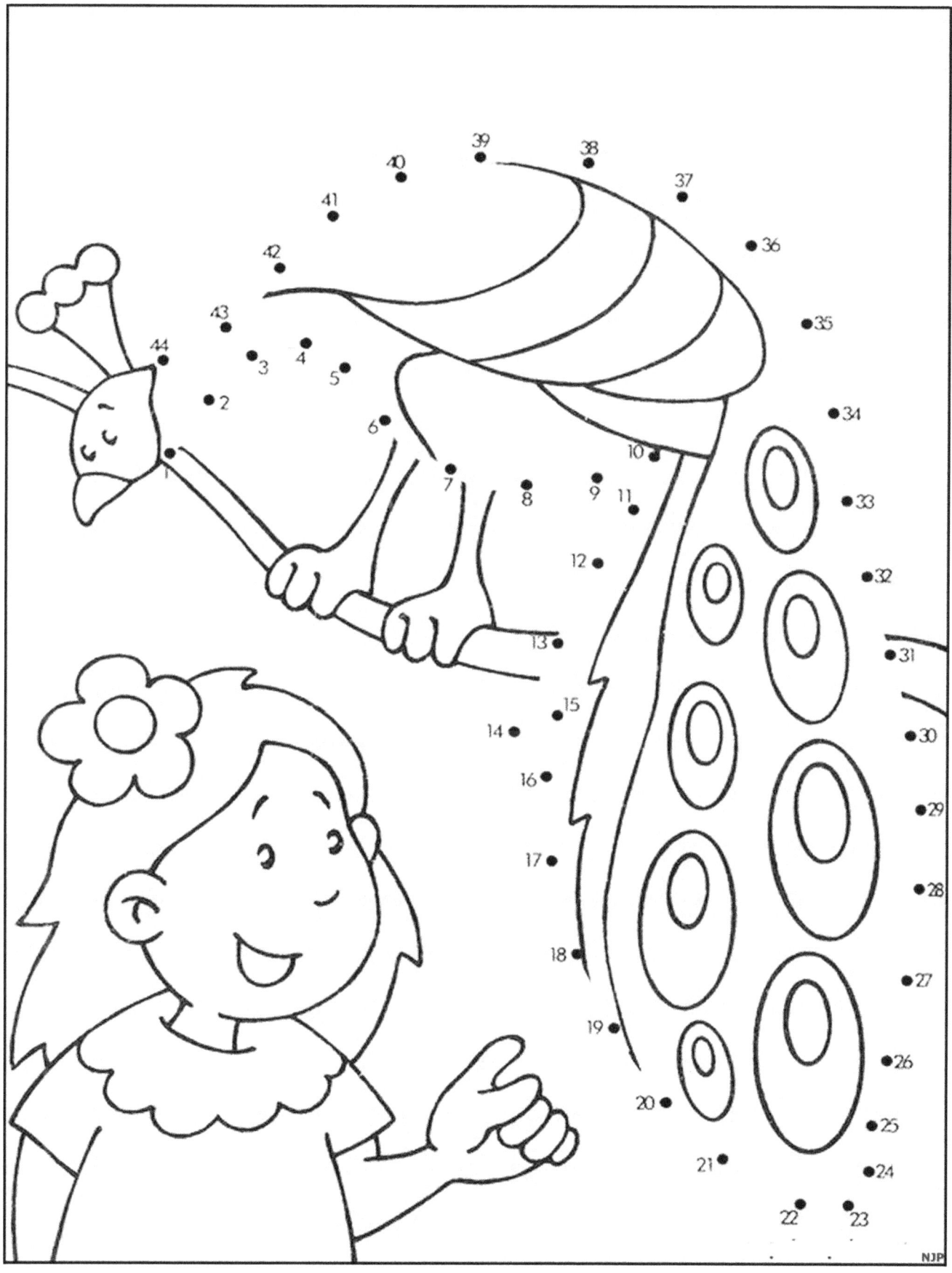

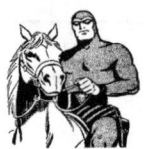

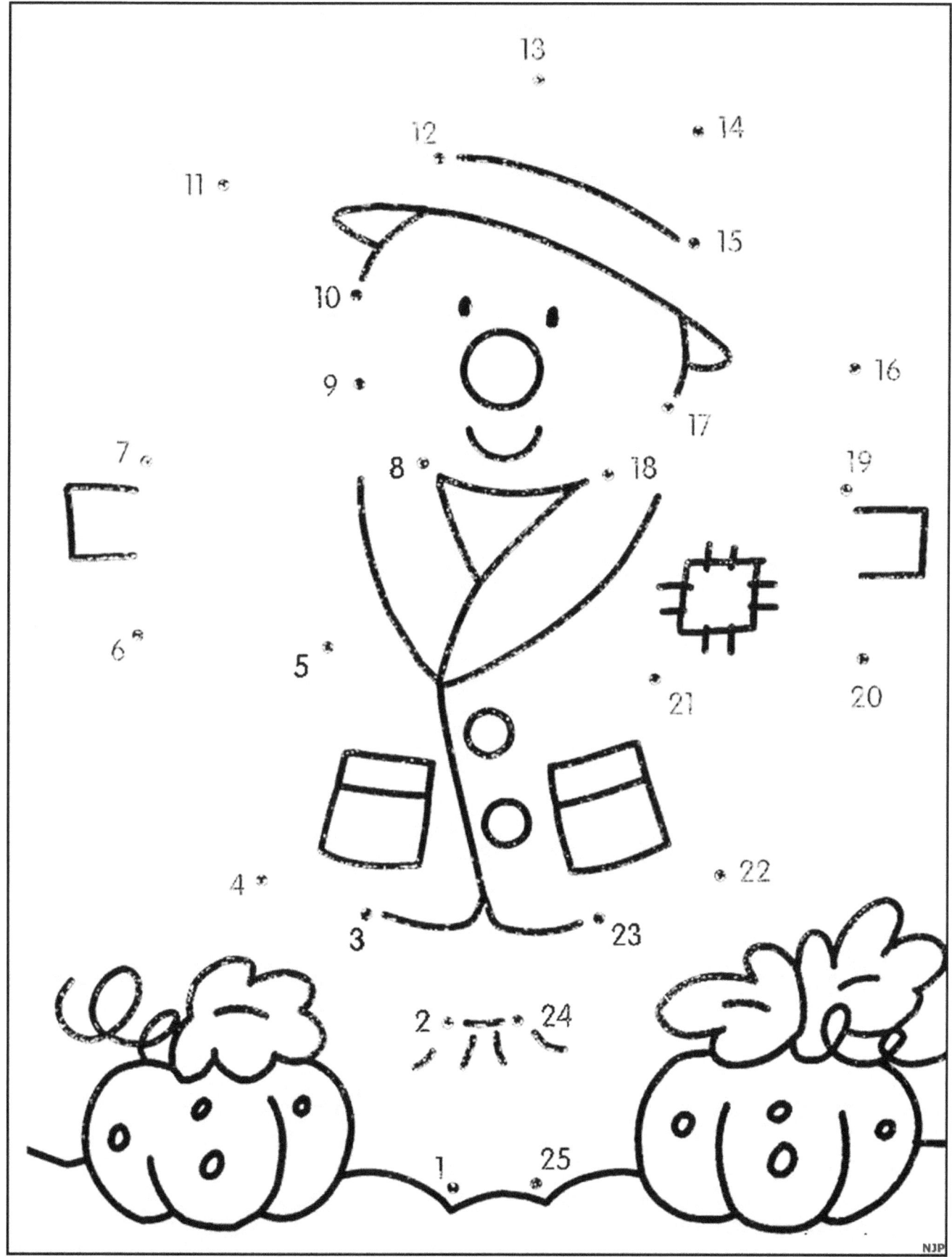

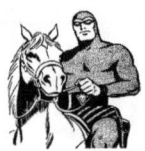

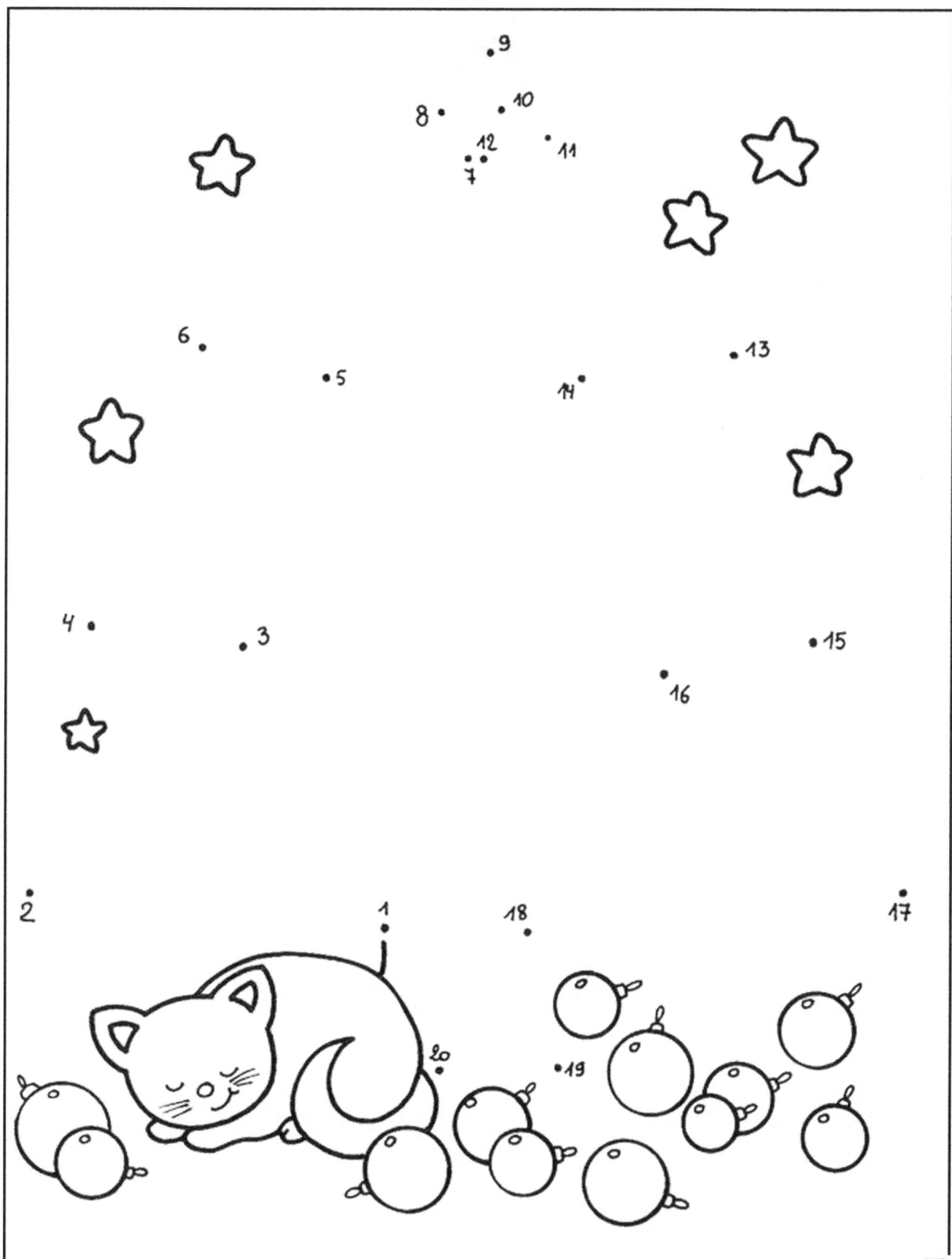

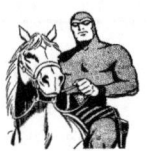

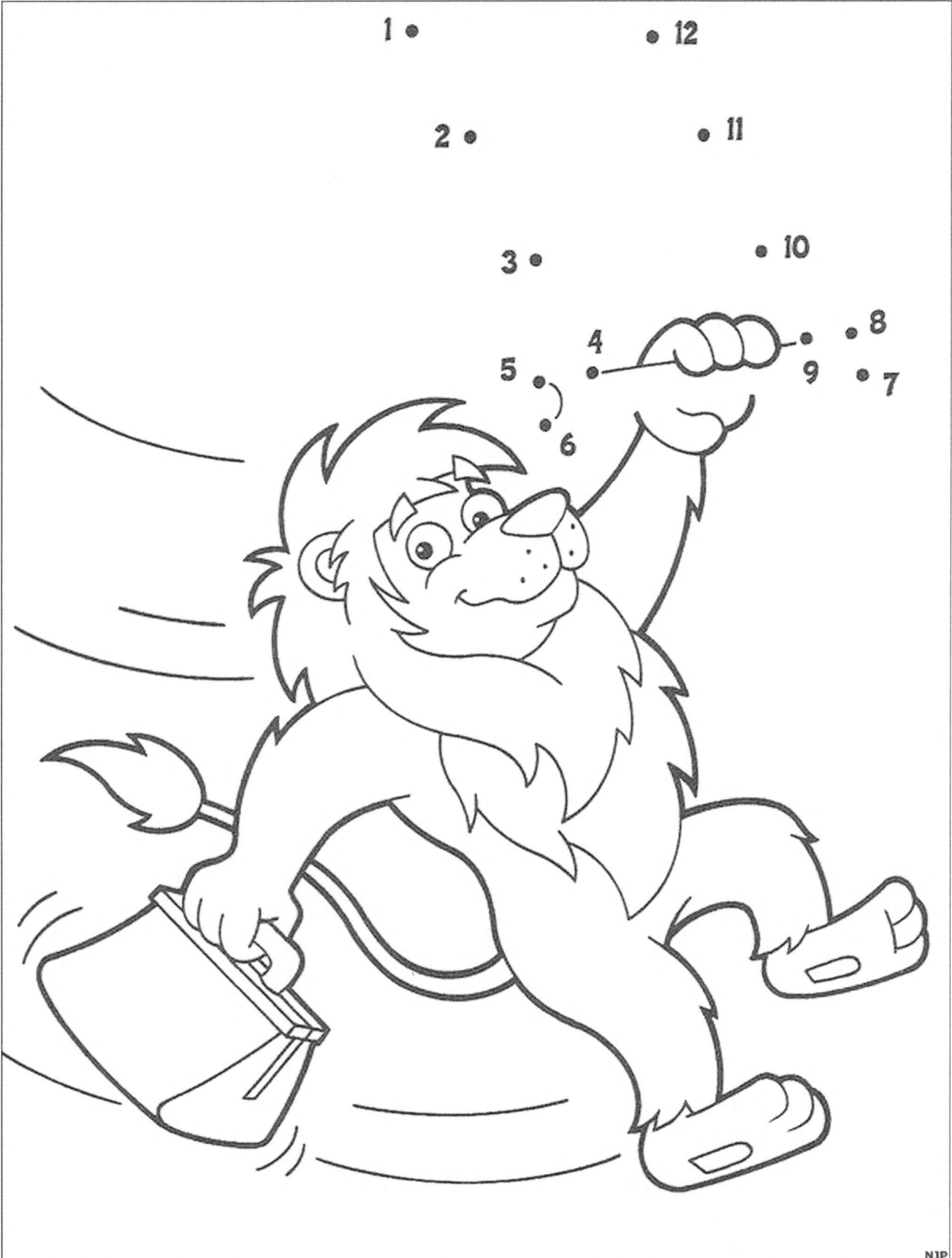

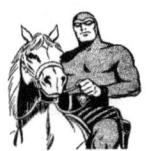

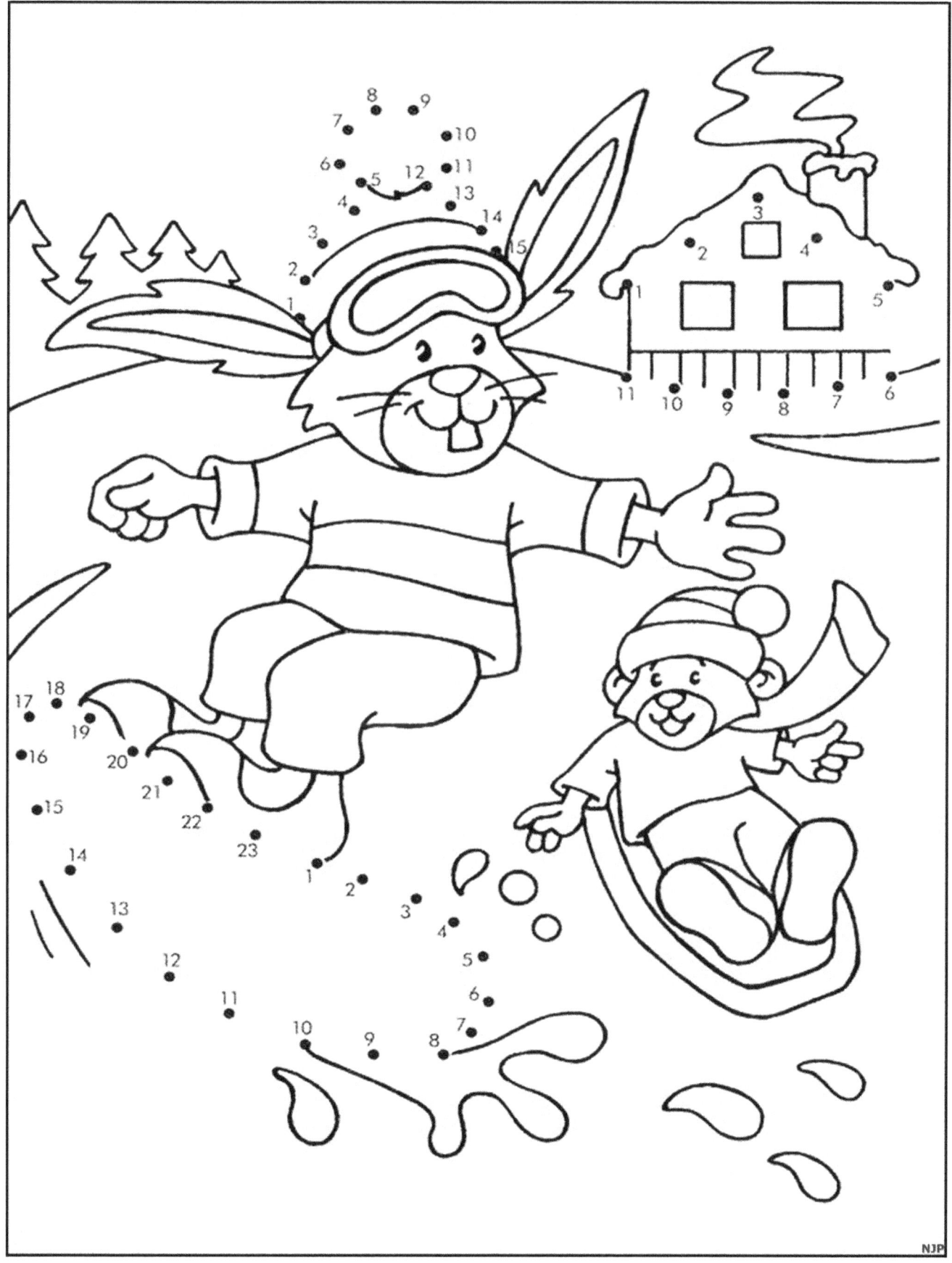

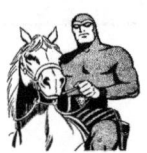

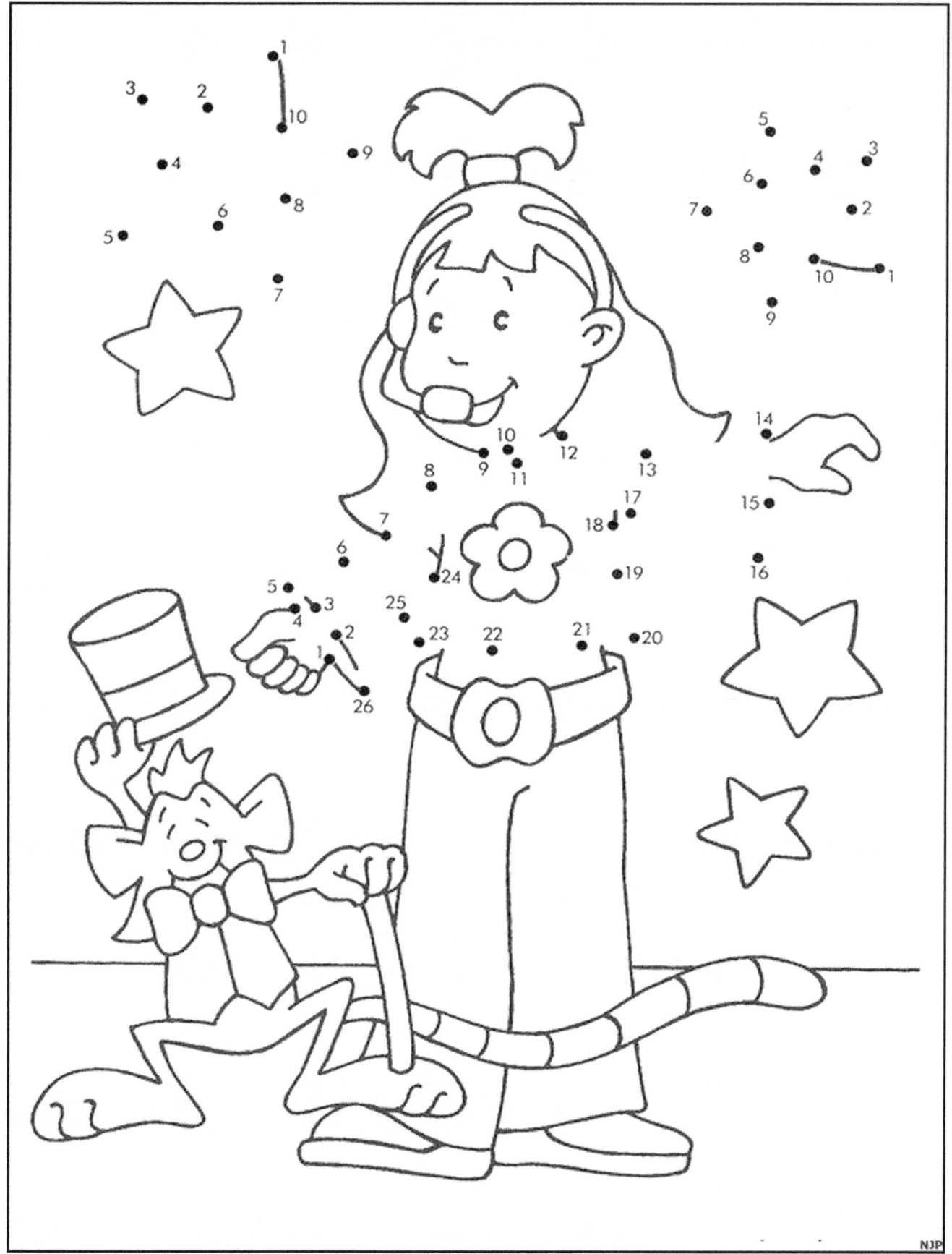

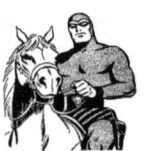

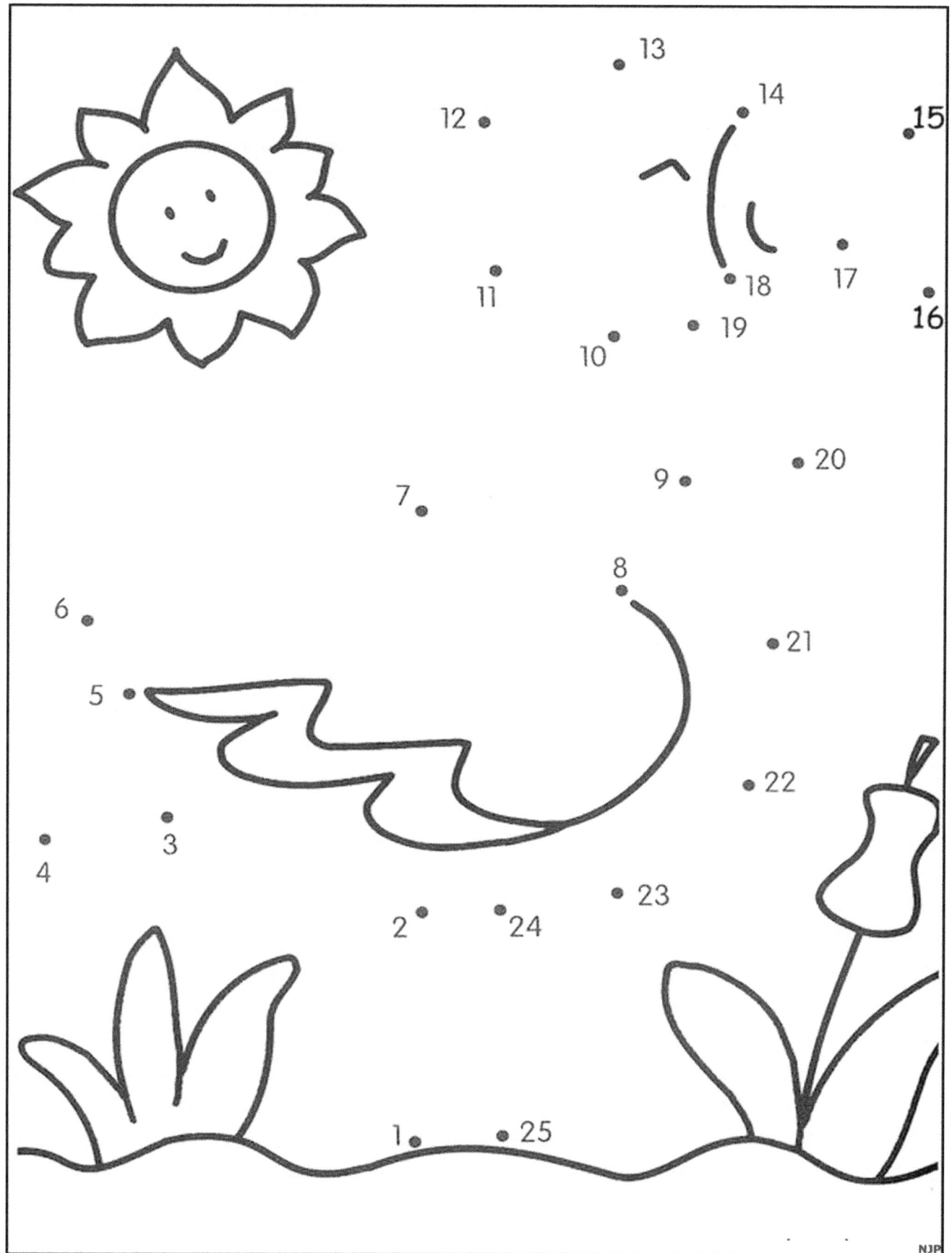

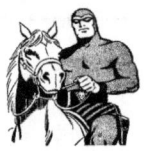

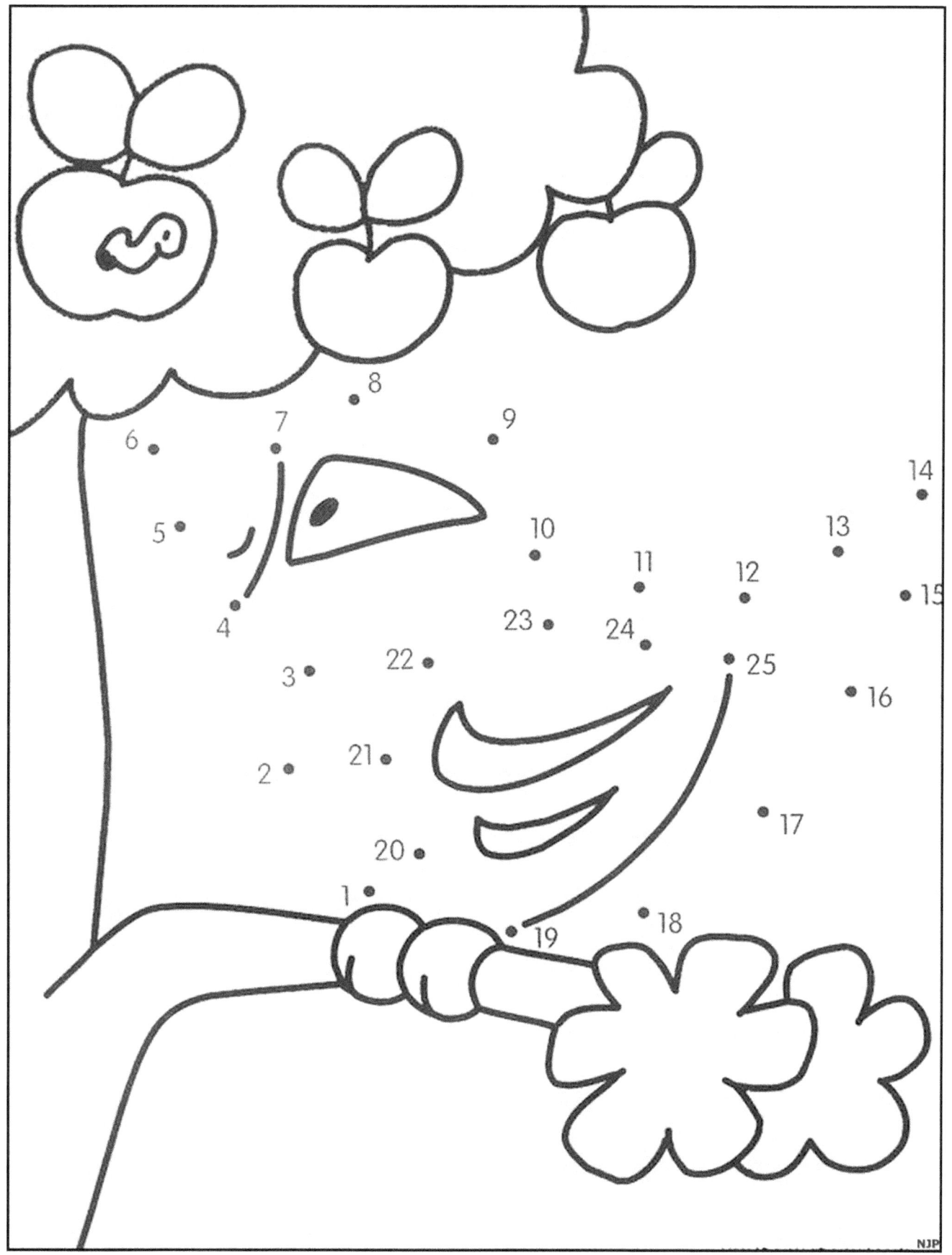

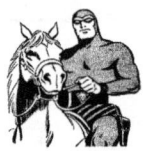

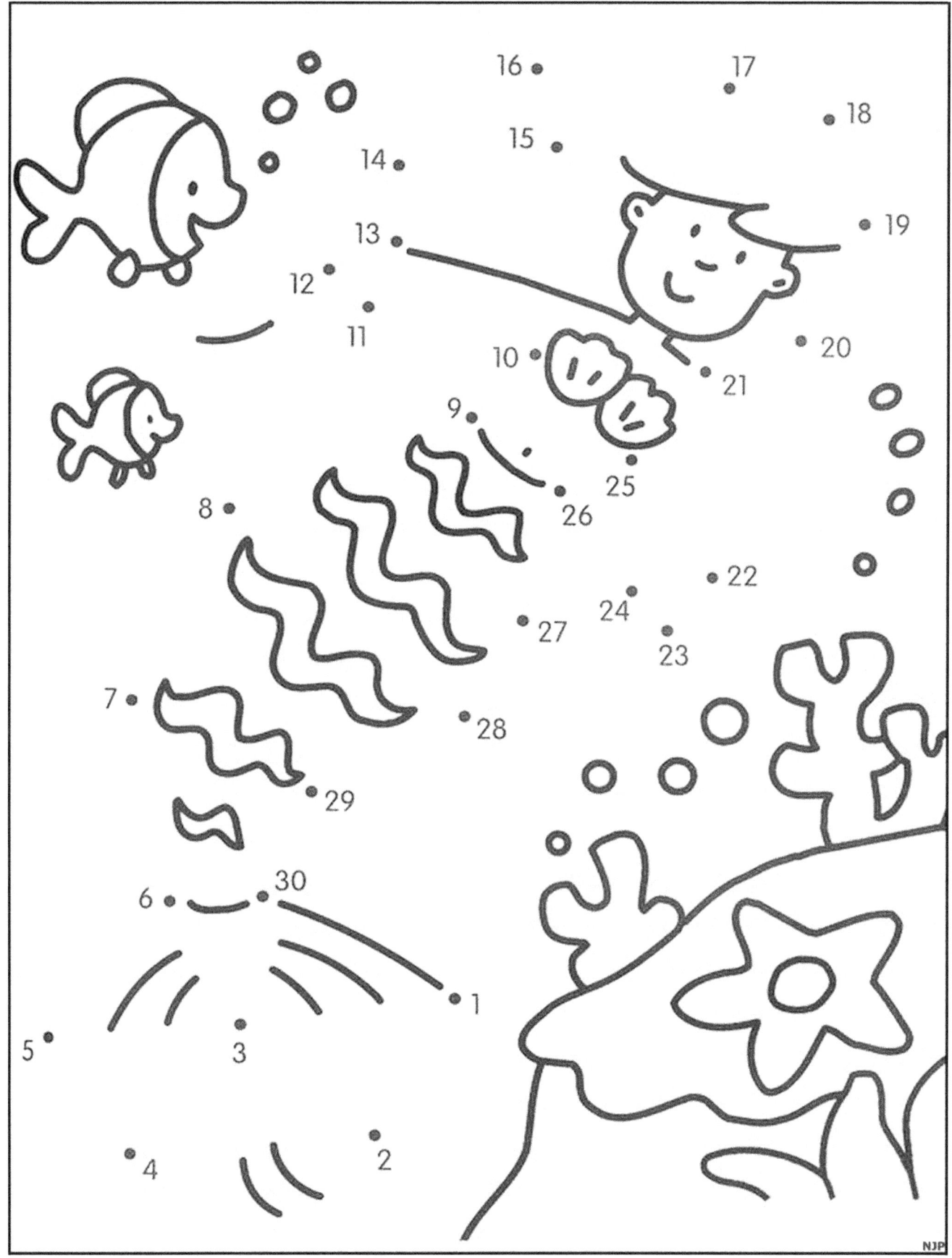

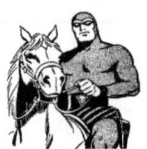

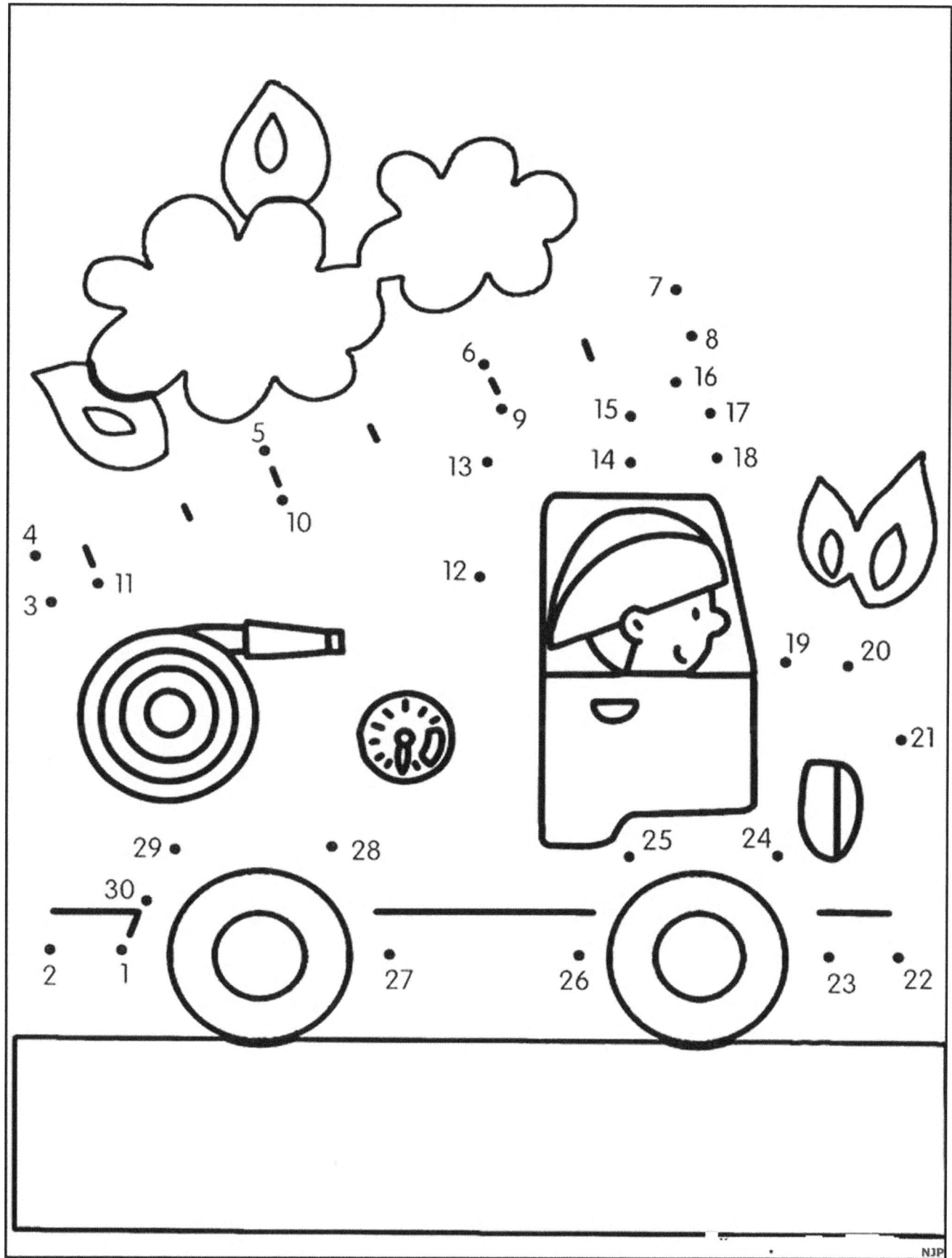

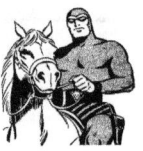

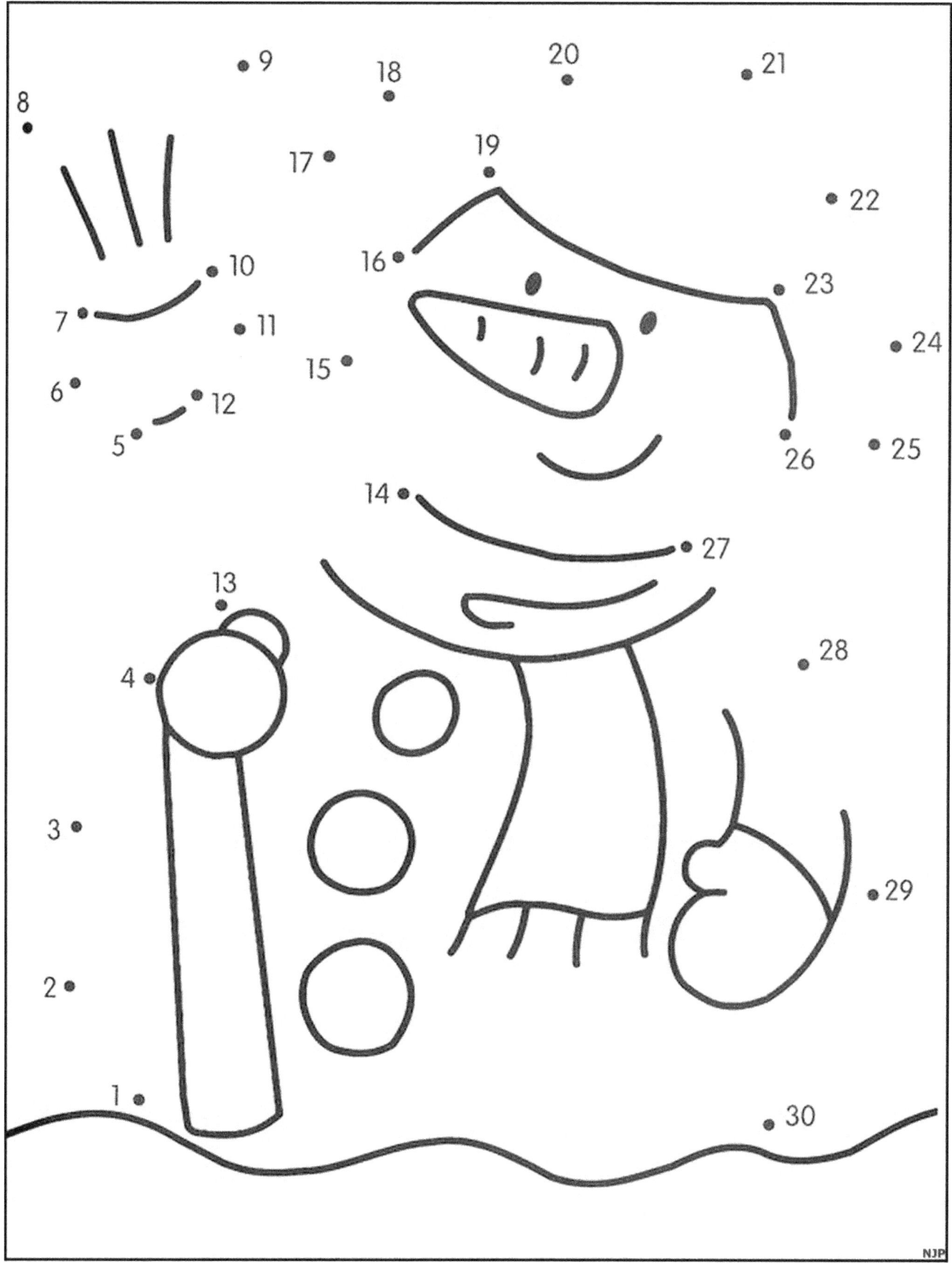

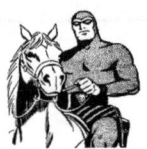

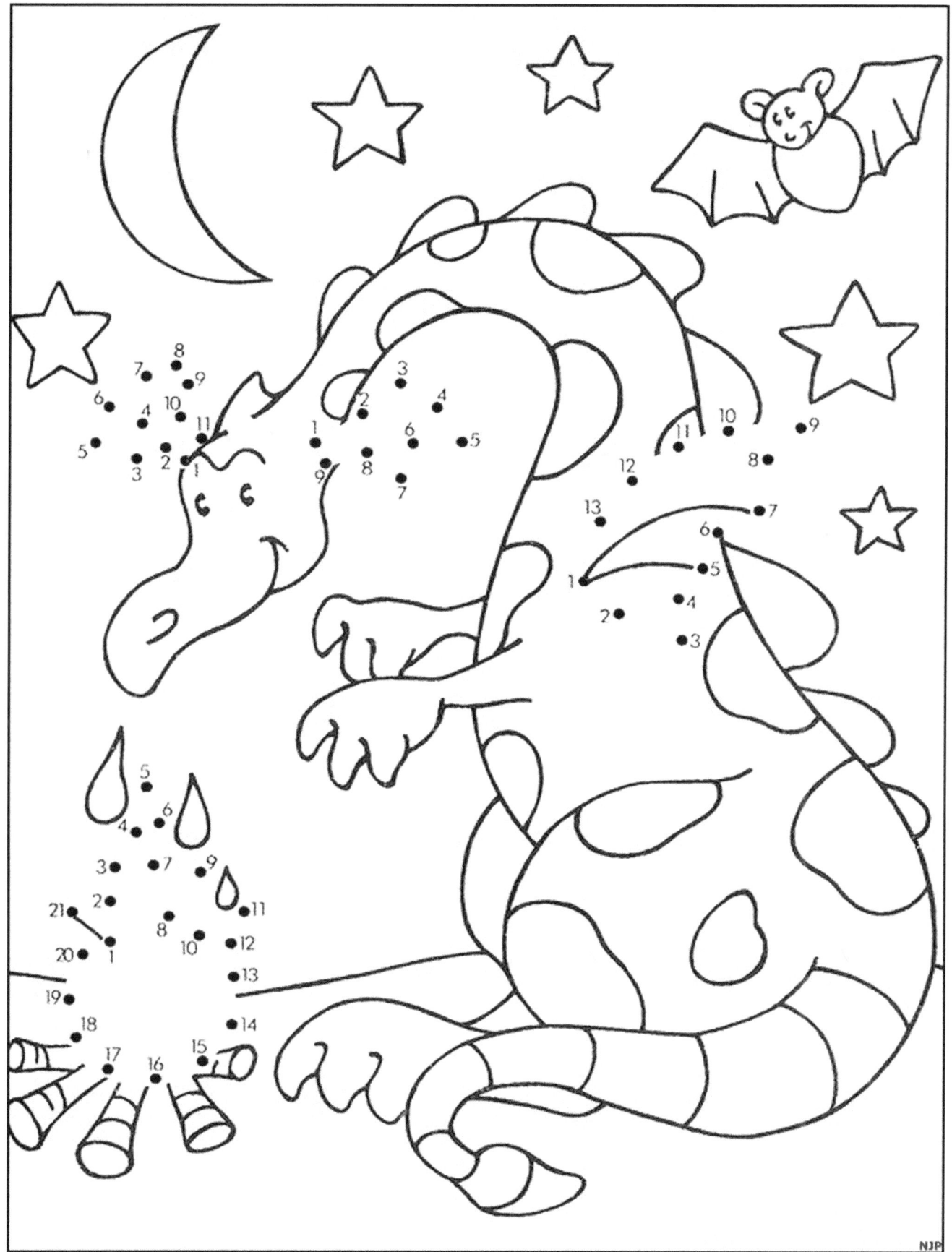

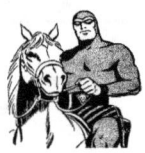

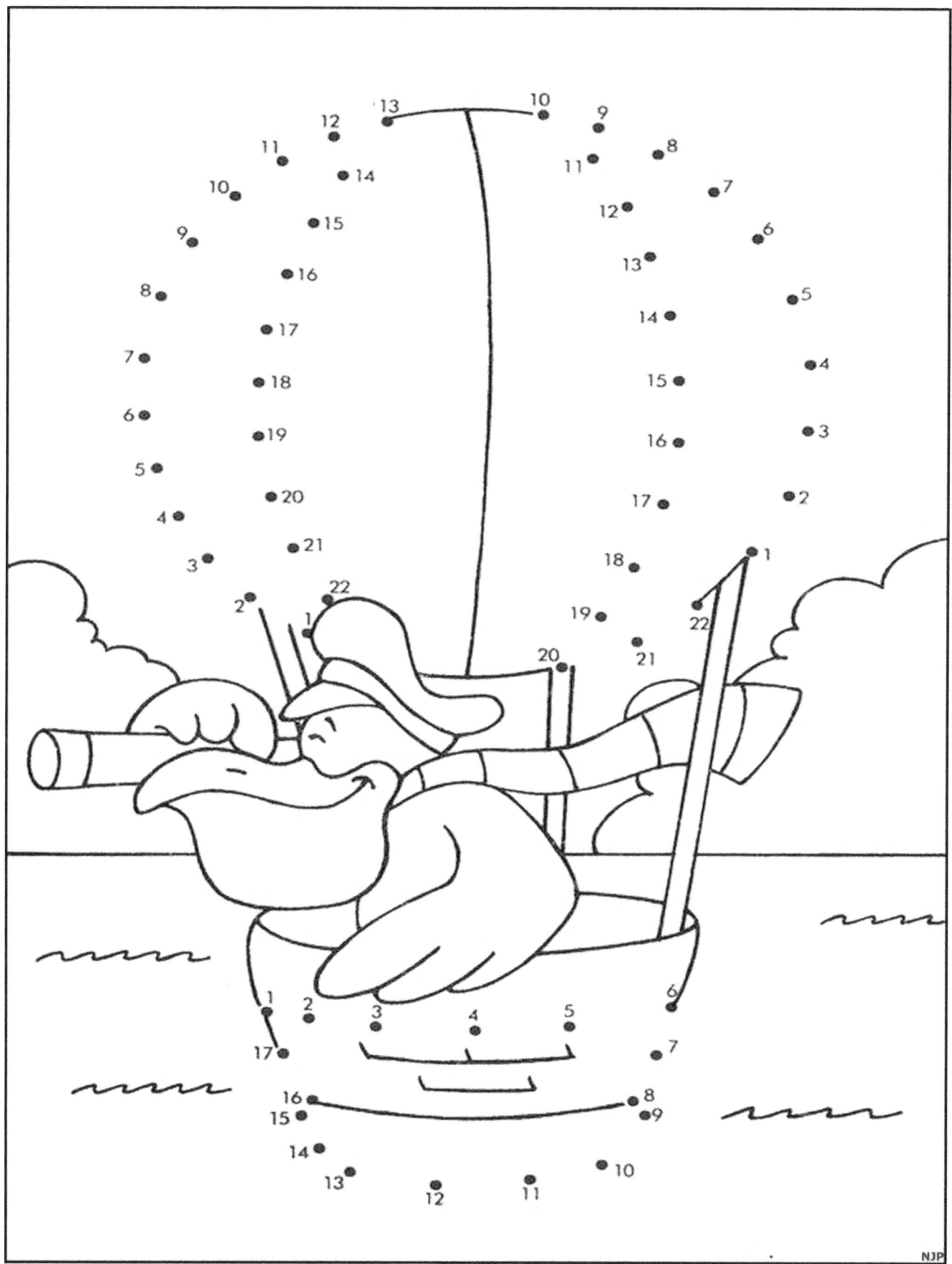

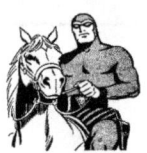

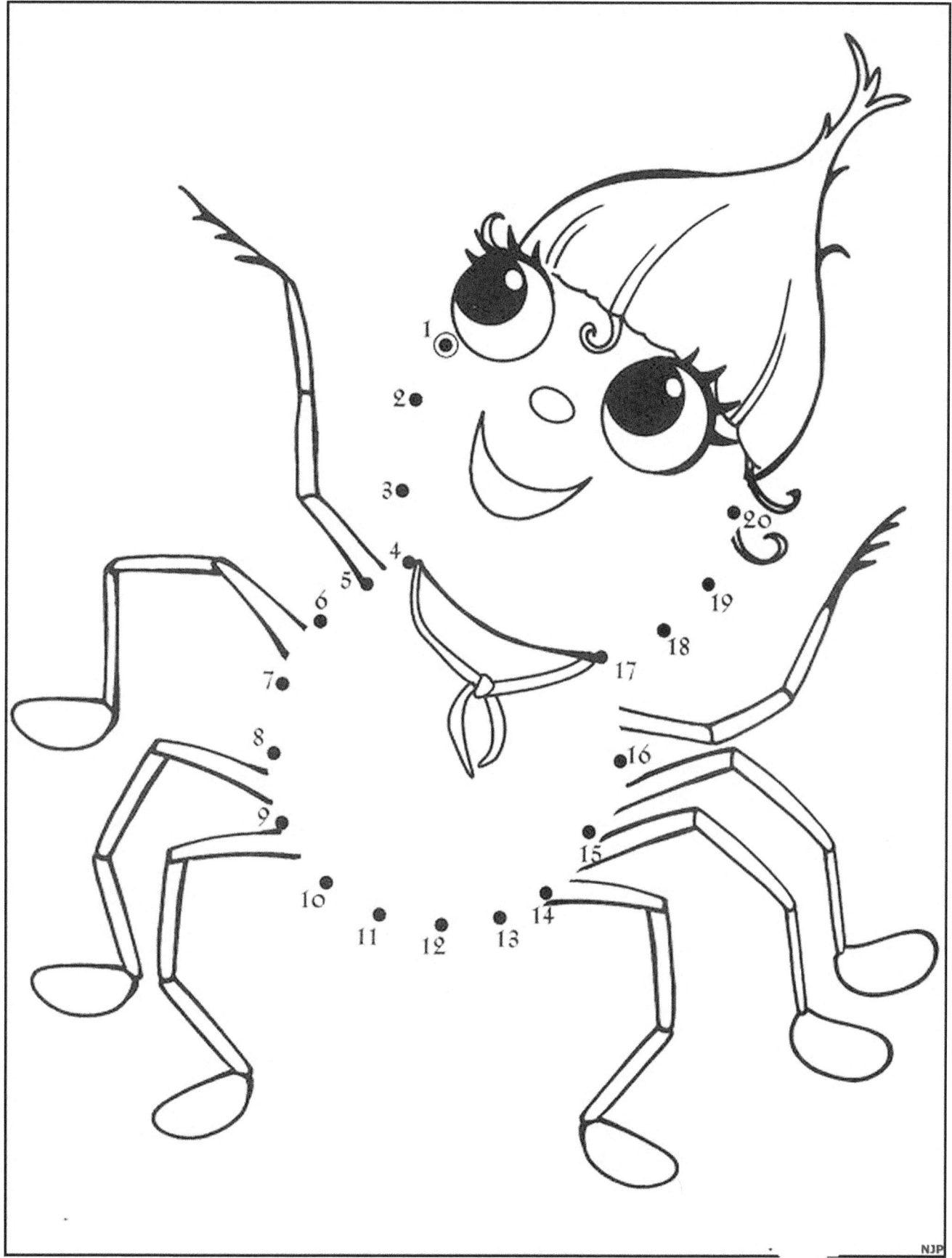

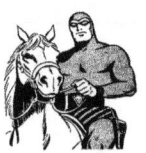

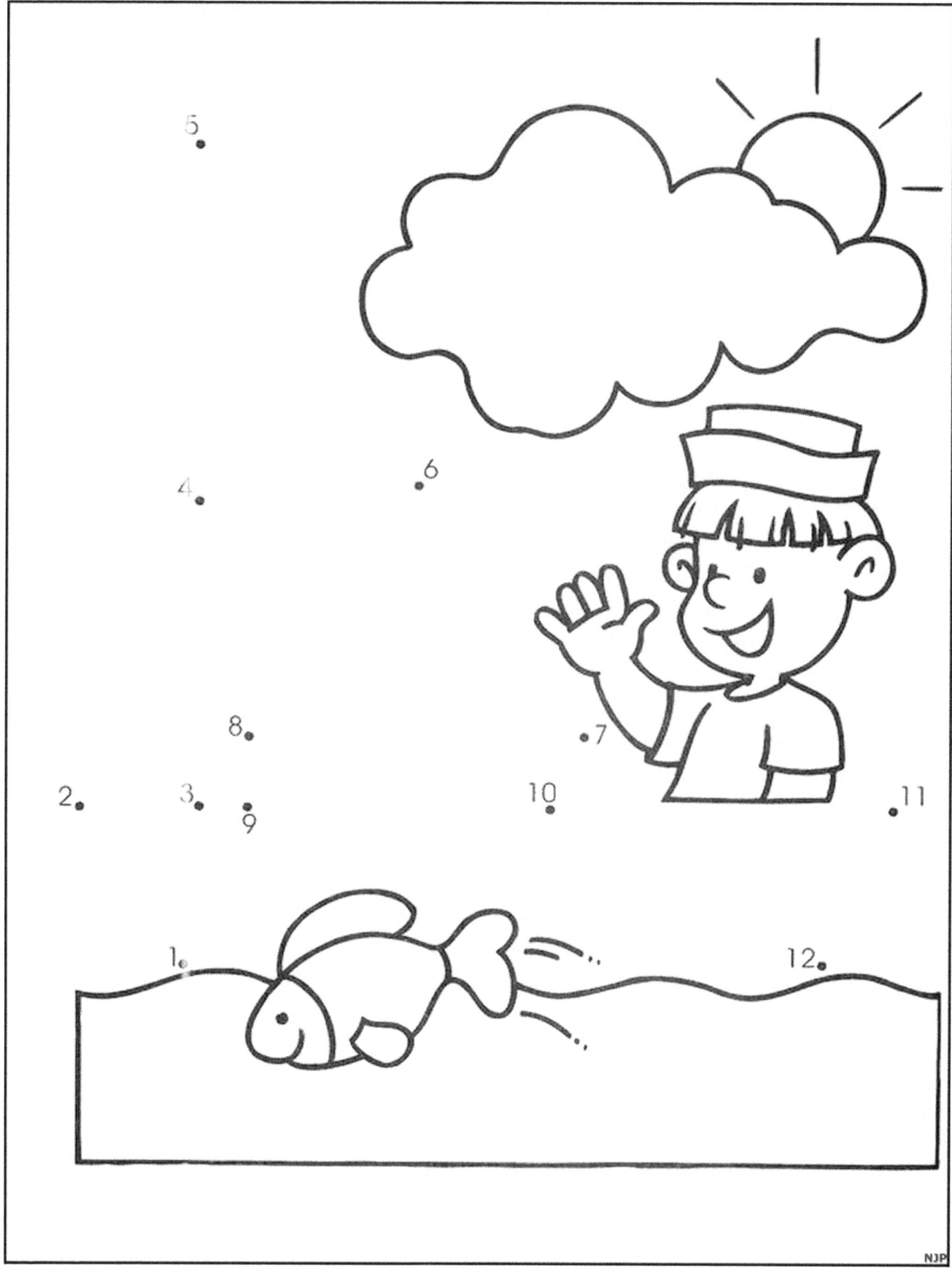

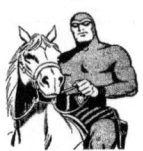

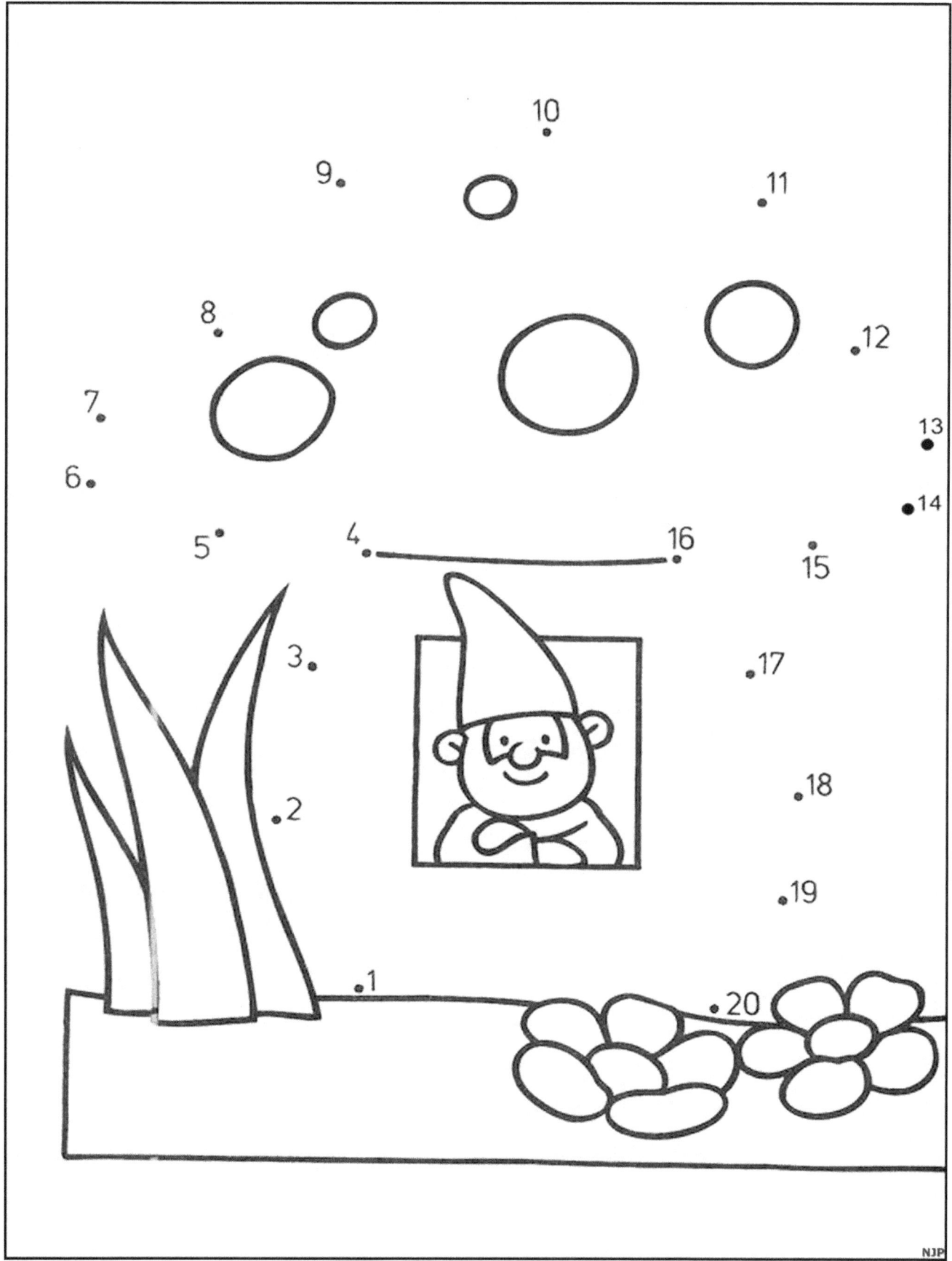

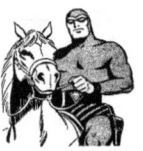

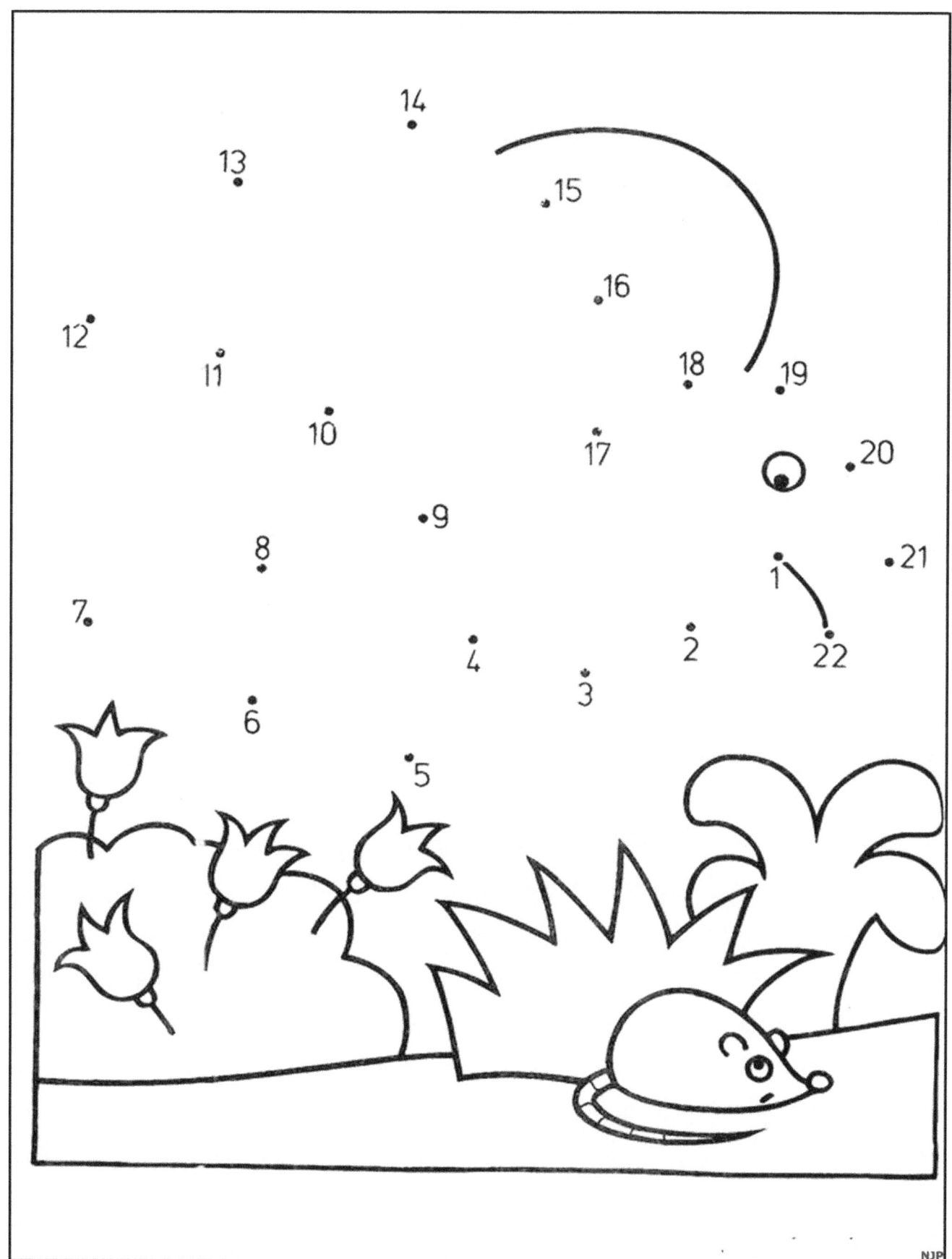

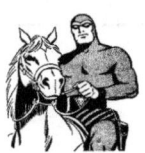

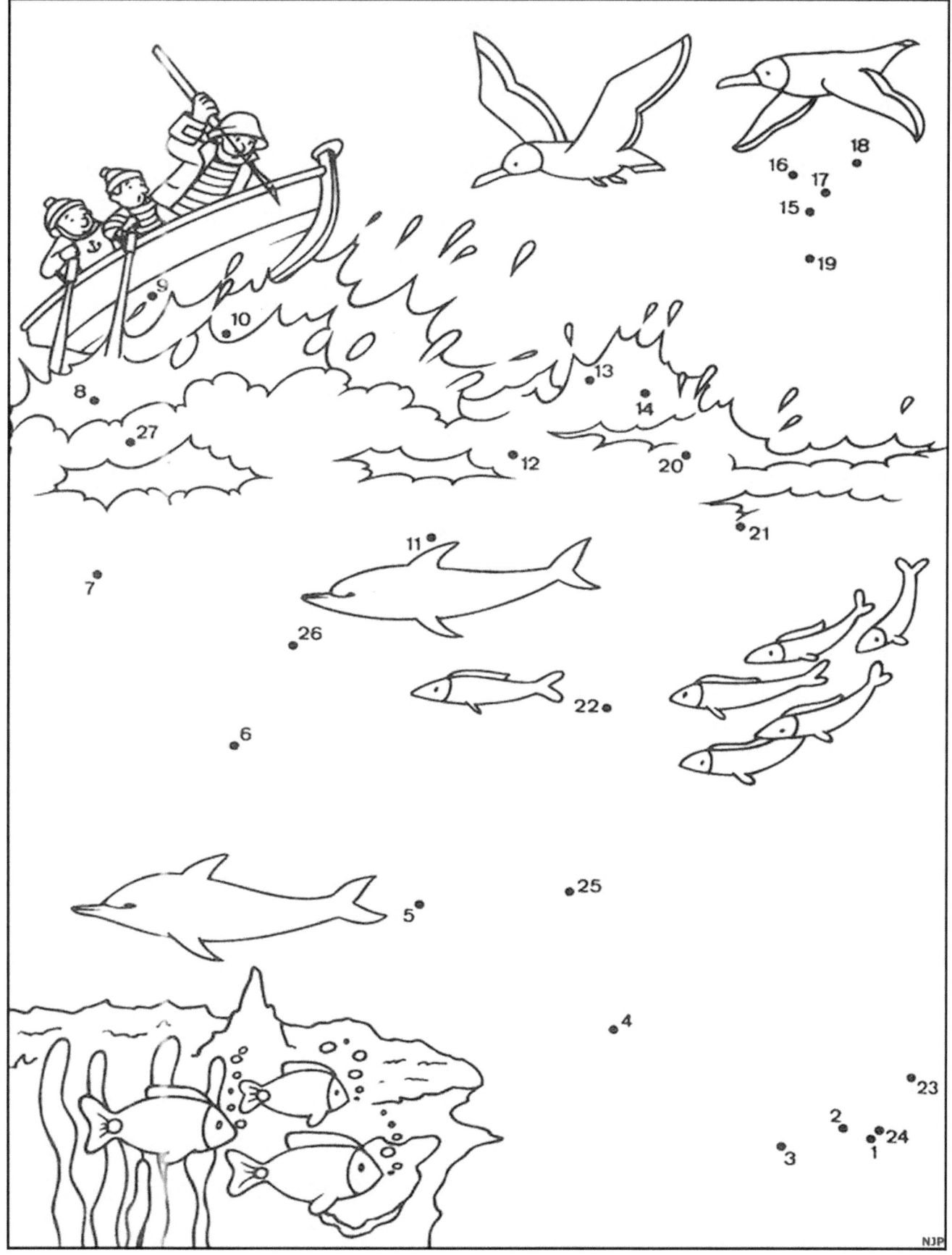

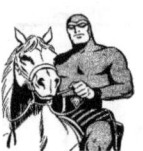

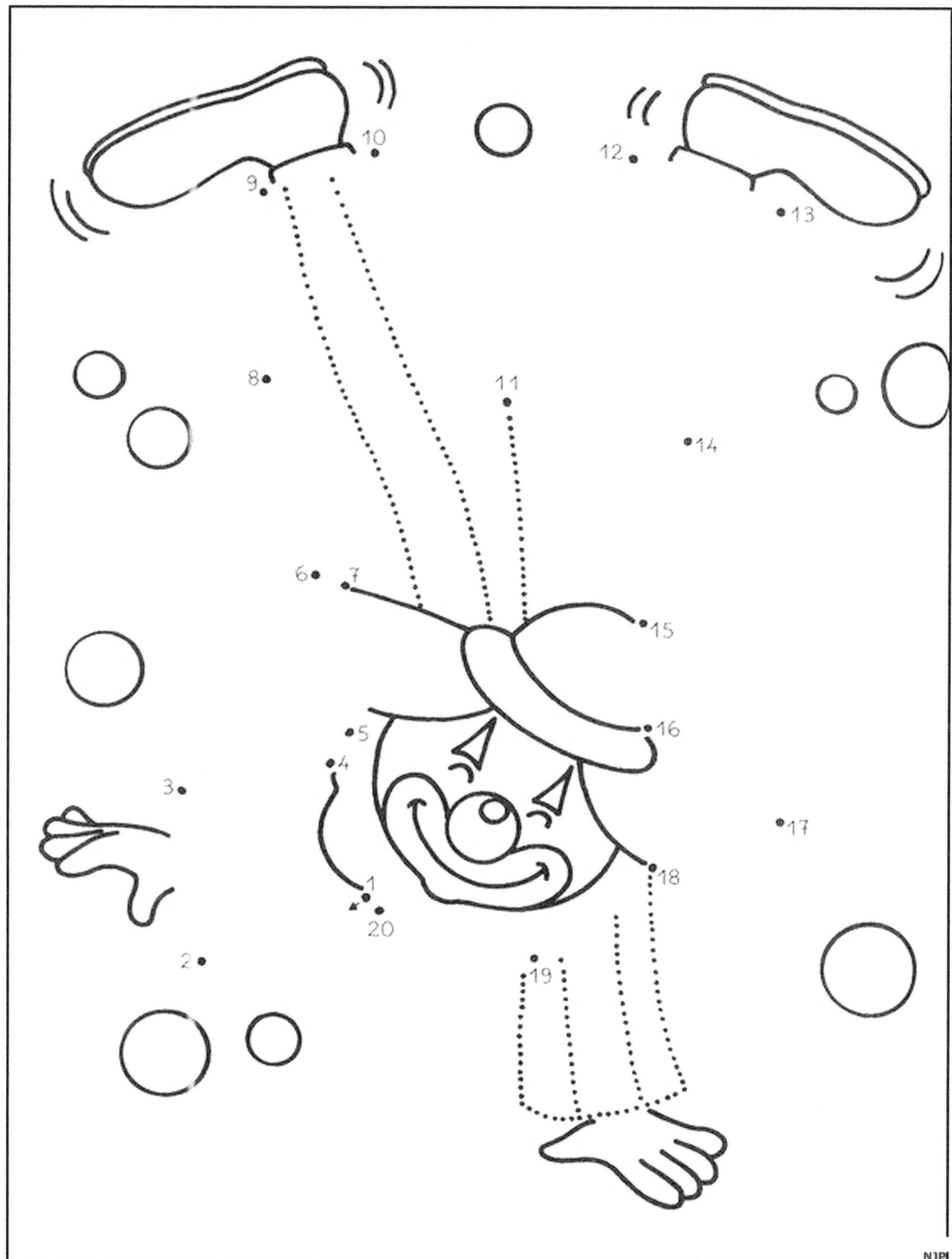

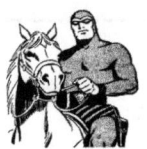

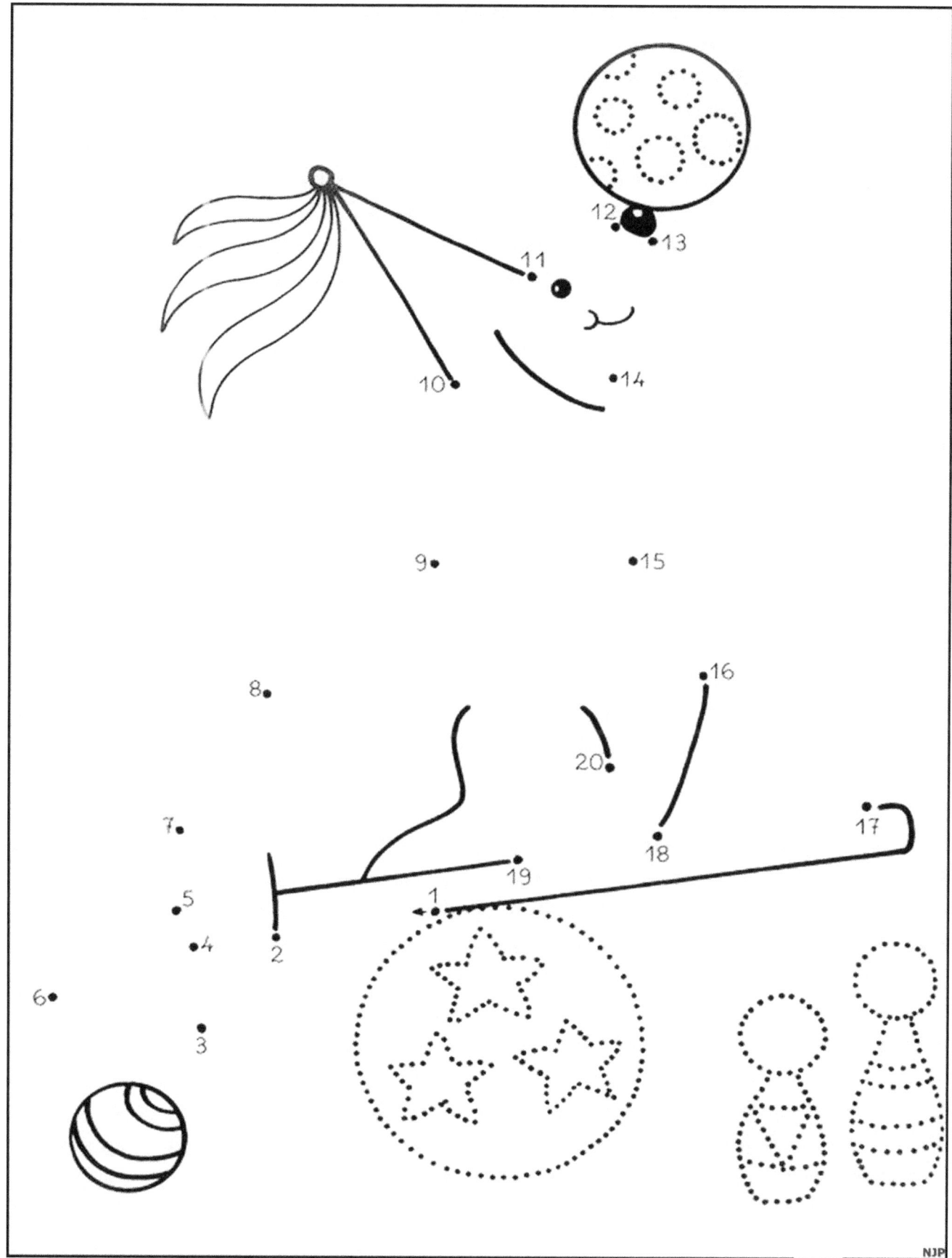

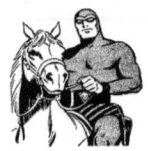

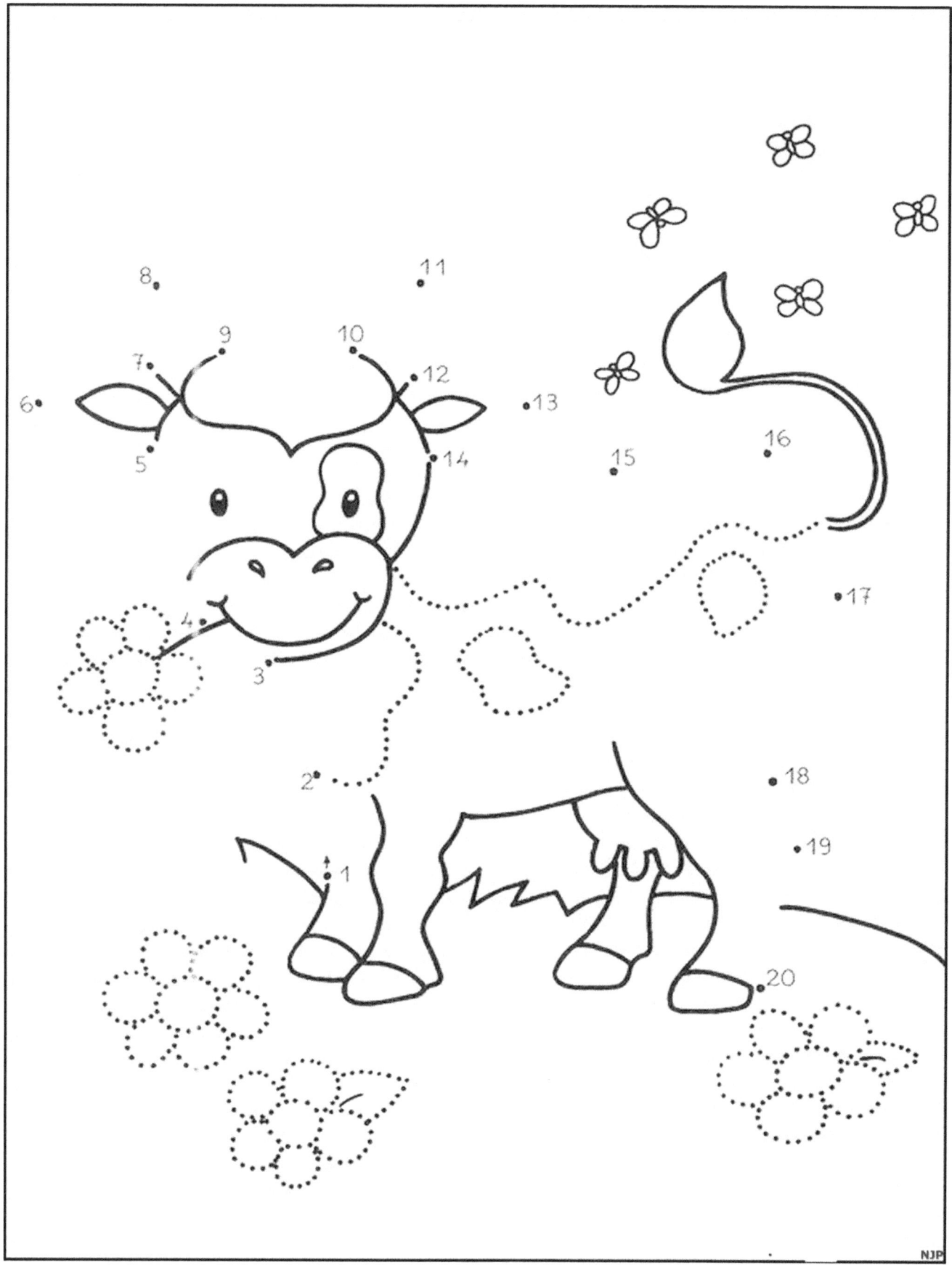

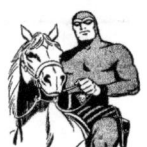

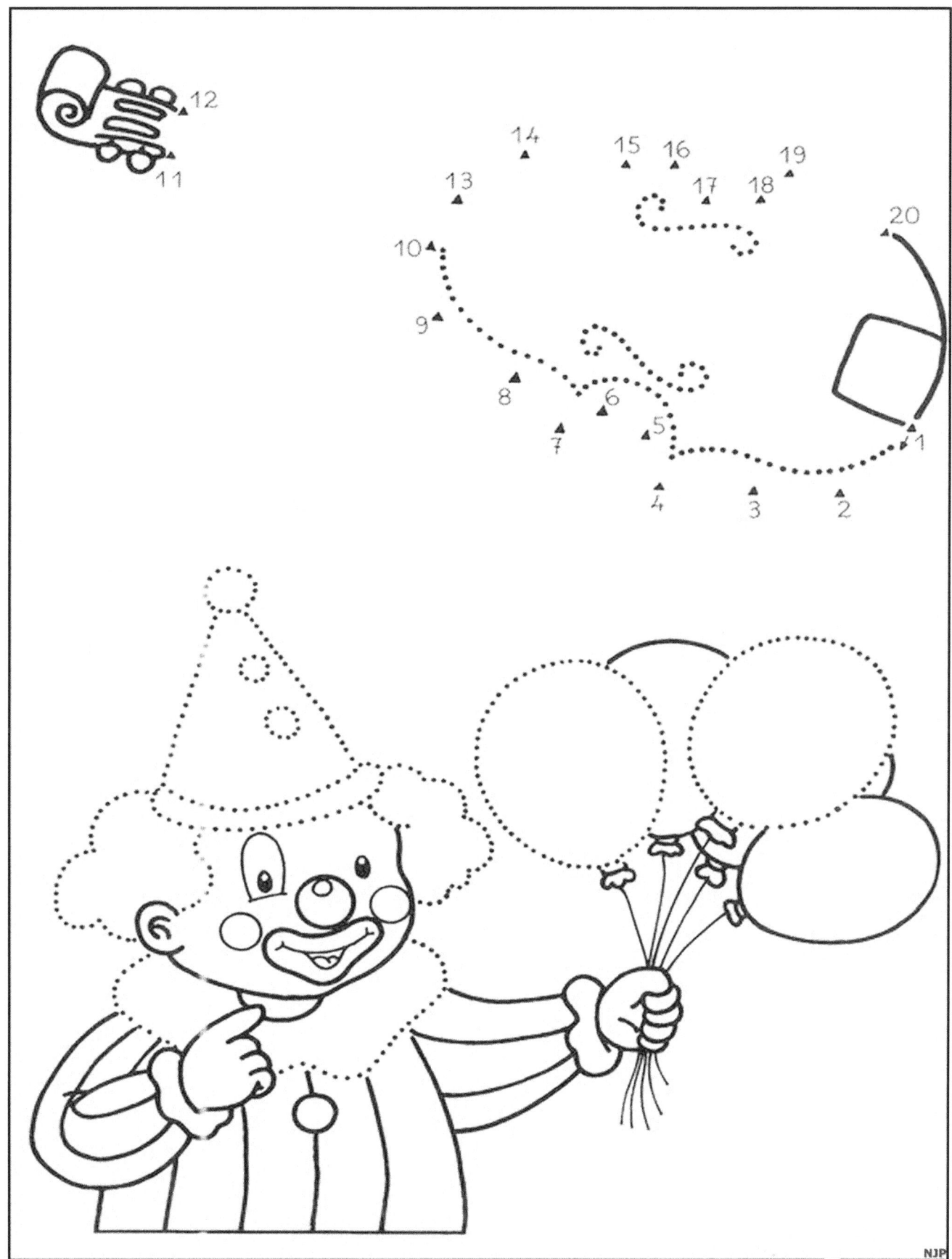

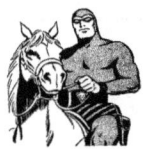

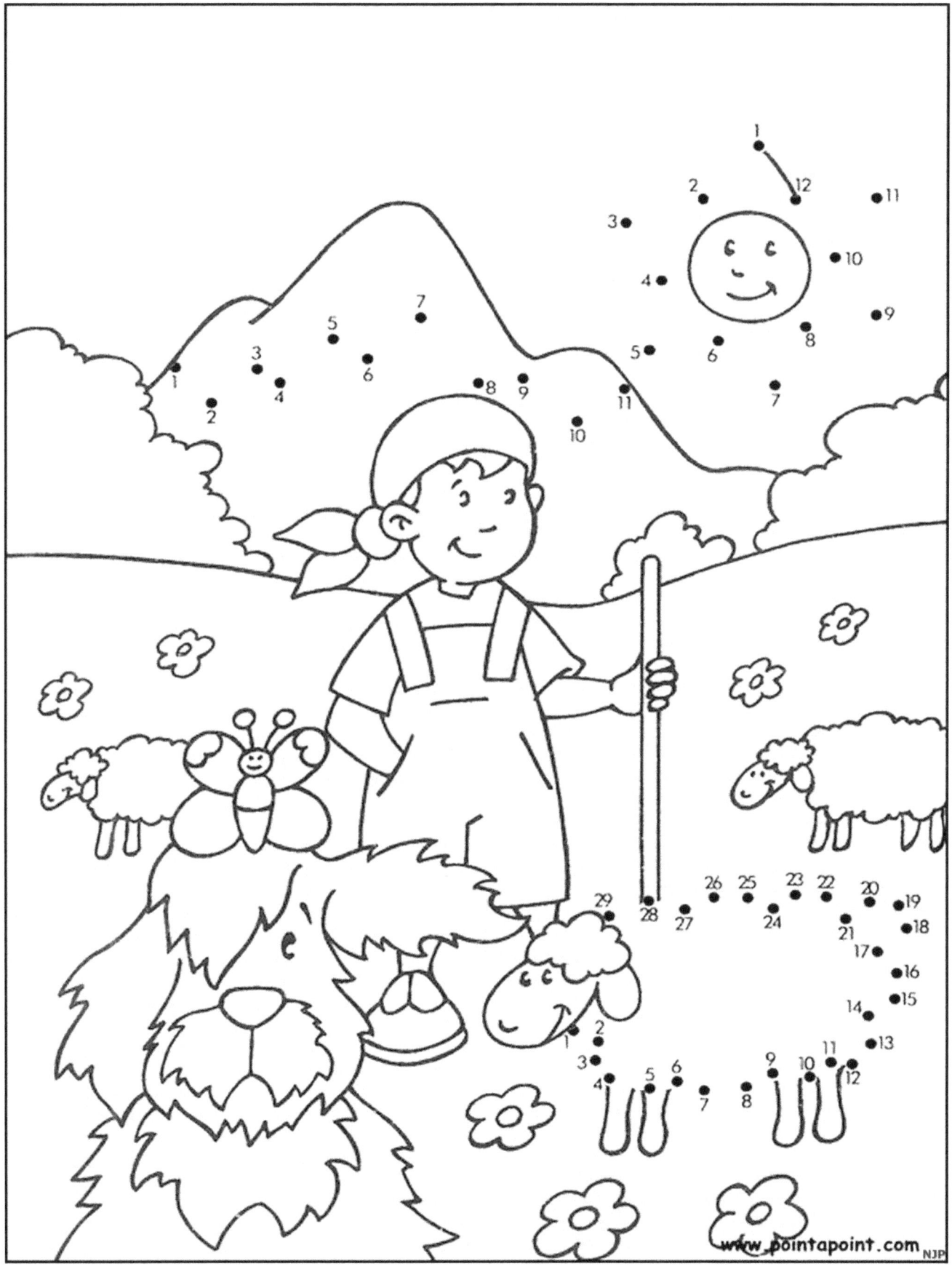

www.pointapoint.com NJP

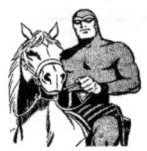

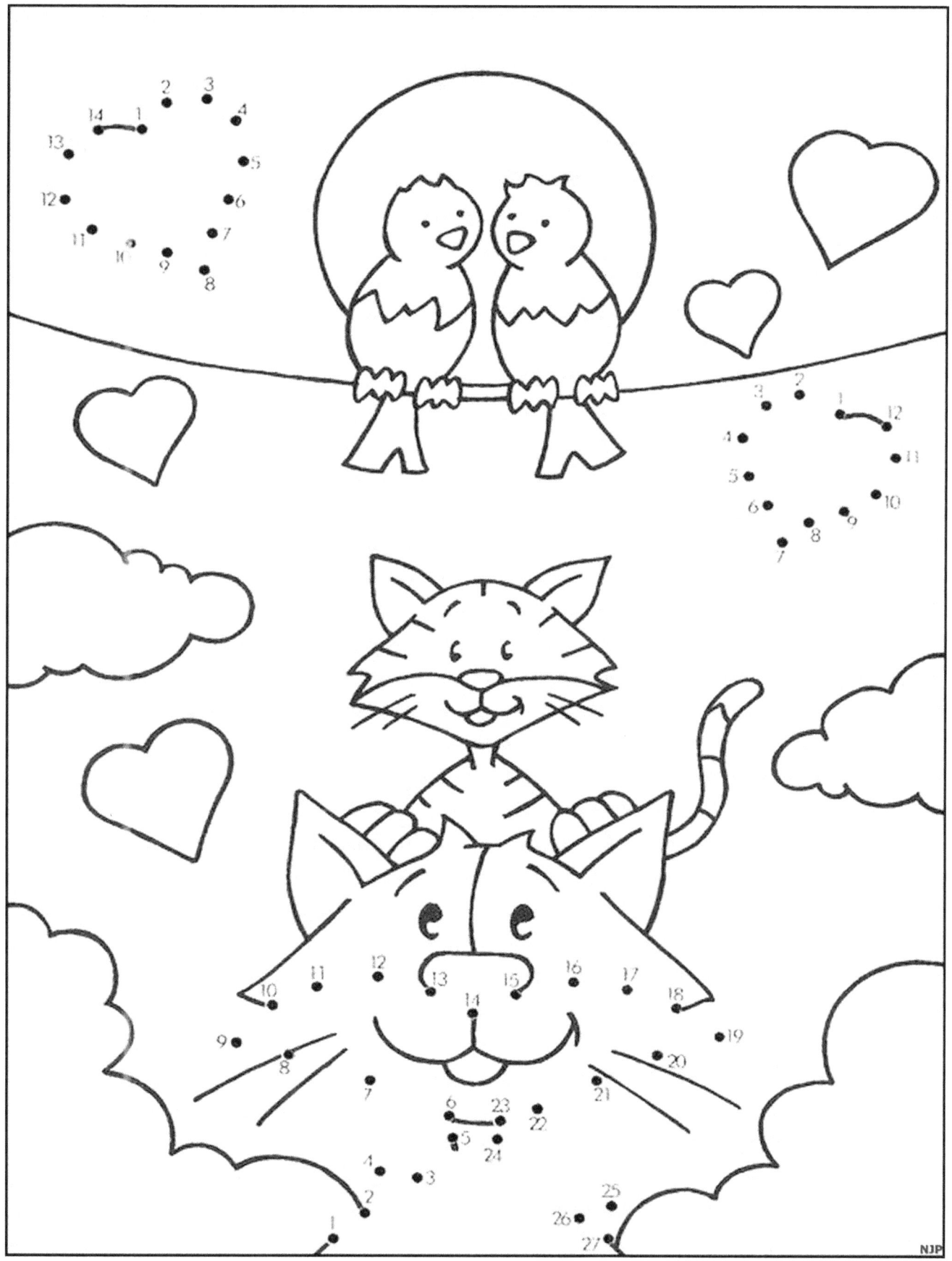

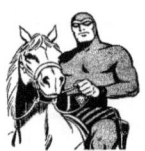

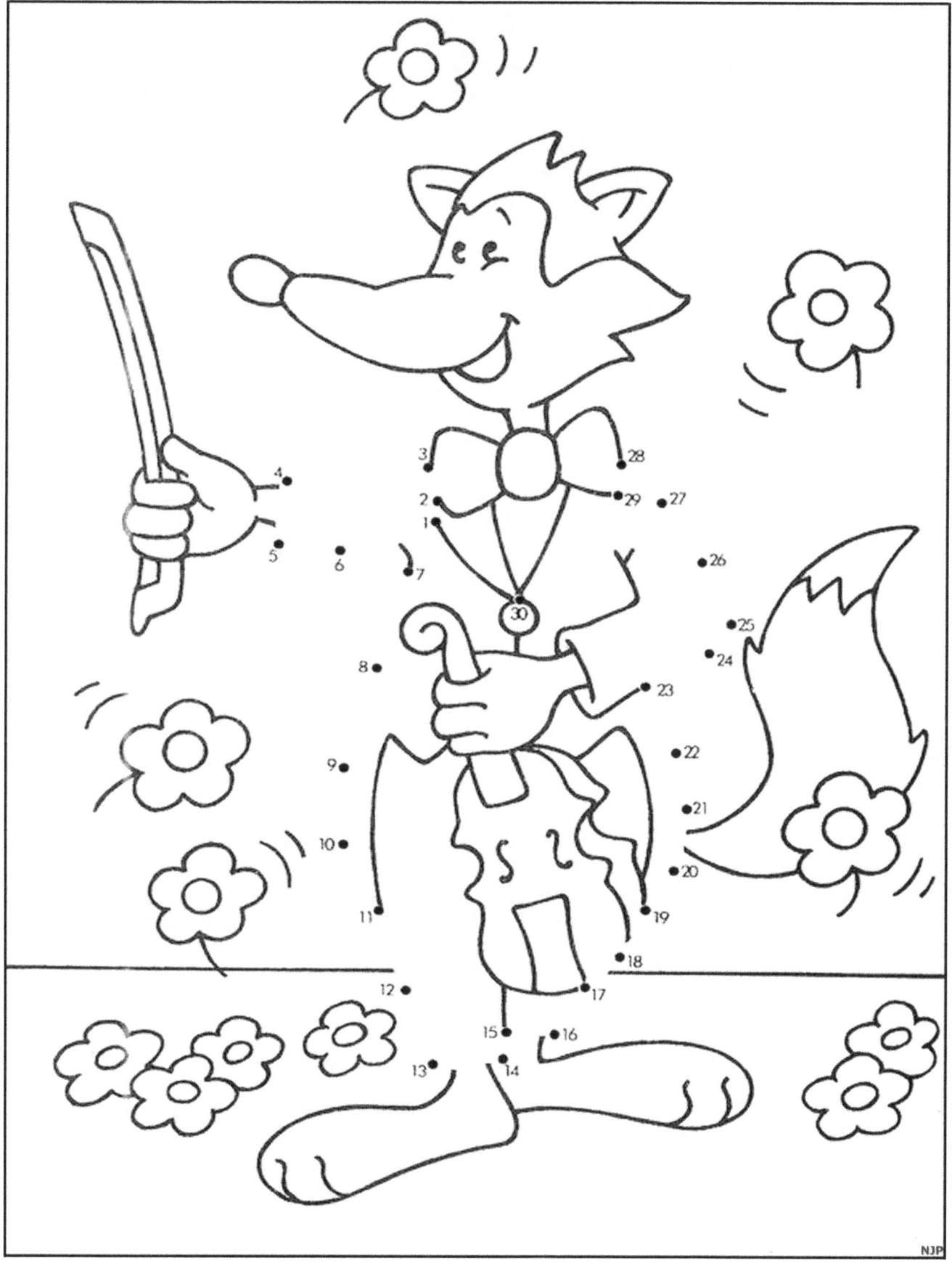

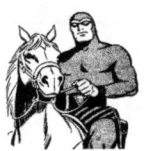

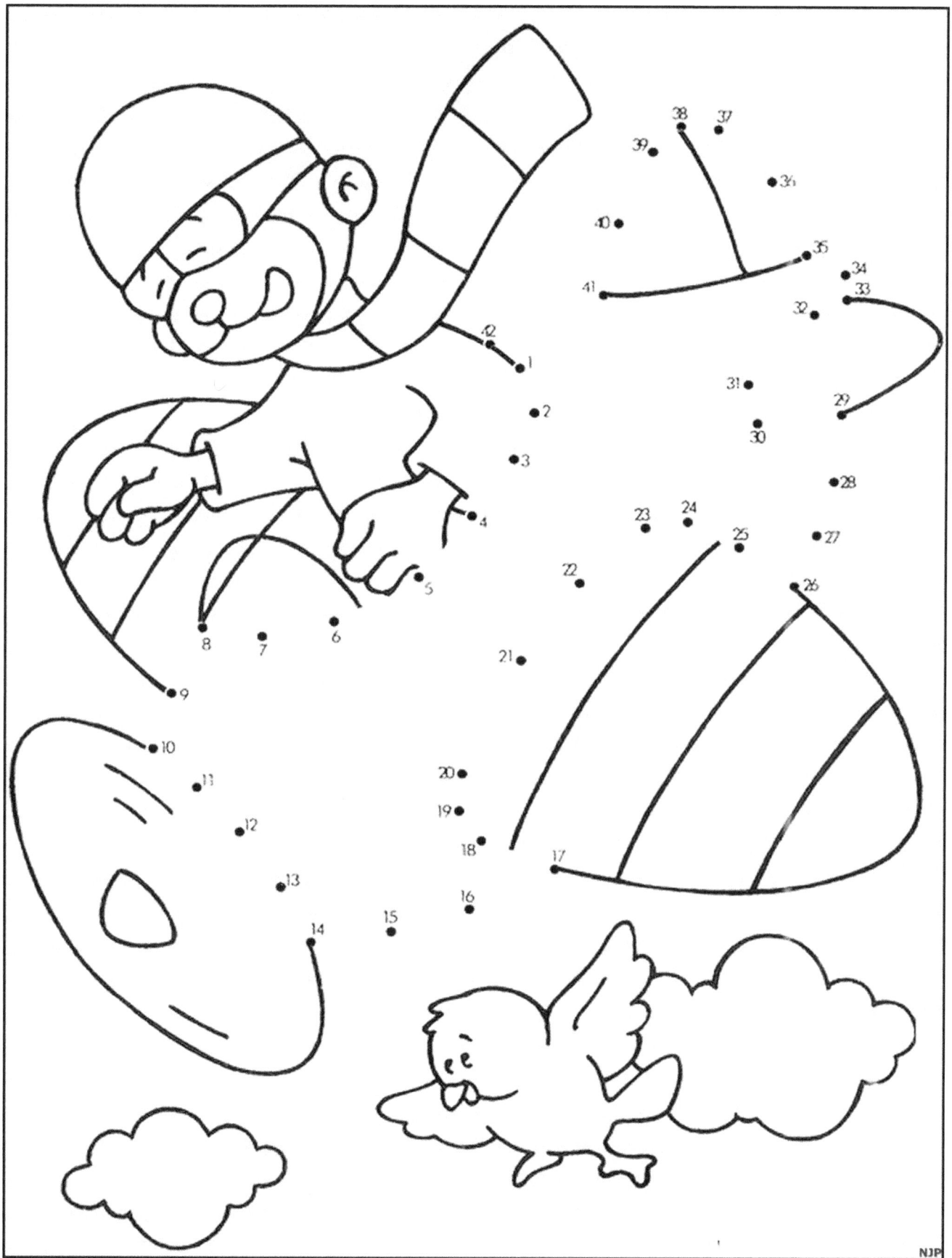

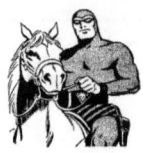

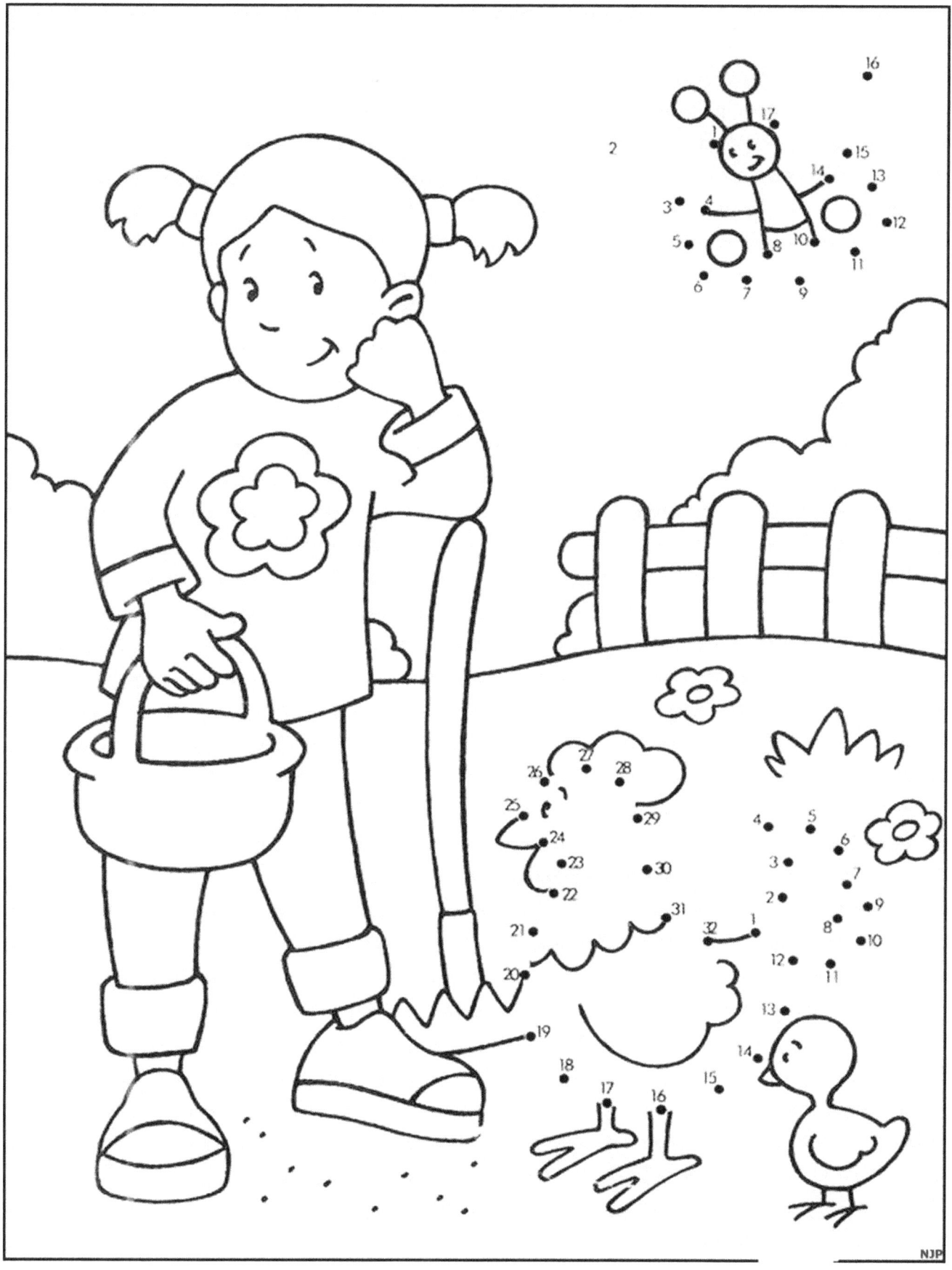

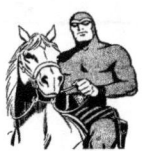

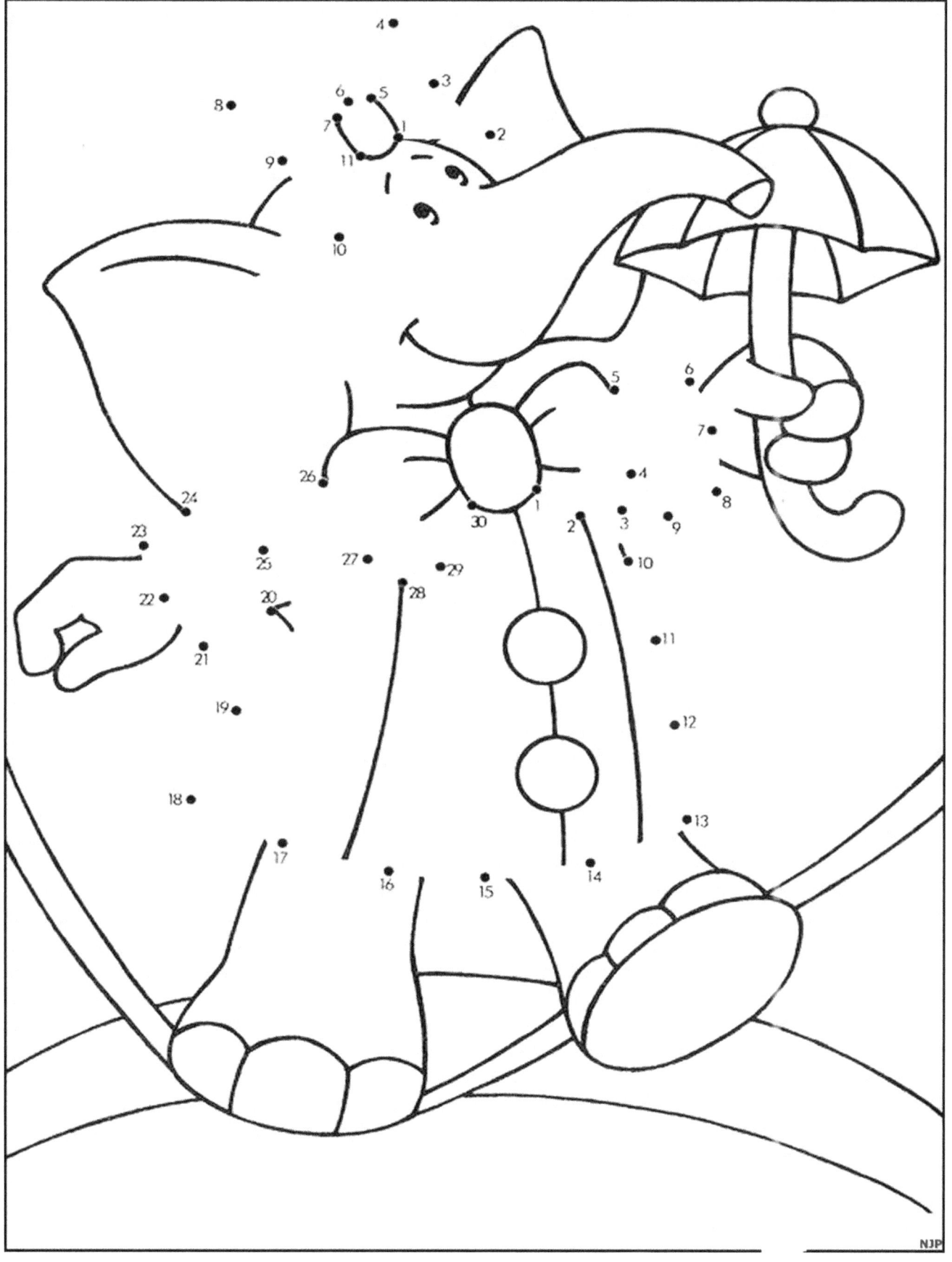

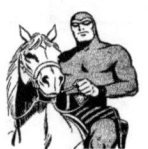

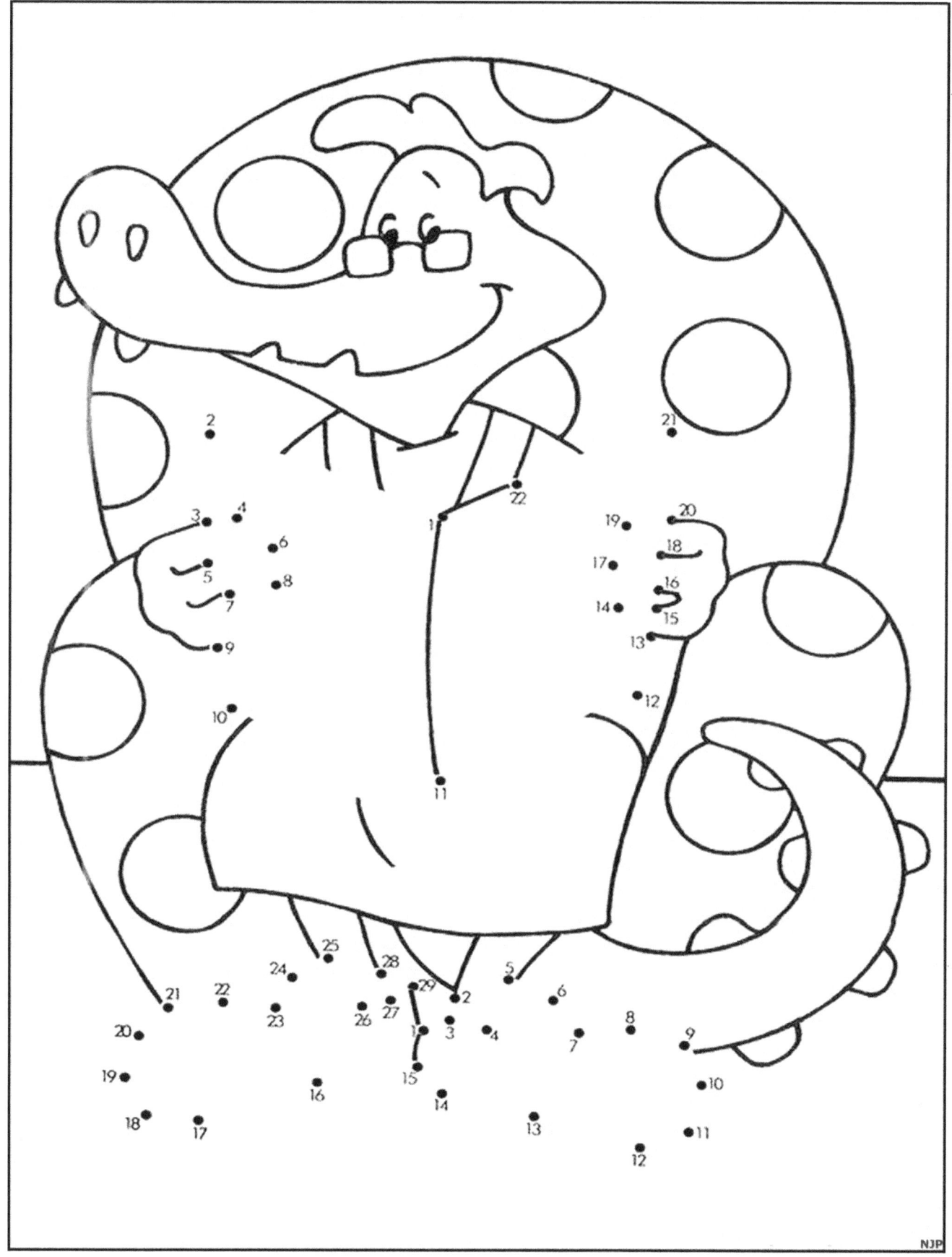

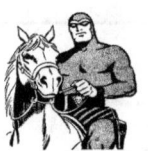

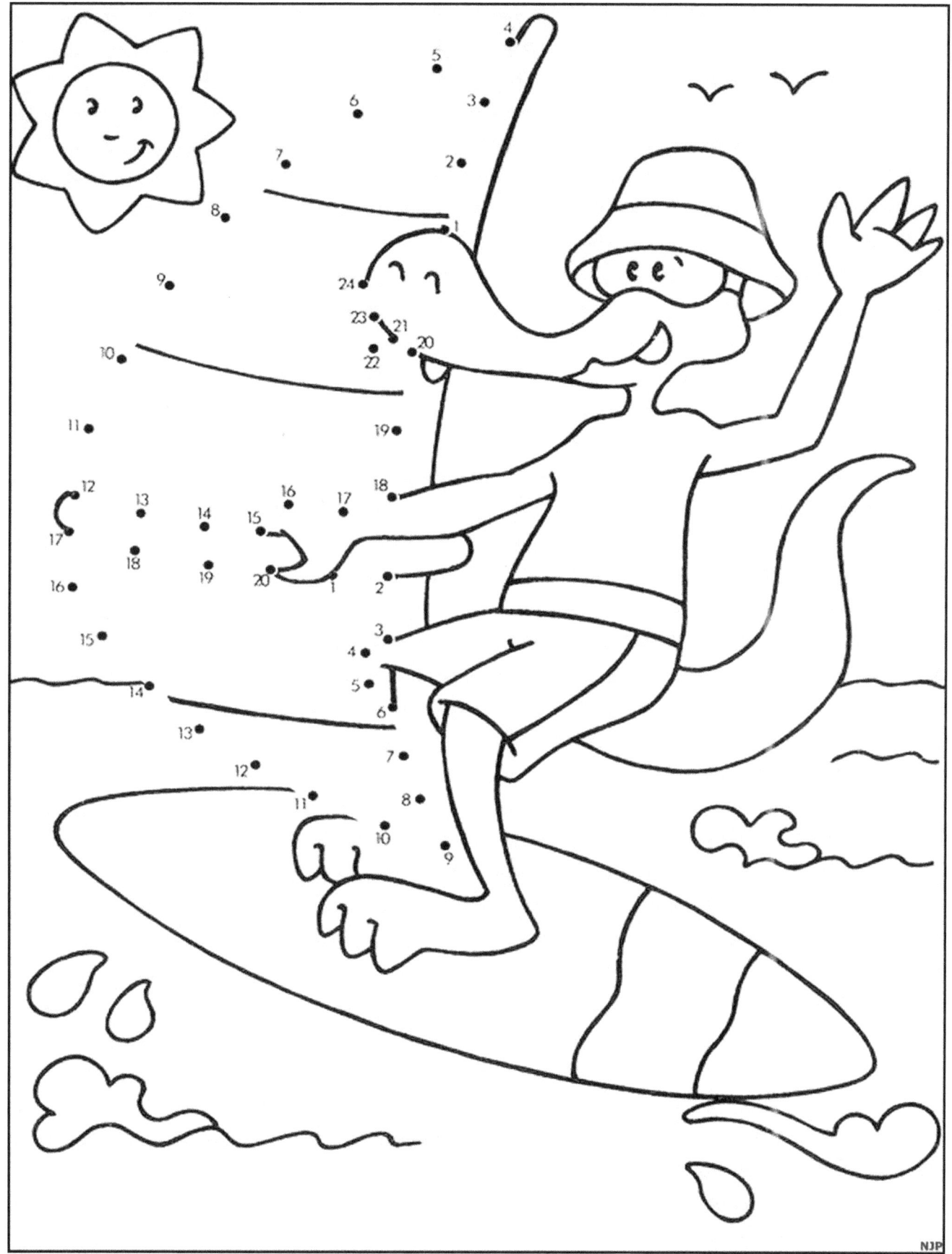

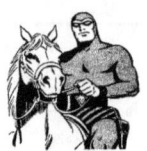

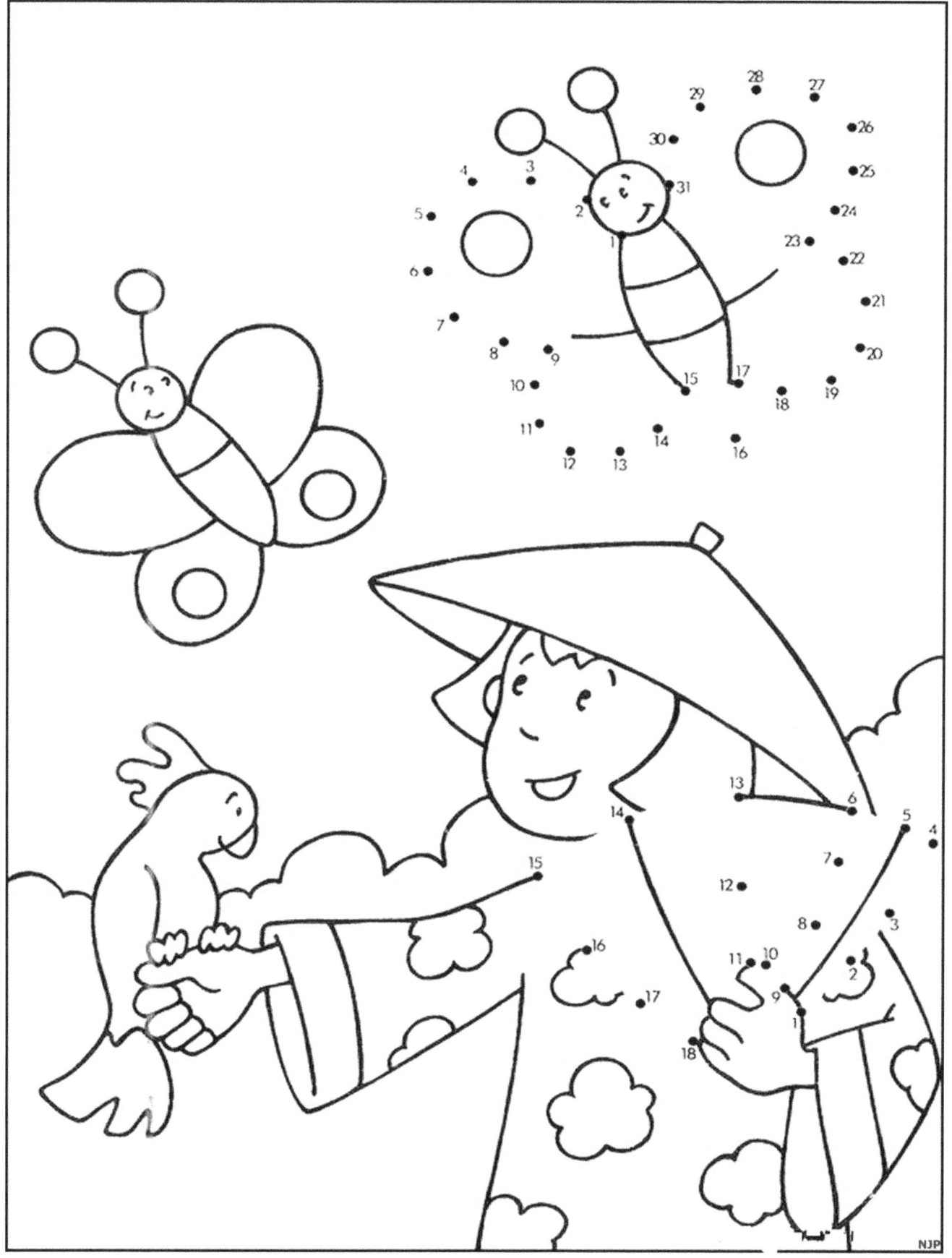

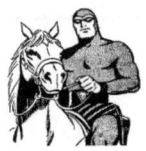

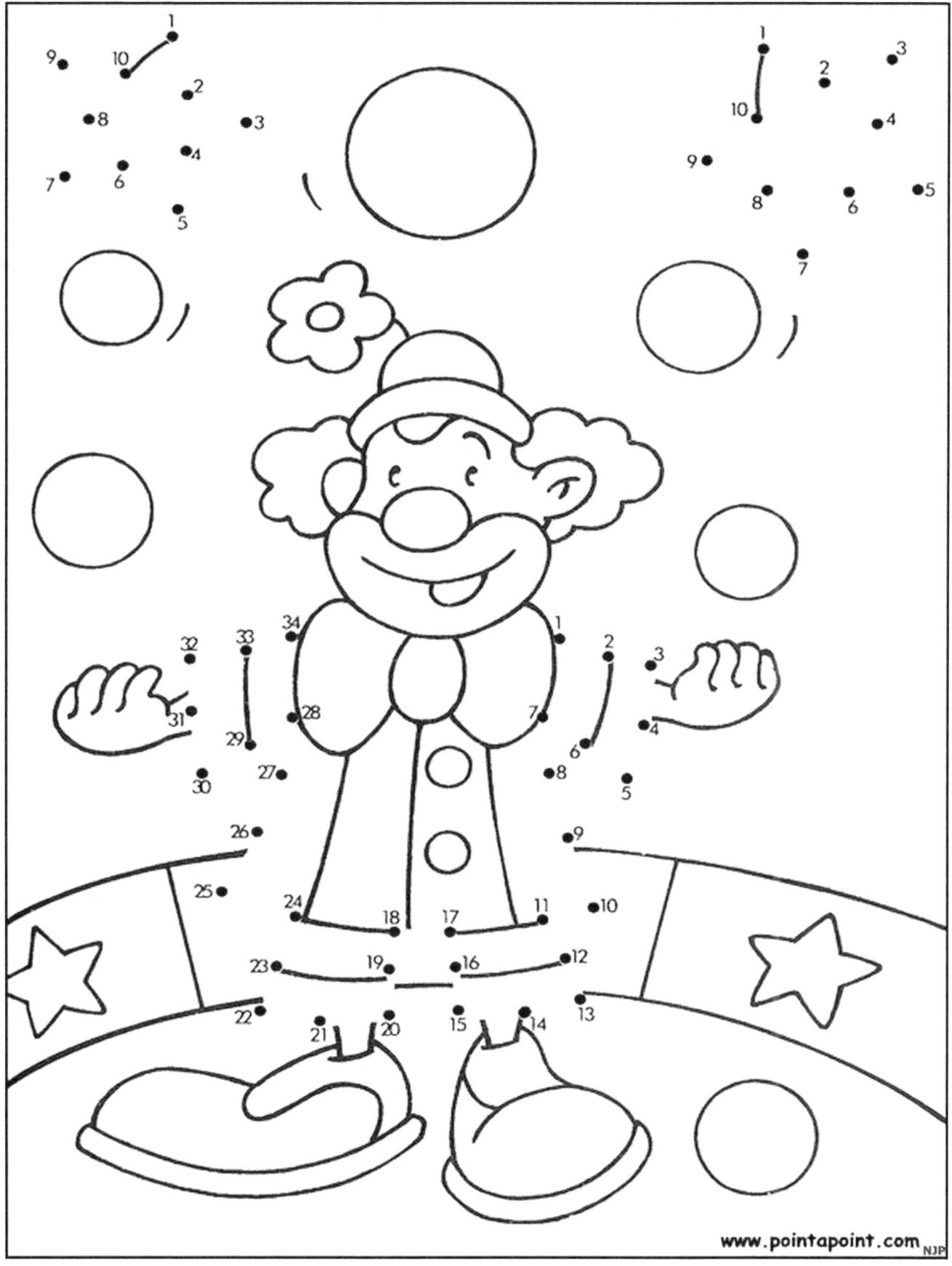

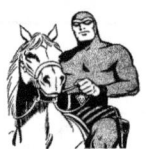

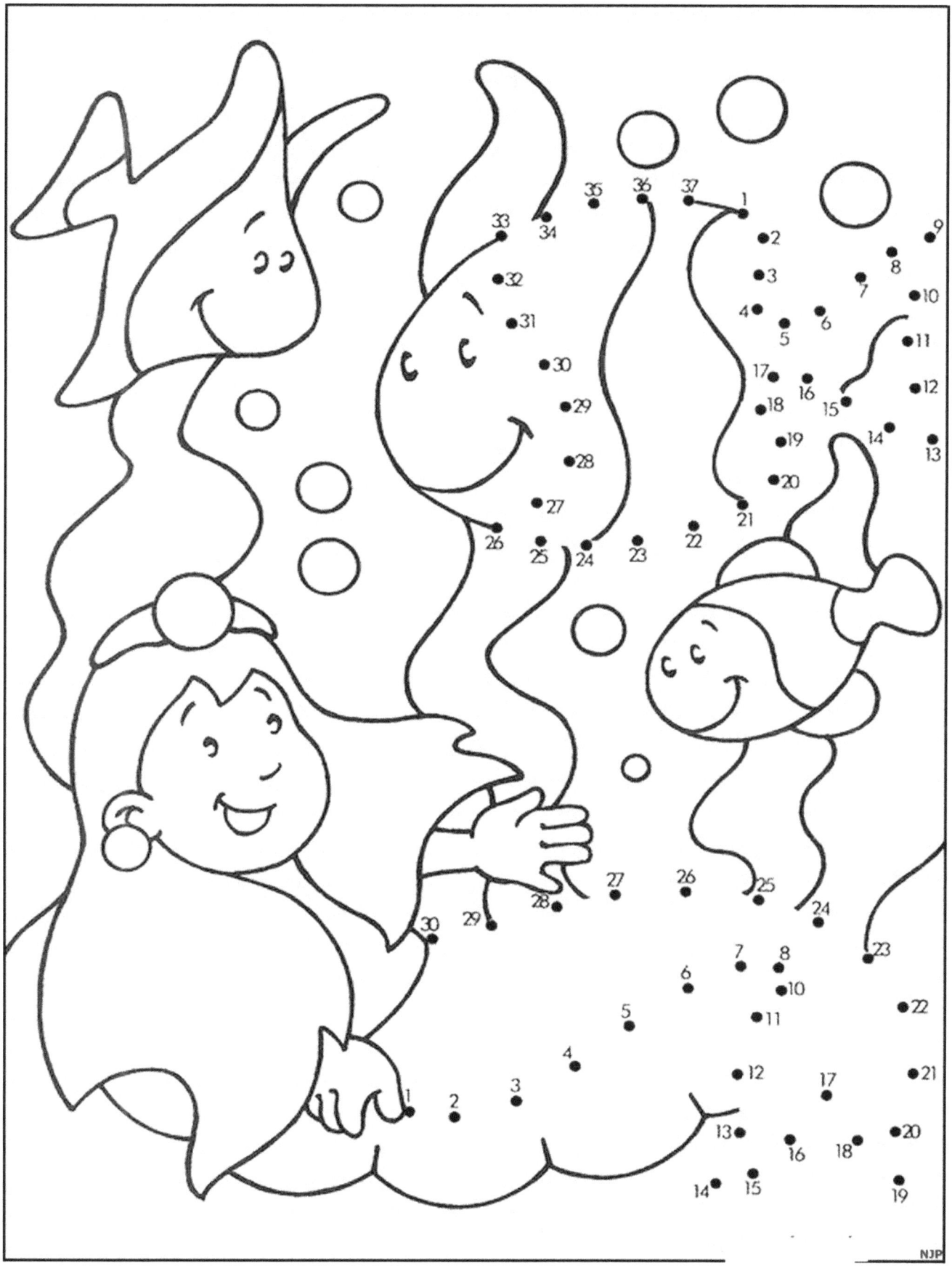

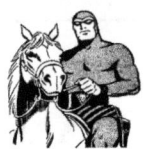

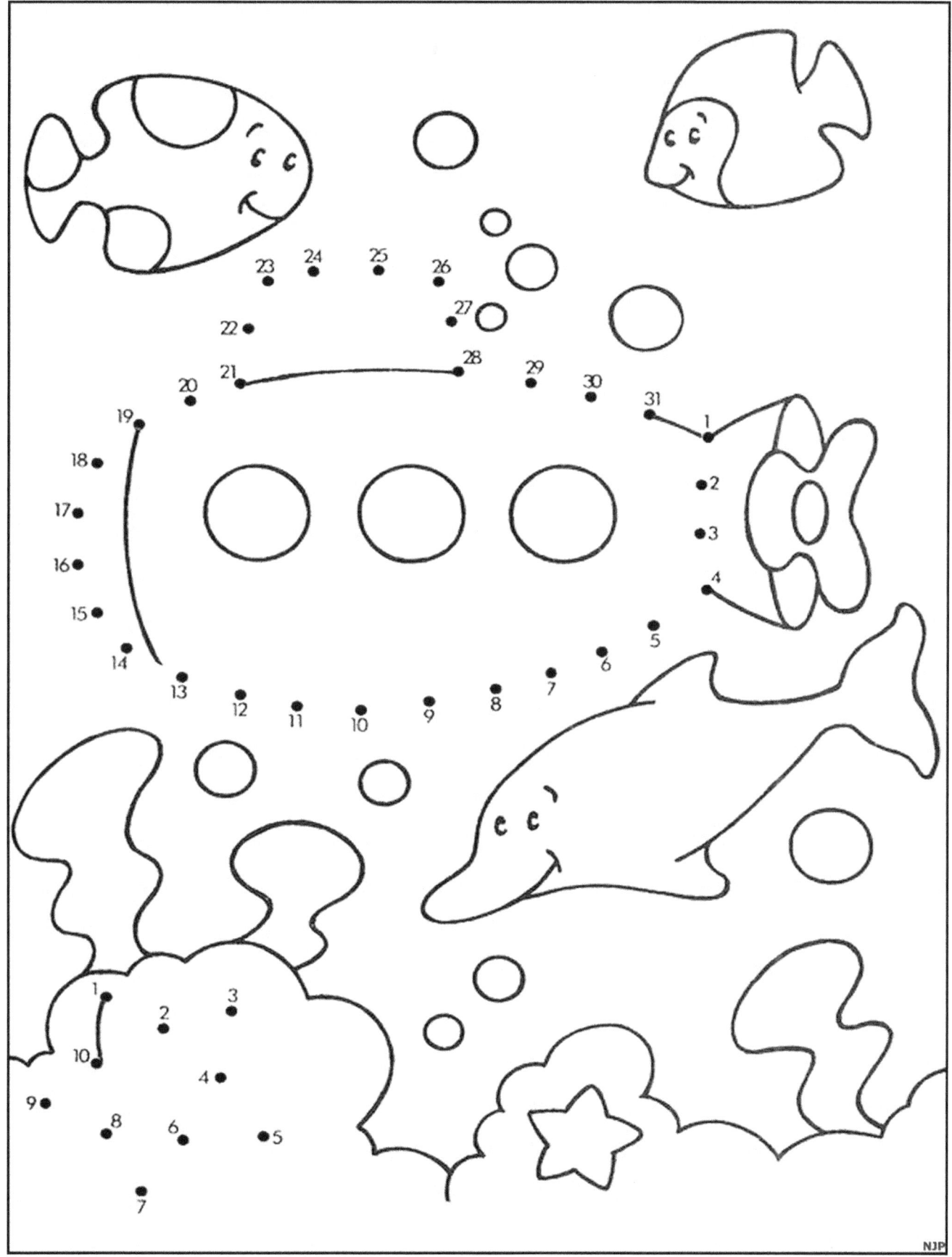

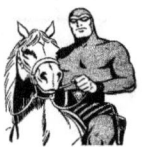

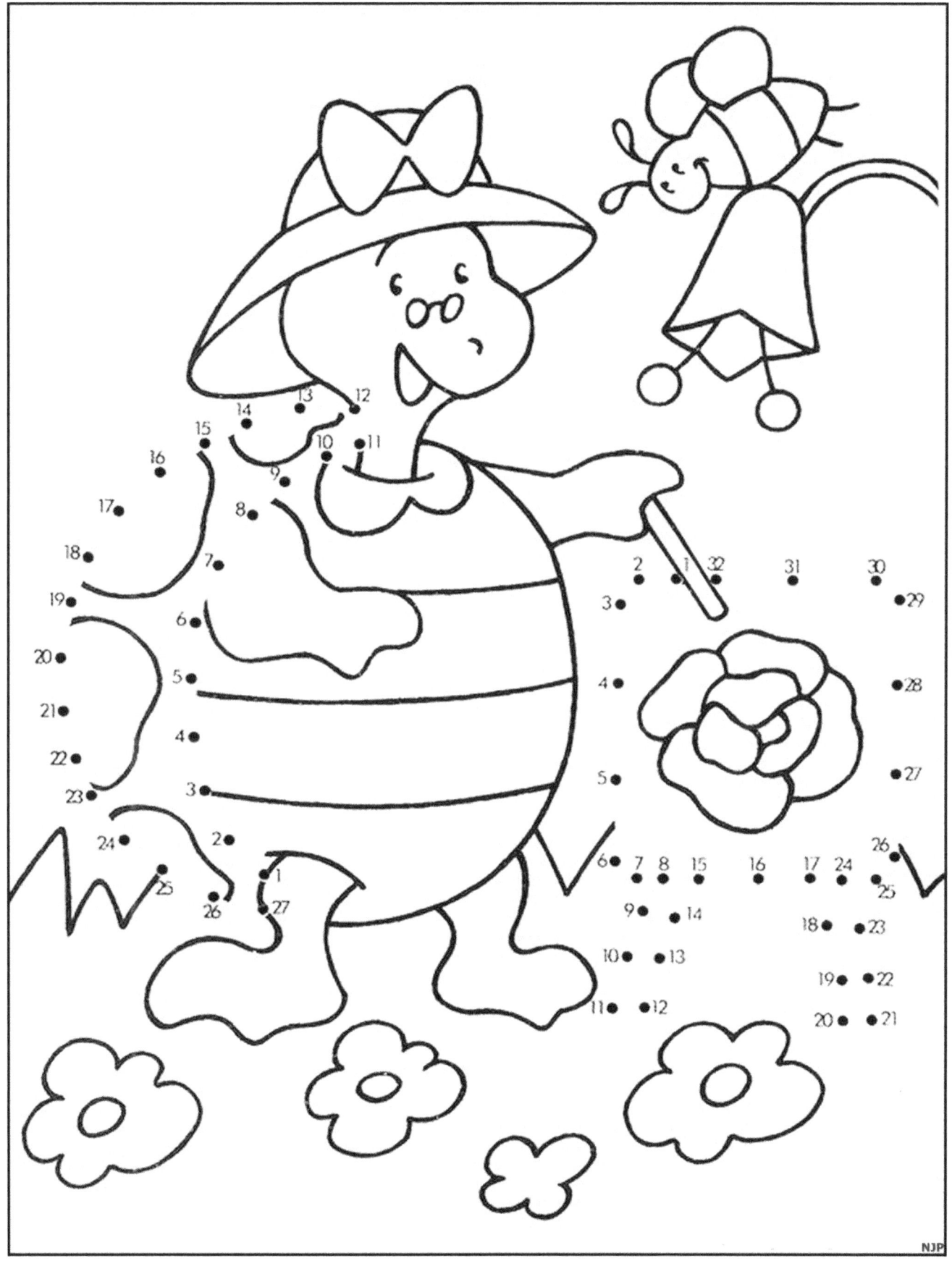

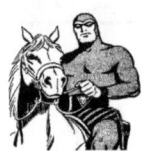

Level – 4

50 Dots per Picture

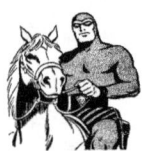

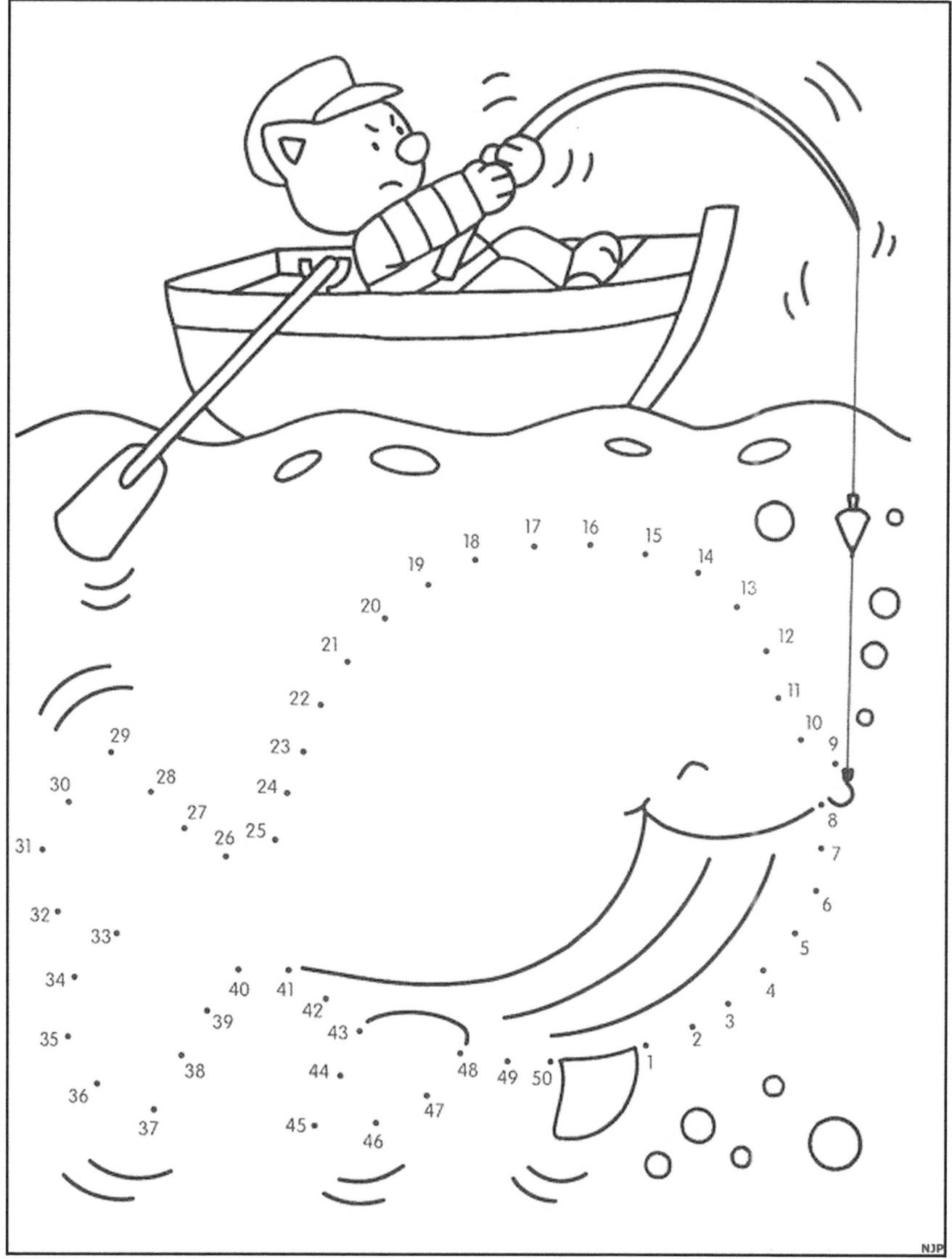

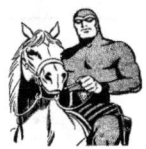

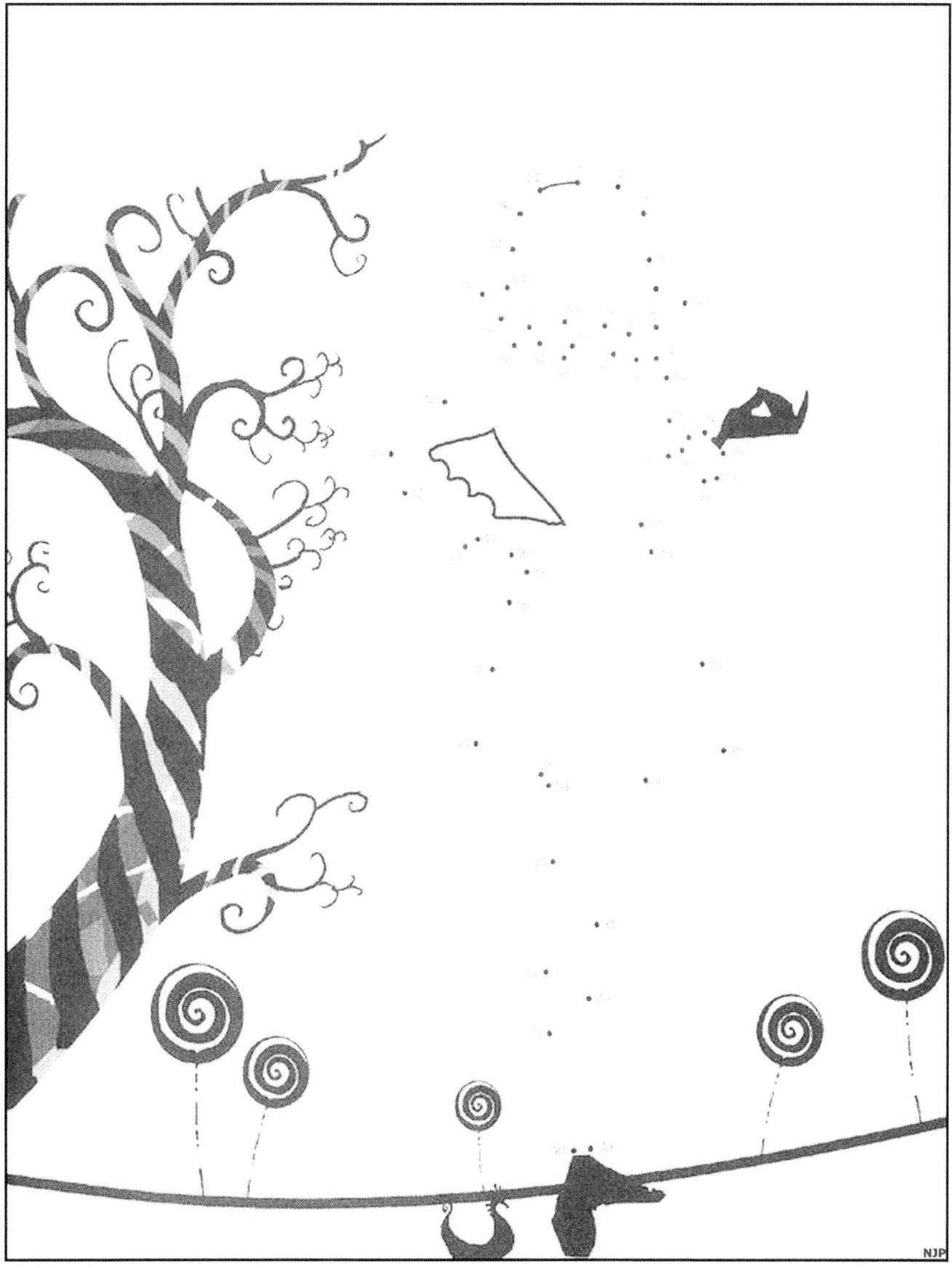

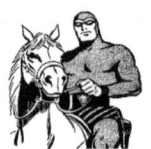

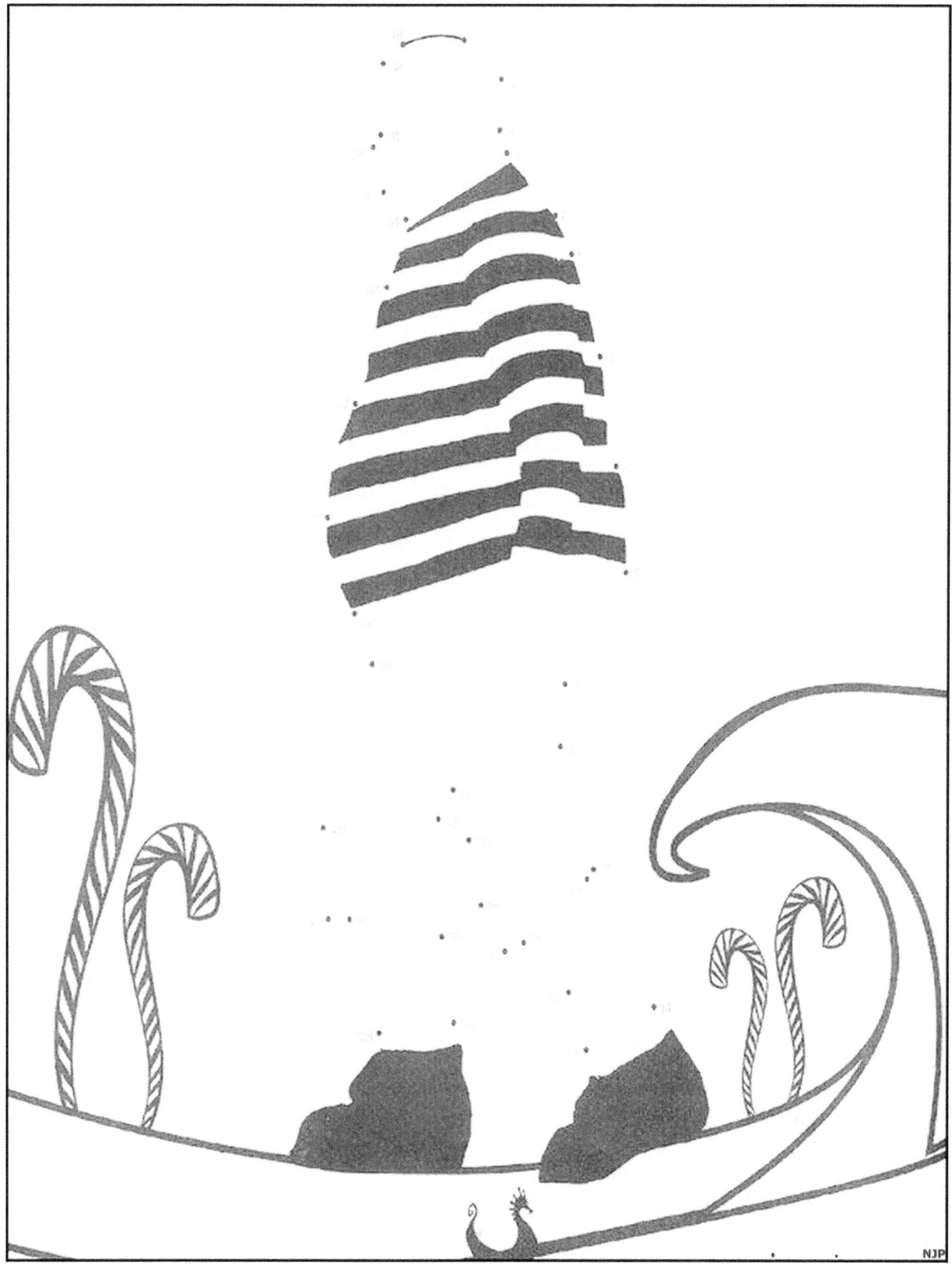

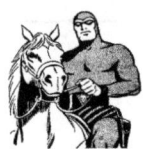

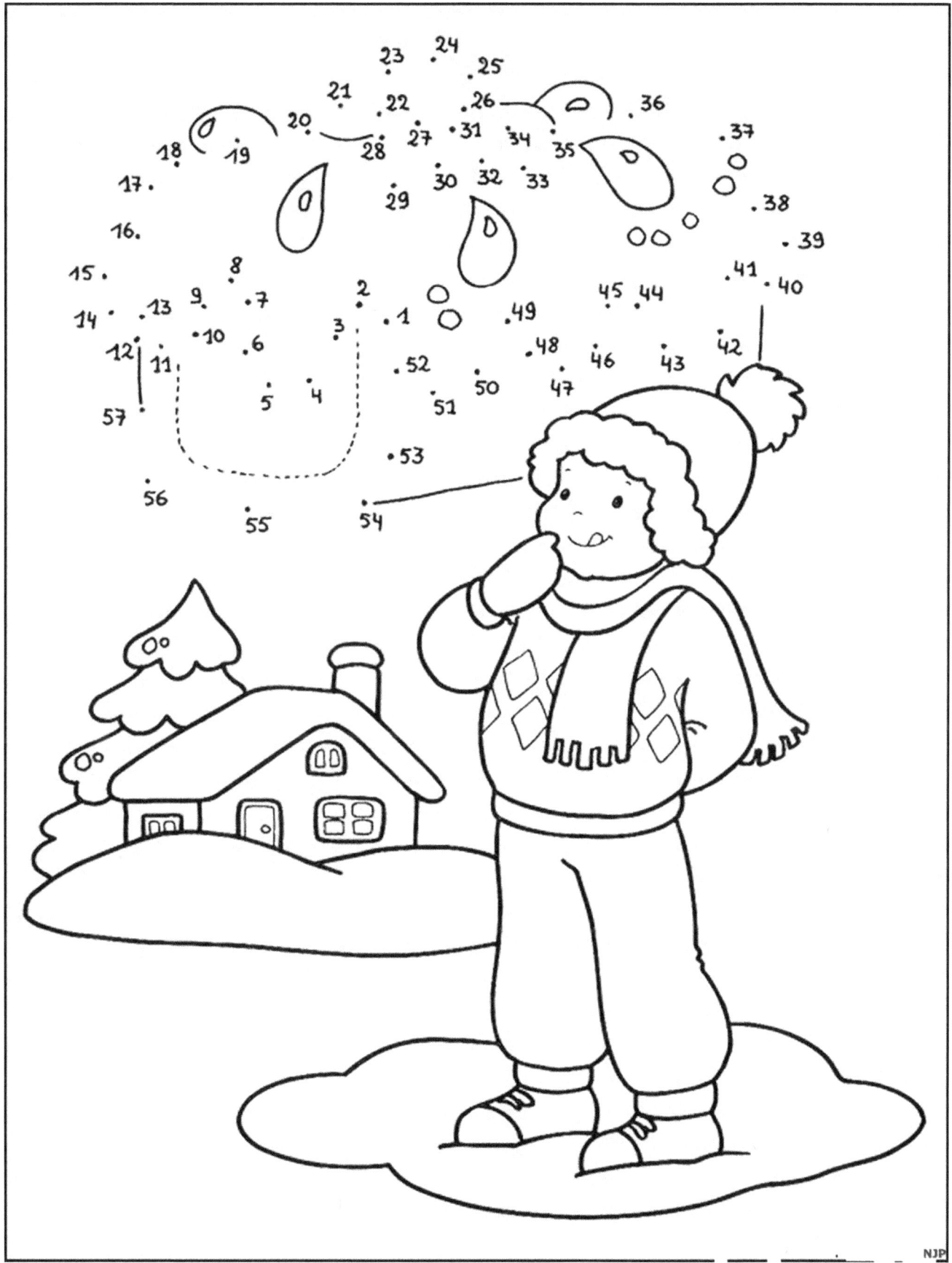

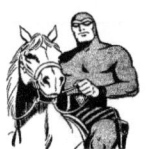

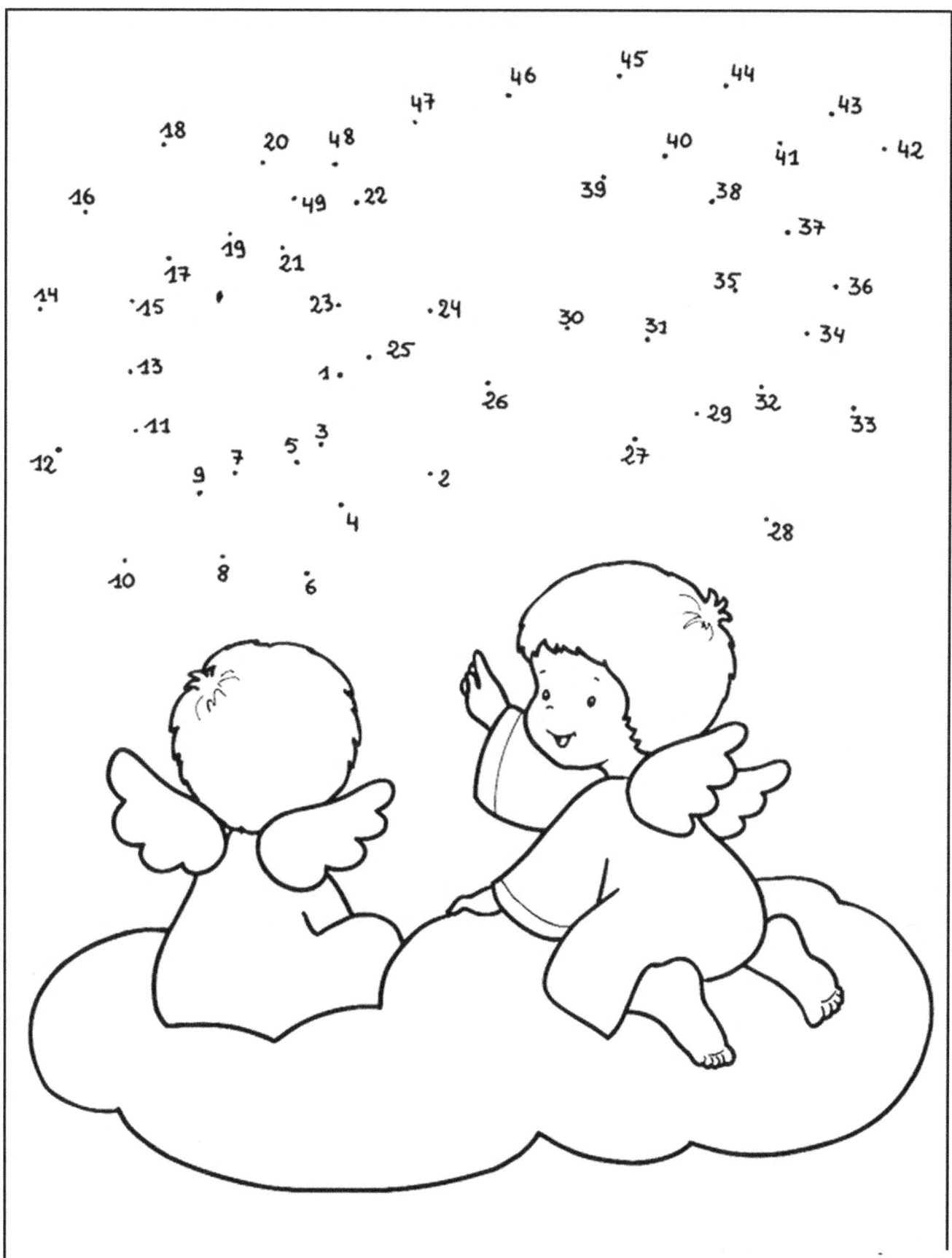

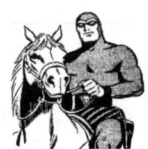

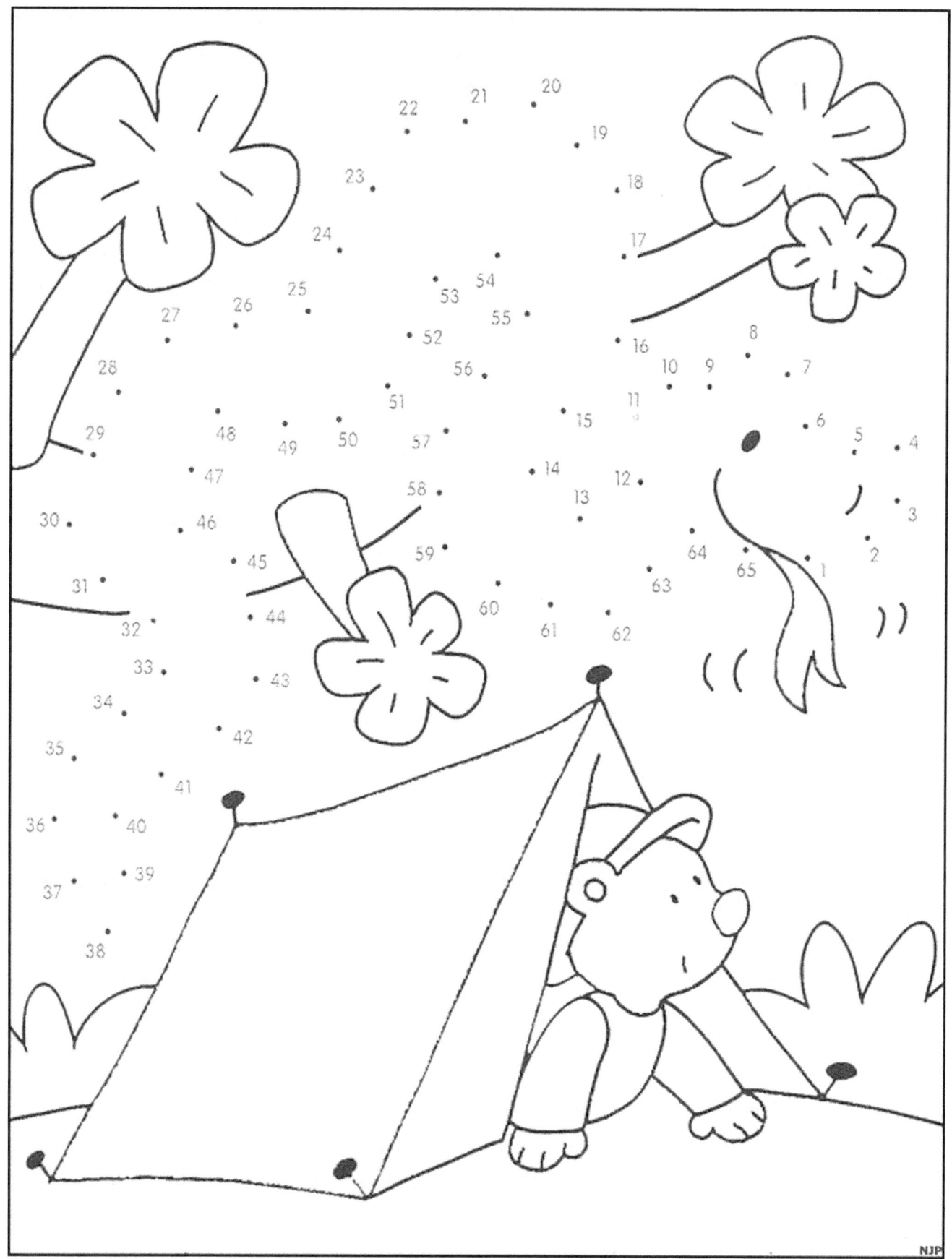

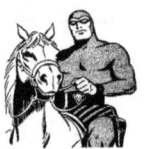

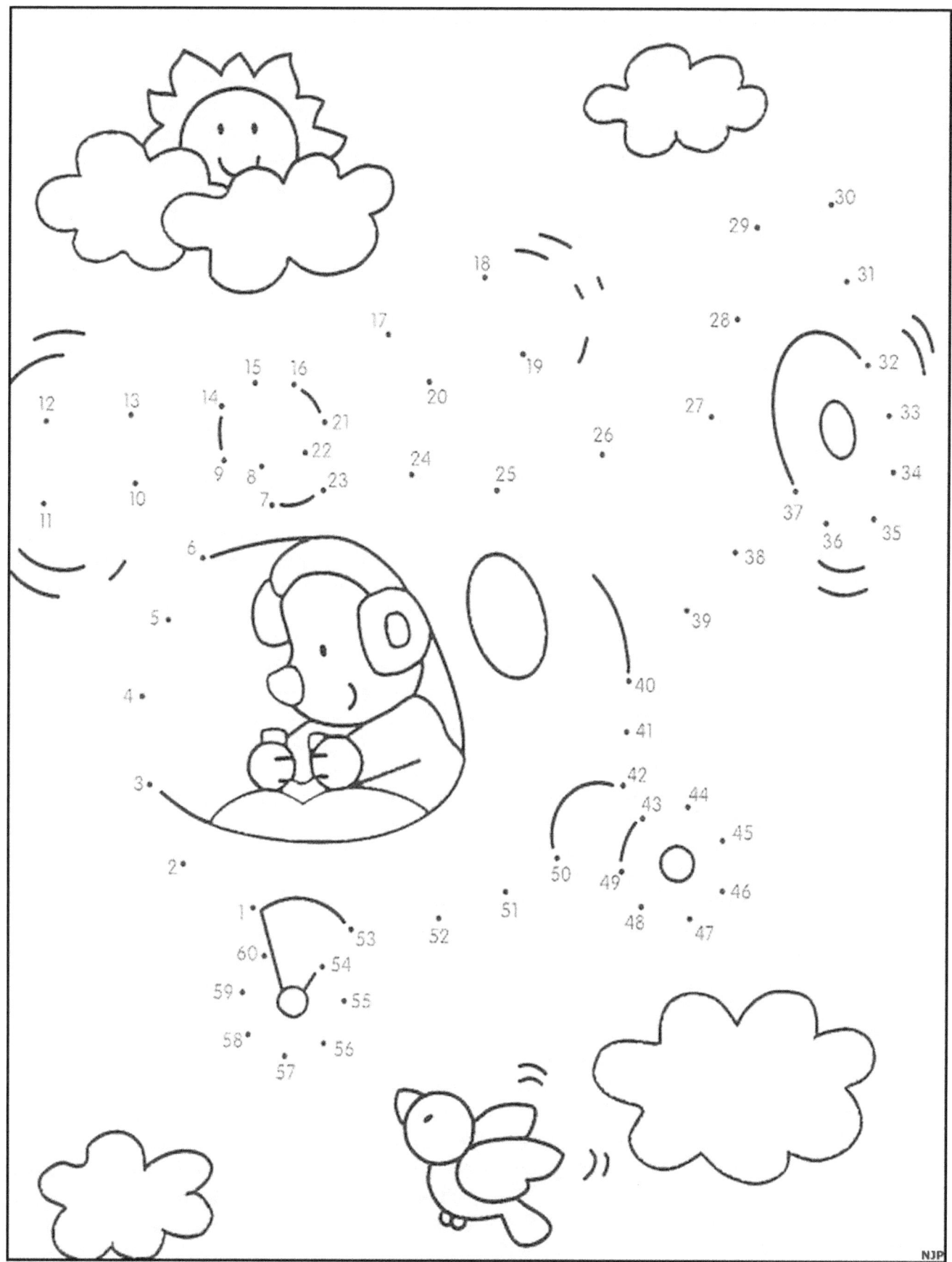

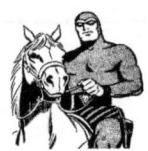

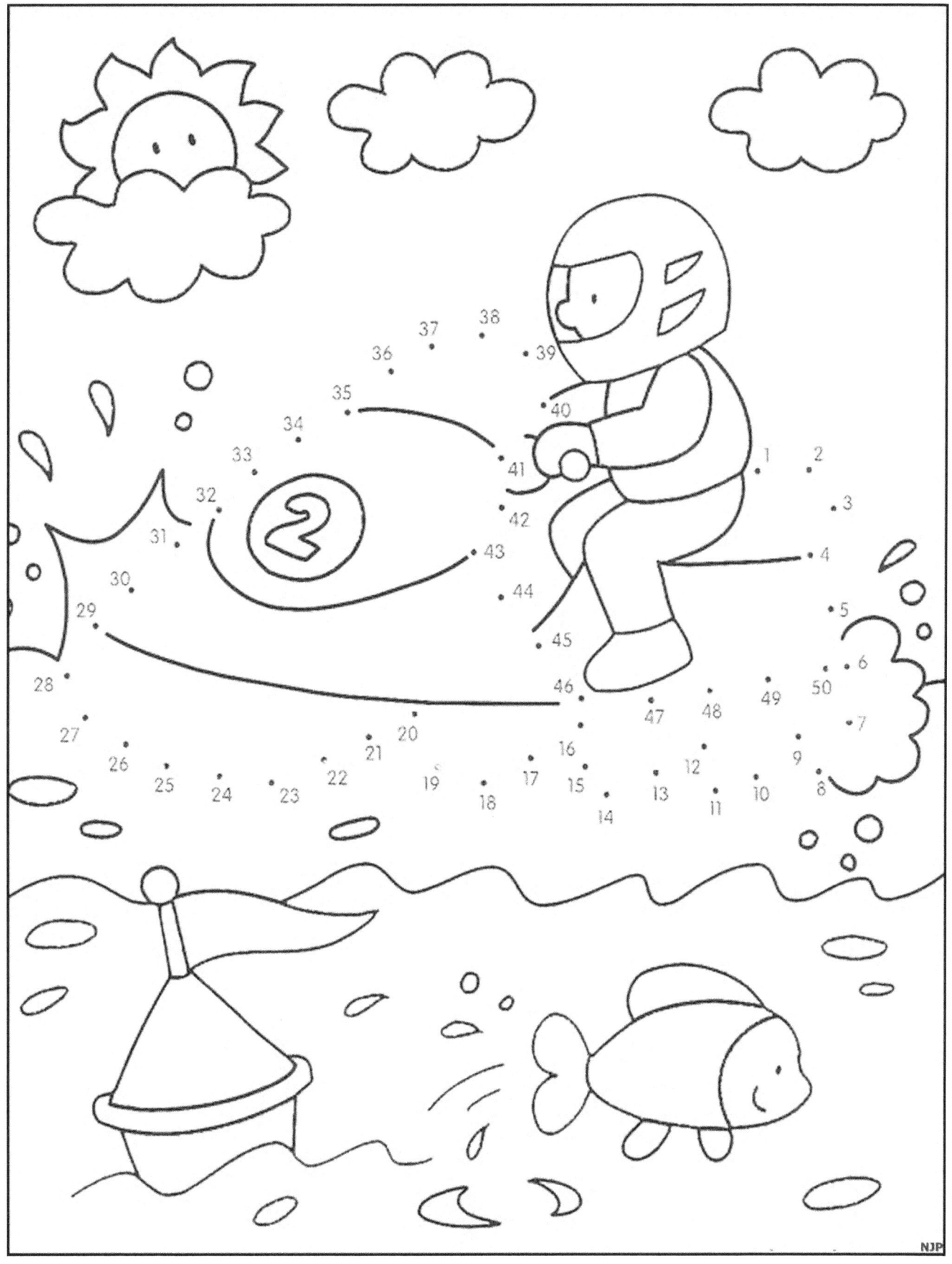

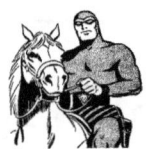

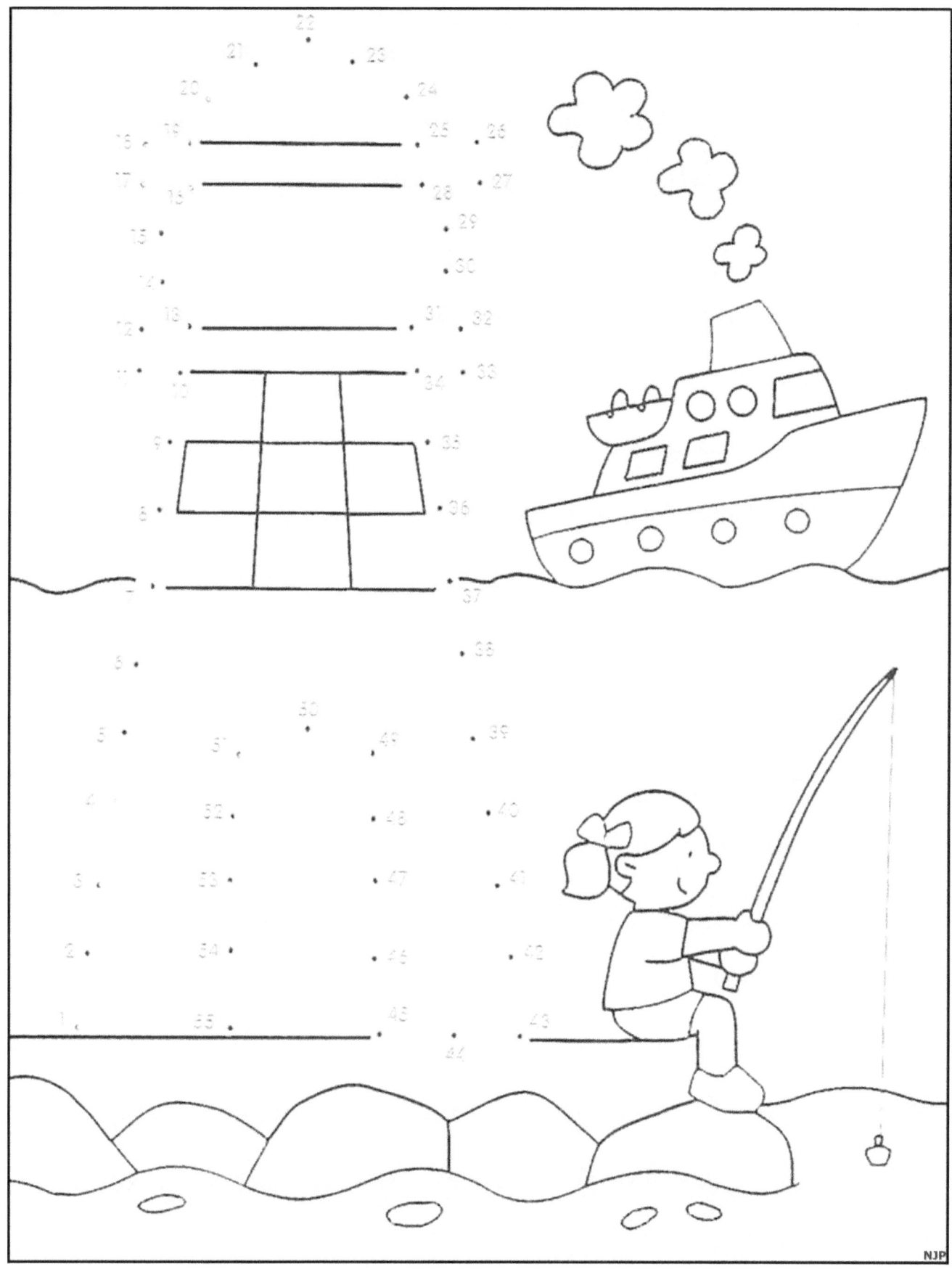

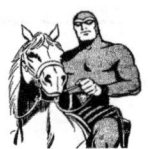

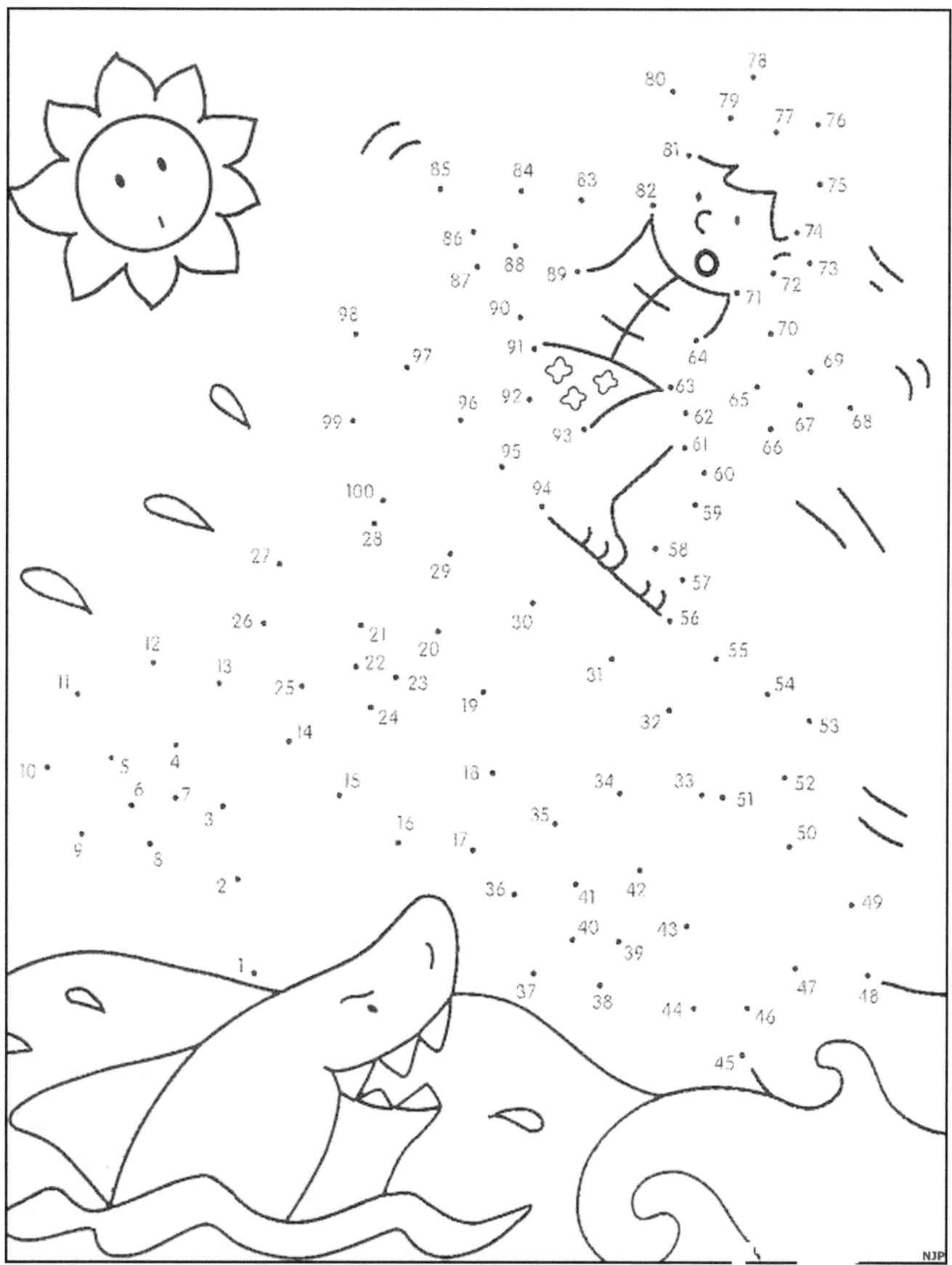

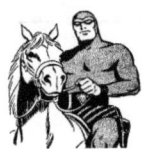

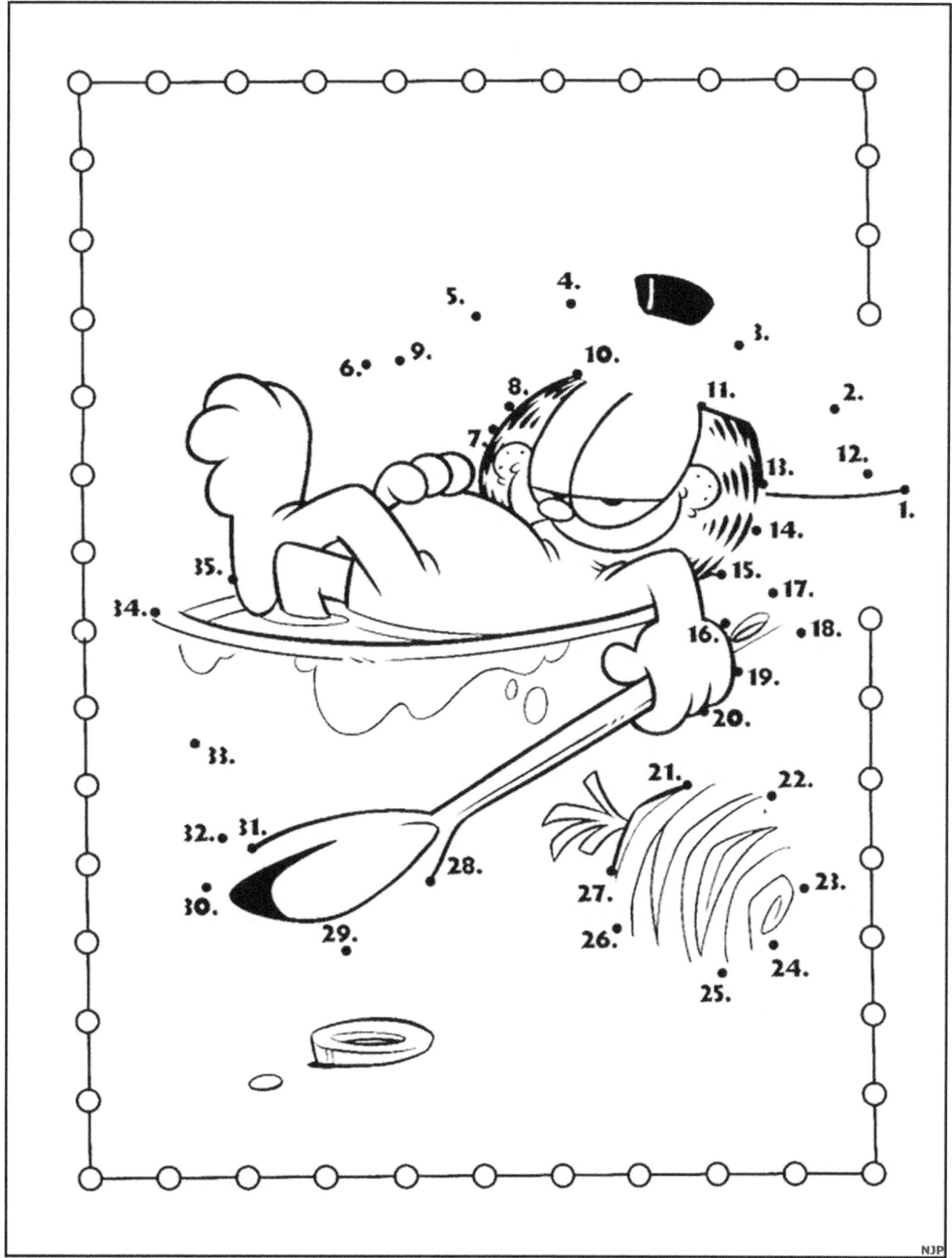

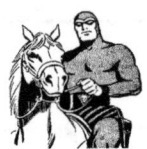

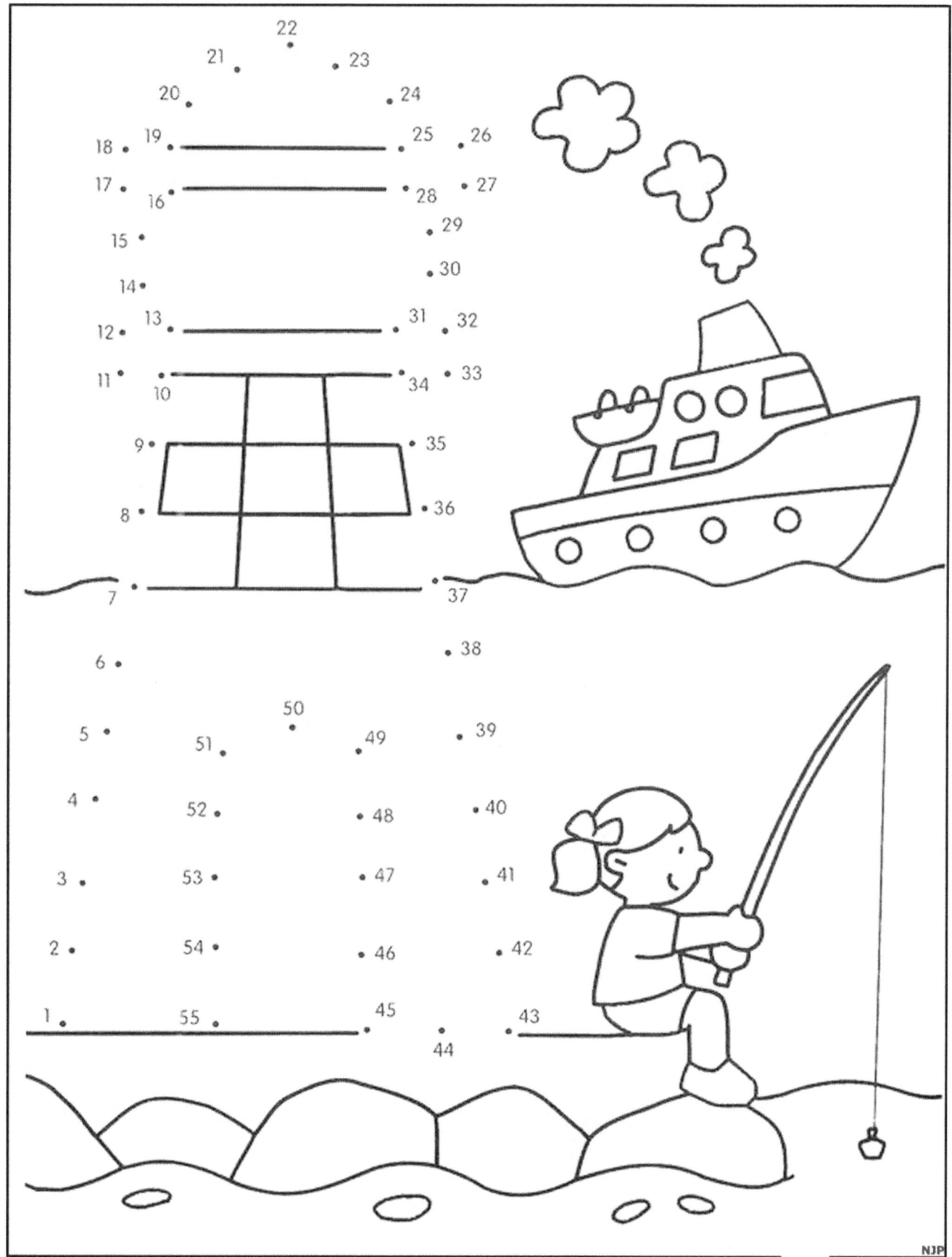

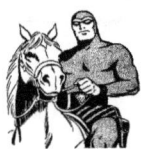

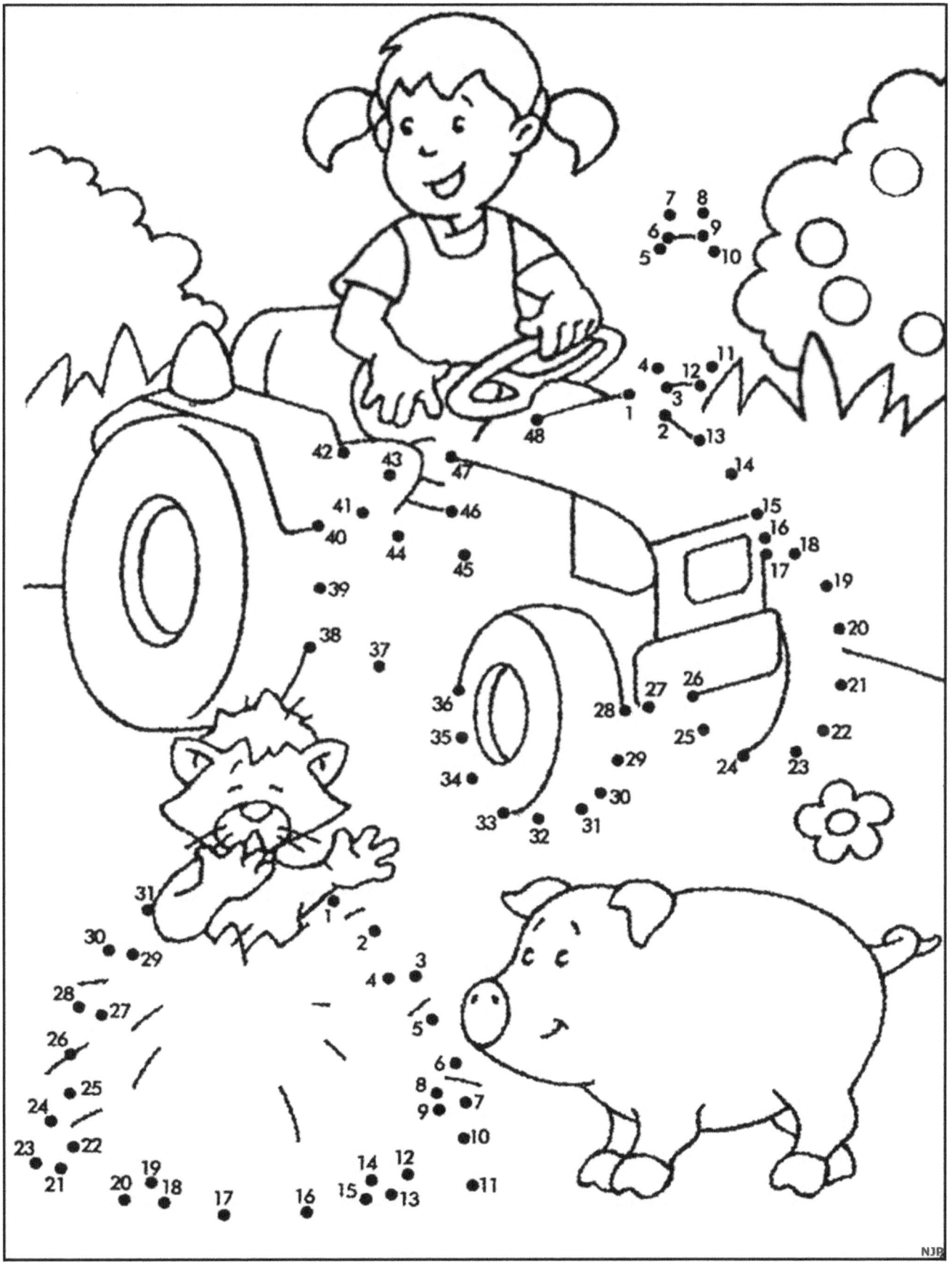

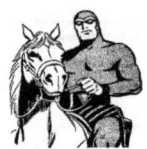

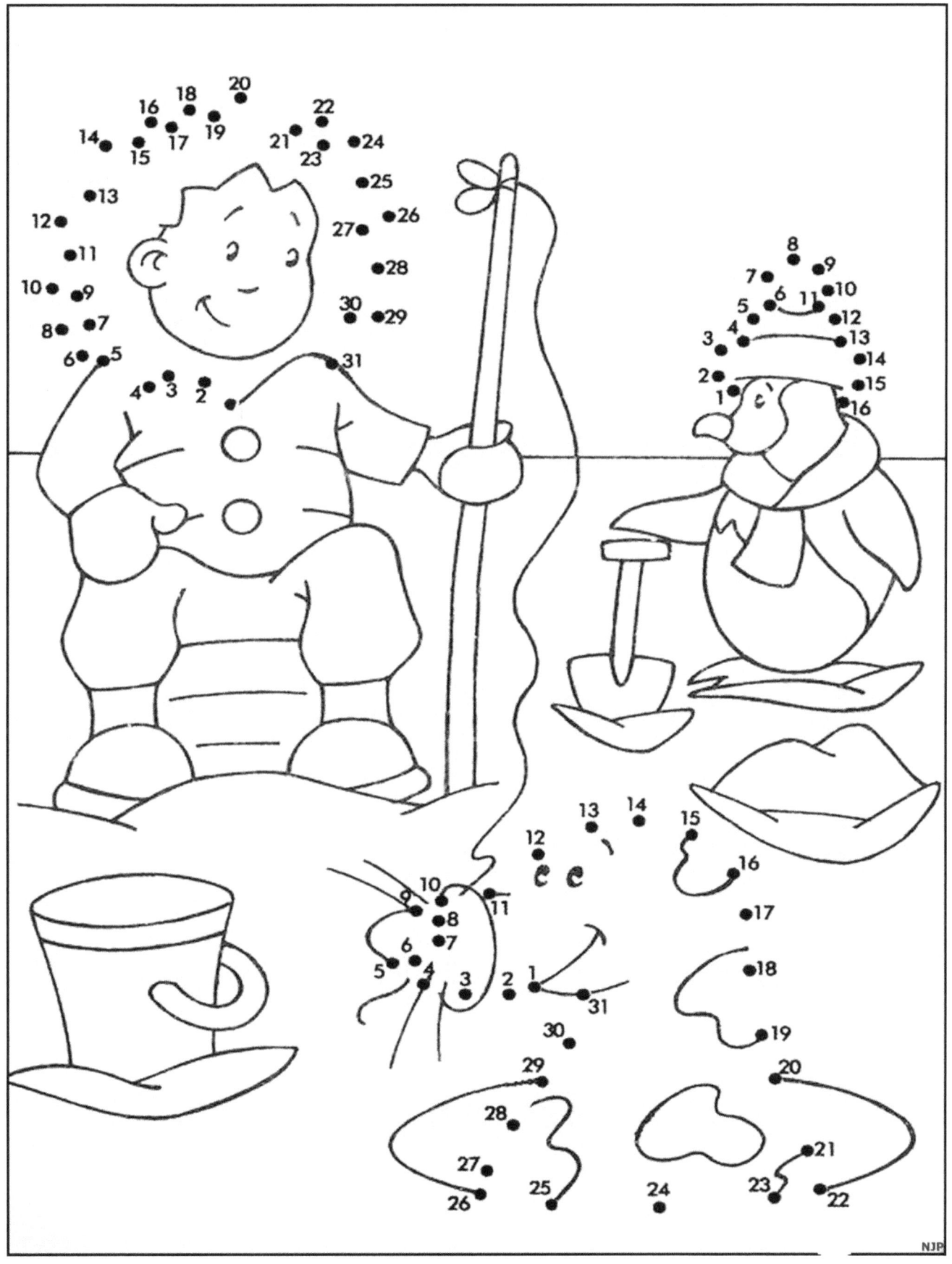

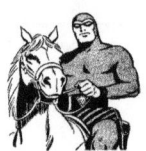

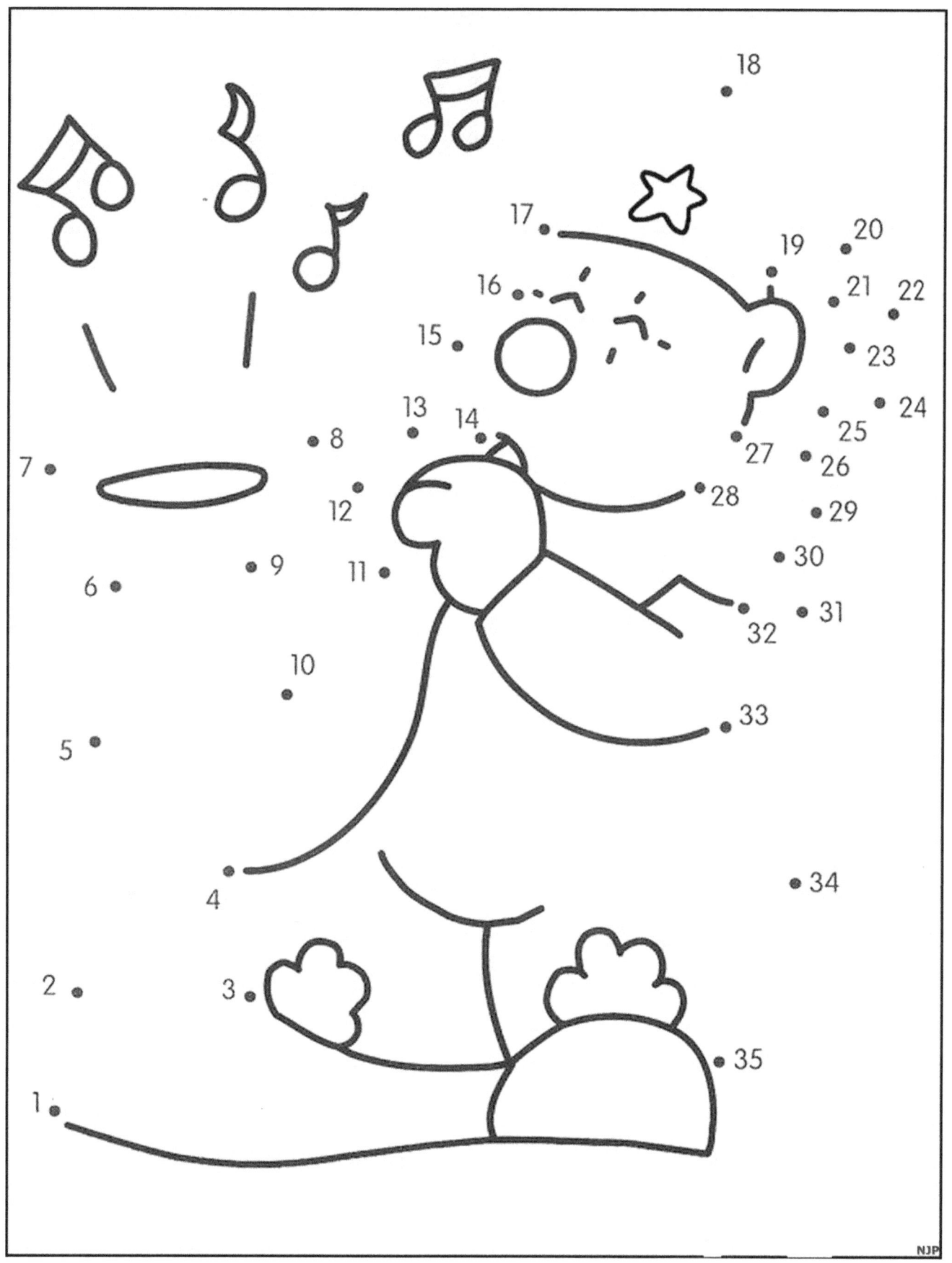

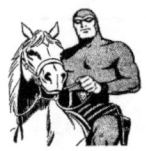

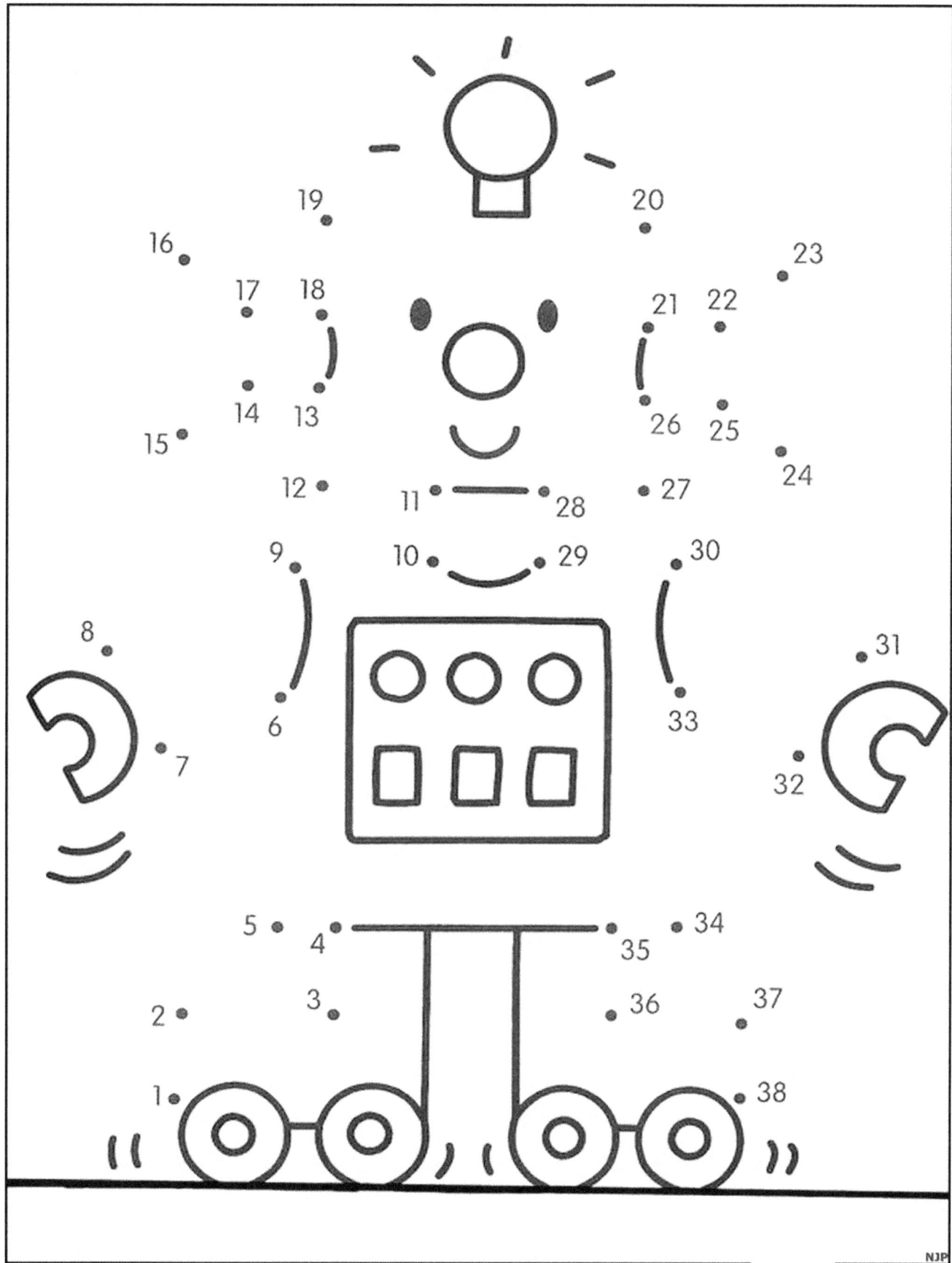

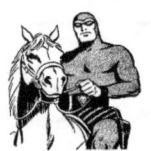

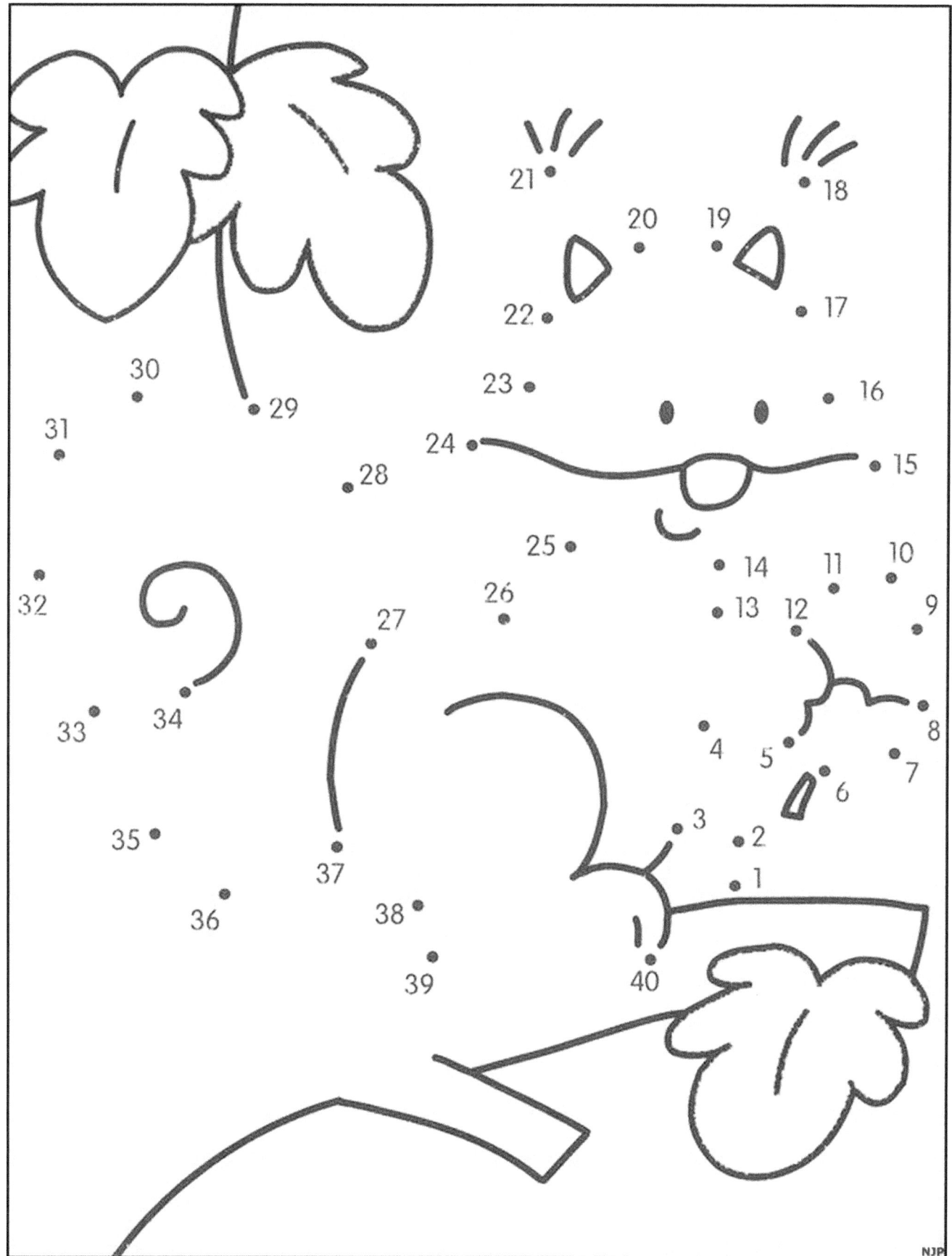

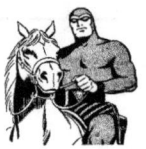

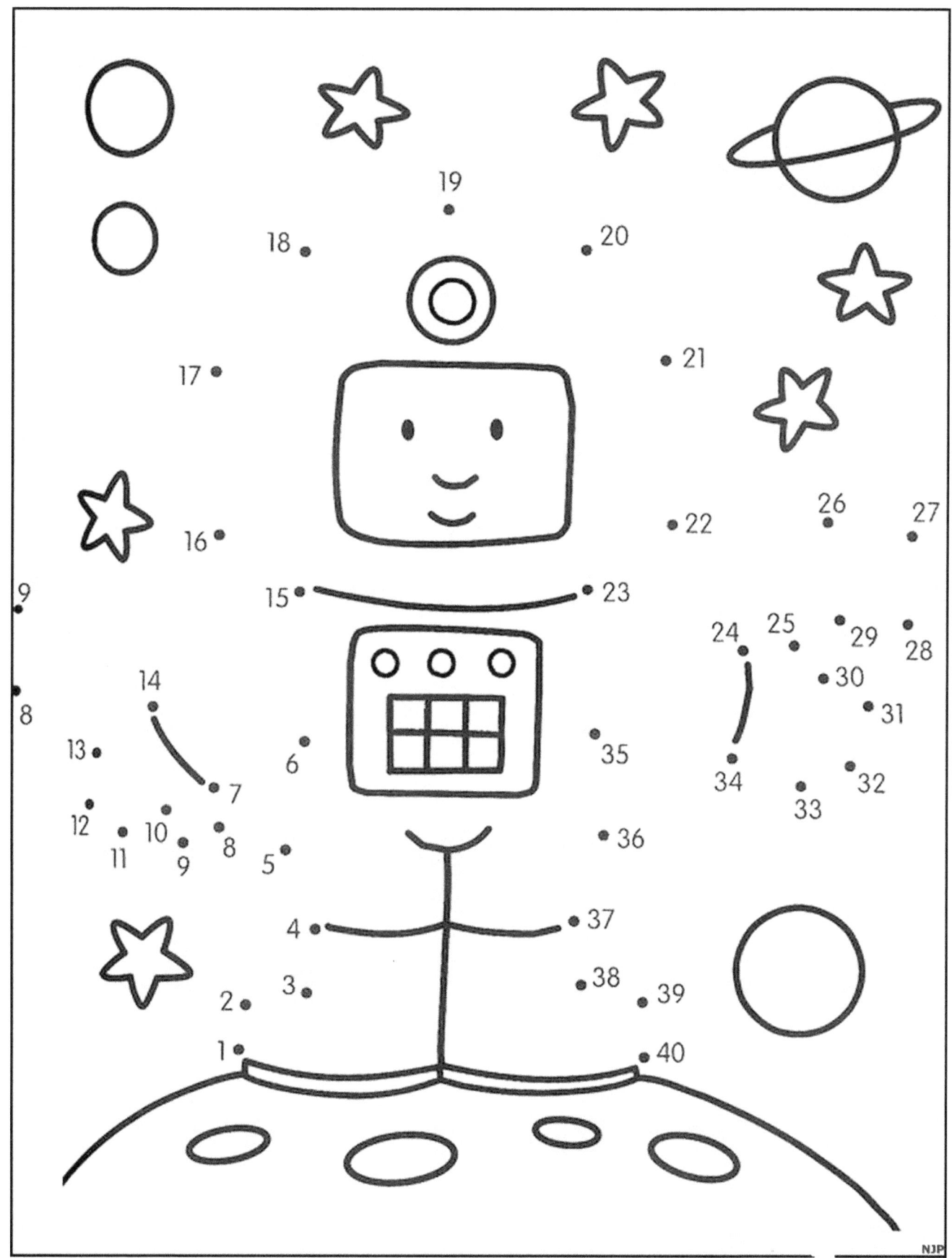

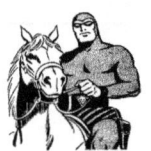

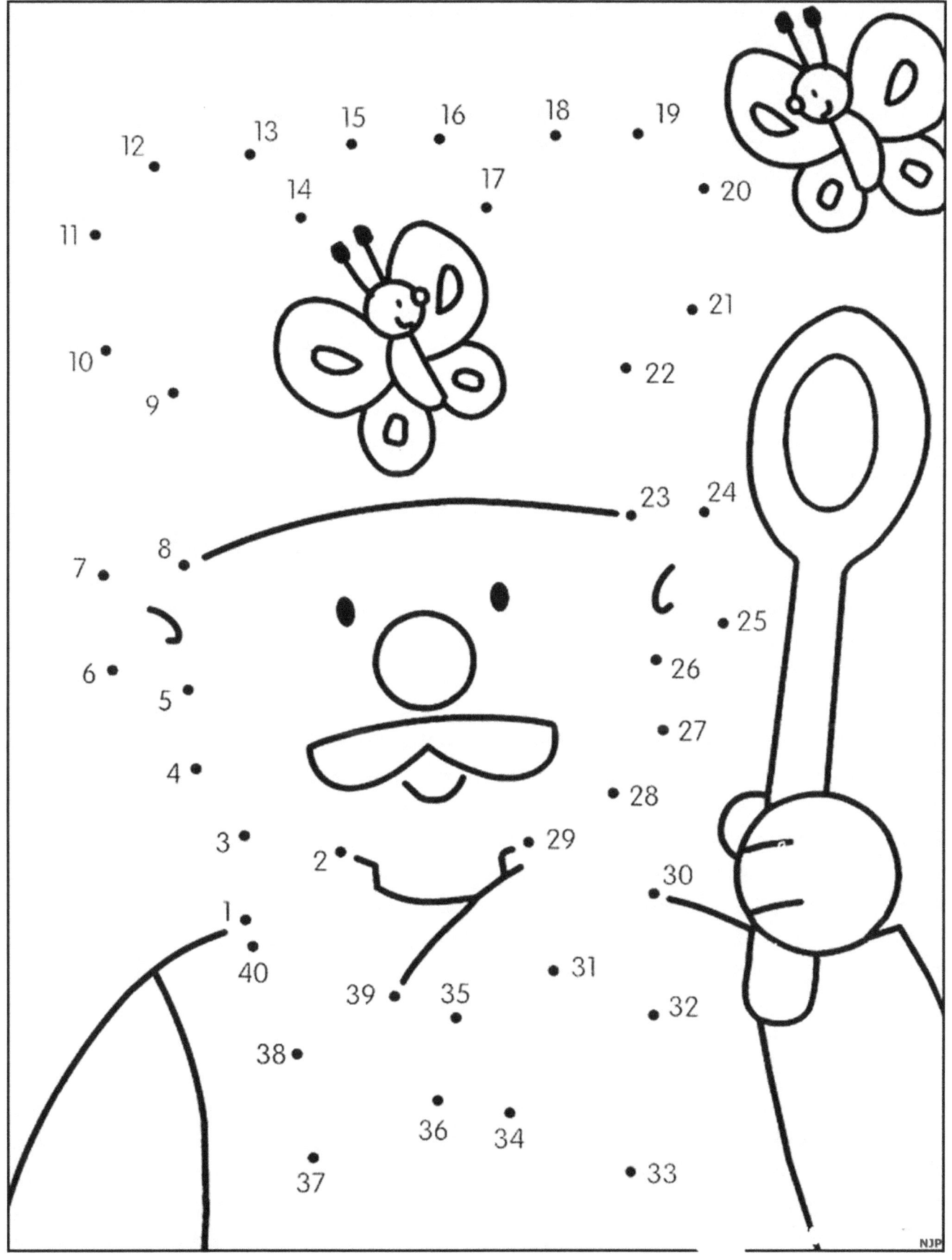

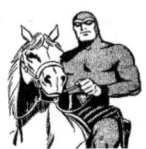

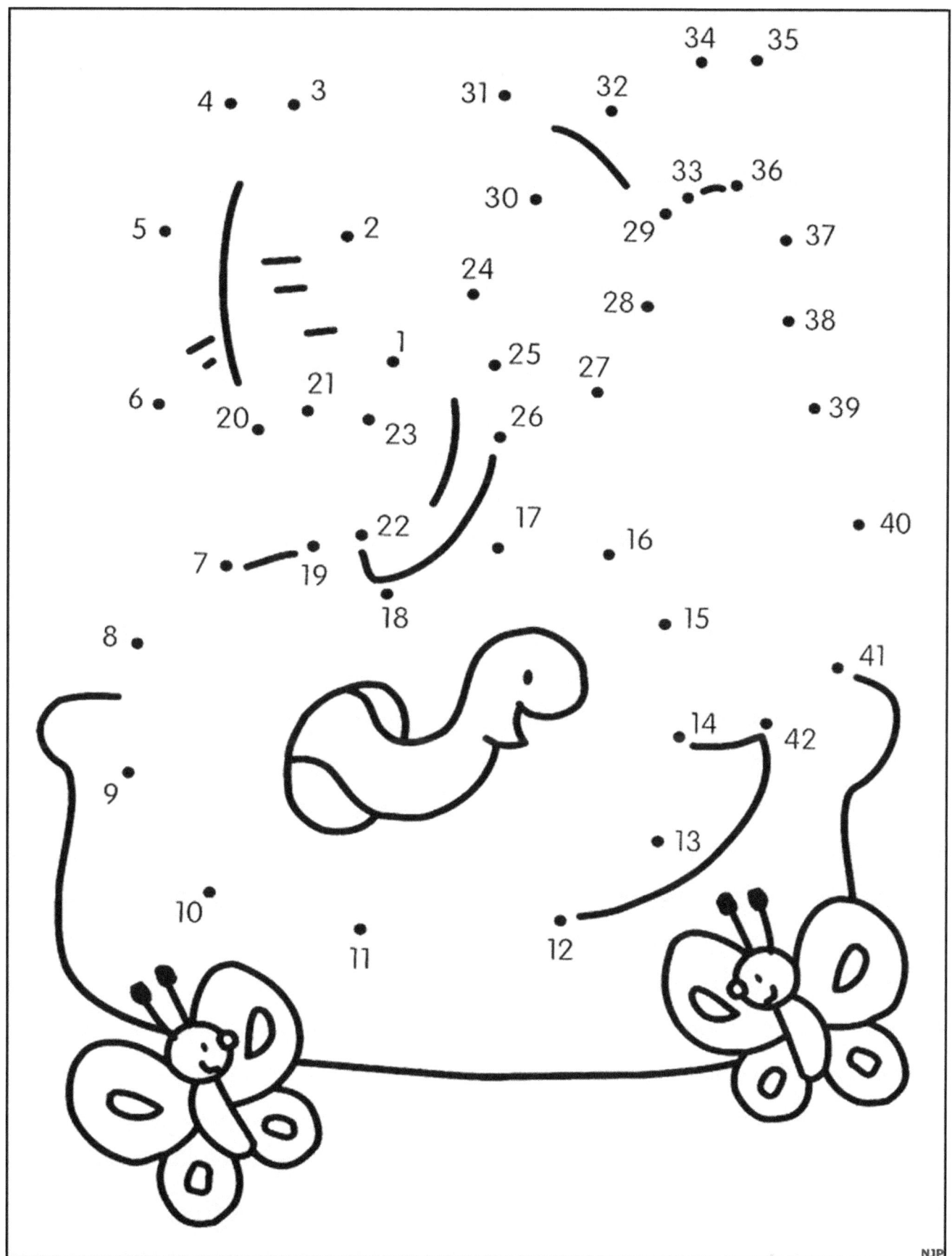

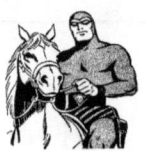

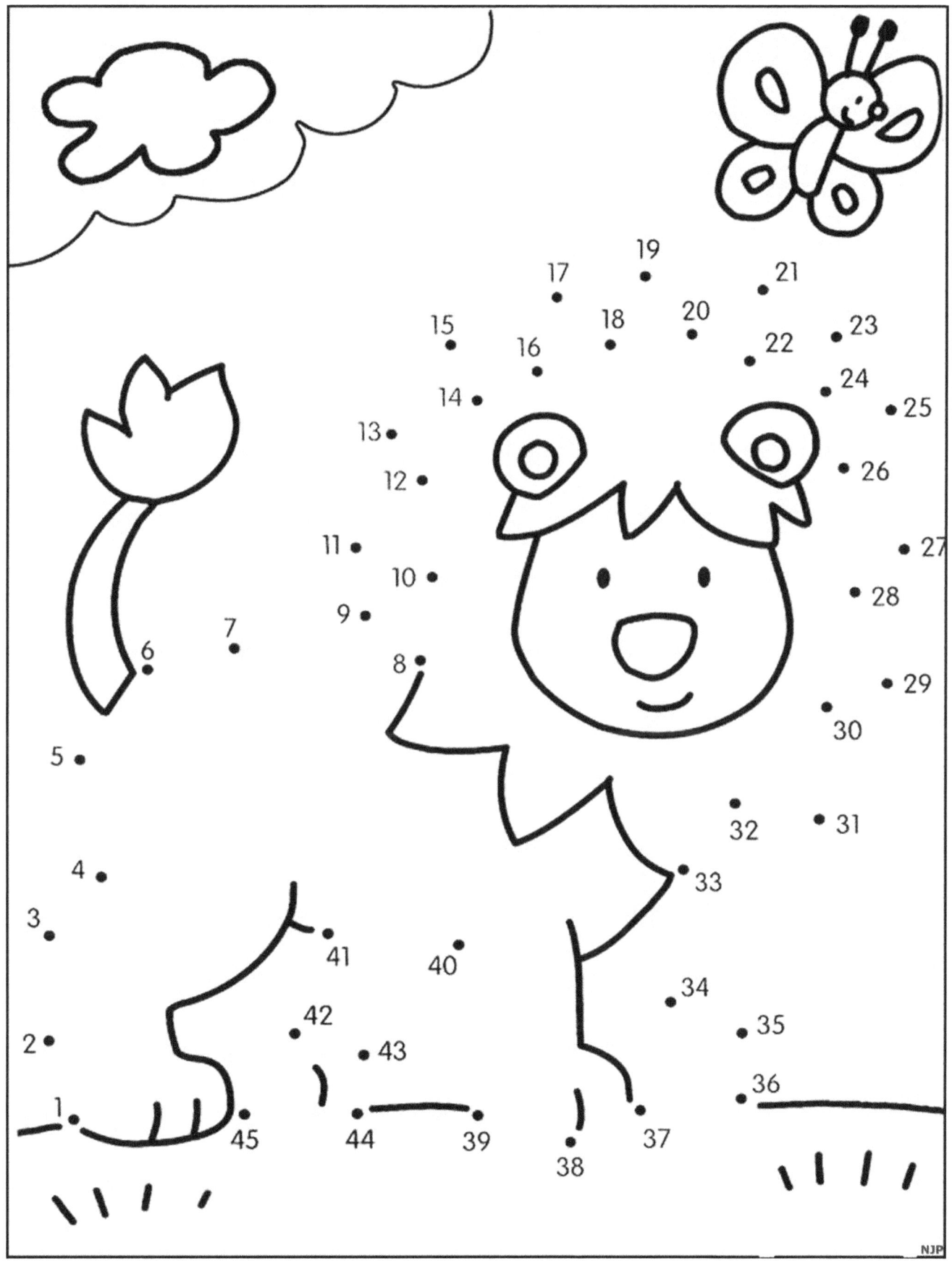

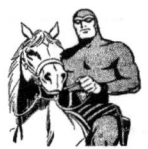

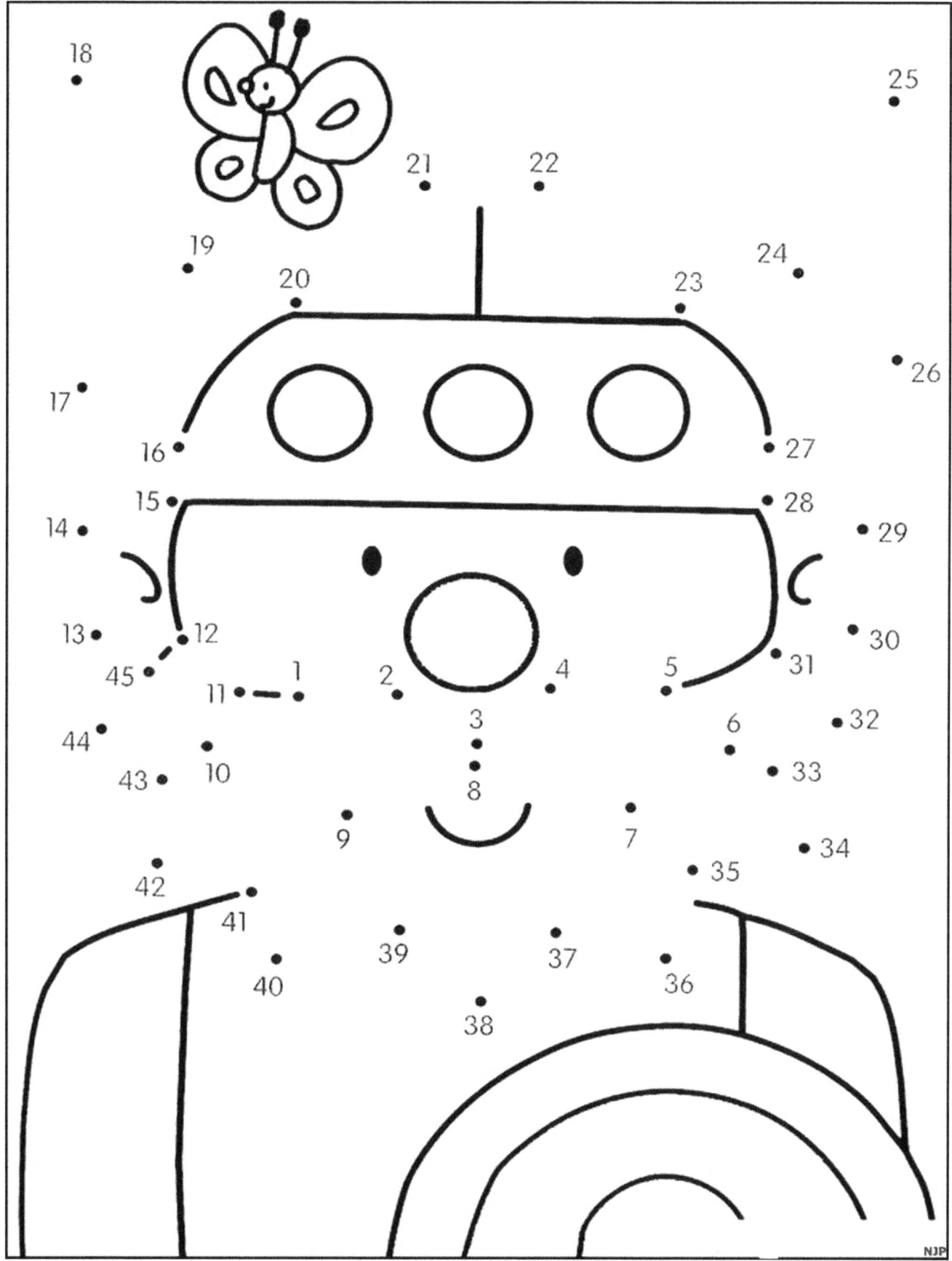

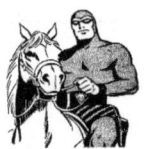

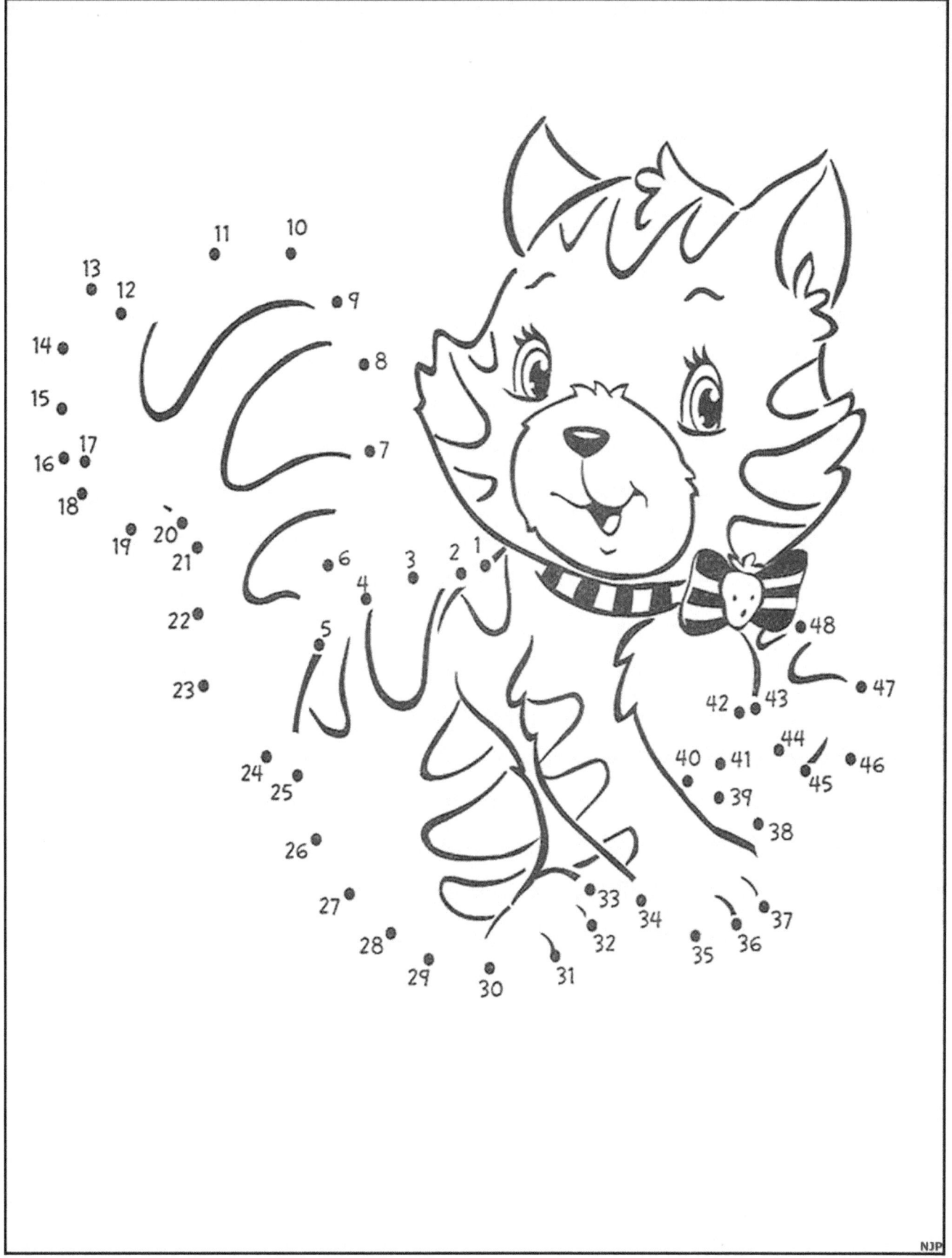

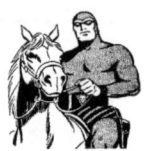

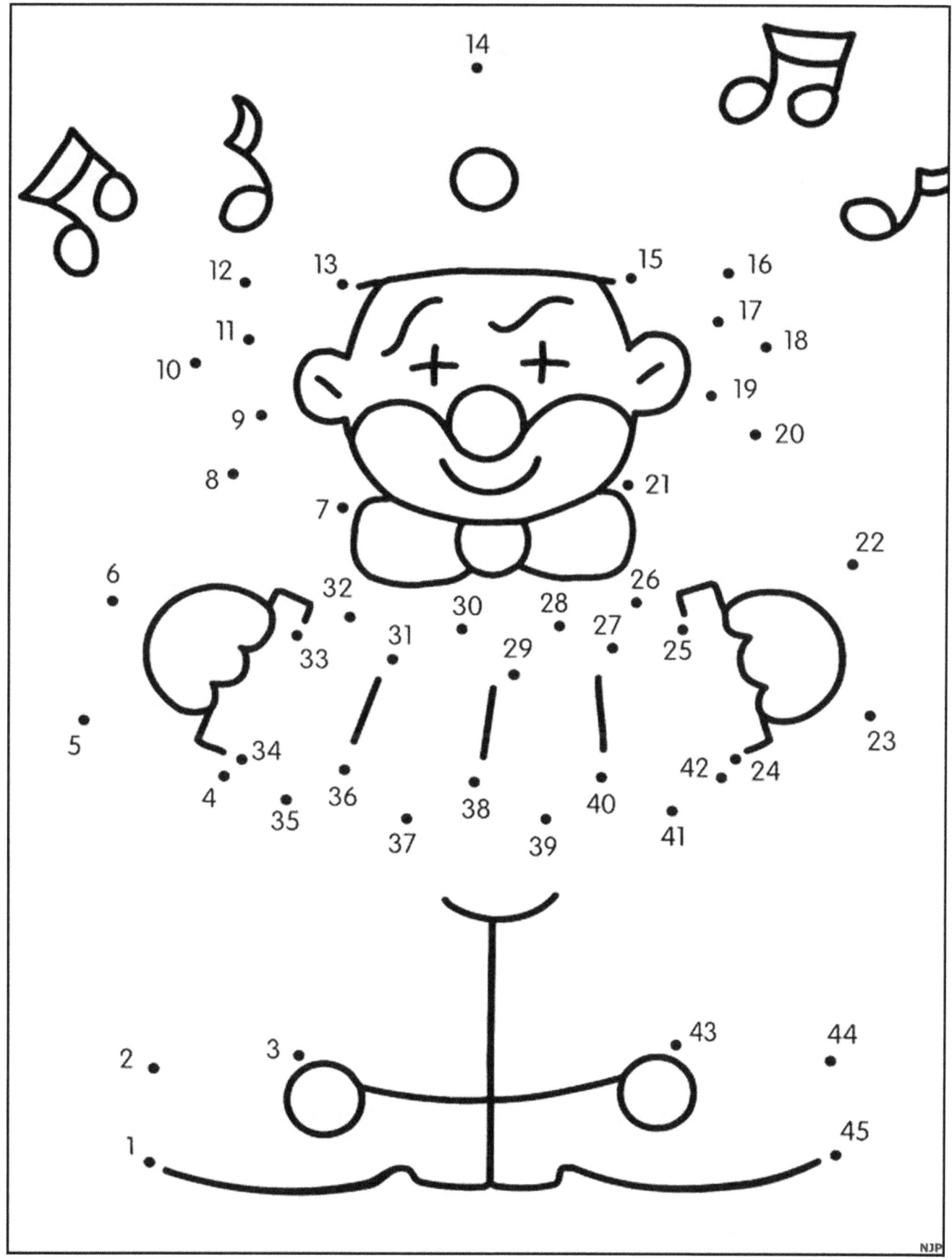

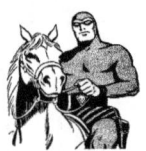

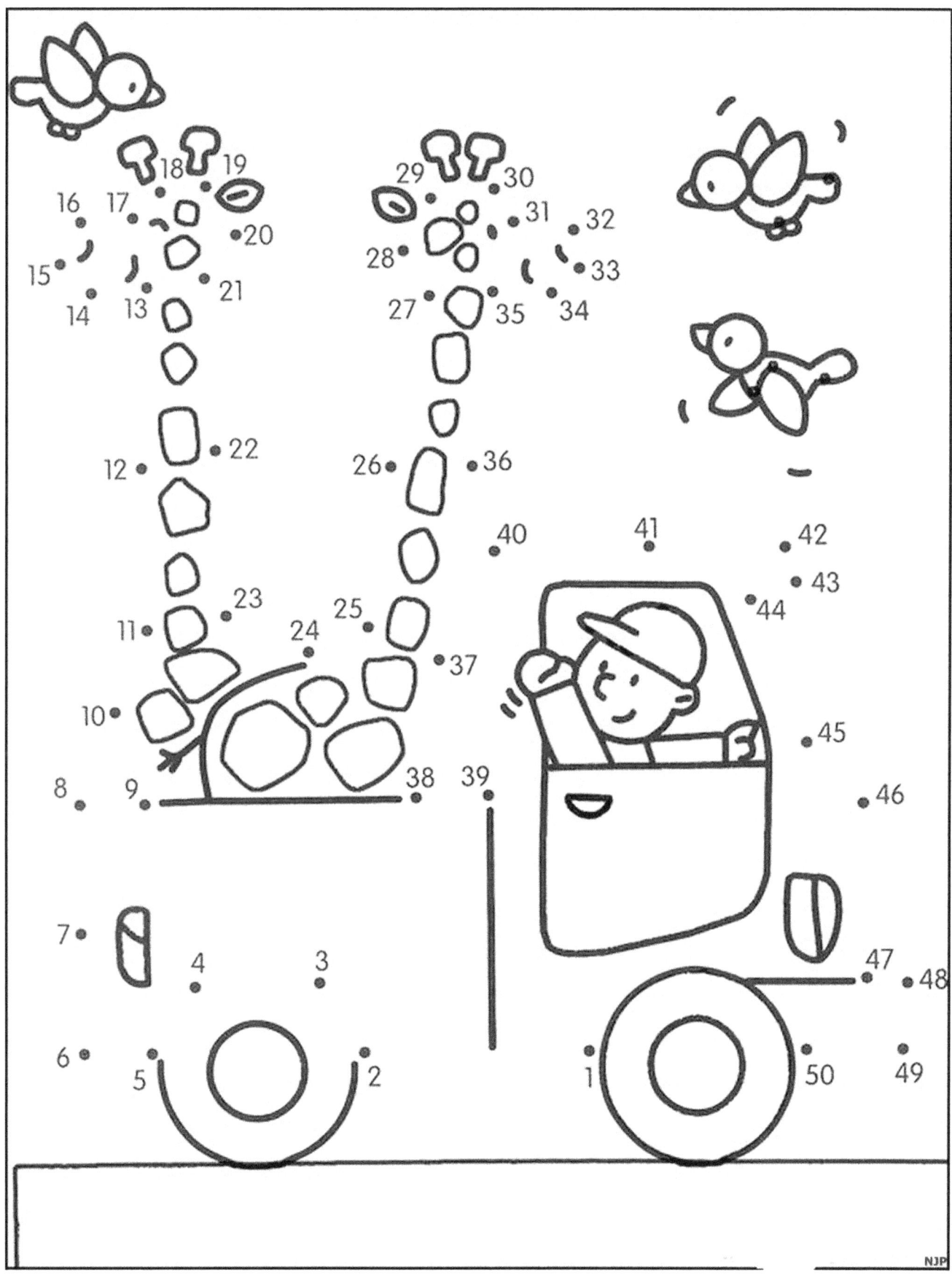

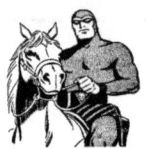

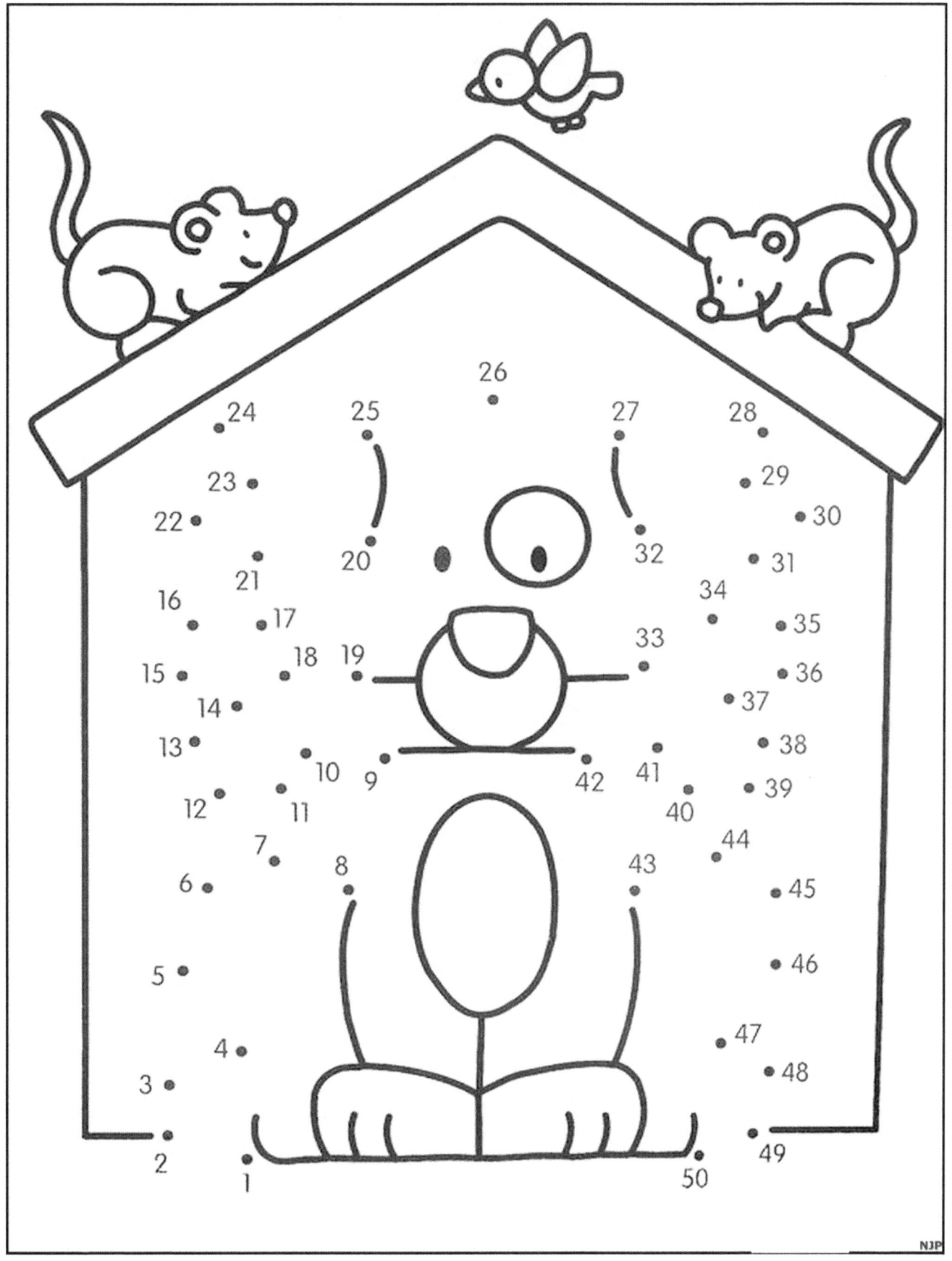

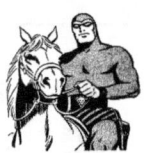

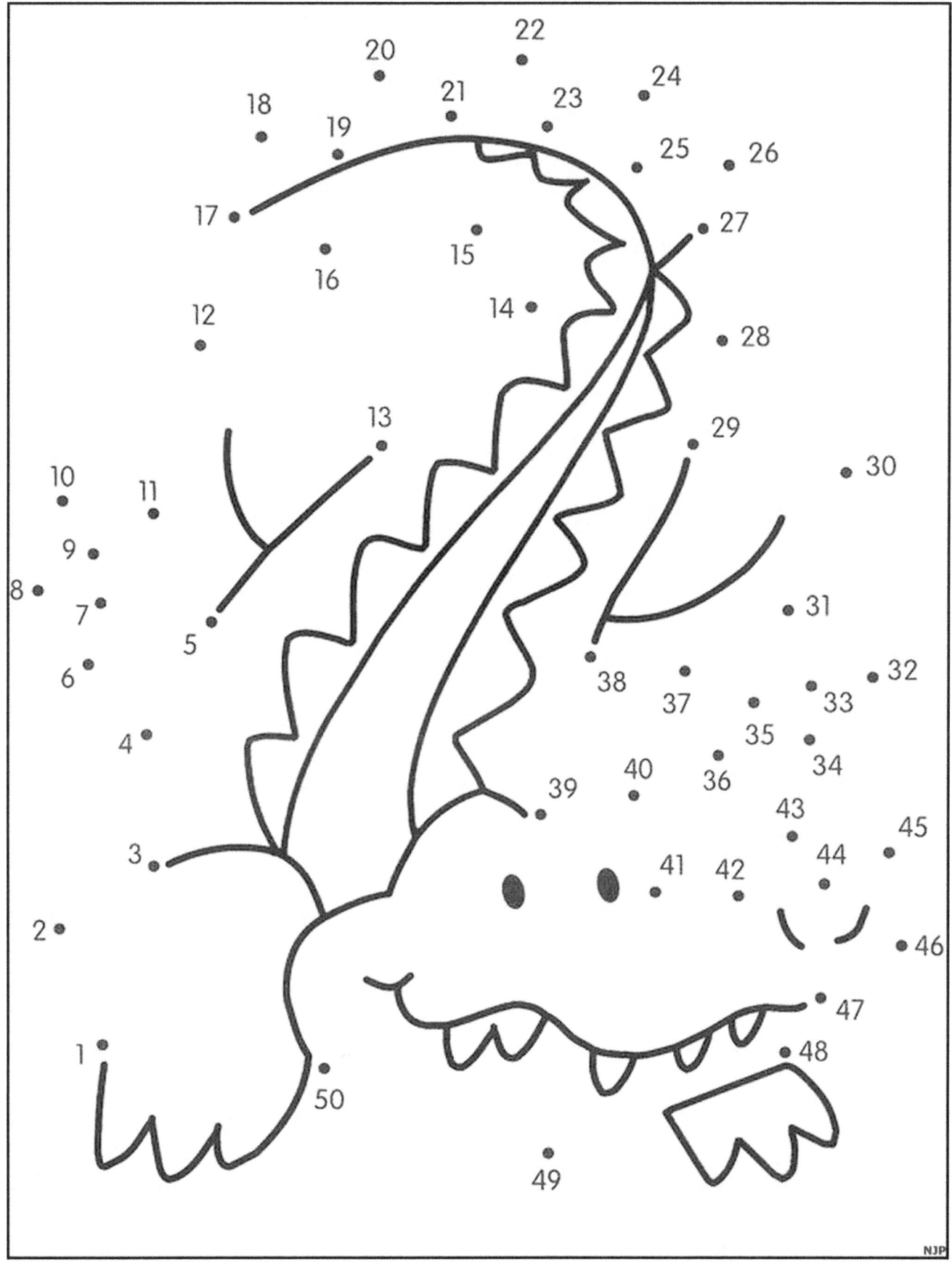

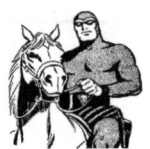

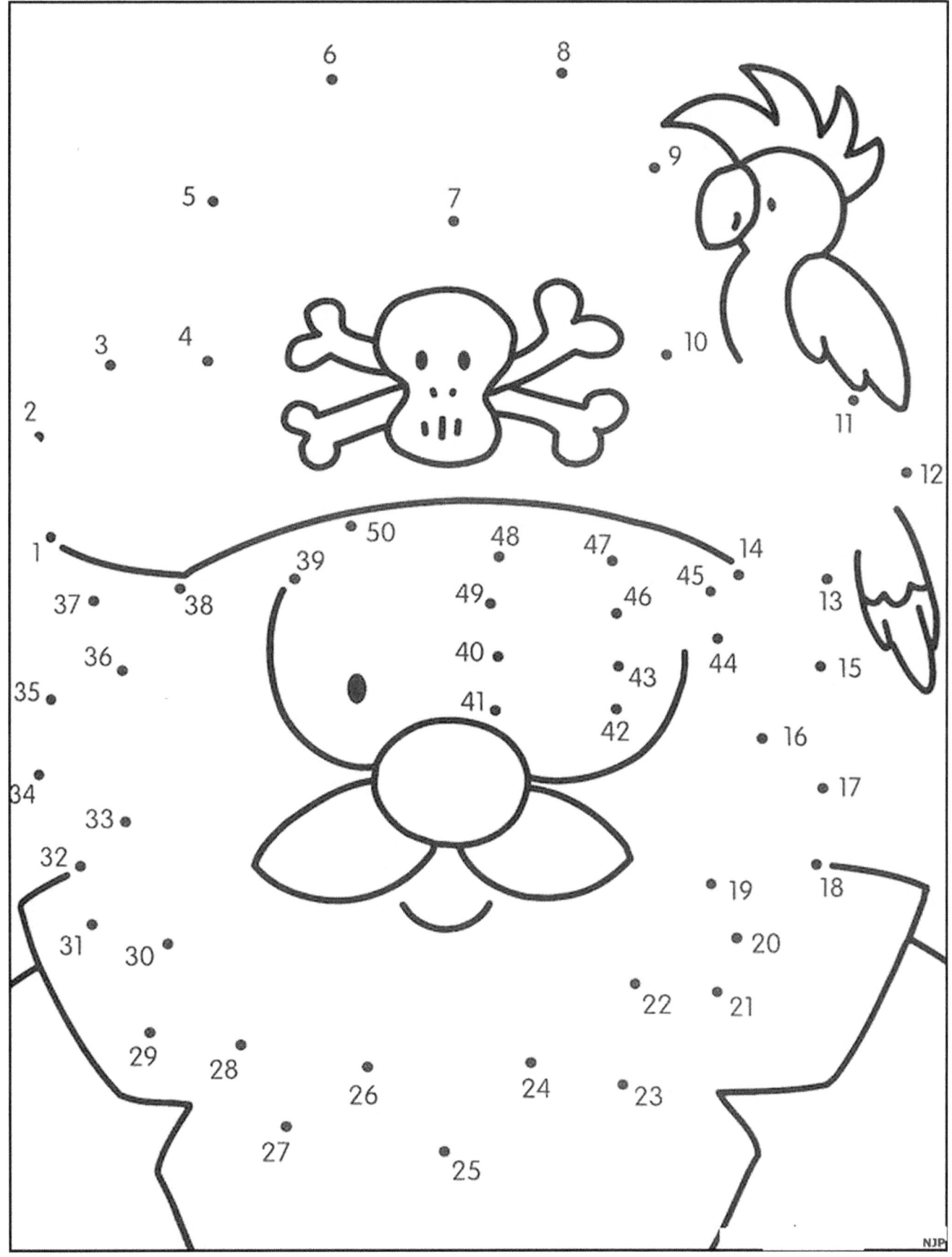

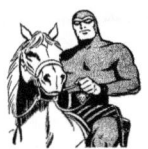

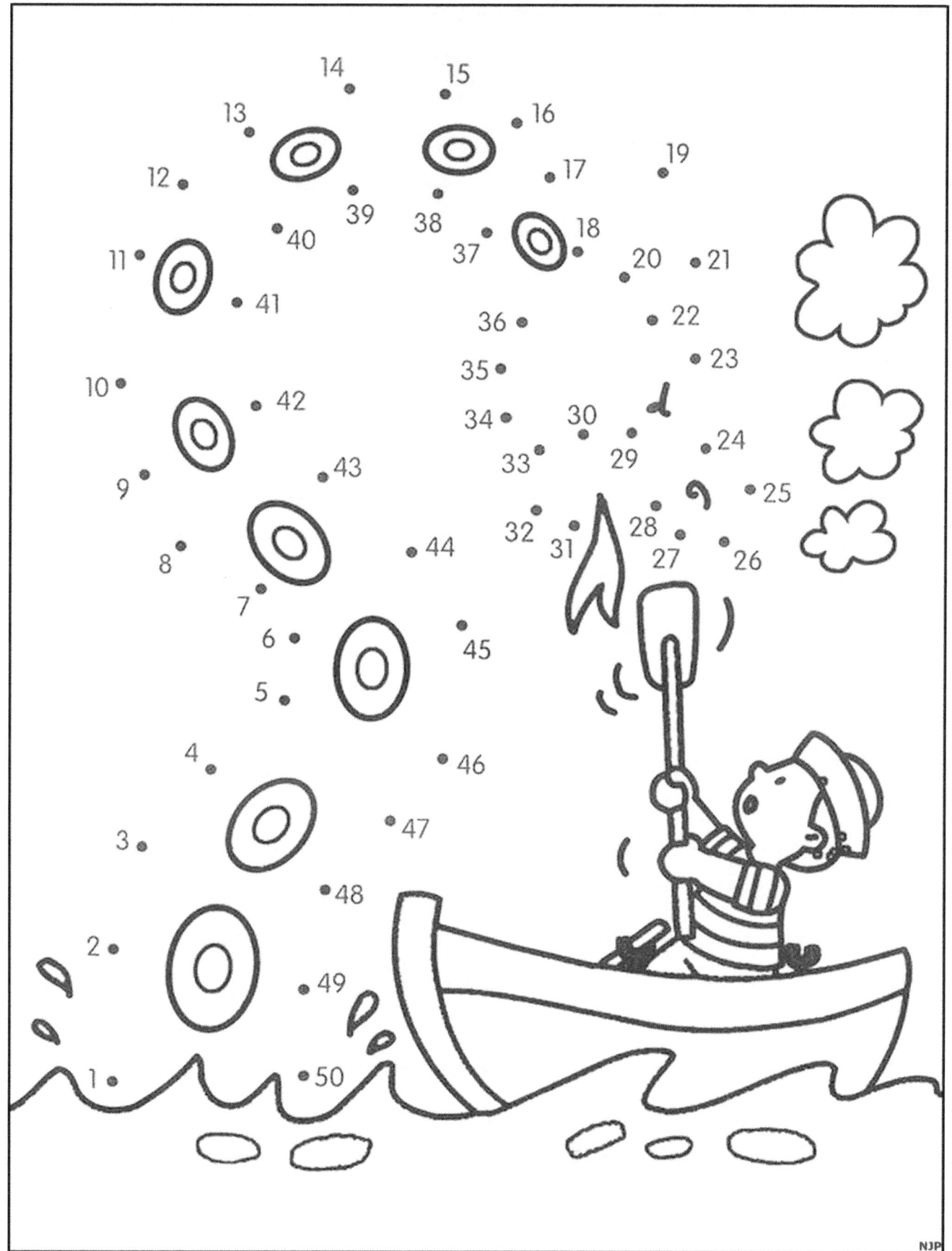

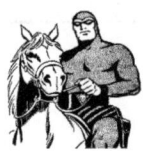

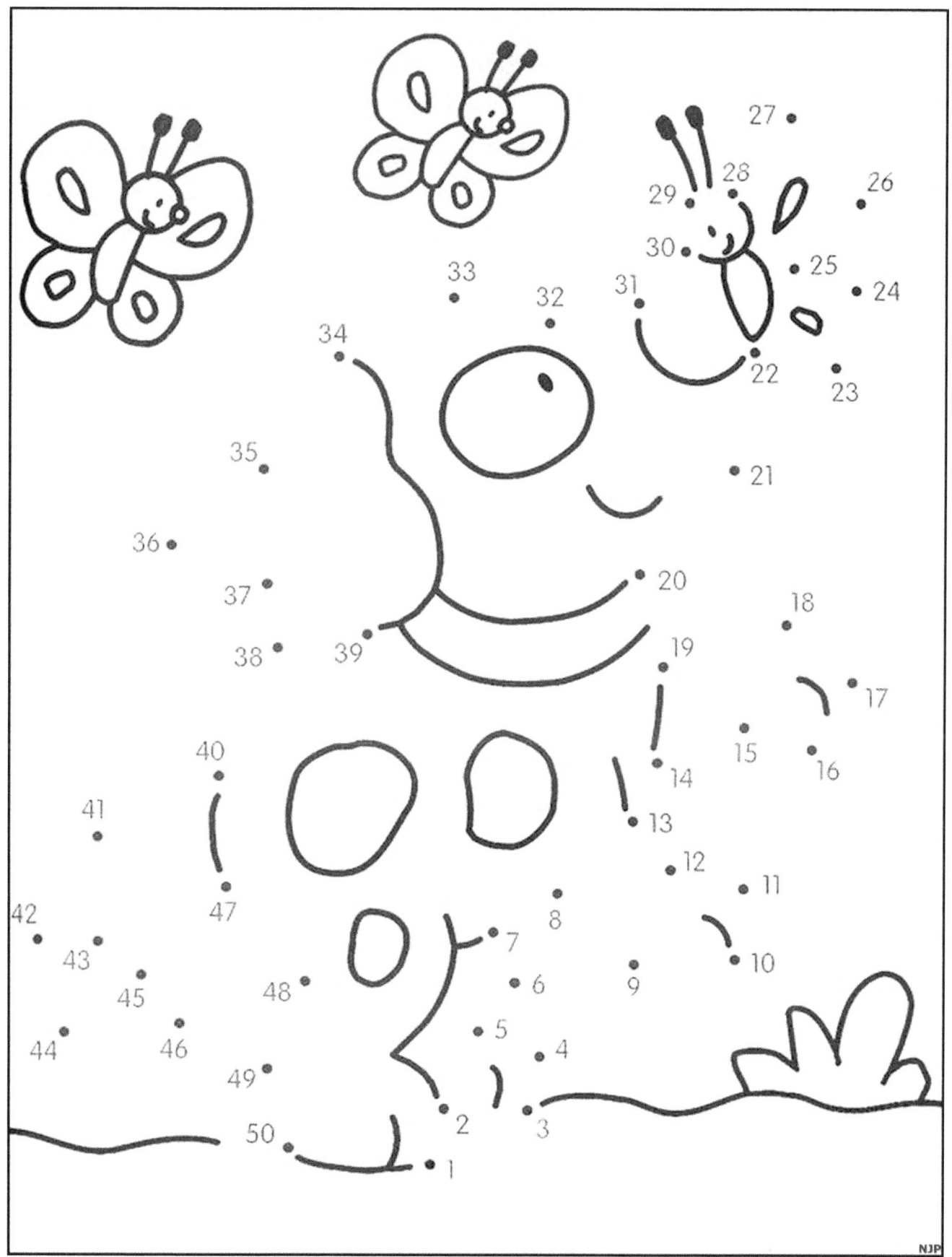

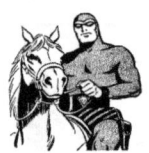

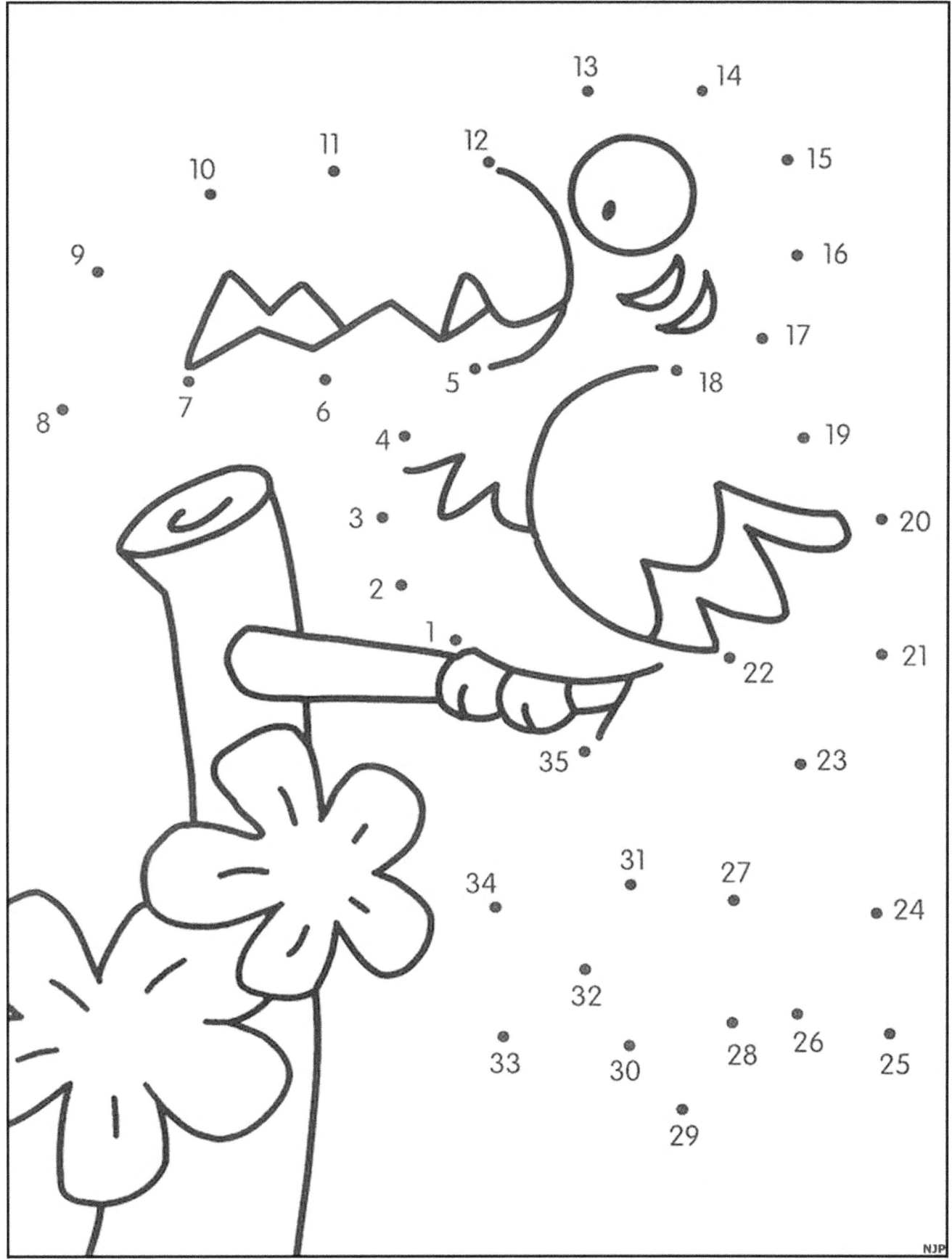

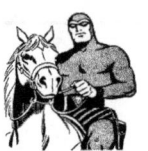

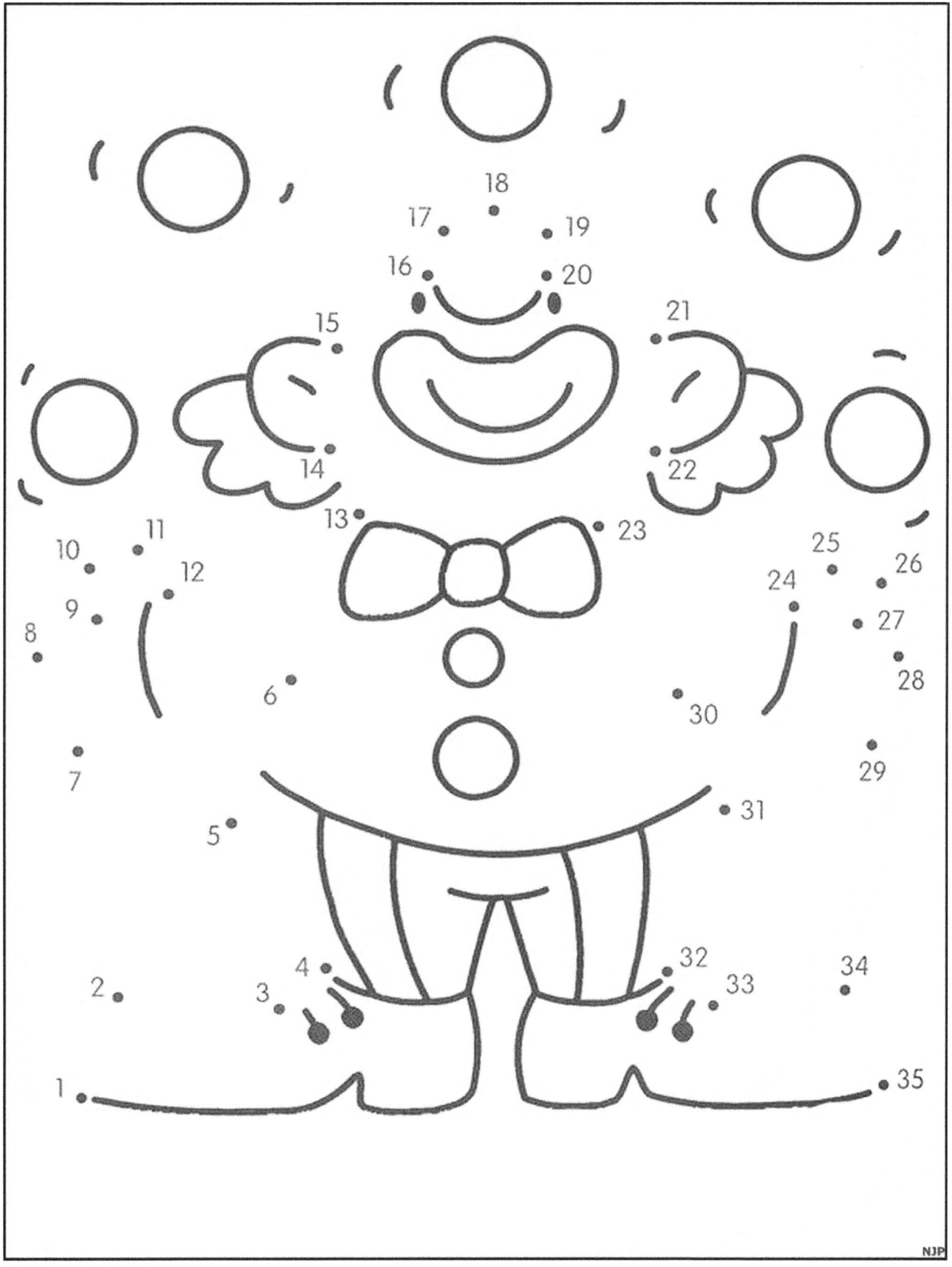

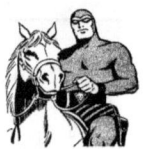

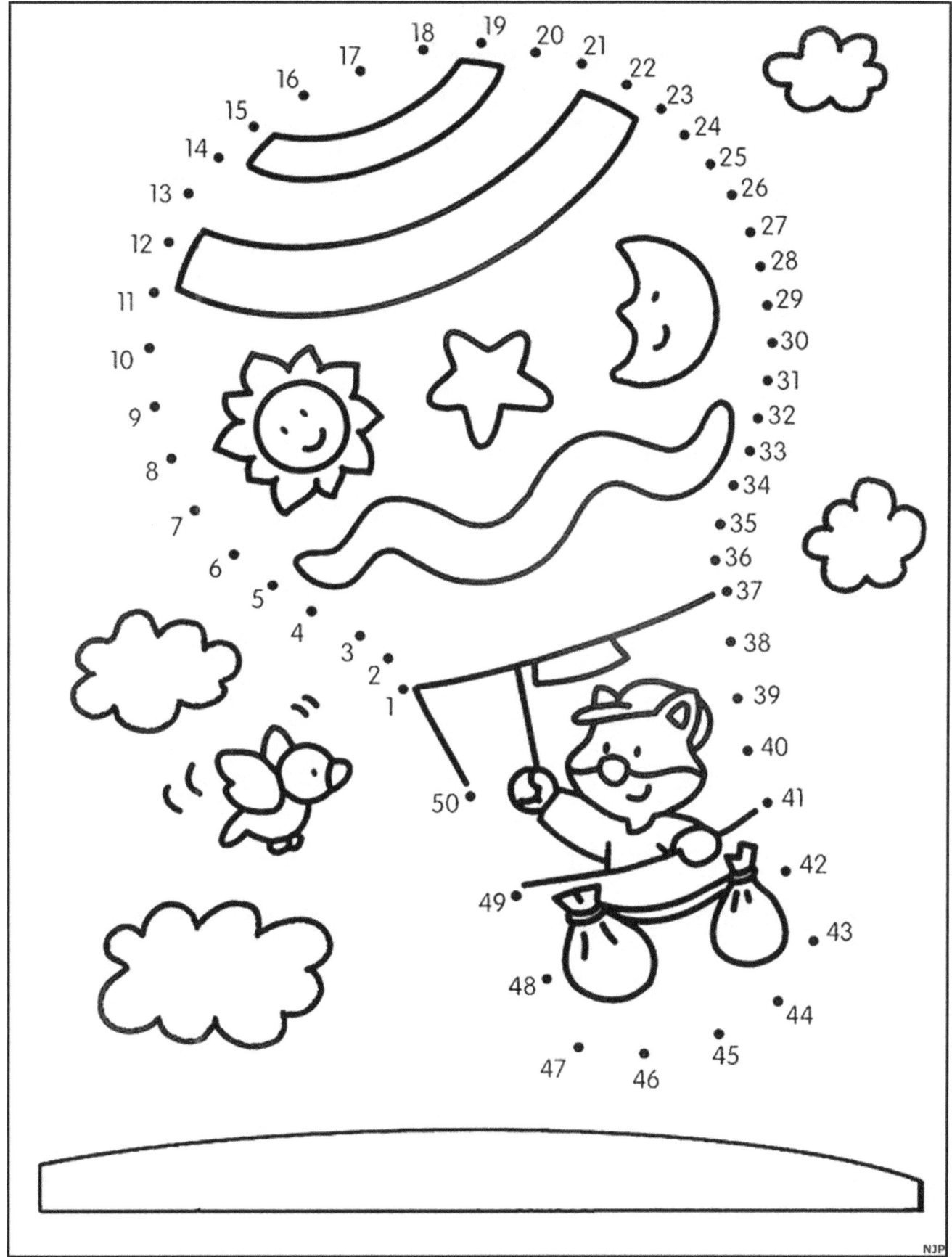

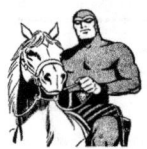

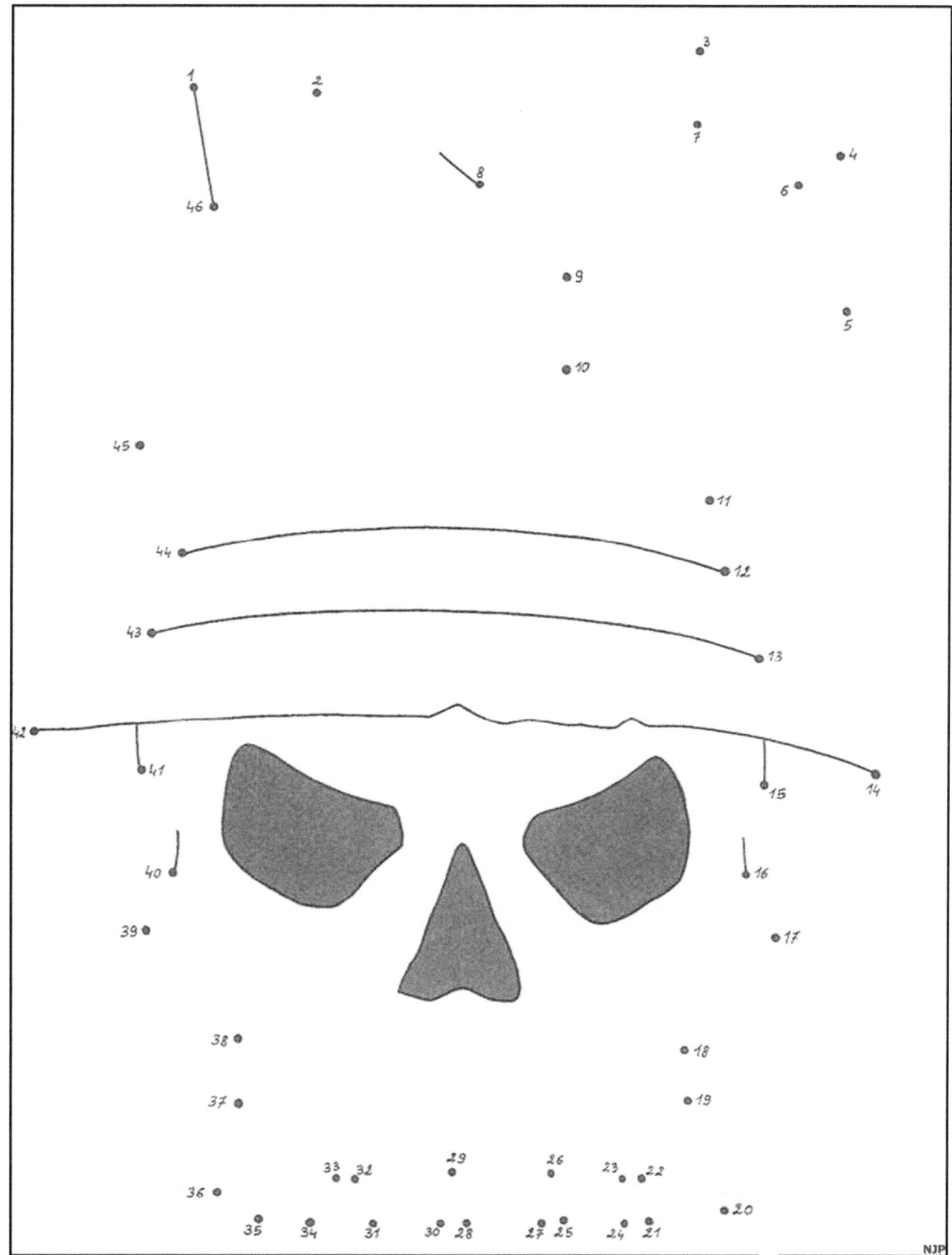

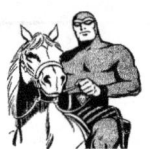

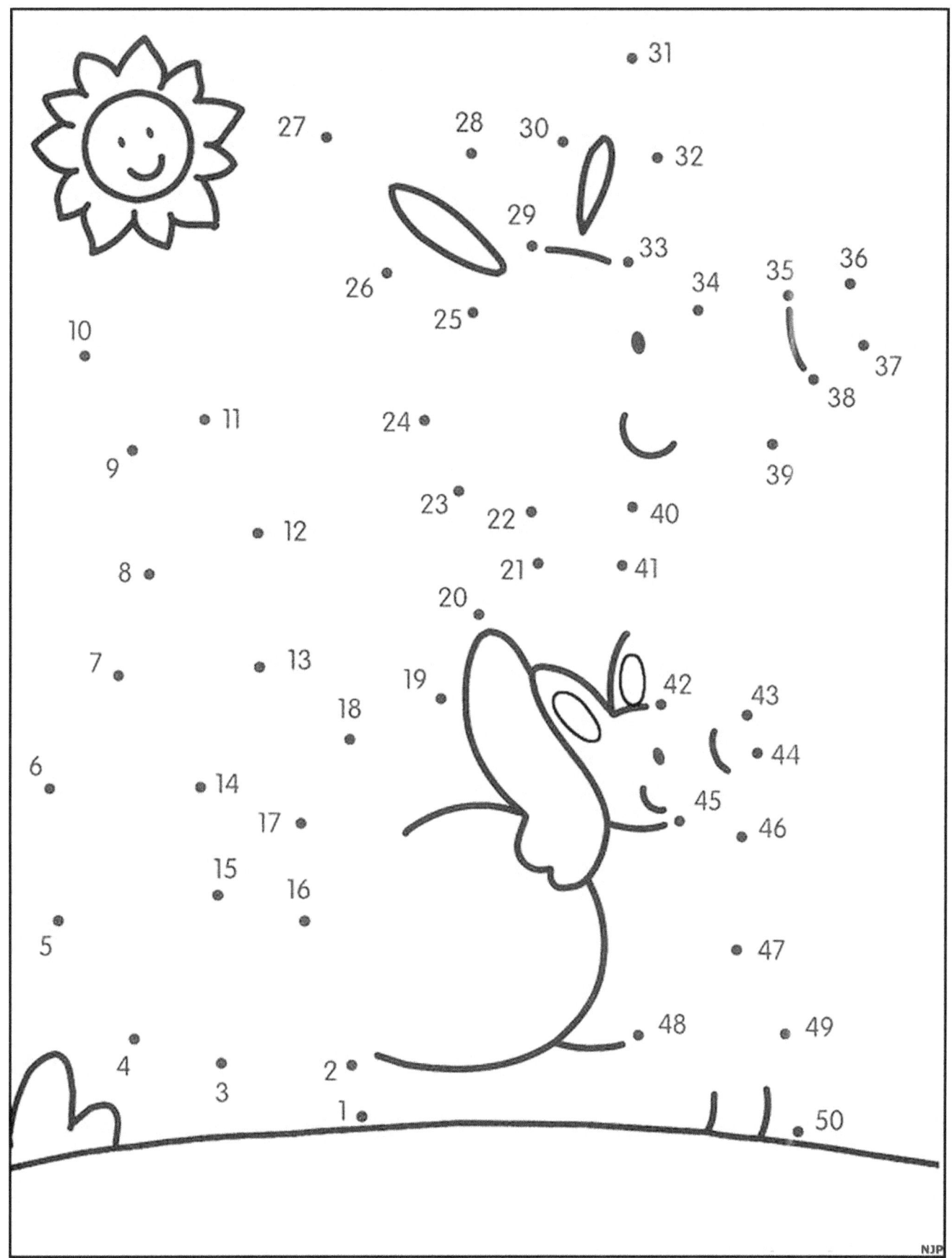

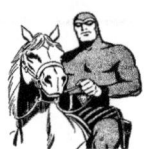

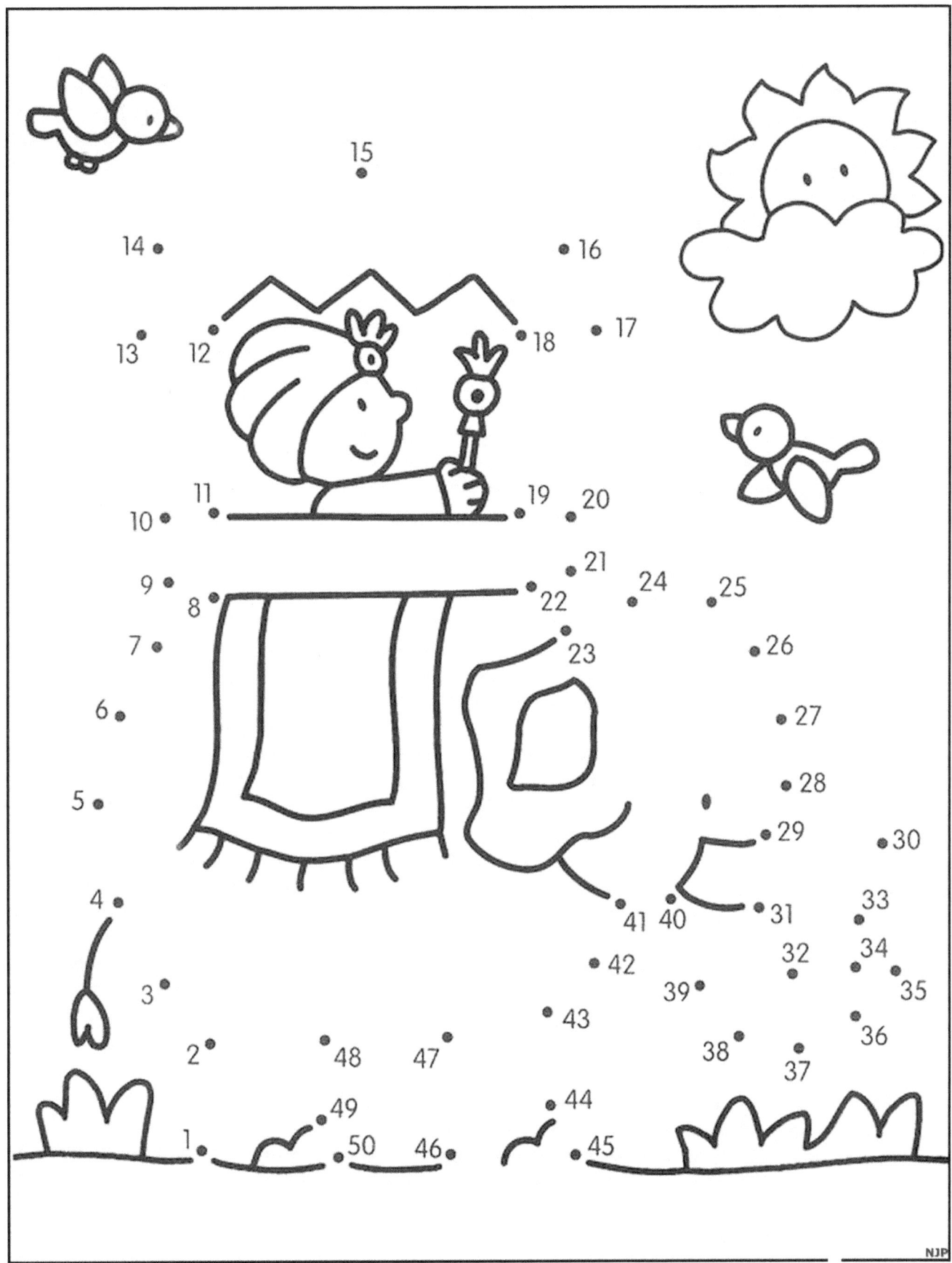

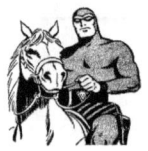

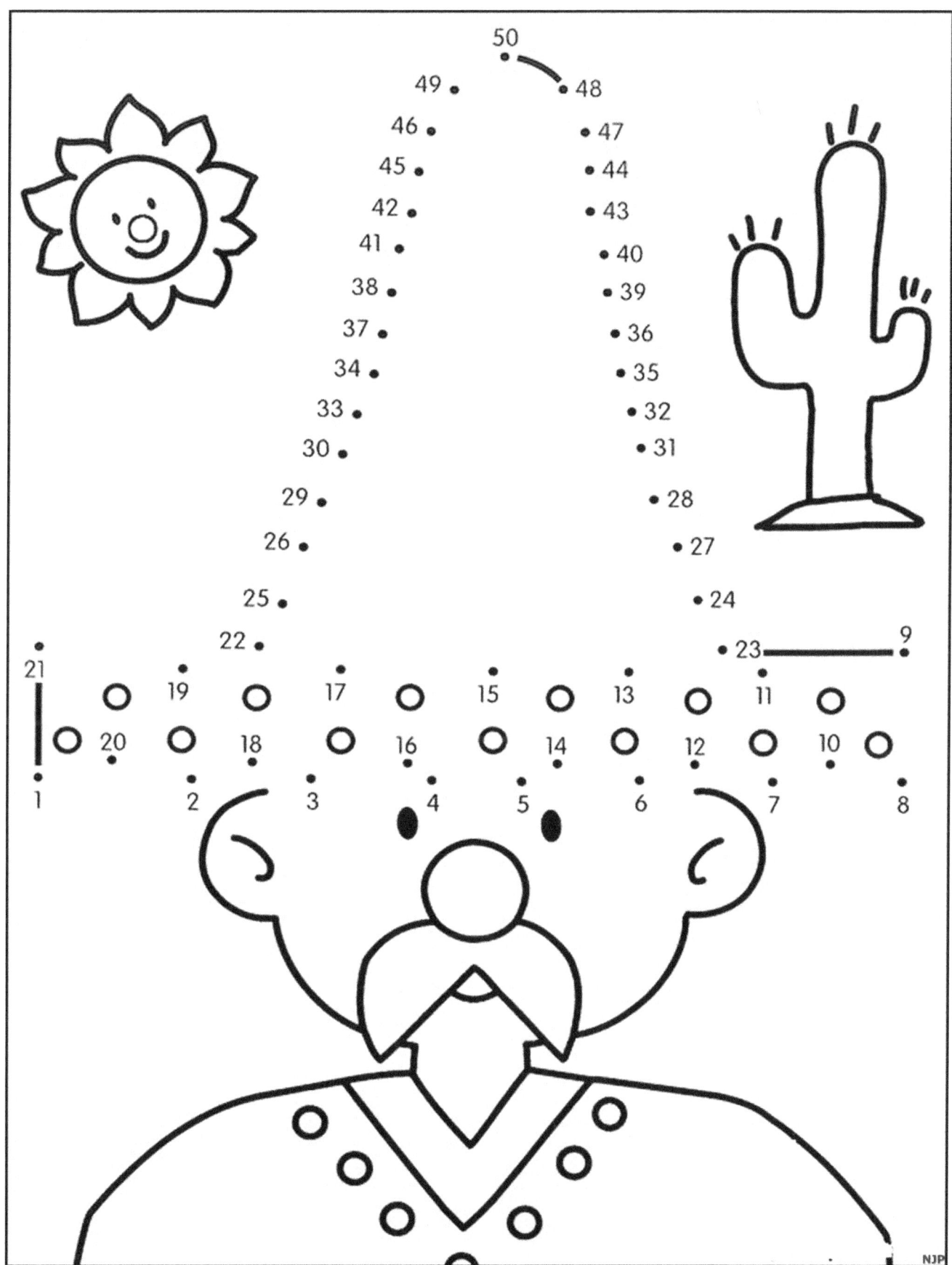

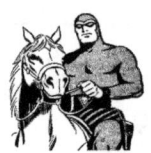

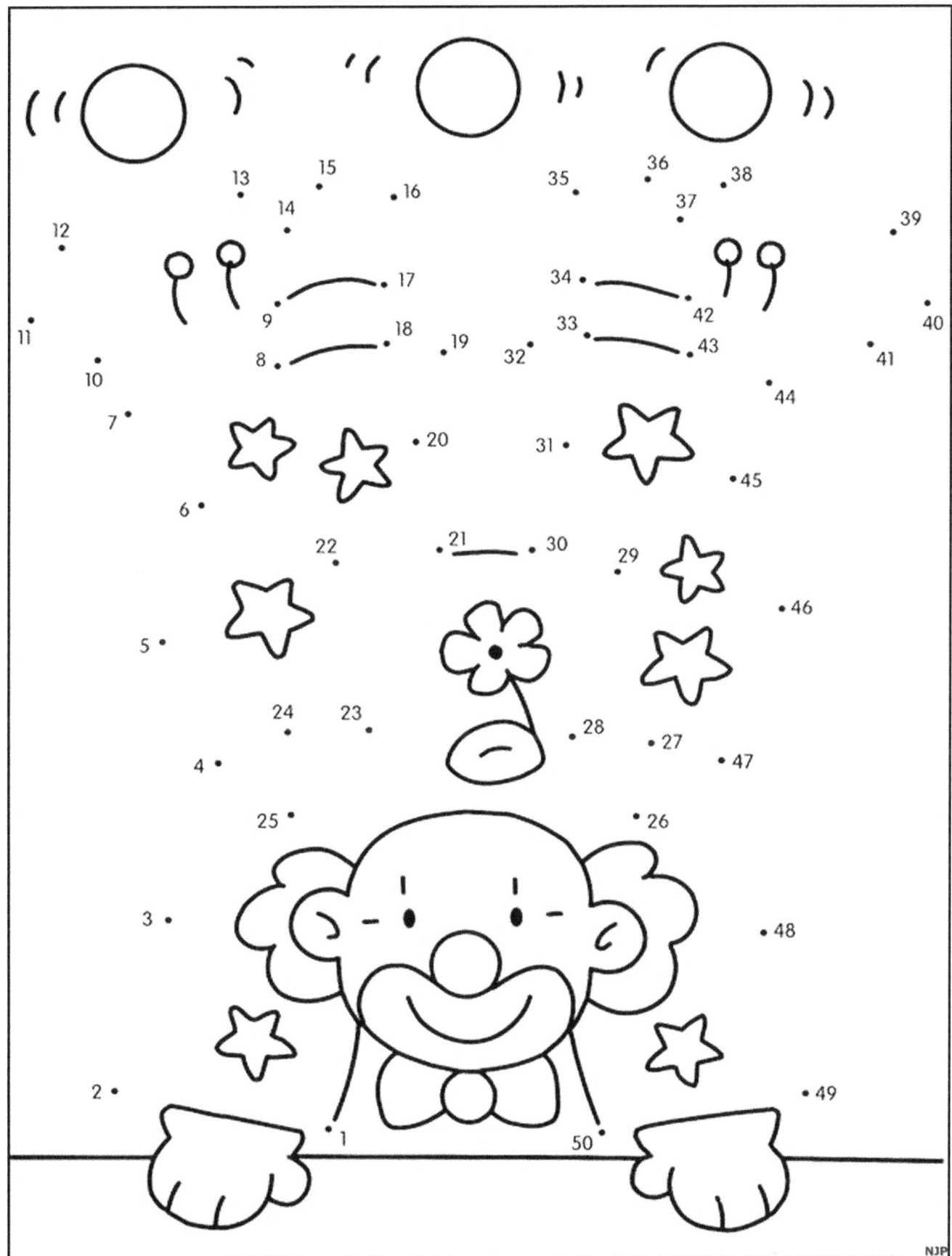

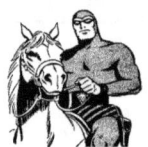

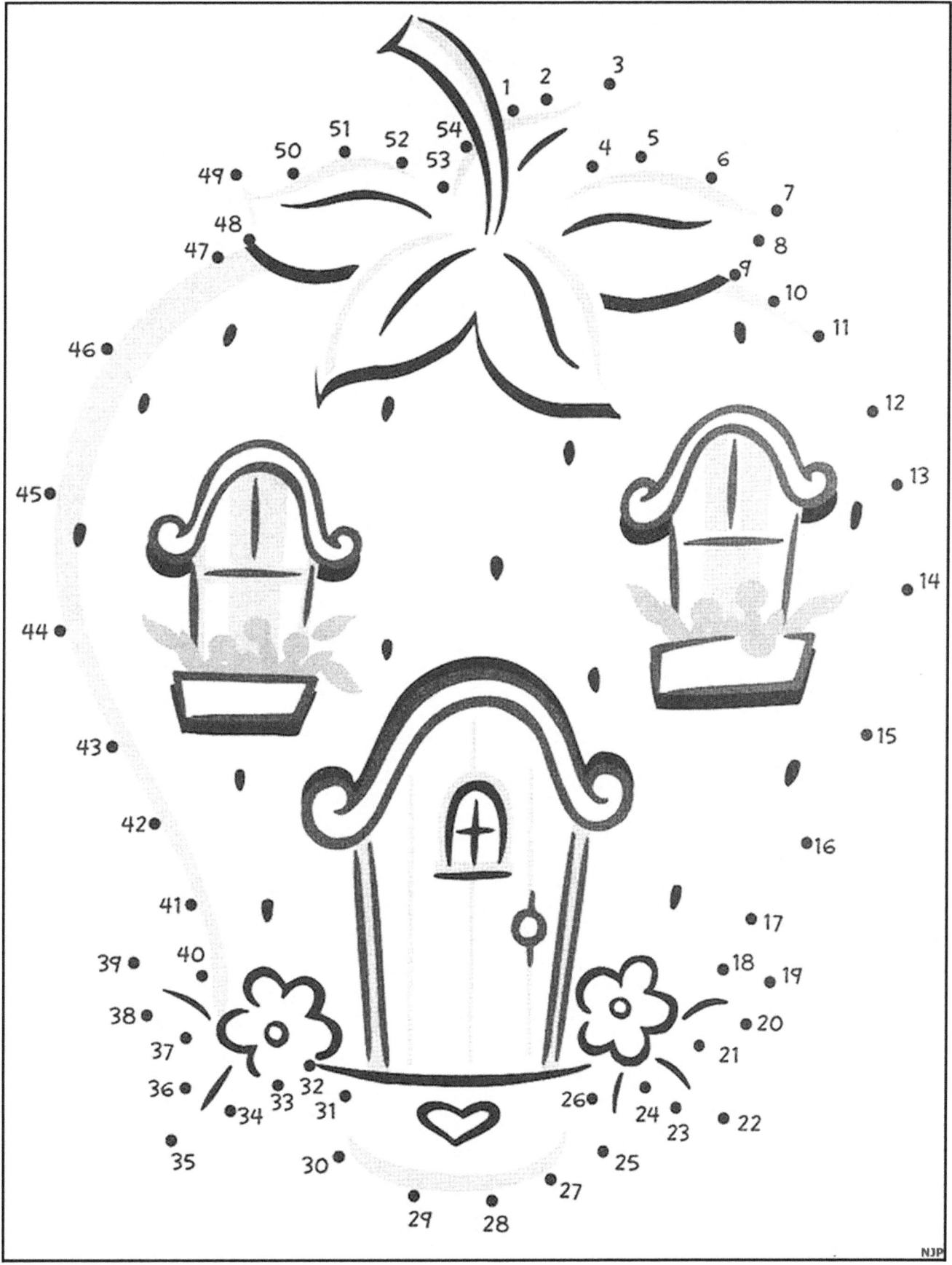

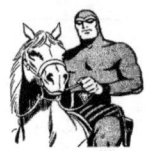

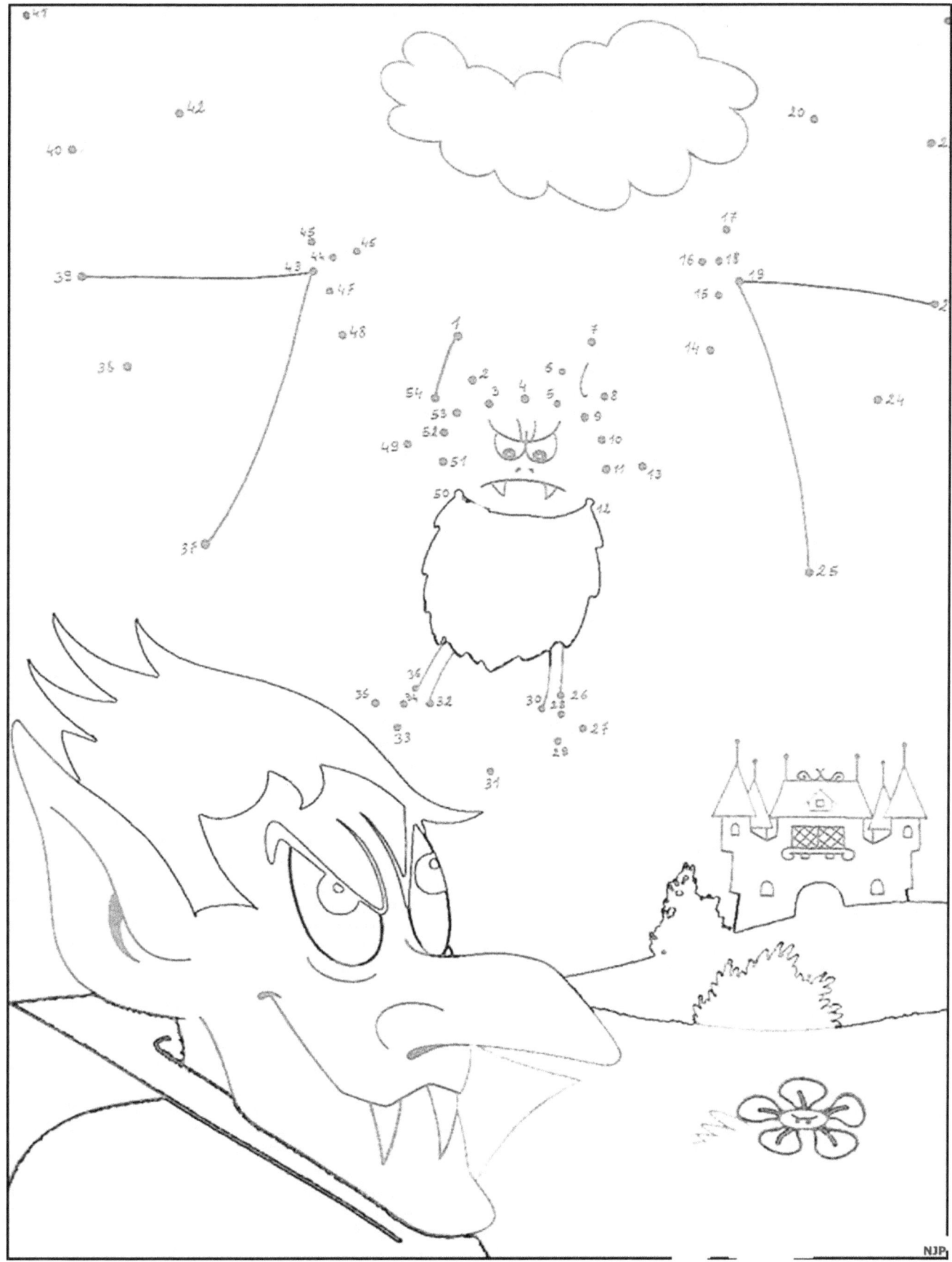

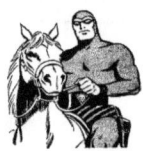

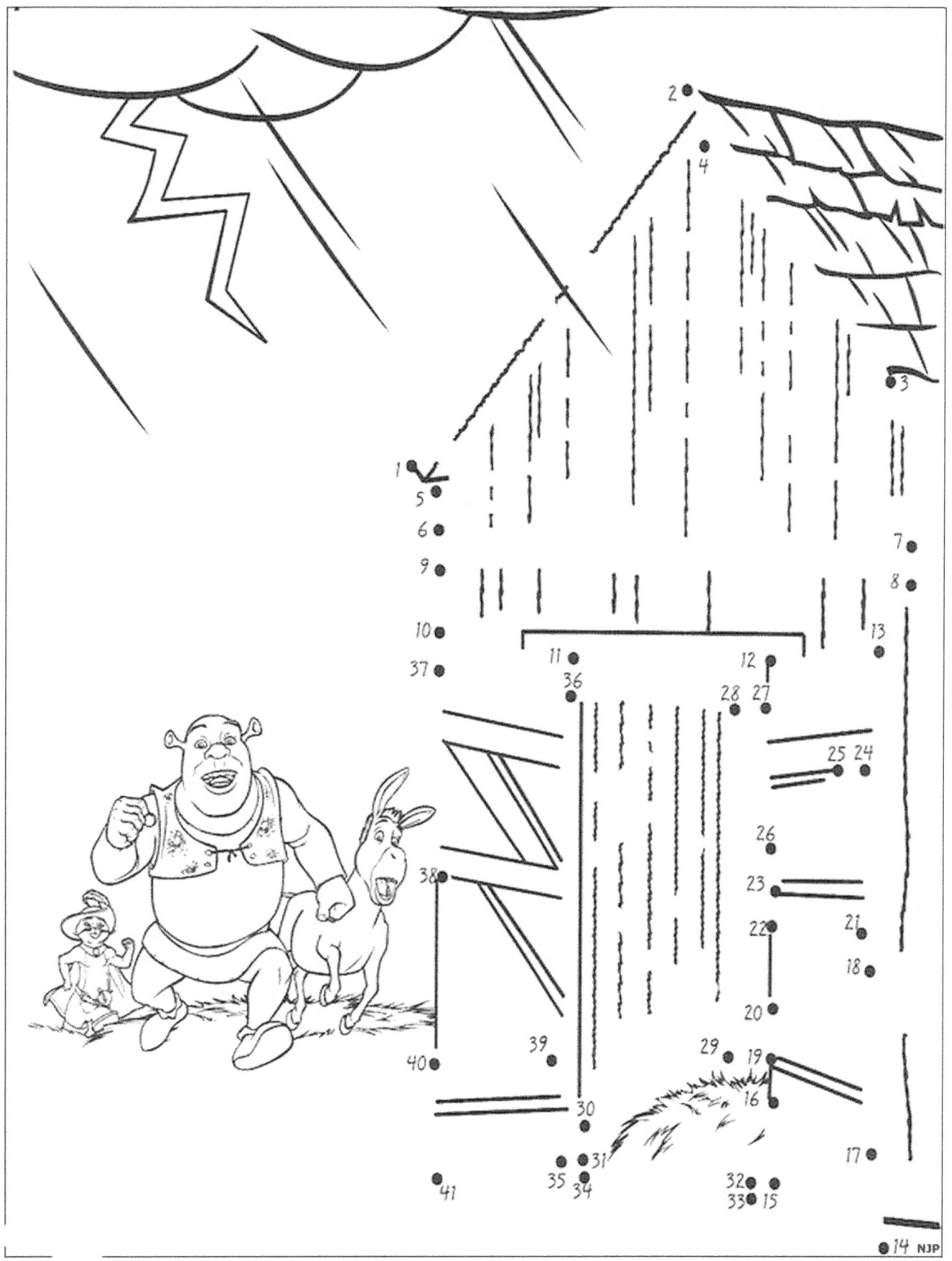

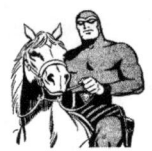

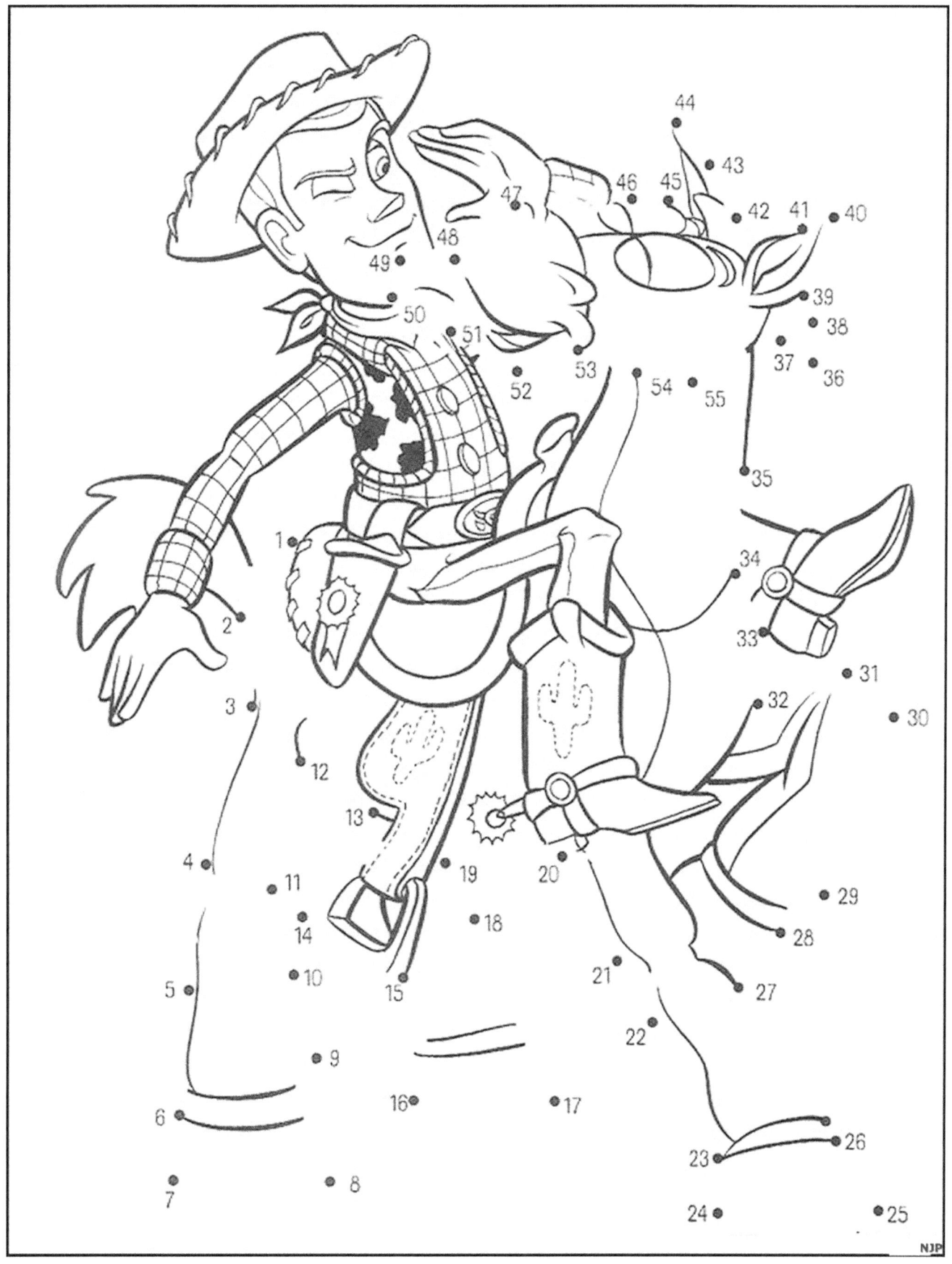

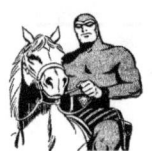

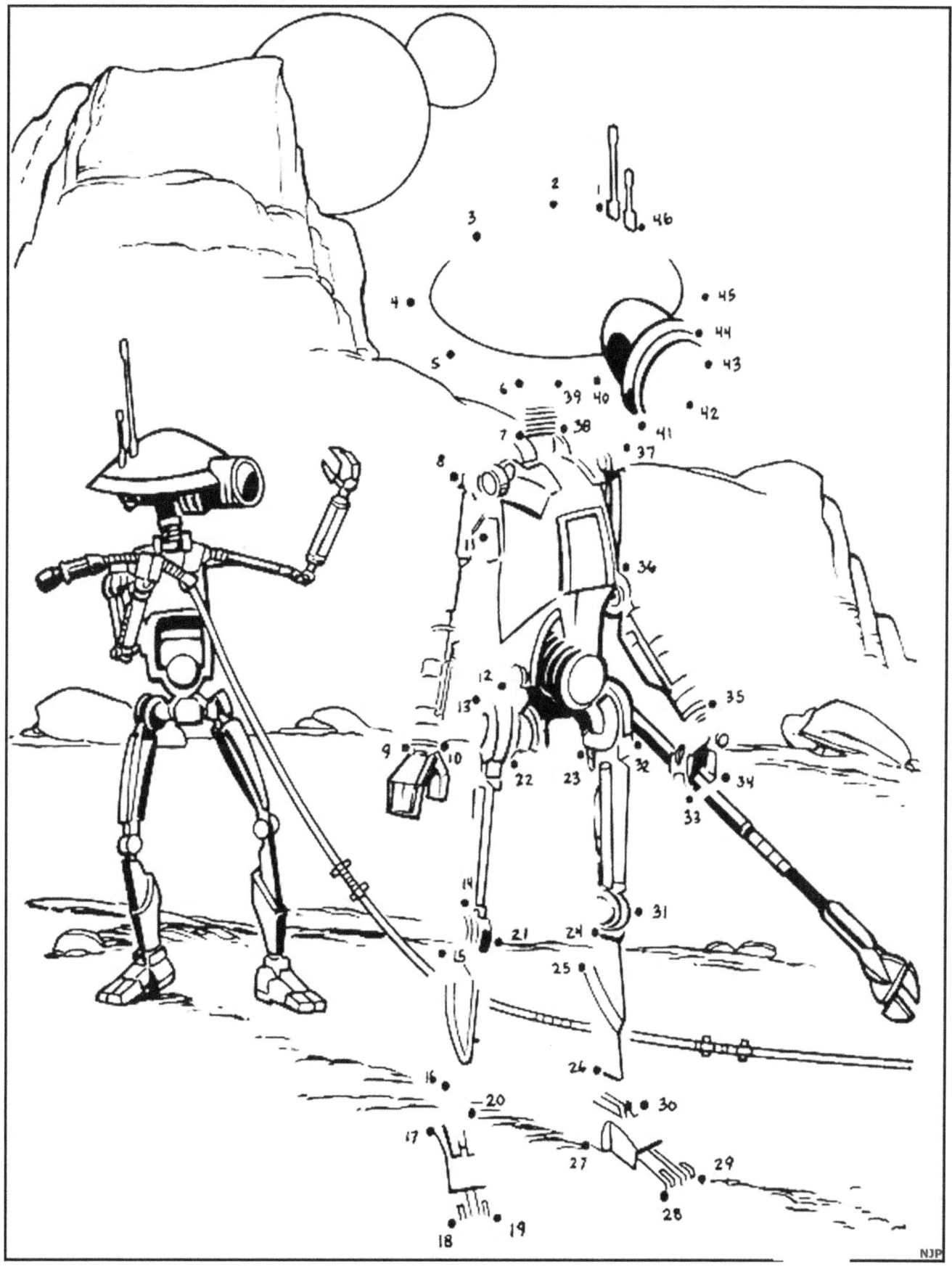

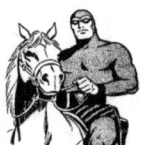